INTRODUCING EARLY CHRISTIANITY

A Topical Survey of Its
Life, Beliefs and Practices

LAURIE GUY

IVP

InterVarsity Press
Downers Grove, Illinois

InterVarsity Press
P.O. Box 1400, Downers Grove, IL 60515-1426
World Wide Web: www.ivpress.com
E-mail: mail@ivpress.com

©2004 by Laurie Guy

InterVarsity Press® is the book-publishing division of InterVarsity Christian Fellowship/USA®, a student movement active on campus at hundreds of universities, colleges and schools of nursing in the United States of America, and a member movement of the International Fellowship of Evangelical Students. For information about local and regional activities, write Public Relations Dept., InterVarsity Christian Fellowship/USA, 6400 Schroeder Rd., P.O. Box 7895, Madison, WI 53707-7895, or visit the IVCF website at <www.intervarsity.org>.

Scripture quotations, unless otherwise noted, are from the New Revised Standard Version of the Bible, copyright 1989 by the Division of Christian Education of the National Council of the Churches of Christ in the USA. Used by permission. All rights reserved.

Quotations from J. Stevenson, A New Eusebius: Documents Illustrating the History of the Early Church to AD 337, rev. ed. by W. H. C. Frend (London: SPCK, 1987) are used by permission of the publisher.

Quotations from B. Ward, trans., The Sayings of the Desert Fathers (Kalamazoo, Mich.: Cistercian Publications, 1975) are used by permission of the publisher. All rights to this material copyrighted by Cistercian Publications are reserved.

Quotations from B. S. Easton, The Apostolic Tradition of Hippolytus (Cambridge: Cambridge University Press, 1934) are used by permission.

Quotations from Egeria's Travels, trans. J. Wilkinson. 3rd ed. 1999. Warminster: Aris & Phillips. Used by permission of Oxbow Books, Oxford.

Cover design: Kathleen Lay Burrows

Cover images: Lourve/BAL; Mauseleo di Galla Placidia, Ravenna, Italy/BAL

ISBN 0-8308-2698-X

Printed in the United States of America ∞

Library of Congress Cataloging-in-Publication Data

Guy, Laurie.
  Introducing early Christianity: a topical survey of its life,
beliefs, and practices / Laurence D. Guy
      p. cm.
Includes bibliographical references and indexes.
ISBN 0-8308-2698-X (hardcover: alk. paper)
1. Church history—Primitive and early church, ca. 30-600 I.
Title.
BR165.G89 2004
270.1—dc22

                                                                                                2004008466

P	20	19	18	17	16	15	14	13	12	11	10	9	8	7	6	5	4	3	2	1
Y	20	19	18	17	16	15	14	13	12	11	10	09	08	07	06	05	04				

CONTENTS

Preface 7

1 IF PAUL COULD SEE US NOW
  Four Centuries of Dramatic Change 9

2 SECOND-GENERATION CHRISTIANITY
  The Churches of the Apostolic Fathers 29

3 SUFFERING AND DYING FOR GOD
  Persecution and Martyrdom 50

4 GETTING ORGANIZED
  Ministry and Structure 83

5 GETTING RECOGNIZED
  Emperor Constantine's Revolution 112

6 RADICAL DISCIPLESHIP
  Asceticism and Monasticism 133

7 WOMEN IN THE EARLY CHURCH
  Liberated or Confined? 165

8 THE EMERGING SHAPE OF WORSHIP
  Eucharist and Liturgy 193

9 GETTING IN AND STAYING IN
  Baptism and Penance 217

10 EXPLORING THE PATHS
  The Development of Early Christian Doctrine 248

11 MAPPING THE MIND OF THE CHURCH
  Orthodoxy Defined 268

Conclusion 295

Glossary 296

Table of Key People and Anonymous Writings 300

Map of Early Christian Sites 304

Modern Author Index 305

Subject Index 307

PREFACE

This is a book for the educated layperson and the undergraduate student. As such it is not addressed to fellow academic historians. It does not claim to present original scholarship from the author. Rather, it is seeking to make modern scholarship available to a more general audience.

A feature of the book is its frequent use of the series *The Ante-Nicene Fathers* *(ANF)* and the *Nicene and Post-Nicene Fathers (NPNF)*. Working from primary sources adds both depth and appreciation in historical studies. While the twin series is now a little dated (English translations primarily from the latter part of the nineteenth century), I have chosen largely to utilize and provide references to these volumes as the most accessible source for the beginning student to find most of the texts referred to in this book (especially as *ANF* and *NPNF* can also now be easily accessed at a number of Internet websites).[1]

Another feature of this book is its topical approach. At a popular level, history is commonly viewed as a narration of successive events. When using such an approach, it too often overwhelms the reader with a mass of detail. Often too this approach makes for boring reading. In addition, one can easily miss the big picture; one cannot see the forest for the trees. An alternative method is to engage far more in analysis and to explore themes within one's period of study. This is the preferred approach of this book. It focuses more on thematic developments in church history rather than on progressive chronicling of events century by century. In exploring topics as this book does, some readers may find it helpful to also read a more chronologically focused text alongside this one to fill gaps in their overall knowledge.[2] Many, however, may prefer to immerse themselves in this thematic approach from the start.

To foster coherence, this book focuses on Christianity within the Roman Empire, even though Christianity early on spilled beyond those bounds. It did so especially with conversion of various Germanic tribes in the fourth and fifth centu-

---

[1] <www.ccel.org/fathers2/>; also <http://graciouscall.com/books/fathers/fathers.html#anf>.
[2] A good starter is H. Chadwick, *The Early Church*, 2nd ed. (London: Penguin, 1993).

ries, albeit to an Arian form of Christianity. A nice chronological boundedness would examine five full centuries, to take this study to A.D. 500. However, the Western Roman Empire collapsed within two or three decades after the Council of Chalcedon (A.D. 451) through Germanic invasion. This left the religious scene in the West far more complex and confused in A.D. 500. To gain a coherent picture it is therefore better to conclude the study at 451, by which time most of the early church's evolution had occurred and much of the church's great debates over the nature of the Trinity and of Christ had been largely resolved.

Study of the early church provides insight not only into the church's beliefs and practices during that period, it also enhances understanding of Christian doctrine and serves as a rich resource for Christian spirituality. It is my desire that this book will serve these varied purposes.

1

IF PAUL COULD SEE US NOW
Four Centuries of Dramatic Change

Imagine one of the earliest apostles, Paul say, having a Rip-Van-Winkle-type sleep for four centuries. Imagine him then awakening in the fifth century and entering into the life of the church of that century. Would he be astonished at all the changes and developments in doctrine and in practice? Would he undergo a profound sense of spiritual culture shock? Would he recognize the Christianity of the fifth century as very similar to his Christianity of the first century? Where a major difference or development had occurred, would he sense an essential connectedness between the two forms of Christianity? Would he feel that fifth-century Christianity was a richer form of his own Christianity or would he feel that somehow Christianity had lost its way? These questions indicate that although Christianity changed little by little, cumulatively the changes over four centuries or more were in some aspects indeed profound.

At the risk of great oversimplification, this chapter will seek to give a very brief overview of developments as a whole, to provide a framework for the exploration of particular themes in more detail. The chapter serves as an overture to this book's symphony, touching on themes that will be developed in greater depth in succeeding chapters. Thus it will be a big-picture chapter. What follows is a brief discussion of a few striking developments during those first centuries of the church's existence.

Numerical Growth

The most obvious shift in Christianity in its first centuries was its change in size. The numerical legacy of the earthly Jesus left followers numbering in the hundreds at most (1 Cor 15:6; Acts 1:15). At the end of the period of study, Christianity was the religion of the whole empire, at least in a formal sense, though significant numbers remained pagan or barely Christian. However, to have become the public religion of the empire and to have captured the allegiance of a majority of the inhabitants of that empire in four centuries demonstrates remarkable growth. That increase was slow at

first. Christians were a barely noticeable blip on the screen of religious presence in
the first century of Christianity's existence. While missionaries like Paul planted
many churches in a way designed to disperse the faith widely, adherents of those
churches were small in number. One estimate of the size of the church at Corinth
when Paul wrote his letters, for example, is that it comprised about fifty persons.[1]
Significant increase occurred in the next century, though absolute numbers in relation to the population as a whole remained minuscule. However, a letter from Pliny
the Younger, governor of Bithynia, to the emperor Trajan, suggests much greater
Christian presence in Northern Asia Minor in about A.D. 112:

> The contagion of that superstition has penetrated not the cities only, but the villages
> and country; yet it seems possible to stop it and set it right. At any rate it is certain
> enough that the almost deserted temples begin to be resorted to, that long disused
> ceremonies of religion are restored, and that fodder for victims finds a market,
> whereas buyers till now were few.[2]

Allowing for rhetorical exaggeration, the language indicates significant growth
of the church in that region. However, the almost total silence of pagan writers for
another half-century in relation to (threat from) Christianity, suggests that the
church overall was too small for public notice. Greater challenges to the church
occurred toward the end of the second century, notably in the literary attack of the
pagan philosopher Celsus in the 170s. This new development points to a church
now sufficiently large to start posing a threat to paganism.

Further Christian growth led to the first empire-wide attacks on the church,
launched by two emperors in the 250s, followed by a third wave of persecution in
the early 300s. The church was growing indeed. Bishop Cornelius evidenced this
growth about A.D. 250, noting that the church of Rome included "above fifteen
hundred widows and persons in distress."[3] This suggests the Christian community
there now comprised many thousands of people. However, the now-large Christian community still remained a small percentage of the total population. At the
time of Constantine's gaining of imperial power in A.D. 312, scholars commonly
estimate the proportion of Christians in society at about ten percent.[4]

Christian growth was not distributed evenly through the empire or within social strata. At the time of Constantine's succession, the church was much stronger
in the eastern half of the empire, especially around Asia Minor. It was a markedly

---

[1]J. Murphy-O'Connor, *St. Paul's Corinth: Text and Archaeology* (London: Michael Glazier, 1983), p. 156.
[2]Pliny *Letter* 10.96 (in J. Stevenson, ed., *A New Eusebius: Documents Illustrating the History of the Church to A.D. 337*, rev. ed. by W. H. C. Frend [London: SPCK, 1987], p. 19).
[3]Eusebius *Church History* 6.43.11 (*NPNF*[2] 1:288).
[4]R. Stark, *The Rise of Christianity* (San Francisco: Harper, 1997), pp. 6-7.

Key Historians in the Early Church:

Lactantius (c. 250-c. 320). Born in North Africa, he was a rhetorician for a time in Nicomedia. Later, in Gaul, he tutored Crispus, the eldest son of Constantine. At the time of the "great persecution" he wrote to uphold Christianity against paganism. His *On the Deaths of the Persecutors* is an important source for the persecution that commenced in A.D. 303.

Eusebius of Caesarea (c. 265-c. 339). In addition to being bishop of Caesarea in Palestine from c. A.D. 313, Eusebius was the foremost church historian of his time. His writings incorporate much earlier material, for example that of the second-century writer Hegesippus, which would otherwise be lost to us. His main writings include his ten-volume *Church History* and his *Life of Constantine.* Socrates, Sozomen and Theodoret tend to begin their studies at the time when Eusebius's study concludes.

Socrates (died c. A.D. 440s). A lawyer from Constantinople, he wrote a *Church History,* spanning the period 305-439. He also preserved a number of original documents.

Sozomen (died c. A.D. 450). Also a lawyer from Constantinople, he wrote a *Church History,* spanning the period 324-439. His history is very dependent on that of Socrates, but it does incorporate original documents. It also incorporates more legendary material.

Theodoret (c. 393-c. 460). Bishop of the minor see of Cyrrhus in Syria, he supported the Antiochene school in the fifth-century Christological debates and thus sympathized with the theology of Nestorius. He wrote a *Church History* covering the period 324-428.

urban phenomenon, with rural populations being much slower to convert. This has been a frequent feature of religious movements, probably because of the greater conservatism of peasants. A similar pattern was evident when Calvinism came close to gaining control of France in the sixteenth century. The slowness of the rural areas to convert in the first centuries left its mark in the English language: a "pagan" is someone who is a *paganus,* a rural villager.

A common perception sees early Christianity as fundamentally a religion of slaves and the poor. This does have significant truth. Paul in 1 Corinthians 1:26 drew attention to the lowly backgrounds of most of that Christian community.

Likewise, Minucius Felix readily conceded the charge about A.D. 230 that most
Christians were called poor persons.[5] This, however, should be no surprise in the
light of the fact that by far the greatest percentage of the entire empire was poor.
Balancing this observation, nevertheless, is an increasing recognition that the
church had significant strength among the lower middle class and a sprinkling of
people of higher social level and wealth. The strata lacking was the Roman male
elite, a lack not corrected until the end of the fourth century when imperial decree
increasingly suppressed paganism, and when it therefore became more and more
expedient to declare oneself Christian. The earlier relative scarcity of high-born
Christian men even led Callistus, bishop of Rome in the early third century, to
sanction Christian women of rank to live in "just concubinage" with a lower-born
male. A factor in Callistus's decision seems to have been that there was a scarcity
of Christian men of class, and if high-born Christian women formally married men
of lower rank they would lose status and property rights.

Once the new emperor Constantine declared himself Christian and gave favor
to Christians in the early fourth century, the church grew apace, though motives
for conversion often now had a more worldly aspect. As Augustine was to note at
the end of the fourth century, "crowds of heathen" who joined Christianity at
Hippo (North Africa) once persecution ceased unfortunately brought their old
practice of drunken revelry with them.[6] Growth there certainly was. Hilary of Poitiers highlighted the advance of Christianity in the fourth century:

> Every day the believing people increase and professions of faith are multiplied. Pagan
> superstitions are abandoned together with the impious fables of mythology and the
> altars of the demons and the vanity of idols. Every one is moving along the road to
> salvation.[7]

This is not to say that in the fourth century the masses turned their allegiance
to Christianity rapidly and totally. Toward the end of that century John Chrysostom's comments indicate that only about half of the population of Antioch (a
strong center for Christianity from its earliest days) gave allegiance to Christianity.[8]

---

[5]Minucius Felix *Octavius* 36 (*ANF* 4:195).
[6]Augustine *Letter* 29.9 (*NPNF*[1] 1:255-56).
[7]Hilary of Poitiers *Homily on the Psalms* 67.20 (in W. H. C. Frend, *The Rise of Christianity* [Philadelphia: Fortress, 1984], p. 560).
[8]John Chrysostom *Homily 85 on the Gospel of Matthew* 4 (*NPNF*[1] 10:510); *Homily 11 on the Acts of the Apostles* 3 (*NPNF*[1] 11:74). Chrysostom estimated the figure for the combined Christian congregations of the city at 100,000. The total population of Antioch at this time is estimated at 200,000. The figure supplied by Chrysostom needs to be treated with caution as ancient writers were often loose with numbers, especially as they commonly quoted them in rhetorical fashion with an end in view. Elsewhere (*Homilies on 1 Timothy* 10 [*NPNF*[1] 13:440]), Chrysostom indicated that Christians were more numerous than heathens. Chrysostom is evidence simply for the fact that many people were still pagans in his time.

The Christianization of the Roman Empire continued apace in the fifth century but was still not complete, especially in rural areas, when waves of invading barbarians interrupted the process, creating the need for a new wave of Christianization in the early Middle Ages. We must also recognize that with "secondary" conversion commonly occurring through marriage (becoming a Christian through the influence of one's believing spouse) and with social conversion (becoming a Christian because society as a whole was moving in this direction), conversion was now often more superficial. Though Christian conversion was booming, pagan views often remained strong—within the church as well as in wider society.

Identity

Christianity at first appearance seemed to be a sect within Judaism. Increasingly, though, it came to stand over against Judaism, asserting its own identity in contrast to Judaism. However, with Christianity and Judaism sharing common traditions and common Scriptures, the two faiths intersected and influenced each other from time to time, despite the overall relationship becoming increasingly bitter. How and why did this occur?

A fundamental aspect of Christianity was its emergence from the matrix of Judaism. Its relationship with its parent was a complex one, involving aspects of both continuity and disjunction. This raised the question of whether Christianity was a form of Judaism or something else.

Initially Christianity was probably perceived as a Jewish sect. Paul in Acts 24:14 indicated that Jews called the Christian community a *hairesis,* "sect," of the Jews. Such a perception should not surprise us. Judaism was far from monolithic in the first century. In many ways it was a jungle of competing sects. Earliest Christianity tended to see itself as a fulfillment of Judaism, built on, rather than rejecting, its past. It used the same Scriptures. In the middle of the second century, Justin Martyr described the Scriptures being read in worship services as "the memoirs of the apostles" and "the writings of the prophets."[9] The latter term, "writings of the prophets," indicates the early church perception that the Old Testament of the Jews was now Christian Scripture.

The earliest Christians continued to practice temple worship alongside fellow Jews (e.g., Acts 2:46; 3:1; 5:12; 21:26). Paul's evangelistic strategy in a new location commonly began with his preaching in the synagogue and remaining there until forced out (Acts 13:5, 14; 14:1; 17:1-2). A consequence was that he suffered thirty-nine lashes on five occasions (2 Cor 11:24). Such lashes could not be administered to any person, but only to those within the Jewish community. This in-

---

[9]Justin Martyr *First Apology* 67 (ANF 1:186).

dicates Paul's continuing place, albeit ambiguously, within Judaism.

Sharper separation between Jews and Christians occurred toward the end of the first century. In part this resulted from the crushing of the Jewish revolt by the Roman legions in A.D. 70. The destruction of the temple, so central to Jewish worship and identity, triggered deep crisis and reflection within Judaism. The collapse of the sect of the Sadducees, whose identity was so tied to the temple, left the Pharisees with even greater influence within Judaism. This fostered narrower and more closely defined Jewish boundaries. From such a perspective, Christians were increasingly seen as "out," not "in." One outcome seems to have been Jewish modification of the twelfth of their eighteen benedictions of daily prayer, to add a curse on the "heretics" (minim) and an imprecation that "Nazarenes be blotted out of the book of life."[10] Under such circumstances many Christians felt they could no longer worship with Jews without compromising their faith.

In some places, total or partial separation occurred early (e.g., Thessalonica: 1 Thess 2:14-16). The "curse of the minim" accelerated this process. Expulsion from the synagogues left Christians exposed to pressure to worship the Roman gods or the emperor, a requirement from which the Jews were exempt. This accounts for the depth of bitterness expressed in the book of Revelation against the Jews: they had forfeited the right to be called Jews; they were "synagogues of Satan" (Rev 2:9; 3:9).

Despite some ongoing interrelationship at a popular level, the chasm between the two communities at higher levels became increasingly deep and permanent. This gave Christians a powerful sense of identity quite separate from the Jews. While Christianity fulfilled Judaism, Christians were not Jews. They were something else. In terms of Judeo-Christian identity in a pagan world, they were a "third race." They were not pagan Greeks and neither were they Jews. When Jews joined in the cry, "Death to the third race," an apologist like Tertullian, while rejecting the sentiment, accepted the classification of being a third race—Christians stood over against Judaism.[11]

Jewish-Christian hostility intensified when Jews aided the persecution of Christians, for example, gathering firewood on the sabbath in mid-second-century Smyrna for the burning of Bishop Polycarp.[12] Christians for their part increasingly thundered against any hybrid version of Christianity that might allow for accommodation with Judaism. The late first- or early second-century Didache expressed

---

[10]See W. Horbury, "The Benediction of the Minim and Early Jewish-Christian Controversy," Journal of Theological Studies 33, no 1 (1982): 19-61.
[11]Tertullian Scorpiace 10; To the Nations 1.8 (ANF 3:643, 116-17).
[12]The Martyrdom of Polycarp 13 (ANF 1:42).

Reflective Christians in the modern era are deeply ashamed of the way the gospel has at times been subverted for use as an anti-Jewish diatribe. The gospel certainly is not such a diatribe. It is good news for all, first for Jews and then for the rest of humanity. However, we have to recognize that from early times, otherwise outstanding Christians have sometimes been disgracefully anti-Semitic. The following extract from John Chrysostom (from *Homily I* of his sermons against the Jews, urging fourth-century Christians in Antioch not to attend Jewish festivals) is part of our past:

Moses himself said, "Israel ate, and he was well fed and grew fat and the beloved became recalcitrant" (Deut 32.15). Just as animals, when they are allowed to eat as much as they want, grow fat and become stubborn and hard to hold, and neither the yoke, nor the bridle, nor the hand of the driver can restrain them, so also the Jewish people, by drunkenness and overeating have been driven to the ultimate evil. They have kicked up their hooves refusing to bear the yoke of Christ and to draw the plough of his teaching. One prophet intimated this when he said, "Israel has run wild, wild as a heifer" (Hos 4.16). Another called Israel an "unbroken calf" (Jer 31.18). Such animals, unfit for any useful work, are fit only for slaughter. This is what has happened since they made themselves unsuitable for any task. They are suited only for slaughter. This is why Christ said, "Those enemies of mine who did not want me for their king, bring them here and slaughter them" (Lk 19.27). . . . If they are ignorant of the Father, if they crucified the Son, and spurned the aid of the Spirit, can one not declare with confidence that the synagogue is a dwelling place of demons? God is not worshipped there. Far from it! Rather the synagogue is a temple of idolatry. . . . Tell me, if demons dwell there, is it not a place of impiety even if there is not a statue of an idol standing there? Where Christ-killers gather, the cross ridiculed, God blasphemed, the Father unacknowledged, the Son insulted, the grace of the Spirit rejected. Indeed is not the harm even greater where demons are present?[a]

---

[a]John Chrysostom *Homilies Against the Jews* 1.2, 3, 6 (trans. W. A. Meeks and R. L. Wilken, *Jews and Christians in Antioch: In the First Four Centuries of the Common Era* [Ann Arbor, Mich.: Scholars Press, 1978], pp. 88-89, 90, 97).

the gulf between the two communities: the "hypocrites" (i.e., Jews) fasted on Mondays and Thursdays, but true believers must fast on Wednesdays and Fridays (*Did.* 8.1). Around the same time Ignatius was even more pointed: "It is absurd to profess Christ Jesus, and to Judaize."[13]

Use of common Scriptures (the First or Old Testament) and their common stance against paganism, however, created an ongoing temptation at a popular level for Christian believers to confuse their identity with Judaism. Even in the fourth century, John Chrysostom's thundering against the Jews in eight homilies arose largely out of his concern over high levels of respect Christians often gave to the Jews and over continuing Christian participation in Jewish festivals.[14] Such persistent Christian rhetoric was successful. Notwithstanding Christianity's beginnings, by the fifth century it was becoming increasingly impossible at a popular as well as a theological level to imagine anything other than total separation between the two faiths: a believer belonged solely to one faith or to the other.

Relationships with State and Society

Religion, politics and society were all intertwined in the ancient world. Judaism—matrix of Christianity—fit awkwardly into Mediterranean society. The relativism of other faiths stood over against the exclusivism of Judaism. They had elasticity to accommodate each other, and a willingness to participate in collective worship of diverse faith systems to honor and appease the guarding gods of society. Judaism's offspring, Christianity, was stricter even than its mother, especially in not conceding any place for sacrifice at all, in contrast to the universality of sacrifice in other Mediterranean faiths. Such a climate fostered an adversarial stance between church and state that led to periodic persecution and even martyrdom of Christian adherents.

This circumstance enormously shaped Christian views of the world. The relationship between a religion and its surrounding society profoundly affects the religion itself. If a religion is to have any societal influence, it must resonate in some way with its social environment. Religious practices need a degree of fit with the everyday experiences of individuals and with the social milieu of the groups those individuals form. One response to a society whose beliefs and practices seems threatening to one's faith is to wall oneself and one's group off from society. The alternative is to locate oneself at the center of society through modifying one's beliefs in order to maintain resonance with broader social patterns and expectations. Ernst Troeltsch classi-

---

[13]Ignatius *To the Magnesians* 10 (*ANF* 1:63).
[14]John Chrysostom *Homilies Against the Jews* 1.3; 2.3; 4.3. More generally on this point see J. N. D. Kelly, *Golden Mouth: The Story of John Chrysostom: Ascetic, Preacher, Bishop* (Ithaca, N.Y.: Cornell University Press, 1995), pp. 62-66.

fied the two approaches as "sect" (standing over against society) and "church" (embracing of society).[15] On such a classification, Christianity began as a "sect," markedly separate and apart from society in its first three centuries of existence.

This does not mean that Christians ceased to interact with their neighbors. Society interlocked too much for anyone other than hermits to opt out of society. Moreover, Christians felt a strong calling to interact with society, to witness to it, to provide Christian compassion within it. The strength of their influence in ultimately pulling society as whole into Christianity attests to their success in engaging with society. Despised at first as an ugly duckling, Christianity soon showed swan-type possibilities. In a world of powerlessness Christianity offered the hope of positive power, not only for the 90 percent who were poor but also for almost everyone, with regard to nature, illness, the spiritual realm and the often arbitrary expression of state power. Within society's conceptual framework, where so many outcomes were the result of spiritual causes in a world teeming with angels, spirits and demons, Christianity provided solutions. Especially was this so in counteracting demonic power.[16] "[I]f one were to ask for a single, simple proposition that would summarize the meaning of Christianity in the patristic period, it would be: Christ has triumphed over Satan."[17] Justin Martyr testified to that victory in the second century:

> For he [Christ] was made man also . . . for the sake of believing men, and for the destruction of the demons. And now you can learn this from what is under your own observation. For numberless demoniacs throughout the whole world, and in your own city, many of our Christian men exorcising them in the name of Jesus Christ, who was crucified under Pontius Pilate, have healed and do heal, rendering helpless and driving the possessing devils out of the men, though they could not be cured by all the other exorcists, and those who used incantations and drugs.[18]

Exorcism played a very prominent role within the Christian community. It was a repeated ritual in the preparation of Christians for baptism. So significant was the matter that the city of Rome had twenty-two designated exorcists at the end of the fifth century.[19] Through exorcism, the church had a solution to issues of spiritual power.

---

[15]Ernst Troeltsch, *Religion in History,* trans. J. L. Adams and W. F. Bense (Minneapolis: Fortress, 1991), pp. 324-26.
[16]On this point see R. MacMullen, *Christianizing the Roman Empire (A.D. 100-400)* (New Haven, Conn.: Yale University Press, 1984), pp. 25-29.
[17]R. A. Greer, *The Freedom of Fear: A Study of Miracles in the Roman Imperial Church* (University Park: Pennsylvania State University Press, 1989), p. 81.
[18]Justin Martyr *Second Apology* 6 (*ANF* 1:190).
[19]MacMullen, *Christianizing the Roman Empire,* p. 28.

Julian's *Letter 49* urging paganism to imitate Christian and Jewish charitable service:

To Arsacius, High-Priest of Galatia. The Hellenic religion has not yet reached the degree of prosperity that might be desired, owing to the conduct of its adherents. The worship of the gods, however, is conducted on the grandest and most magnificent scale, so far exceeding our very prayer and hope. . . . But are we to rest satisfied with what has been already effected? Ought we not rather to consider that the progress of atheism has been principally owing to the humanity evinced by Christians towards strangers, to the reverence they have manifested towards the dead, and to the delusive gravity which they have assumed in their life? It is requisite that each of us should be diligent in the discharge of duty. . . . Establish hostels in every city, so that strangers from neighboring and foreign countries may reap the benefit of our philanthropy, according to their respective need. I have provided means to meet the necessary expenditure, and have issued directions throughout the whole of Galatia, that you should be furnished annually with thirty thousand bushels of corn and sixty thousand measures of wine, of which the fifth part is to be devoted to the support of the poor who attend upon the priests; and the rest to be distributed among strangers and our own poor. For, while there are no persons in need among the Jews, and while even the impious Galileans provide not only for those of their own party who are in want, but also for those who hold with us, it would indeed be disgraceful if we were to allow our own people to suffer from poverty. . . . Accustom those of the Hellenic faith to the exercise of this liberality, by showing them how such conduct is sanctioned by the practice of remote antiquity. . . . Let us not permit others to excel us in good deeds; let us not dishonor ourselves by violence, but rather let us be foremost in piety towards the gods. If I hear that you act according to my directions, I shall be full of joy.[a]

---

[a]Pontius *Life of Cyprian* 9-10 (ANF 5:270-71).

In addition to Christian access to power, Christians commended themselves to society through their social concern. Largely this was in-house care of their own. Sometimes, however, the caring embraced wider society. Examples include ministering to the sick and dying and the burial of corpses during a terrible plague at Carthage in 252,[20] and the recognition by the pagan emperor Julian in the mid-fourth century that Christians were winning the allegiance of society by their social care for pagans as well as Christians.[21]

Thus, though as a "sect" Christianity stood apart from and over against society in the first three centuries, it gradually gained favor within society, especially through its charismatic and compassionate qualities. It offered cohesive community in a crumbling world. Nevertheless, the church still operated fundamentally from an "us" and "them" attitude. In no way were church and society coterminous.

The conversion of emperor Constantine in A.D. 312 and the ensuing gradual Christianization of the empire marked a huge change in Christian self-identity. Christianity increasingly shifted from the edge of society to its center. Bishops became government officials in their function of hearing appeals from court decisions that involved Christians (increasingly most of the populace). They had prestige similar to that of a state governor. Governors, even emperors, were members of their congregations, and so subject to their moral and religious guidance, which at times could become coercive in nature. Priestly power could corrupt. Christianity began in the face of cruel persecution. By the end of the fourth century Christians were close to the levers of power and were starting to manipulate them in the oppression of heretics and pagans. The persecuted were on the way to become persecutors.

Being at the center of society commonly led Christianity to embrace many previously rejected dimensions of society. Tertullian's famous early third-century denunciation of fraternization with the enemy—"what indeed has Athens to do with Jerusalem?"[22]—now had a positive answer: "everything." While Greco-Roman mythology and cult remained anathema, classical philosophy, rhetoric and literature became integral to the thinking of the church.[23] The great theological creeds, beaten out on the anvil of fourth- and fifth-century struggle, were much more couched in the language of Greek philosophy. Abstract and abstruse propositions and reasoning increasingly displaced the ambiguous yet powerfully evocative language of metaphor more commonly used in the first two centuries. Difficult theo-

---

[20]Pontius *Life of Cyprian* 9-10 (ANF 5:270-71).

[21]Julian *Letter* 49, in Sozomen, *Church History* 5.16 (NPNF² 2:338).

[22]*The Prescription Against Heretics* 7 (ANF 3:246).

[23]G. W. Bowersock, *Hellenism in Late Antiquity* (Ann Arbor: University of Michigan Press, 1990), pp. 10-11.

logical issues could not be resolved by Jesus as "rock," "shepherd," "vine." He was
now "the only begotten Son of God, begotten from the Father before all the ages,
light from light, true God from true God, begotten not made, of one substance
with the Father."[24] This only-begotten was now to be acknowledged

> in two natures, without confusion, without change, without division, without separa-
> tion; the distinction of natures being in no way abolished because of the union, but
> rather the characteristic property of each nature being preserved, and concurring into
> one Person and one substance, not as if Christ were parted or divided into two persons,
> but one and the same Son and only-begotten God, Word, Lord, Jesus Christ.[25]

Although such language had its seeds in Scripture and in the church of the first
two centuries, its evocative flavor now differed greatly. Despite credal thought being deeply rooted in Scripture, the language of the creeds increasingly drew from
the language of the academy. Athens was harnessed in the service of Jerusalem.
Tertullian's warning around A.D. 200, "Away with all attempts to produce a mottled
Christianity of Stoic, Platonic, and dialectic composition," was brushed aside in
the theological wrestling of the fourth and fifth centuries.[26]

Tertullian's disjunction between church and society no longer fit in the later
centuries. In both East and West the church came to stand at the center of society.
In the East the church increasingly became subservient to the state, serving as its
tool, as its religious arm—a tendency of some of the Orthodox churches continuing into the present. In the West there was commonly more recognition of two realities: church and state. Which was the top dog? Depending on social and historical circumstances and strength of particular personalities, at times one, at times
the other prevailed. However, in both East and West a huge shift took place. Over
the centuries, society as a whole came to be viewed as Christian, subject to church
guidance and scrutiny. Most if not all members of society were routinely becoming
members of the church. How different this was from Christian beginnings.

Institutionalization

The Christian church began as a dynamic movement. Institutional structures had a
largely embryonic nature. It would be wrong, however, to say that at its beginnings
the church was totally spontaneous and institutionally unformed. Judas, after all,
was the designated treasurer for the Jesus group (Jn 12:6). Moreover, care for widows in the fledgling church soon led to the appointment of seven deacons (Acts 6:1-

---

[24]Creed of the Council of Constantinople, 381 (*NPNF*[2] 14:163).
[25]Definition of the two natures of Christ at the Council of Chalcedon, 451. A version of this statement
may be found in *NPNF*[2] 14:264-65.
[26]Tertullian *Prescription Against Heretics* 7 (*ANF* 3:246).

6). Recognized office was a part of early Christianity (e.g., Phil 1:1; Acts 14:23; 1 Tim 3; Tit 1:5). Commonly, however, such office had fluidity and lacked sharp definition, as Paul's variously labeled lists of gifts and ministries indicate (Rom 12:6-8; 1 Cor 12:4-11; 12:28-30; Eph 4:11). Furthermore, much ministry emerged within a charismatic frame of understanding. It was seen as self-authenticating, stemming from direct connection with God (2 Cor 12:12; Rom 15:18-19).

Some of that ministry had a significant itinerant dimension, beginning with the Gospels, continuing in Paul, and persisting in the late first-century *Didache* (Lk 9:1-6; 10:1-20; Acts 8:4; Rom 15:19; *Did.* 11—13). Itinerancy played a vital role in the spread of the gospel. What, however, was the relationship of itinerants to a church they visited, seeking to provide direction to and gain support from that church? What authority did prophets have in relation to formally appointed leaders? For a couple of centuries the church struggled with the relationship between institutional and charismatic ministry.

By the time of Constantine the answer was pretty clear: the church was the institutional church, though sometimes supplemented by other, self-authenticating ministry. That ministry was clearly subject, however, to the institutional church. For example, the rise of monasticism initially took place outside and away from the institutional church. When, however, monasticism was drawn into the church, its looser and more spontaneous qualities became very much subject to church direction. Holy men and women were welcome additional guests to the church banquet, but they could not upset the meal.

These changes occurred in the context of an increasingly hierarchical church structure. As early as the second century the need for institutionally identified authority figures was recognized. Without such development the church would splinter, relationally and doctrinally. Institutional containers were needed for the heady wine of the Spirit. "Do nothing without the bishop," was the cry of Bishop Ignatius at the start of the second century.[27] The aggressive promotion of this claim suggests that it was a contested matter; Ignatius was advancing into disputed territory. A century and a half later, the matter was not in dispute, at least not in the mainstream of church life. Cyprian viewed the bishop as the center of a church life that was united and held together by the mutual cohesion of its bishops.[28] Bishops embodied the church: "You ought to know that the bishop is in the church and the church in the bishop; and if anyone be not with the bishop that he is not in the church."[29]

---

[27]Ignatius *To the Philadelphians* 7; *To the Trallians* 2; *To the Magnesians* 7 (ANF 1:83, 66, 62).
[28]Cyprian *Epistle* 66.3 (ANF 5:368).
[29]Cyprian *Epistle* 68.8 (ANF 5:374-75).

Bishops became exceedingly powerful, especially after the church received imperial favor. By the end of the fourth century the bishop was equal in status with a provincial governor. The see of the metropolitan bishop occupied the same territory as that of the governor. Senior bishops and governors received the same salary. A senior bishop was now a great officer of state. As Gregory of Nazianzus stated of popular expectation when he resigned from the see of Constantinople in 381:

> I was not aware that we ought to rival the consuls, the governors, the most illustrious generals, who have no opportunity of lavishing their incomes; or that our belly ought to hunger for the enjoyment of the goods of the poor, and to expend their necessaries on superfluities, and belch forth over the altars. I did not know that we ought to ride on splendid horses, and drive in magnificent carriages, and be preceded by a procession and surrounded by applause, and have everyone make way for us, as if we were wild beasts, and open out a passage so that our approach might be seen afar.[30]

The pomp and prestige were a far cry, as Gregory uncomfortably knew, from the lifestyle of the Son of Man who had nowhere to lay his head, as well as from Gregory's own monastically oriented lifestyle.

The emergence of powerful bishops occurred alongside an increasingly vertical framework of layers within the episcopate: metropolitans (senior bishops occupying the chair of the provincial capital), patriarchs (senior metropolitans of a handful of key cities) and a pope (the bishop of Rome) as the keystone. Some, especially in the East, disputed the place or role of the papacy at the apex of the ecclesiastical pyramid. However, by the end of our period of study the church had constructed a foundation of ecclesiastical doctrine and structure adequate to bear the medieval papacy that was later to emerge. Rustic Simon Peter's leadership had transmuted to the point where his claimed successors, the bishops of Rome, came to assert their standing as "the head of the world through the blessed Peter's Holy See."[31]

Setting

Christianity began as a reform movement within Judaism. As such, its earliest identity remained linked with synagogue and temple. Alongside this connection was also a sense of separate identity, intensified by Jewish hostility toward the new movement. Thus from the beginning Christianity had its own gatherings. While meetings outdoors and in rented halls were a possibility (Acts 16:13; 19:9), the natural church meeting place was the home. The periodic persecution after the first generation meant that the church must exist largely out of the public eye. Further, the small size of the intensely relational Christian community made homes a

---

[30]Gregory of Nazianzus *Oration 42: The Last Farewell* 24 (NPNF[2] 7:393).
[31]Leo *Sermon* 82.1 (NPNF[2] 12:195).

fitting gathering place. Moreover, synagogues were initially located in homes;[32] so churches located there reflected continuity on this matter with their original Jewish roots.

The New Testament gives clear evidence of house church meetings. The Acts of the Apostles records home meetings (Acts 2:46; 12:12; 20:8). Paul's letters also point to houses as the common location for church meetings (Rom 16:5, 23; 1 Cor 16:19; Col 4:15; Philem 2). Conceptually, there was one church for one city. Thus while Paul would refer to the "churches" (plural) of a region (Gal 1:2, 22; 1 Cor 16:19; 2 Cor 8:1), when he referred to Christians in one city he wrote of the "church" (singular) of that city (1 Cor 1:2; Col 4:16; 1 Thess 1:1). While the church of a city might meet together as a whole unit on occasion (Rom 16:23; 1 Cor 14:23), typically it met in several smaller house churches. Because social dynamics commonly led to household conversion (extended families, which in wealthier families might include slaves and clients of the wealthy patron), rather than conversion simply of solitary individuals, household meetings were a natural outcome of this conversion pattern.

Meetings in limited-size homes fostered multiple meeting locations in any one city. Jerome Murphy-O'Connor notes that excavations of wealthy first-century homes in Corinth had an *atrium* (central court) averaging 55 square meters and a *triclinium* (dining room) averaging 36 square meters. From this he deduced that the church at Corinth would not include more than 50 persons as it could still meet in one home (Rom 16:23).[33] One house would soon, however, be too small to accommodate a meeting of all the Christians in one city—hence the feature of multiple house meetings.

Justin Martyr in mid second-century Rome provides clear evidence that his church met in a home: "I live above one Martinus, at the Timiotinian Bath; and . . . I am unaware of any other meeting than his."[34] The earliest evidence for Christians meeting in a specially designated building comes from Dura-Europos on the eastern edge of the Roman Empire in the third century. Somewhere between A.D. 232 and 256 (when the city was sacked), a house was remodeled and specifically set aside for church use. An interior room was removed to create a hall 12.9 m x 5.15 m (estimated to be large enough to accommodate about 70 persons), and a baptistery room was created.[35] Significantly the building was a *domus ecclesiae* (a

---

[32]H. C. Kee, "Defining the First-Century C.E. Synagogue: Problems and Progress," *New Testament Studies* 41 (1995): 481-500.

[33]Murphy-O'Connor, *St. Paul's Corinth,* pp. 156-57.

[34]*The Martyrdom of Justin* 2 (*ANF* 1:305).

[35]For example, G. F. Snyder, *Ante Pacem: Archaeological Evidence of Church Life before Constantine* (Macon, Ga.: Mercer University Press, 1985), pp. 68-71.

house church). It has been argued that there is no evidence of any specially constructed church building prior to Constantine.[36] However, the fourth-century account of Lactantius of the razing of the church building at Nicomedia asserted that it was "on rising ground . . . within view of the palace," surrounded by other large buildings.[37] This suggests a prominent public building.[38] Nevertheless, the experience of most Christians in the first three centuries of the church was gathering for meetings in homes (or, in the final fifty years, in converted homes).

Such patterns enormously shaped earliest Christianity. Largely it "was nurtured in non-sacred space at the heart of daily life."[39] The home setting fostered the relational dimension of the faith. Christians were "brothers" and "sisters" together.

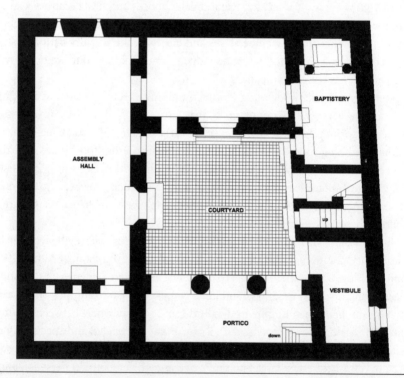

Figure 1.1. Plan of the first known church building (a modified house) at Dura-Europos (mid-third century) (Drawing by William Caulton)

[36]Ibid., p. 67.

[37]Lactantius Of the Manner in Which the Persecutors Died 12 (ANF 7:305).

[38]See also R. Lane Fox, Pagans and Christians (New York: Knopf, 1986), p. 587, for evidence of other public Christian buildings prior to the reign of Constantine.

[39]R. Aguirre, "Early Christian House Churches," Theology Digest 32, no. 2 (1985): 151-55.

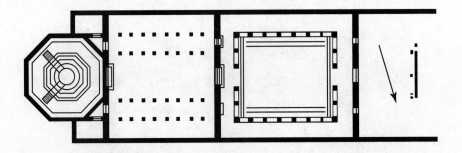

Figure 1.2. Plan of a basilica: The Church of the Nativity, Bethlehem, erected during the reign of Constantine (d. A.D. 337) (Drawing by William Caulton)

They were brought into a *koinonia*, "fellowship," which included radical sharing of resources with those in need. The home setting placed a brake on hierarchy and formality. Setting markedly influences worship. The shift from homes in the third century to impressive basilicas in the fourth allowed for a great flowering of formality, ritual and structuring. Consider a formal processional entrance, for example. Whether such an entrance opened into a house or into a grand building would make an enormous difference as to how a processional took place, or whether it even took place in a formal sense at all.

As a consequence of Constantine's favoring Christianity in the fourth century, the building of church basilicas proceeded apace. Constantine commissioned or subsidized numerous church buildings throughout the empire, including seven basilicas in Rome. Grand Christian buildings sent a message to pagan society that Christianity was substantial and worth consideration, providing a "deluge of Christian publicity."[40] Such buildings also lifted Christian self-image, providing a sense of dignity and self-respect. The danger, however, was that they risked diverting attention from what was central, fostering a sense of opulence and selfishness. Hilary of Poitiers, writing to his bishops in the mid fourth century, was very much aware of the downside of grand buildings: "Let me warn you of one thing: beware of Antichrist. What an evil it is, this love of building that possesses you."[41]

Worship
Three things markedly influenced early Christian worship: One was its awareness

---

[40]Fox, *Pagans and Christians*, p. 623.
[41]*Against Auxentius* 3 (quoted in P. Rousseau, *Ascetics, Authority, and the Church in the Age of Jerome and Cassian* [Oxford: Oxford University Press, 1978], p. 3).

Figure 1.3. The basilica of St. Sabina, Rome, built during the pontificate of Celestine I (422-432)
(Scala/Art Resource, NY)

of the presence and ongoing activity of the Spirit, fostering dimensions of spontaneity and immediacy. The second was Christianity's Jewish roots, fostering continuity with the past and a richness of formal liturgy. The third was the home setting, fostering informality and congregational participation. It was the Jewish strand (or that part of human nature that desires order, continuity and repetition) that became predominant. By the end of the first century there was a suggested structure for liturgy and a form of words to use. It was formal, but it was not a rigid system. Some flexibility remained. Praying was simply to be "after this manner" (*Did.* 8.2; 9.1; 10.1). Elements of flexibility persisted along with fixity of form. A century later (early third century) Hippolytus, after setting down an array of prayers for particular occasions, acknowledged that they were a guide only. One did not need to recite the exact words, and those gifted with language creativity could use that gifting to pray in an elevated fashion. For others, however, adhering closely to standard prayers would be best. And whether one used the standard prayers or not, one should pray according to the sound doctrine that the standard prayers of the church embodied.[42]

The trend, however, moved away from flexibility and toward formalization. The

---

[42]A loose précis of ideas contained in Hippolytus *The Apostolic Tradition* 10.

new architectural context of grand buildings accelerated this process. Choirs, elaborately robed bishops, ornate furnishings, processions and other rituals all contributed to a rich complexity of worship. It was a very different atmosphere from the world of the first Christians breaking bread in each other's homes (Acts 2:46).

Conclusion

This chapter has highlighted some of the enormous shifts that occurred in the life of the church in its first centuries of existence. At the end, as at the start, the core of the creed still declared that Jesus is Lord. Bread was still broken and baptism was still performed. But in atmosphere, in size, in relationship with society, the church in the fifth century had become in many ways another world from the church of the first century.

This is not to pine for "the good old days" of the first-century church. They were both good old days and bad old days. A much less structured church was also a much more fractured church. Greater levels of institutionalization were needed in the long run if the church was to survive and flourish. Greater definitions and cohesiveness were required if the church was not to splinter into myriads of pieces. Change was necessary as the church grew and faced new contexts. Change was both good and bad. How and why those changes occurred will be explored at greater depth in subsequent chapters.

For Further Reading

Each chapter will have a list of suggested readings at its conclusion. The one that follows lists major titles (either of a more general nature or relating to topics not focused on in detail in the following chapters).

Brown, P. *Augustine of Hippo.* London: Faber, 1967.

Chadwick, H. *The Early Church,* rev. ed. London: Penguin, 1993. (Originally published 1967.)

Ferguson, E., ed. *Encyclopedia of Early Christianity.* 2 vols. New York: Garland, 1997.

Fox, R. Lane. *Pagans and Christians.* London: Penguin, 1986.

Frend, W. H. C. *The Early Church,* 3rd ed. London: SCM Press, 1991. (Originally published 1965.)

———. *The Rise of Christianity.* London: Darton, Longman & Todd, 1984.

Hall, S. G. *Doctrine and Practice in the Early Church.* London: SPCK, 1991.

Kelly, J. N. D. *Jerome: His Life, Writings and Controversies.* London: Duckworth, 1975.

———. *Golden Mouth: The Story of John Chrysostom—Ascetic, Preacher, Bishop.* New York: Cornell University Press, 1995.

Moorhead, J. *Ambrose: Church and Society in the Late Roman World.* London: Longman, 1999.

Rousseau, P. *Basil of Caesarea.* Berkeley: University of California Press, 1994.

Skarsaune, O. *In the Shadow of the Temple: Jewish Influences on Early Christianity.* Downers Grove, Ill.: InterVarsity Press, 2002.

Stevenson, J., ed. *A New Eusebius,* rev. ed. by W. H. C. Frend. London: SPCK, 1987. (Originally published 1957.)

————, ed. *Creeds, Councils and Controversies,* rev. ed. by W. H. C. Frend. London: SPCK, 1989. (Originally published 1966.)

SECOND-GENERATION CHRISTIANITY
The Churches of the Apostolic Fathers

Historians love evidence. Modern history is very suspicious of sweeping statements and grand theory unless it sees clear and substantial evidence to support it. The problem is that especially with early historical periods there is often a great paucity of evidence. In that circumstance, evidence that does exist is treasured all the more.

This chapter focuses on a few documents that emerged in the late first and early second centuries. The main reason for looking at these documents is that prior to focusing on thematic developments in the early church, it is helpful to clarify the nature of Christianity in its earliest years, to provide a point of reference against which to measure later developments. To quite an extent this means a focus on the New Testament itself, whose contents were largely, if not totally, set down by the end of the first century. That inquiry belongs, however, more to the discipline of New Testament studies, and a vast array of accessible literature deals with that material. Of more profit here is to focus on extrabiblical church documents that emerged in the earlier part of the second century.

The amount of surviving Christian literature from that time period is scanty. What survives is a wonderful treasure, invaluable in opening windows into Christian life and thought of that period. Especially is this the case because the material of the early second-century period can sometimes be helpful to project back and illuminate unclear aspects of the New Testament itself. While some of the documents may at first appear a little dull, the scarcity factor makes them priceless.

Undertaking this study carries the danger of overemphasizing differences between the early second-century situation and that of the New Testament. We need to recognize that there was no one standard church situation either in the New Testament or in the early second century. We need also to acknowledge that there was likely chronological overlap between the last-written New Testament documents and the first-written second-century documents (a few of which may in fact have been written a little before the close of the first century).

This chapter will look at the life of the church as evidenced in four sets of writings, chosen because of their value in providing windows into the life and practices of the early church:

- The *Didache*

- The *First Epistle of Clement*

- The letters of Ignatius of Antioch

- The *Shepherd* of Hermas

These writings, with a few others, are commonly called the writings of the Apostolic Fathers or the writings of the subapostolic era, that is, the second generation of church leadership after the apostles. Sometimes some of the second-century "apologies" justifying Christianity in the face of paganism are also included. The apologies are probably, however, best regarded as a separate matter.

Apostolic Fathers	Date
1 Clement	c. 95
Didache	c. 100
Hermas, *The Shepherd*	c. 100 (at least in part)
Epistle of Barnabas (so-called)	c. 100-120
Ignatius, *Letters*	c. 110
Polycarp, *To the Philippians*	c. 110 (at least in part)
2 Clement (so-called)	c. 120-140
Martyrdom of Polycarp	c. 155-160

I will confine major discussion to the four sets of writings I have already singled out as being the most illuminating of the Apostolic Fathers' writings. It is significant that none of them deal in a major way with what we would call systematic theology. Their concern is much more applied, particularly relating to the life of the earliest churches. A prominent concern emerging from the documents as a whole is that of unity. This should be of no surprise, for the same concern is marked in most of the New Testament letters. Without an emphasis on unity and without the establishing of structure, the church could become sundered into hundreds of fragments.

It is possible that the *Didache* was written as early as A.D. 70 and the *Shepherd* of Hermas as late as A.D. 150. Increasingly, however, both documents are dated about the turn of the century,[1] while *Clement* is dated just before that date and the letters of Ignatius a little after. It is quite likely that all four sets of materials date within a twenty-year period, between A.D. 95 and 115. Two emanate from Rome (*Clement* and the *Shepherd* of Hermas) and two from western Asia (the *Didache* and the letters of Ignatius). We will quarry these writings to gain insight into the life of churches at the start of the second century.

The "Didache"

The full title of the work is *The Teaching [Didache] of the Twelve Apostles*. Despite its title, the work does not really pretend that its authors were the twelve apostles. Rather, it is claiming that its teaching faithfully reflects the original teaching given to the church by those apostles. The material probably comes from the region of Syria, written somewhere between A.D. 70 and 120, with an estimate of A.D. 100 being as good as any. The *Didache* is fundamentally a manual of church order, spelling out right behavior, individually and collectively. The document can be divided into three parts:

- a moral code based on the two ways of life and death

- a liturgical section dealing with baptism, fasting and the Eucharist/worship

- a concern for church order: apostles, prophets, teachers, bishops and deacons

The moral code. The *Didache* utilizes "two-ways" teaching, a traditional form of moral instruction. Each person has two options: to follow what leads to life or to follow what leads to death. It places a major focus on love, which includes giving within the community. New Testament fellowship (*koinonia*) had commonly been expressed in radical sharing between rich and poor.[2] The language of the *Didache* indicates that this was not simply idealized rhetoric, but an ongoing fundamental dimension of Christian community. The obligation is general: "Give to everyone who asks, and don't ask for it back" (*Did.* 1.5).[3] Free giving always runs the risk of giving to those who are irresponsible or wasteful, and won't be helped in the long run by the gift. The *Didache* seems to be aware of this problem. However, instead of cautioning donors to hold back their giving, it places a burden on recipients: if they receive unnecessarily they will face discipline, presumably by God (*Did.* 1.5-6). The *Didache* displays major concern with sexual sin, singling out pedophilia, fornication, abortion, infanticide and adultery for condemnation (*Did.* 2.2; 3.3).

---

[1]Part of the problem in dating these documents is that they may have existed in shorter versions and subsequently had additional material added to them.

[2]Acts 2:44-45; 4:32; 11:27-30; 20:35; Gal 2:10; Rom 15:25-27; 2 Cor 8—9.

[3]The *Didache,* trans. C. H. Hoole, The Saint Pachomius Library, <http://ocf.org/OrthodoxPage/reading/St.Pachomius/Liturgical/didache.html>.

The moral concern of the *Didache,* especially regarding sexual matters:

You shall not kill; you shall not commit adultery; you shall not corrupt youth; you shall not commit fornication; you shall not steal; you shall not use divination; you shall not practice sorcery; you shall not kill a child by abortion, neither shall you slay it when born; you shall not covet the goods of your neighbor. (*Did.* 2.2)[a]

[a]*Didache*, trans. C. H. Hoole, The Saint Pachomius Library, <http://ocf.org/OrthodoxPage/reading/St.Pachomius/Liturgical/didache.html>. English modernized.

The contamination of paganism is also a peril. Thus enchantments, sorcery, augury and astrology are all denounced: "from all these things idolatry is generated" (*Did.* 2.2; 3.4).

What is significant about these three moral concerns—love, sexual purity and avoidance of idolatry—is that these values were not unique to Christianity but also deeply rooted in Judaism. The overlap of these concerns is not surprising given that many scholars believe that the two-ways section of the *Didache* utilized an extant Jewish document.[4] If one removes from the moral code *Didache* 1.3-5 (material also found in the Matthean Sermon on the Mount material), one is left with a document that could be purely Jewish in origin (similar to that found in the Christian *Epistle of Barnabas* 18—20). The Jewishness of the moral code highlights the marked extent of early Christian dependence on Judaism on matters of morality. On many matters, Christian morality was simply Jewish morality. Thus to identify early Christian teaching on a topic of moral behavior, a good starting point is to ask about Jewish understanding and practice on the topic in the first century. We see major implications of this overlap, for example, on the topic of homosexuality, which first-century Judaism strongly condemned in keeping with its deep concern with its strict code on sexual transgression.[5]

Liturgical practices. The earliest baptisms in the New Testament appear to have occurred immediately upon response to the gospel (Acts 2:41; 8:12; 8:38;

[4]See, for example, O. Skarsaune, *In the Shadow of the Temple: Jewish Influences on Early Christianity* (Downers Grove, Ill.: InterVarsity Press, 2002), pp. 212-13.
[5]A point that struck the author in considering the issue while researching and writing his Ph.D. thesis: "Worlds in Collision: The Gay Debate in New Zealand 1960-86," University of Auckland, 2000 (since published under the same title, Wellington: Victoria University Press, 2002).

9:18; 10:47-48; 16:15, 33). However, the later church interposed a lengthy period of instruction and trial prior to baptism. When did the change occur? The *Didache* is evidence of the change coming early. Baptism was to occur "having gone over all these instructions," that is, the instructions of the "two ways." This suggests a catechetical period of unknown duration (*Did.* 7.1). The earliest Christian converts were Jews or Gentiles with extensive exposure to Judaism (the "God-fearers"). As Christianity increasingly drew its converts from more pagan backgrounds, the church likely felt the need to teach its new converts the moral implications of being a Christian prior to administering baptism—hence the "two-ways" material of the *Didache*.

Another puzzle on which the *Didache* sheds light is the fact that Acts (and probably Paul) shows that baptism took place "in the name of Jesus" (Acts 10:48; 19:5; Rom 6:3; cf. Gal 3:27; Col 2:12), whereas the evidence of Matthew's Gospel is that baptism was "in the name of the Father and of the Son and of the Holy Spirit" (Mt 28:19). The *Didache* shows a number of signs of significant influence from Matthew's Gospel; so unsurprisingly it indicates that baptism is to be into the threefold name, a universal practice in the later church. Baptism in the *Didache* was to be in "living," that is, in running water. This suggests that baptism at this time was normally by immersion.[6] Such a conclusion is based on the emphasis placed on the nature of the water medium, and the acknowledgment that if living/running water is not available then pouring is a valid alternative (*Did.* 7.1-3). At the same time one should note that the language echoes that of the Torah, where ritual purity commonly required use of living/running/pure water (Lev 14:5-6, 50-51; 15:13; Num 19:17). This underscores an aspect of the significance of baptism: it is the instrument of cleansing. The *Didache* also demonstrates a solemnity regarding the administration of baptism: the baptizer, the baptized and others are to fast one or two days prior to the baptism (*Did.* 7.4).

The Eucharist appears to be celebrated in the context of a fellowship meal (the *agapē* or love feast). Evidence consists of the fact that the instruction on the Eucharist follows the words "after you are filled" (*Did.* 10.1). There is repeated focus on giving thanks (*eucharisteō*), indicating that the primary focus is on gratitude for God's act in Christ. The meal is a sacred rite, reserved for the baptized (*Did.* 9.5). It appears to have central focus within the worship gathering. The fact that the cup was taken before the bread (in contrast to later universal practice) suggests diversity in how the Eucharist was celebrated or that these aspects of worship were not particularly fixed (*Did.* 9.2-3).

---

[6]W. Rordorf, "Baptism According to the Didache," in *The Didache in Modern Research*, ed. J. A. Draper (Leiden: Brill, 1996), pp. 212-22, at p. 219.

Church order. Itinerant ministries appear to be at the heart of church life. Three itinerant ministries—ministries who "come" (to the church)—are mentioned: apostles, prophets and teachers (*Did.* 11.1, 4; 12.1, 2). These are not precisely defined roles, and there is significant overlap. Thus *Didache* 11.4-6 discusses "apostles," but concludes by saying that the "apostle" who asks for money is a "false *prophet.*"

The *Didache* demonstrates ambiguity and tension with regard to the value of these ministries. On the one hand the prophets are tremendously elevated. They are to receive the first fruits of produce, "for they are your chief priests" (*Did.* 13.3). Their utterances are not to be challenged: "every prophet who speaks in the Spirit you shall not try or judge; for every sin shall be forgiven, but this sin shall not be forgiven" (*Did.* 11.7). Their high value is also suggested in that the *Didache* feels the need to urge the congregation to elect also bishops and deacons, "for they are honoured with the prophets and teachers" (*Did.* 15.1-2). This gives an impression that charismatics were so honored that regular ministries such as those of overseers (bishops/*episkopoi*) and deacons were seen as of secondary importance. The same conclusion can also be drawn from the description of the ministry of the two groups. The description of the itinerant charismatics places them in the highest order, in that their function is that of "chief priests" (*Did.* 13.3), while the function of the institutional bishops and deacons is simply that of "ministering to you the ministry of the prophets and teachers" (*Did.* 15.1). Thus the prophets and teachers were felt to exercise a crucial ministry, which the bishops and deacons would exercise in the absence of such itinerant ministries.[7]

Against this high value for charismatics, there seems also to be deep concern at prophets who give false teaching or who sponge off the community. Specifying that wandering charismatics should stay for two days only or get a job to become self-supporting ("if he remain for three days he is a false prophet," *Did.* 11.5) hardly indicates unqualified approval. Similar comment could be made in relation to warnings against prophets directly seeking money or food from the community (*Did.* 11.6, 9, 12). Moreover, balancing the exhortation not to try utterances in the Spirit (*Did.* 11.7) is the exhortation to reject false teaching (*Did.* 11.2). The charismatic must be tested before he (or perhaps she) is to be received (*Did.* 12.1). How does one know whether the teaching is "in the Spirit" or is false? The teaching must line up with what the community already knows (*Did.* 11.1-2), and the teacher must live a godly life, having "the ways of the Lord" (*Did.* 11.8) and practicing what he/she preaches (*Did.* 11.10).

---

[7]G. L. C. Frank, "Iconic Leadership in the Early Christian Tradition," *Acta Patristica et Byzantia* 2 (1991): 38.

Tension in the *Didache* over the value of prophetic ministry:

Let every apostle who comes to you be received as the Lord. (*Did.* 11.4)

He will remain one day, and if it be necessary, a second; but if he remain three days, he is a false prophet. (*Did.* 11.5)

And let the apostle when departing take nothing but bread until he arrive at his resting-place; but if he ask for money, he is a false prophet. (*Did.* 11.6)

And you shall not test or dispute with any prophet who speaks in the spirit; for every sin shall be forgiven, but this sin shall not be forgiven. (*Did.* 11.7)

But not every one who speaks in the spirit is a prophet, but he is so who has the disposition of the Lord; by their dispositions they therefore shall be known, the false prophet and the prophet. (*Did.* 11.8)

And every prophet who orders in the spirit that a table shall be laid, shall not eat of it himself, but if he do otherwise, he is a false prophet. (*Did.* 11.9)

And every prophet who teaches the truth, but fails to do what he teaches is a false prophet. (*Did.* 11.10)

But whoever shall say in the spirit, Give me money, or things of that kind, do not listen to him; but if he tell you to give to others that are in need, let no one judge him. (*Did.* 11.12)[a]

---

[a]Trans. C. H. Hoole, English modernized.

The extremely affirmative and extremely negative perspectives on wandering charismatics suggest a community in tension. On the one hand, prophecy—utterance under the direct inspiration of the Holy Spirit—is enormously valued. On the other hand, some apparently prophetic utterance is evidently false. How does one reject bad prophecy without rejecting good prophecy? And how does one elevate good prophecy without elevating bad prophecy? That is the dilemma of the *Didache*. The text does not come up with a clear-cut solution, but rather expresses the tension. It is an issue that has plagued the church in various forms throughout the centuries.

The First Epistle of Clement

Despite use of the term *first*, there is no "second" epistle by the same author. Al-

Testimony from the fourth-century historian Eusebius concerning *1 Clement* and *2 Clement*:

There is extant an epistle of this Clement which is acknowledged to be genuine and is of considerable length and of remarkable merit. He wrote it in the name of the church of Rome to the church of Corinth, when a sedition had arisen in the latter church. We know that this epistle also has been publicly used in a great many churches both in former times and in our own. And of the fact that a sedition did take place in the church of Corinth at the time referred to Hegesippus is a trustworthy witness.[a]

But it must be observed also that there is said to be a second epistle of Clement. But we do not know that this is recognized like the former, for we do not find that the ancients have made any use of it.[b]

[a]Eusebius *Church History* 3.16 (*NPNF*[2] 1:147).
[b]Ibid., 3.38 (*NPNF*[2] 1:169).

though the early church linked a second writing to "Clement," its fundamentally different style suggests there is no authorial connection between the two works.

While church tradition attributed *1 Clement* to a church leader at Rome named Clement, the epistle itself does not make this authorship evident. Rather, the letter indicates it comes from the church leadership at Rome (*1 Clem.* 1) who sent it to the church at Corinth via three messengers (*1 Clem.* 59). Thus, although this chapter will use the traditional ascription of the letter to "Clement," it is with a sense of communal authorship (although the historical figure Clement may have been its primary scribe).[8]

At this time, various congregations had no formal linking into a unified universal church. However, the very fact that the Corinthian church (or some of its members) sought assistance from Rome, and that the Roman church then sought to guide this relatively distant church as it faced turmoil, shows some sense of catholicity and interlinking between churches from the beginning. While the letter seeks simply to persuade Corinth of the steps they must take, rather than laying down the law, it is perhaps a hint of Rome's subsequent emerging leading role among the churches.

---

[8]B. E. Bowe, *A Church in Crisis: Ecclesiology and Paraenesis in Clement of Rome* (Minneapolis: Fortress, 1988), p. 1.

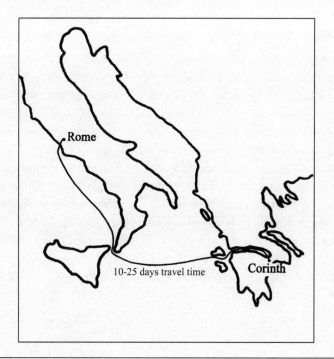

Map 2.1. Rome and Corinth

This was the situation at Corinth: certain presbyters had been ejected from their ministries (*1 Clem.* 44), with a great deal of strife, unrest and instability in the Corinthian church as a result. Why the leaders were ejected, we are not told. The epistle notes the proper appointment, the longstanding ministry, and the godly lives of these presbyters. Maybe there was a factional power struggle with the replacement leaders displaying a charismatic quality that was less evident in their predecessors.

If the situation involved the latter, then Clement's letter is very significant in coming down on the side of order and tradition. Tension between order and charism, which in the *Didache* seems weighted in favor of charism, is here clearly weighted in favor of order and institution. Clement is not very impressed with the new leaders' ability to sway others: it smacks of "proud and arrogant self-confidence" (*1 Clem.* 57).

A great deal of Clement's argument seems based on Old Testament parallels. The elect people of God are now the church (*1 Clem.* 46). Ministry was reserved for the high priest, the priests and the Levites, each with their own function (*1 Clem.* 40). Consequently laypeople should not be presumptuous: they are "bound by the laws that pertain to lay-people" (*1 Clem.* 40.5). Religion was ordered: the Jewish daily sacrifices were to be offered "in Jerusalem only" (*1 Clem.* 41.2). In his

Clement's vision of rightful ministry:

Our apostles also knew, through our Lord Jesus Christ, and there would be strife on account of the office of the episcopate. For this reason, therefore, inasmuch as they had obtained a perfect fore-knowledge of this, they appointed those [ministers] already mentioned, and afterwards gave instructions, that when these should fall asleep, other approved men should succeed them in their ministry. We are of opinion, therefore, that those appointed by them, or afterwards by other eminent men, with the consent of the whole Church, and who have blamelessly served the flock of Christ in a humble, peaceable, and disinterested spirit, and have for a long time possessed the good opinion of all, cannot be justly dismissed from the ministry. For our sin will not be small, if we eject from the episcopate those who have blamelessly and holily fulfilled its duties.[a]

---

[a] *1 Clem.* 44 (*ANF* 1:17).

arguments Clement drew clear parallels between Old Testament ministry and that of the church. The apostles were the authorized leaders, and they in turn appointed bishops and deacons (*1 Clem.* 42)—some of whom have now been displaced. While it is not fully articulated, the parallel between Israel's ministry and the church's suggests that, in Clement's understanding, appointed ministry was for life provided there was good and godly leadership (*1 Clem.* 44).

Another strong image in *1 Clement* in favor of communal stability and against individualism is that of the city-state (*politeia*).[9] Use of the term *politeia* in *1 Clement* 3.4 "indicates Clement's intent to contrast their individualistic motives with those of the true 'citizen' whose care should be for the common good of the *polis*."[10] Clement repeatedly calls for the civic virtues of peace and harmony (*eirēnē* and *homonoia*, literally "same mind")[11] and warns against the dangers of discord (*stasis*, a term with significant political overtones).[12] The church needs to be a good, socially cohesive unit, like the Hellenistic city-state.

---

[9] *1 Clem.* 3.4; 6.1; 21.1; 44.6; 54.4.
[10] Bowe, *A Church in Crisis*, p. 86.
[11] *1 Clem.* 20.3, 10, 11; 60.4; 61.1; 63.2; 65.1.
[12] For example, *1 Clem.* 2.6; 3.2; 14.2; 46.9; 49.5; 51.1; 54.2.

Division, particularly in the first hundred years of the church, imperiled congregations. The blessing of Spirit inspiration could also be a Trojan horse, concealing self-seeking one-upmanship. What mesh could filter out the chaos, while preserving the life? Clement's solution was to honor and buttress established leadership. The letter represents the routinization of charismatic authority: it comes through properly appointed leaders.[13] In the long term, this solution would push charismatic spontaneity to the margins of the church's life.

The Letters of Ignatius of Antioch

When Ignatius, bishop of Antioch, wrote his letters, he was on his way to Rome, a prisoner facing execution at Rome about A.D. 110 for the sake of "the name."[14] On his enforced journey he met with groups from a number of churches. In that situation he wrote letters to five of those churches; a sixth letter went to the church at Rome to prepare them for his arrival; a seventh letter went to the later-famous Polycarp, bishop of Smyrna. The extreme personal crisis Ignatius was facing and his deep pastoral concern for the churches of western Asia make up the frame within which the seven letters were written.

Figure 2.1. Image of Ignatius (Courtesy of Holy Transfiguration Monastery)

---

[13]J. S. Jeffers, *Conflict at Rome: Social Order and Hierarchy in Early Christianity* (Minneapolis: Fortress, 1991), p. 199.

[14]Ignatius *To the Ephesians* 3 (*ANF* 1:50).

Ignatius expressed major theological concerns in relation to some of the churches. Two major issues were involved. One related to the nature of Christ. Docetist ideas (from *dokein,* "to seem") had sprung up, arguing that, as Christ was divine, he only *seemed* to be a man. Docetic argument had roots in Greek dualism, which sharply contrasted spirit and matter. The Docetists' cultural modification of Christianity led them to the view that the real Christ belonged to the realm of the spirit and only seemed to take flesh. Thus many of the "events" of his life were in pretence only and not in reality. The response of Ignatius to these "deceivers" is that they "slander his being born of the Virgin; they deny his passion . . . and they do not believe his resurrection."[15] Against this, Ignatius insisted that Christ "was truly born of the Virgin," and that he "really died and was buried and rose from the dead."[16] Docetic argument had implications for the Eucharist: "they do not confess the eucharist to be the flesh of our savior Jesus Christ."[17] Ignatius affirmed that Christ was really present in the elements, which had a tremendous potency, being "the medicine of immortality and the antidote which prevents us from dying."[18]

The other theological concern was the relationship of Christianity to Judaism. Ignatius took a hard-line, separating stance. To live according to Judaism, for example to live according to the sabbath rather than the Lord's day (Sunday), was to "deny that we have received grace."[19] Ignatius slammed shut any possible door of compromise: "it is absurd to speak of Jesus Christ with the tongue, and to cherish in the mind a Judaism which has now come to an end."[20]

That theological issues should have arisen is not surprising. Any belief system is capable of more than one interpretation. Especially was this the case with early Christianity, which was transmitted largely in oral rather than in written form.[21] Furthermore, a faith that placed strong emphasis on grace and spirit was less likely to nail down all truths and dot every *i* and cross every *t*. Moreover, there was the question of how Christianity related to what already existed: to culture, to thought, to other religions. Almost inevitably, attempts at syncretism or harmonization would emerge. The church had to address a host of issues on the relationship between Christianity and popular belief and practice. Appropriate

---

[15]Ignatius *To the Trallians* 6 (*ANF* 1:68, English modernized).

[16]Ibid., 10 (*ANF* 1:71).

[17]Ignatius *To the Smyrneans* 7 (*ANF* 1:89, English modernized).

[18]Ignatius *To the Ephesians* 20 (*ANF* 1:57).

[19]Ignatius *To the Magnesians* 8.1; 9.1 (both *ANF* 1:62).

[20]Ibid., 10.3 (*ANF* 1:63).

[21]Papias, bishop of Hierapolis, for example, writing about A.D. 120, expressed his preference for oral rather than written gospel tradition: "For I did not think that what was to be gotten from the books would profit me as much as what came from the living and abiding voice" (*Fragments* 1, in Eusebius *Church History* 3.39.4 [*NPNF*[2] 1:171]).

Christian responses to Judaism and to Greek dualistic thought were two major issues. A major challenge for the early church was to identify the sources of authority that would advise the (commonly illiterate) faithful as to who and what was right and wrong.

Over the centuries, church history has thrown up three main answers on the locus of authority: the church, Scripture and the guidance of the Spirit (emphases embodied most strongly in the Roman Catholic, Protestant and Pentecostal traditions respectively). Written Scripture (the New as well as the Old Testament) was not the primary self-evident option for Ignatius: it was of great influence, but only decades later was anything like a list of authoritative New Testament books drawn up. The authority of the Spirit was a significant buttress to Ignatius's arguments. His elevated view of the bishop's role was heightened through a claim to Spirit inspiration: "The Spirit made an announcement to me, saying as follows: 'Do nothing without the bishop.'"[22] Ignatius urged fellow bishop Polycarp of Smyrna to seek divine revelation in order to guide his flock in perilous times: "Pray that God would reveal the things that are concealed from you, so that you may be deficient in nothing but may abound in all gifts."[23]

Fundamentally, however, authority for Ignatius lay with the bishop rather than with charism (though in his view the bishop would have that charism). A major factor in this perspective was that Ignatius saw himself as "a man devoted to unity."[24] His all-encompassing concern for unity forced him to wrestle with the peril of Christian fragmentation. How could unity be preserved? Ignatius's solution was a hierarchical one: the vesting of spiritual authority in one man, the bishop. Ignatius was the first writer to show with certainty three clearly defined, settled ministries in the church: bishop, presbyters and deacons. This contrasts with the earlier confusion and overlap—probably even the full identity—between the roles of bishop and presbyter. The Ignatian concept was that each city had one bishop who was the linchpin of the church. At times Ignatius appeared to give the bishop absolute authority. At other times this authority was recognized as exercised in collegiality, particularly in conjunction with his presbyters.[25] This approach suggests a tension: the bishop rules, but this rule is effective only within a team and with the goodwill of the congregation.

In Ignatius's eyes the bishop's position was extremely elevated: "We should look upon the bishop even as we would look upon the Lord himself."[26] The church was

---

[22]Ignatius *To the Philadelphians* 7 (*ANF* 1: 83).
[23]Ignatius *To Polycarp* 2 (*ANF* 1:94, English modernized).
[24]Ignatius *To the Philadelphians* 8:1 (*ANF* 1:84).
[25]Ignatius *To the Magnesians* 7 (*ANF* 1:62); *To the Trallians* 2; 7 (*ANF* 1:66-67, 69).
[26]Ignatius *To the Ephesians* 6 (*ANF* 1:51).

to "follow . . . the bishop even as Jesus Christ does the Father."[27] No baptism, Eucharist or love feast was to be held in his absence, or at least without his sanction.[28] Christians who were separated from the bishop were separated from Christ: "As many as are of God and Jesus Christ are also with the bishop. . . . If any man follows him that makes a schism in the church, he shall not inherit the kingdom of God."[29] In discussing the importance of linkage with the bishop, Ignatius used the term "catholic [i.e., universal] church." His use of the term seems to imply that

---

The hierarchical and unifying vision of Ignatius:

See that you all follow the bishop, even as Jesus Christ does the Father, and follow the presbyters as you would the apostles; and reverence the deacons, as being the institution of God. Let no one do anything connected with the church without the bishop. Let that be deemed a proper Eucharist, which is [administered] either by the bishop, or by one to whom he has entrusted it. Wherever the bishop shall appear, there let the multitude [of the people] also be; even as, wherever Jesus Christ is, there is the catholic church. It is not lawful without the bishop either to baptize or to celebrate a love-feast; but whatsoever he shall approve of, that is also pleasing to God, so that everything that is done may be secure and valid.[a]

---

[a]Ignatius *To the Smyrnaeans* 8 (*ANF* 1:89-90, English modernized).

---

there were competing groups. Only through communion with the bishop, however, is one connected to the catholic church.

All this suggests that the church had now become markedly hierarchical in a monoepiscopal framework. Such a conclusion, however, is not necessarily valid. In the early church positions were often asserted, not because they had been settled with certainty, but rather because they were matters of controversy. Ignatius's repeated assertions in relation to the bishop may indicate that his perspective was not universally held and was perhaps of fairly recent origin. The fact that he exhorted Polycarp to be a strong bishop may suggest that this younger fellow bishop

---

[27]Ignatius *To the Smyrnaeans* 8.1 (*ANF* 1:89).
[28]Ignatius *To the Smyrnaeans* 8.2 (*ANF* 1:89-90).
[29]Ignatius *To the Philadelphians* 3 (*ANF* 1:80).

had a more modest view of his leadership role than that held by Ignatius.

Although Ignatius noted the presence of the bishop and gave prominence to that role in five of his letters to churches, his letter to the Romans contains no indication of a single bishop at Rome, nor any reference to the theme of submission to the bishop. In part, the difference may be explained by the different purpose of the letter. Ignatius had not had major previous contact with that church and wrote to it to prepare it for his arrival and to urge it not to intervene to save him from impending martyrdom. However, the silence of Ignatius in relation to a single bishop at Rome matches evidence from both *1 Clement* and the *Shepherd* of Hermas, each of which indicate that the church of Rome in the first part of the second century was led by presbyters (plural). Again this points to Ignatius's position being innovative and controversial. Ignatius's solution, his dying legacy, for churches in danger of doctrinal derailment and organizational fragmentation, was a disciplined structure led by the bishop. His innovation was to be the way of the future.

The "Shepherd" of Hermas

The *Shepherd* of Hermas has been difficult to date because of conflict between the internal and the external evidence. The external evidence comes from the Muratorian fragment, a document commonly regarded as from the late second century, which dated the *Shepherd* as being from the middle of that century. However, more recent scholarship has persuasively suggested that the Muratorian fragment is actually from the fourth century and of little value in determining the dating of the *Shepherd*.[30] Internally the *Shepherd* refers to sending one of the books to Clement, who is likely a presbyter at Rome.[31] This seems to connect the *Shepherd* with the Clement of Rome of church tradition. Hermas apparently assumes the existence of plural presbyterial rather than monoepiscopal leadership.[32] While the *Shepherd* was likely written over a period of time, the internal evidence points to a dating of the major portion of the document around the turn of the first century.

If the *Shepherd* was written close to the time of *1 Clement,* its contrasting approach to charisma is striking. *1 Clement* espouses institutional authority, a looking to past tradition and to institutional office. In contrast, the *Shepherd* focuses much more on divinely inspired authority. Hermas's message stems directly from divine mandate: "a revelation was given to me, my brethren," and an "angel of repentance" told me to "write down my commandments and the parables."[33] Whereas

---

[30]A. J. Sundberg, "Canon Muratori: A Fourth-Century List," *Harvard Theological Review* 66 (1973): 1-41; R. M. Grant, *Jesus after the Gospels* (London: SCM Press, 1990), p. 56.
[31]Hermas *Visions* 2.4 (*ANF* 2:12).
[32]Ibid., 2.2, 4; 4.9 (*ANF* 2:11, 12, 16).
[33]Ibid., 2.4; 5.5 (*ANF* 2:12, 19).

1 Clement urges deference to the established leaders, revelation given to Hermas starkly challenges their sinfulness:

> Wherefore I now say to you who preside over the church and love the first seats, "Be not like to drug-mixers. For the drug-mixers carry their drugs in boxes, but you carry your drugs and poisons in your heart. You are hardened and do not wish to cleanse your hearts."[34]

Part of the divergence between *1 Clement* and the *Shepherd* on this point may be explained in terms of the particular circumstances each addressed. Nevertheless, the divergence illuminates the issue of inspired versus institutional authority and how this underlying issue should be resolved.

When assessed against later orthodoxy, the *Shepherd* seems a rather inadequate document. Hermas's understanding of Christ appears to be adoptionist in places: Jesus became a partner with the Father and Spirit because of his cooperating faithfully with the indwelling Spirit.[35] Elsewhere, however, he describes the incarnation as the manifestation of the preexistent Son.[36] In his interpretation of the parable of the vineyard, the Holy Spirit is the master's son, while Christ is merely the servant.[37] There, the *Shepherd* lacks a consistent or coherent Christology. However, the *Shepherd* needs to be assessed against its purpose, and that purpose was not to articulate systematic theology. Rather, as with the other documents studied in this chapter, its concern was practical, focusing on the life of the congregation.

Another factor in the *Shepherd*'s lacking a systematic expression of theology is its apocalyptic form. By nature, apocalyptic writing is allusive rather than direct—by no means a weakness. Its pictures tend to communicate evocatively, with less emphasis on clearly enunciating propositional truths. Despite his limited educational background, Hermas produced a work that was immensely popular in its first centuries of existence—in fact more popular before the fourth century than any other noncanonical writing.[38] Clearly its images and message resonated with the ordinary person for whom it was written. It can be aptly described as a kind of *Pilgrim's Progress* for the early church.[39]

The social setting of the *Shepherd* is very significant. Hermas seems to have lived in a context of Christian sluggishness. He attributed the problem to the sapping in-

---

[34]Ibid., 3.9 (*ANF* 2:16, English modernized).

[35]Hermas *Similitudes* 5.6 (*ANF* 2:35).

[36]Ibid., 9.12 (*ANF* 2:47).

[37]Ibid., 5.5 (*ANF* 2:35).

[38]C. Osiek, "The *Shepherd* of Hermas in Context," *Acta Patristica et Byzantia* 8 (1997): 115-34, see p. 115.

[39]J. Orr, *The Early Church*, 2nd ed. (London: Hodder & Stoughton, 1903), p. 44.

Testimony of Eusebius showing the importance of the *Shepherd* in the life of the early church:

But as the same apostle [Paul], in the salutations at the end of the Epistle to the Romans, has made mention among others of Hermas, to whom the book called *The Shepherd* is ascribed, it should be observed that this too has been disputed by some, and on their account cannot be placed among the acknowledged books; while by others it is considered quite indispensable, especially to those who need instruction in the elements of the faith. Hence, as we know, it has been publicly read in churches, and I have found that some of the most ancient writers used it.[a]

---

[a]Eusebius *Church History* 3.3.6 (*NPNF*[2] 1:135).

fluence of business and wealth.[40] The result was that many Christians were divided in focus and purpose. Hermas used some form of the term *di-psychia* (literally "double-mindedness") in the *Shepherd* over fifty times.[41] It was a perilous state to be in:

And they who gave in their branches half-green and half-withered, are those who are immersed in business, and do not cleave to the saints. For this reason, the one half of them is living, and the other half dead.[42]

The antidote to the seductive poison of prosperity and pleasure was to "refrain from much business" and to "abide in your simplicity *[haplotēs]*."[43]

How does one achieve that? Hermas put the focus more on human effort than on God's activity. He called for repentance, for a fresh keeping of the commandments of God: "Obey his commands and you will have a cure for your former sins."[44] Could the commandments be kept? Quite easily, said Hermas: "If you lay it down as certain that they can be kept, then you will easily keep them, and they will not be hard."[45] Overall, the *Shepherd* is a very moralizing, "can-do" document.

---

[40]Hermas *Visions* 1.3; 2.3; 3.11; *Mandates* 5.2; 6.2; *Similitudes* 4.5; 8.8: 9.19 (*ANF* 2:10, 12, 17, 23, 24, 33, 42, 50).

[41]D. P. O'Brien, "The Cumaean Sibyl as the Revelation-bearer in the *Shepherd of Hermas*," *Journal of Early Christian Studies* 5, no. 4 (1997): 473-96, see p. 488n58.

[42]Hermas *Similitudes* 8.8 (*ANF* 2:42).

[43]Ibid., 4 (*ANF* 2:33); *Visions* 3.1 (*ANF* 2:13). R. J. Hauck, "The Great Fast: Christology in the *Shepherd* of Hermas," *Anglican Theological Review* 75, no. 2 (1993): 187-98, quote p. 192.

[44]Hermas *Similitudes* 10.2 (*ANF* 2:55); also *Similitudes* 10.4.

[45]Hermas *Mandates* 12.3 (*ANF* 2:29).

This "can-do" philosophy emerges too in relation to postbaptismal sin. This presented a particular problem for the early church, as baptism was understood only to remove sins committed prior to baptism.[46] While Hermas carefully limits his solution to prevent abuse, his understanding is clear: the way to deal with such sin is the route of penance (for fuller comments on this topic see chapter 9).

The growing gap between rich and poor within the Christian community also appears as a major concern for Hermas. The earliest church was very egalitarian. However, disparities of wealth were weakening its cohesiveness. Those immersed in business "do not cleave to the saints."[47] What should be done? Hermas gave two answers: one said that wealth was evil and must be reduced and eliminated; the other said that wealth was good when used in meeting the needs of the poor. Hermas's negative view of wealth can be seen in his image of the church being built as a great tower. In the construction of the tower, stones were treated in three different ways. Square ones (apostles, bishops, teachers, deacons and other good Christians) were utilized without being polished. Others (the wicked) were rejected altogether. Rough ones (those involved in discord) and white and round ones (those with wealth and in business), although rejected as being the wrong shape, were potentially useable if they were reshaped:

> When the riches that now seduce them have been circumscribed they will be of use to God. For as a round stone cannot become square unless portions be cut off and cast away, so also those who are rich cannot be useful to the Lord unless their riches be cut down.[48]

Significantly, church leaders were among the wealthy. In challenging the rich to share, Hermas directly addressed "you who preside over the church and love the first seats."[49] Why might they be among the wealthy? We need to recall that the church of the first centuries largely met in homes. The home needed to be sizeable and was therefore normally that of a wealthy person. This made it "quite natural that the person who gave shelter to the church should also be its leader."[50] Evidence of leadership wealth also appears in Hermas's description of the attributes of good bishops: given to hospitality and caring for the poor and needy.[51] Clearly, wealth had permeated the church. Could one simply be negative about it, especially when some of its leaders were among the better-off members?

---

[46]See, for example, Cyprian *Treatise 8: On Works and Alms* 2 (*ANF* 5:476).

[47]Hermas *Similitudes* 8.8 (*ANF* 2:42).

[48]Hermas *Visions* 3.6 (*ANF* 2:15).

[49]Ibid., 3.9 (*ANF* 2:16).

[50]R. Aguirre, "Early Christian House Churches," *Theology Digest* 32, no. 2 (1985): 151-55, quote pp. 154-55.

[51]Hermas *Similitudes* 9.27 (*ANF* 2:52).

In warning against the perils of prosperity, Hermas also affirmed the positive value of wealth. He noted how vines grow over elm trees. On their own, elm trees are unfruitful. Likewise, on their own, vines trail on the ground and the fruit they produce rots. Fruitfulness comes through a symbiotic relationship between the two: the elm is useful in supporting the vine, and the vine bears fruit. Likewise, the rich contribute to the poor and vice versa:

> But when the rich man refreshes the poor, and assists him in his necessities, believing that what he does to the poor man will be able to find its reward with God—because the poor man is rich in intercession and confession, and his intercession has great power with God—then the rich man helps the poor in all things without hesitation; and the poor man, being helped by the rich, intercedes for him, giving thanks to God for him who bestows gifts upon him. . . . Both accordingly accomplish their work. The poor man makes intercession; a work in which he is rich, which he received from the Lord. . . . And the rich man in like manner unhesitatingly bestows upon the poor man the riches which he received from the Lord.[52]

In the *Shepherd* Hermas points a way to future accommodation with wider society: the wealthy would also be welcome—so long as they were generous and used their money in caring for the needy.

While not the dominant theme, Hermas's writings, like the other Apostolic Fathers, also show concern about strife and disunity. We have already noted that part of his concern about the wealthy was that they were aloof from their brothers and sisters in Christ. In Hermas's view disunity was a crucial issue. It disqualified people from being useful in the church. Disruptive members were "torn" stones that needed repairing before they could be useful.[53]

How was the church to be preserved in wholeness and unity? Hermas's argument does not explicitly use scriptural mandates, though their teaching undergirds much of his views. What of Spirit inspiration as an authoritative guide? Hermas recognized the perils of prophecy. Prophets commonly told their hearers what they wanted to hear: "answers according to their inquiries and according to their wicked desires."[54] Such prophets were arrogant, luxury-loving and seeking enrichment from their prophetic ministry.[55] But Hermas did not reject prophecy on that account. After all, he himself received visions and revelations that he viewed as authoritative. The crucial test was that a genuine prophet would have a godly life: "He who has the Divine Spirit proceeding from above is meek, and peaceable, and

---

[52]Ibid., 2 (*ANF* 2:32).
[53]Hermas *Visions* 3.6 (*ANF* 2:14-15).
[54]Hermas *Mandates* 11 (*ANF* 2:27).
[55]Ibid.

humble, and refrains from all iniquity and the vain desire of this world, and contents himself with fewer wants than those of other men."[56] Thus Hermas displayed an ambivalent attitude toward claimed charismatic inspiration: it was problematical, but the genuine gift was of high value.

Hermas's most significant answer to error and fragmentation was perhaps the authority of the church. Revelations came to Hermas through two figures: an old woman and an angel in the form of a shepherd. The first four visions of the book came to Hermas through an old and venerable matron who was the church. The church received a very elevated status: it was for her that the world was created, and the Lord sent his revelations to Hermas through "his holy church."[57] It was thus in the collective body that God was at work and through which he gave guidance. This answer seems to be a common thread in the Apostolic Fathers. The church was the repository of truth and the sure guide to belief and behavior. Protection against distorted teaching and divisive behavior rested in the duly appointed church leadership.

Conclusion

The early churches were close-knit communities. However, human frailty, ambition and factionalism meant that these churches soon and repeatedly faced the peril of fragmentation and even disintegration. How could the problem be solved? What authority could preserve unity and truth? Two of the documents studied in this chapter largely favored an institutional solution. Thus 1 Clement stressed due appointment and Ignatius emphasized the authority of the bishop. On the other hand, the Didache and the Shepherd of Hermas gave greater weight to prophetic inspiration. However, in honoring the inspiration of the Spirit who would "guide into all truth," the identification and outworking of that inspiration were clearly often problematic. The Apostolic Fathers are evidence of churches in tension between the attractions of charism and order. In the long-run it was the latter that was to prevail.

For Further Reading

Bowe, B. E. A Church in Crisis: Ecclesiology and Paraenesis in Clement of Rome. Minneapolis: Fortress, 1988.

Draper, J. A., ed. The Didache in Modern Research. Leiden: Brill, 1996.

Draper, J. A. "Weber, Theissen, and 'Wandering Charismatics' in the Didache." Journal of Early Christian Studies 6, no. 4 (1998): 541-76.

---

[56]Ibid.
[57]Hermas Visions 2.4; 4.1 (ANF 2:12, 17).

Hauck, R. J. "The Great Fast: Christology in the *Shepherd* of Hermas." *Anglican Theological Review* 75, no. 2 (1993): 187-98.

Jefford, C. N. *Reading the Apostolic Fathers: An Introduction.* Peabody, Mass.: Hendrickson, 1996.

Maier, H. O. *The Social Setting of the Ministry as Reflected in the Writings of Hermas, Clement and Ignatius.* Waterloo, Ont.: Wilfred Laurier University Press, 1991.

Niederwimmer, K. *The Didache: A Commentary.* Translated by L. M. Maloney. Minneapolis: Fortress, 1998.

Osiek, C. "The Oral World of Early Christianity in Rome: The Case of Hermas." In *Judaism and Christianity in First-Century Rome,* edited by K. P. Donfried and P. Richardson, pp. 151-72. Grand Rapids, Mich.: Eerdmans, 1998.

————. "The Second Century through the Eyes of Hermas: Continuity and Change." *Biblical Theology Bulletin* 20, no. 3 (1990): 116-22.

Schoedel, W. R. *Ignatius of Antioch: A Commentary on the Letters of Ignatius of Antioch.* Philadelphia: Fortress, 1985.

Trevett, C. *A Study of Ignatius of Antioch in Syria and Asia.* Lewiston: Edwin Mellen, 1992.

Weinrich, W. C. "The Concept of the Church in Ignatius of Antioch." In *Good News in History: Essays in Honor of Bo Reicke,* edited by L. Miller, pp. 137-50. Atlanta: Scholars Press, 1993.

Wilken, R. L. *The Christians as the Romans Saw Them.* New Haven, Conn.: Yale University Press, 1984.

3

SUFFERING AND DYING FOR GOD
Persecution and Martyrdom

With modern medicine some illnesses are easy to treat at any stage. Others, however, once they have a grip, are extremely difficult to dispel. So also with myths. Despite mountains of contrary evidence, many myths are so deeply embedded in consciousness that they are almost impossible to dislodge. Such is the case with the mountains of myths surrounding the topic of the persecution of the early church.

The Myth and the Reality

One popular misperception sees the church locked in a continuous ongoing struggle throughout its first three centuries of existence, subject to wave upon wave of relentless state-inspired persecution. This myth portrays a continual bloodbath of myriads upon myriads of numberless Christians, all of whom died bravely for their faith. The courage of their deaths finally cracked the power of the Roman Empire, leading masses of people to conversion and finally leading the empire as a whole to become Christian.

Over against such popular understandings, the reality is that persecution was typically local rather than empire-wide. The reason persecution was not universal is that so much of it, especially in the first two centuries of the church, was the result of mob pressure stirring local governors to action, rather than the result of direct imperial policy. The death of Jesus himself highlights the role of the mob. The execution of Jesus involved the complex interplay of the hatred of Jewish leaders and crowd pressure as well as Pilate's own initiative. Similarly, the famous martyrdom of Polycarp in the second century occurred through the governor's meekly following the will of the mob when the populace cried out, "Away with the atheists. Search for Polycarp."[1] Likewise, mob violence was the trigger for persecution

---

[1]*The Martyrdom of Polycarp* 3.2 (in J. Stevenson, ed., *A New Eusebius: Documents Illustrating the History of the Church to A.D. 337*, rev. ed. by W. H. C. Frend [London: SPCK, 1987], p. 24).

at Lyons and Vienne in 177. The fact that these persecutions arose locally indicates that it is quite inappropriate to characterize the reigns of different emperors as periods of either unbroken peace or incessant persecution. For example, one of the worst pogroms against Christians occurred in Alexandria in 248 during the reign of an emperor who was perceived as sympathetic toward the Christians.[2] Much persecution stemmed not from any official program, but rather from neighbors reacting to the perceived threat of Christianity to the well-being of society.[3]

Key Events Regarding Early Christian Persecution

30/33	Crucifixion of Jesus
64-65	Nero's persecution in Rome
c. 95	Probable persecution under Domitian
	Writing of the Book of Revelation
c. 110	Letters of Ignatius on his way to martyrdom
c. 112	Letters between Pliny and Trajan regarding Christians
c. 156	Polycarp martyred in Smyrna
165	Justin Martyr executed in Rome
177	Martyrdoms at Lyons
202-203	Persecution aimed at new converts
	Perpetua and Felicitas martyred at Carthage
249-251	General persecution under Decius
257-259	General persecution under Valerian
303	Beginning of the "great persecution"
305	Cessation of persecution in the West
311	Nearly complete cessation of persecution in the East
312	Constantine's embrace of Christianity; era of persecution basically ceases

In its first two centuries Christianity was a relatively tiny sect, seldom the focus of rulers who had multitudes of concerns. Persecuting Christians fell at the lower end of imperial priorities. The demands of other business commonly made governors reluctant to respond to mob pressure against Christians. With few staff, governors could do little more than handle important cases and maintain order.[4]

---

[2]T. D. Barnes, *Tertullian: A Historical and Literary Study* (Oxford: Clarendon, 1971), p. 151.

[3]P. J. J. Botha, "God, Emperor Worship and Society: Contemporary Experiences and the Book of Revelation," *Neotestamentica* 22 (1988): 87-102, see p. 99.

[4]S. R. F. Price, *Rituals and Power: The Roman Imperial Cult in Asia Minor* (Cambridge: Cambridge University Press, 1984), p. 2.

Governors would visit major towns, maybe once a year. It was during such visits that Christians would need to be arraigned for trial. But often a whole raft of other concerns were presented to the governor at the same time. At Arsinoë in Egypt, more than 1804 petitions were presented in two days when the governor came to visit in A.D. 209.[5] How keen would the governor be to look into complaints concerning a tiny peaceful group in the context of all that other business?

Even when an imperial edict called for direct confrontation with Christians, a lot depended on the perspective of the local governor. Rome was a long way off, and communications were slow. Modern states commonly ensure the laws they pass are in fact enforced, but Roman imperial decrees were much less certain of implementation. Thus, when the so-called great persecution took place in A.D. 303-311, it affected the western half of the empire until 305 only. Within the West, it hardly affected areas like Britain, Gaul and Spain at all. Their ruler, Constantius Chlorus (father of the future Christian emperor Constantine) took virtually no action against Christians apart from the token destruction of a few Christian buildings.

In Christianity's first three hundred years of existence, persecution was typically sporadic rather than sustained. For long periods almost no persecution at all occurred within the empire, for example, the period 260-303. At other times persecution might occur in one area but not another. There were sporadic outbreaks of anti-Christian violence in the years 195-200, 208 and 212/213, but these were basically limited to the Roman province of (North) Africa.[6] The weather pattern was one of scattered showers of persecution rather than a general rain bloodbath.

Also contrary to some popular myths, Christians were not uniformly heroic in facing persecution. Certainly many were. At times, however, many compromised their faith in the face of threatened death. In A.D. 250, for example, when the emperor Decius decreed that all free citizens must sacrifice to the gods of the Empire, Christians crumpled under the threat of death and lapsed by the thousands. Cyprian indicated that in North Africa the number of Christians willing to sacrifice to the gods was so great that the officials had to ask many of them to return the following day in order to be processed.[7] The failure of so many Christians under persecution during the third and early fourth centuries led to major theological difficulty for the church when peace returned. What do you do with those who lapsed? Do you allow them to return to the church easily, or do you impose rigorous discipline—even keeping some excommunicate throughout their lives? Controversies

[5]R. Lane Fox, *Pagans and Christians* (New York: Knopf, 1986), p. 423.
[6]W. H. C. Frend, *Martyrdom and Persecution in the Early Church: A Study of a Conflict from the Maccabees to Donatus* (Oxford: Blackwell, 1965), pp. 321, 323.
[7]Cyprian *On the Lapsed* 8 (ANF 5:439).

over such issues led to significant schisms within the church during this period.

Another feature of martyrdom was that it often resulted from Christians deliberately courting trial and death rather than being hunted and arrested by the authorities. One analysis of martyrdoms in early fourth-century Palestine under Maximin indicates that of the 47 of Eusebius's list of 91 martyrs who could be classified, at least 13 were volunteers; at least 18 more drew attention to themselves without going so far as to demand martyrdom; thus only 16 at most were sought out by the local authorities.[8]

Eusebius's idealized account of multitudes of martyrdoms in early fourth-century Egypt:

We, also being on the spot ourselves, have observed large crowds in one day; some suffering decapitation, others torture by fire; so that the murderous sword was blunted, and becoming weak, was broken, and the very executioners grew weary and relieved each other. And we beheld the most wonderful ardor, and the truly divine energy and zeal of those who believed in the Christ of God. For as soon as sentence was pronounced against the first, one after another rushed to the judgment seat, and confessed themselves Christians. And regarding with indifference the terrible things and the multiform tortures, they declared themselves boldly and undauntedly for the religion of the God of the universe. And they received the final sentence of death with joy and laughter and cheerfulness; so that they sang and offered up hymns and thanksgiv ings to the God of the universe till their very last breath.[a]

---

[a]Eusebius *Church History* 8.9 (*NPNF*[2] 1:330).

Some of those hankering after martyrdom were "lucky" and got what they wanted, others not so. Early in the second century, the soon-to-be-"lucky" Ignatius, describing in graphic detail his unbalanced "lusting for death," urged the Christians at Rome to take no measures to help him escape execution:

Permit me to become food for the wild beasts through whose instrumentality it will

---

[8]G. E. M. de Ste. Croix, "Aspects of the 'Great' Persecution," in *Church and State in the Early Church*, ed. E. Ferguson (New York: Garland, 1993), pp. 185-223, see pp. 211-12 (originally published in *Harvard Theological Review* 47 [1954]: 75-113, see pp. 101-2).

Figure 3.1. Second-century floor mosaic showing young man attacked by wild beast (Gilles Mermet/Art Resource, NY)

be granted me to attain to God. I am the wheat of God, and let me be ground by the teeth of the wild beasts, that I may be found the pure bread of Christ. . . . Let fire and the cross; let the crowds of wild beasts, let tearings, breakings, and dislocations of bones, let cutting off of members; let shatterings of the whole body; and let all the dreadful torments of the devil come upon me: only let me gain Jesus Christ.[9]

Very early then, martyrdom became a prized state, at least for some Christians. In A.D. 185 a number of Christians courted death by presenting themselves before Arrius Antoninus, proconsul of the Roman province of Asia. Obliging a few with death, he dismissed the rest with the words, "You wretched men, if you wish to die, you have your own cliffs [to jump off] or nooses [to hang yourselves with]."[10]

Eusebius recorded the differing fortunes of Origen and his father in Alexandria in the persecutions that arose after the emperor Septimius Severus forbade conversion to Judaism or Christianity in 202:

---

[9]Ignatius *To the Romans* 4 and 5 (*ANF* 1:75-76, English modernized).
[10]Tertullian *To Scapula* 5 (*ANF* 3:107, English modernized).

> As the flame of persecution had been kindled greatly, and multitudes had gained the
> crown of martyrdom, such desire for martyrdom seized the soul of Origen, although
> yet a boy, that he went close to danger, springing forward and rushing to the conflict
> in his eagerness.
>
> And truly the termination of his life had been very near had not the divine and heav-
> enly Providence, for the benefit of many, prevented his desire through the agency of
> his mother.
>
> For, at first, entreating him, she begged him to have compassion on her motherly
> feelings toward him; but finding, that when he had learned that his father had been
> seized and imprisoned, he was set the more resolutely, and completely carried away
> with his zeal for martyrdom, she hid all his clothing, and thus compelled him to re-
> main at home.
>
> But, as there was nothing else that he could do, and his zeal beyond his age would not
> suffer him to be quiet, he sent to his father an encouraging letter on martyrdom, in
> which he exhorted him, saying, "Take heed not to change your mind on our account."[11]

For Origen, martyrdom was a desired fate; only the shame of public nakedness
prevented his gaining his goal. A century later, desire for martyrdom caused the
great hermit Antony to leave his desert abode to go to Alexandria at the time of the
Maximin persecution.[12] He hoped that by mingling with imprisoned Christians
and attending their trials, he would come under official notice and through this
gain his sought-after martyrdom. "Unlucky" man, he was disappointed.

Some voices spoke out against this courting of death. To early third-century
Clement of Alexandria, voluntarily appearing before a magistrate to provoke the
death penalty was sinful, suicidal self-destruction.[13] Clement sought to cause focus
to return to the original sense of *martyria,* the bearing of witness. It was the faithful
speaking out for Christ when on trial, not the death itself, which was the com-
mendable act.[14] For most Christians, however, it was probably death for Christ
which was the praiseworthy focus.

Two obvious questions are raised by this discussion. Why were many Christians eager to die? And why did the state persecute? To answer the first question
we need to look back in history; to answer the second we need to consider the
waves of persecution that the church underwent, and reflect on the worldview of
society, and on the politics of imperial rule.

---

[11]Eusebius *Church History* 6.2-6 (*NPNF*[2] 1:250).
[12]Athanasius *Life of Antony* 46.
[13]Clement of Alexandria *Stromata or Miscellanies* 4.4 (*ANF* 2:412).
[14]Ibid., 4.9 (*ANF* 2:421-22).

The Prizing of Christian Martyrdom

To understand the almost fanatical desire for martyrdom in many Christians, we need to consider the matrix of Christianity, especially Judaism, the key formative factor out of which Christianity emerged. It is significant that W. H. C. Frend's narrative of martyrdom and persecution in the early church takes the period of the Maccabees (165 B.C.) as his starting point.[15] While this period predated the Christian movement by two centuries, Frend's taking it as his starting point underscores both the occasional ongoing pogroms against Judaism during that time period (something that could easily become pogroms against Christians) and the tradition of heroic steadfastness embedded in Judaism (a tradition drawn upon by Christians). The Book of Daniel, which probably assumed its final form at the time of the Maccabees in the 160s B.C., was a model for Jew and Christian alike of how to behave under religious persecution.

A martyrdom narrative from _2 Maccabees:_

It happened also that seven brothers and their mother were arrested and were being compelled by the king, under torture with whips and thongs, to partake of unlawful swine's flesh. One of them, acting as their spokesman, said, "What do you intend to ask and learn from us? For we are ready to die rather than transgress the laws of our ancestors." The king fell into a rage, and gave orders to have pans and caldrons heated. These were heated immediately, and he commanded that the tongue of their spokesman be cut out and that they scalp him and cut off his hands and feet, while the rest of the brothers and the mother looked on. When he was utterly helpless, the king ordered them to take him to the fire, still breathing, and to fry him in a pan. The smoke from the pan spread widely, but the brothers and their mother encouraged one another to die nobly, saying, "The Lord God is watching over us and in truth has compassion on us, as Moses declared in his song that bore witness against the people to their faces, when he said, 'And he will have compassion on his servants.'" (2 Macc 7:1-6 NRSV). [The narrative goes on to detail the death of each of the seven sons and finally the mother. It is an exemplar of being true to the faith and dying courageously.]

---

[15]W. H. C. Frend, _Martyrdom and Persecution._

Figure 3.2. *The Christian Martyrs' Last Prayer* by Jean-Léon Gérôme (1883) (Walters Art Museum, Baltimore, USA/Bridgeman Art Library)

A feature of Christianity that tended to make Christianity more suspect in the empire is that Roman authority executed its founder. In addition, Jesus' death provided a model for Christians. Jesus was the great exemplar. Scriptural passages urging Christians to follow his example commonly link this with his death (Mk 8:31-35; Heb 12:1-3; 1 Pet 2:18-25). To follow Jesus in death meant the ultimate in Christian perfection (Rev 20:4-5).

The basic call for Christians was to be faithful witnesses. Originally the word *martys,* "martyr," signified only that: witness. However, already the book of Revelation hints that the true witness will be the "martyred" witness. Thus Jesus is called "the faithful witness," which is followed by allusion to his death (Rev 1:5). From such seed thinking, the role of the Christian *martys* came to be not only testimony but also death for the faith.

In church understanding, the notion soon arose that only martyrs had immediate access to heaven (based on Rev 20:4-5). As Tertullian explained, "The sole key to unlock Paradise is your own life's blood."[16] All nonmartyrs went to Hades in the cavernous depths of the earth. This had two regions, that of the good and that of the bad.[17] In the good region there would be not only consolation but also

---

[16]Tertullian *On the Soul* 55; *On the Resurrection of the Flesh* 43 (ANF 3:231, 576).
[17]Tertullian *On the Soul* 56 (ANF 3:233).

punishment, some "compensatory discipline" for earthly sins, to prepare the deceased for ultimate Paradise.[18] Only with Christ's return could the ordinary Christian attain to the presence of God. How much incentive then to shortcut the process and gain heaven now.

Furthermore, martyrdom gained enormous spiritual importance as a substitute baptism. Since baptism itself was a crucial component of salvation, what about Christians who died while under prebaptismal instruction? Was martyrdom itself a baptism (as Lk 12:50 might suggest)? Writing about A.D. 220, Hippolytus gave reassurance on this matter: "if it should happen that they treat him shamefully and kill him [before his baptism], he will be justified, for he has been baptized in his own blood."[19] A little earlier, Tertullian viewed martyrdom as equivalent to baptism. Calling it "a second font," Tertullian saw it as efficacious for those who were soiled with postbaptismal sin and lacked any other cleansing agent because they had already used the once-only washing remedy of baptism.[20]

Martyrdom came to be seen as spiritually potent not only for the victim but also for those around him or her. In the mid third century, Origen dared to compare its efficacy with that of the death of Christ: "baptism in the form of martyrdom, as received by the Saviour, is a purgation for the world; so too, when we receive it, it becomes a purgation for many."[21] He went on to claim:

> Perhaps just as we have been purchased by the precious blood of Jesus, when Jesus received the name that is above every name, so some will be purchased by the precious blood of the martyrs; for they themselves are exalted higher than they would have been if they had only been justified and not also become martyrs.[22]

No wonder then that a cult of martyrdom quickly sprang up. By the end of the second century, churches had their rolls of martyrs whose "birthdays" (*natalicia*, actually the date of their martyrdom) were celebrated each year.[23] According to Tertullian, "the death of martyrs is praised in song."[24] The prizing of relics soon emerged. Polycarp's body was supposed to have been burnt by the Jews to prevent a cult being built around it.[25] However, a sufficient amount of his remains were left

---

[18]Ibid., 58 (ANF 3:235).

[19]Hippolytus *Apostolic Tradition* 19.2 (trans. B. S. Easton, *The Apostolic Tradition of Hippolytus* [Cambridge: Cambridge University Press, 1934]).

[20]Tertullian *On Baptism* 16; *Scorpiace* 6 (ANF 3:677, 639).

[21]Origen *Exhortation to Martyrdom* 30, quoted in B. Ramsey, *Beginning to Read the Fathers* (London: SCM Press, 1993), p. 131.

[22]Origen *Exhortation to Martyrdom* 50 (in Ramsey, *Beginning to Read the Fathers*, p. 132).

[23]Frend, *Martyrdom and Persecution*, p. 257; *Martyrdom of Polycarp* 18—19 (ANF 1:43); Tertullian *On the Crown* 3 (ANF 3:94).

[24]Tertullian *Scorpiace* 7 (ANF 3:639).

[25]*Martyrdom of Polycarp* 18 (ANF 1:43).

to provide tangible connection with the holy martyr: "we afterwards took up his bones, as being more precious than the most exquisite jewels, and more purified than gold, and deposited them in a fitting place, whither, being gathered together as opportunity is allowed us, with joy and rejoicing, the Lord shall grant us to celebrate the anniversary of his martyrdom."[26] The value of relics soon led to the custom of dividing the bodies of the martyrs into fragments, each one of which was thought to have the same virtue as the whole body itself.[27] In A.D. 386 the emperor Theodosius forbade the transference of the bodies of martyrs or their being cut into pieces or the sale of such pieces.[28] Robin Lane Fox cleverly summed up the early church's prizing of relics: "The race for bones and skin began early."[29]

Martyrs, as immediate travelers to paradise, became a unique point of contact between heaven and earth.[30] Soon the faithful called on them as sources of interces-

Figure 3.3. Inscription from the catacomb of Sebastian in Rome: "Pray for Victor." (Scala/Art Resource, NY)

[26]Ibid.
[27]J. A. Jungmann, *The Early Liturgy: To the Time of Gregory the Great* (London: Darton, Longman & Todd, 1959), p. 185.
[28]*Codex Theodosius* 9.17.7 (in Jungmann, *Early Liturgy*, p. 185).
[29]R. Lane Fox, *Pagans and Christians* (New York: Knopf, 1986), p. 446.
[30]Ibid., p. 445.

sory power. Thus graffiti scratched on walls near martyrs' graves has prayers such as, "Peter and Paul, pray for Victor," and, "Lord Crescentio, heal my eyes for me."[31]

Martyrs had power in the eyes of believers, but they were invisible. There were, however, sort-of-martyrs around who were visible, namely the "confessors," who stood firm under arrest but escaped execution. Strictly speaking, confessors were not martyrs, and the soon-to-be-martyrs at Lyons insisted on this distinction, acknowledging that they were confessors, but denying they were martyrs.[32] However, confessors were credited with such access to God that their spiritual stature neared that of the martyrs. At the beginning of the third century, Perpetua as confessor could expect and receive direct revelation from God:

> My brother said to me, "My dear sister, you are already in a position of great dignity, and are such that you may ask for a vision, and that it may be made known to you whether this is to result in a passion or an escape." And I, who knew that I was privileged to converse with the Lord, whose kindness I had found to be so great, boldly promised him, and said, "Tomorrow I will tell you."[33]

Not only did Perpetua receive the appropriate revelation, but she also shifted another brother, deceased, from a place of suffering to a place of joy by her prayers:

> I saw Dinocrates going out from a gloomy place, where also there were several others, and he was parched and very thirsty, with a filthy countenance and pallid colour, and the wound on his face which he had when he died. This Dinocrates had been my brother after the flesh, seven years of age, who died miserably with disease—his face being so eaten out with cancer, that his death caused repugnance to all men. For him I had made my prayer. . . . I was aroused and knew that my brother was in suffering. But I trusted that my prayer would bring help to his suffering; and I prayed for him every day until we passed over into the prison of the camp. . . . I saw that that place which I had formerly observed to be in gloom was now bright; and Dinocrates, with a clean body well clad, was finding refreshment. . . . Dinocrates . . . began to drink . . . and the goblet did not fail. And when he was satisfied, he went away from the water to play joyously, after the manner of children, and I awoke. Then I understood that he was translated from the place of punishment.[34]

The confessors' perceived closeness to God also drew others to them. Tertullian spoke of queues thronging prisons where confessors lay: "No sooner has anyone put on bonds than adulterers beset him, fornicators gain access,

[31]In Jungmann, *Early Liturgy*, p. 182.
[32]Eusebius *History of the Church* 5.2.2 (*NPNF*[2] 1:217-18).
[33]*Passion of Perpetua* 1.3 (*ANF* 3:700).
[34]Ibid., 2.3 (*ANF* 3:701-2).

Figure 3.4. Details of medallion of the martyr Perpetua, Archepiscopal Chapel, Ravenna (Scala/ Art Resource, NY)

prayers echo round him, pools of tears from sinners soak him."[35] This perceived closeness to God gave the confessors a quasi-priestly function, which Hippolytus noted early in the third century: "On a confessor, if he has been in bonds for the name of the Lord, hands shall not be laid for the diaconate or the presbyterate, for he has the honour of the presbyterate by his confession."[36] This led to the situation where confessors took to themselves the right to forgive sins and restore the lapsed to communion. Tertullian appeared to approve this practice:

> Some, not able to find this peace in the Church, have been used to seek it from the imprisoned martyrs. And so you ought to have it dwelling with you, and to cherish it, and to guard it, that you may be able perhaps to bestow it upon others.[37]

Despite Tertullian's approval, Cyprian later rebuked this assuming of priestly func-

---

[35]Tertullian *On Modesty* 22 (ANF 4:100).
[36]Hippolytus *Apostolic Tradition* 10.1 (trans. B. S. Easton).
[37]Tertullian *To the Martyrs* 1 (ANF 3:693).

tion.[38] The fact that the confessors dared to assume such a role, notwithstanding the church's increasing emphasis on discipline and order, underlines the high standing of martyrs and prospective martyrs in the church, a dimension highlighted in the following narrative of some of the more outstanding events and measures relating to persecution.

Persecutions of the Christian Church

The New Testament church. In considering persecution, we should recall the killing of Christianity's founder and how that happened. Religious strife, religious jealousy and mob violence all came into play prior to judicial sentence by the Roman authorities. This became a common pattern for the future. The instigation of persecution of the fledgling church was initially not so much from the state as from the Jewish community. Christianity was birthed in Judaism and for several decades was not totally separate from it. Judaism itself included a jungle of competing sects, and Christianity could easily be viewed as one of those sects (Acts 24:14). Paul's evangelism typically began within the synagogue. His "sheep-stealing" of Jews and God-fearing proselyte Gentiles frequently provoked jealousy and strife, leading to murderous hatred and the driving of the new group into separate identity (e.g., 1 Thess 2:14-16). Paul's ongoing Jewishness can be seen in his receiving thirty-nine lashes on five occasions (2 Cor 11:24). Only those within the Jewish community were liable to such treatment. This suggests that to a significant degree Paul still remained within Judaism.

For much of that earliest period, the Roman state was relatively neutral, even protective of the young church against lynch law (Acts 18:12-17; 19:23-41). This, however, was to change under Nero.

The Neronian persecution. Nero's imperial rule began well in A.D. 54, but his erratic excesses had used up the initial public goodwill by the 60s. In A.D. 64 a fire destroyed half of Rome. Rumor blamed Nero himself as the originator of the fire (alleging that he set the slums on fire to launch a grandiose rebuilding program). Such rumor placed Nero's rule in jeopardy. He quickly diverted attention to a scapegoat: the Christians. Terrible atrocities ensued. Fifty years later the Roman writer Tacitus recorded the savagery:

> Mockery of every sort was added to their deaths. Covered with the skins of beasts, they were torn by dogs and perished, or were nailed to crosses, or were doomed to the flames. These served to illuminate the night when daylight failed. Nero had thrown open his gardens for the spectacle, and was exhibiting a show in the circus,

---

[38]Cyprian *Epistle* 27 (*ANF* 5:306). Cyprian's concerns partly related to the ad hoc nature of such actions, which tended to lead to disorder in the absence of an overall church policy on the matter.

while he mingled with the people in the dress of a charioteer or drove about in a chariot. Hence, even for criminals who deserved extreme and exemplary punishment, there arose a feeling of compassion; for it was not, as it seemed, for the public good, but to glut one man's cruelty, that they were being destroyed.[39]

Among those who probably perished about this time were the apostles Peter and Paul.[40] Why were Christians the chosen scapegoat? Tacitus referred to them as "a class hated for their abominations," and as a "deadly superstition."[41] The early second-century historian Suetonius made no reference to the fire in referring to the persecution, but simply called them "a sect professing a new and mischievous religious belief [superstitio nova et malefica]."[42] Romans had deep distrust of new religions. Thus Cicero indicated in the century before Christ that new religions should not be accepted unless duly authorized.[43] The language of Tacitus and Suetonius suggests that popular prejudice made Christians a natural scapegoat.

The Neronian persecution seems to have been limited to Rome itself. Strictly speaking, the criminal charges were directed at arson, not at being a Christian. However, as the trials required no other proof of arson than that those accused were Christians, a precedent was set for persecution on account of that name alone.

Persecution under Domitian. Church tradition viewed the late first-century emperor Domitian as a second Nero.[44] That tradition, however, is first evidenced at least seventy years after the alleged persecution, and a number of scholars now doubt whether there was any persecution under Domitian.

There are, nevertheless, three pieces of evidence which together provide strong corroboration for the early tradition that persecution did occur under Domitian. The first piece of evidence is that of Clement's *First Epistle to the Corinthians*, written from Rome about A.D. 96. The letter opens with an apology for delay in writing to Corinth, which was caused by "the sudden and successive calamitous events which have happened to ourselves."[45] This reference does not refer with certainty to persecution instigated by Domitian, but it is clearly compatible with it. The letter goes on in chapters five and six to discuss martyrdoms from the past, including those of Peter and Paul. It then states that the Christians at Rome "are struggling in the same arena."[46] Cumulatively, these portions of *1 Clement* provide significant

---

[39]Tacitus *Annals* 15.44.2-8 (in Stevenson, *New Eusebius,* pp. 2-3).
[40]*1 Clem.* 5 (ANF 1:6).
[41]Tacitus *Annals* 15.44.3-4.
[42]Suetonius *Nero* 16.
[43]Cicero *Concerning Laws* 2.8.
[44]Tertullian *Apology* 5.4 (ANF 3:22); Melito of Sardis in Eusebius *Church History* 4.26.9 (NPNF[2] 1:205).
[45]*1 Clem.* 1.1 (ANF 1:5). See also *1 Clem.* 7.1.
[46]*1 Clem.* 7.1.

evidence for some persecution of Christians at Rome under Domitian.[47]

The second piece of evidence comes from the Book of Revelation in the Bible. The earliest tradition is that it dates from the time of Domitian,[48] a dating which most modern scholars accept. The Book of Revelation was written in an atmosphere of persecution. While only one Christian had certainly been martyred (Rev 2:13), many other allusions point to the likelihood of a number of other martyrs (Rev 6:9-10; 7:14; 12:11; 17:6; 20:4). This biblical material suggests persecution of Christians in the Roman province of Asia toward the end of the first century. Although it does not necessarily indicate empire-wide persecution or even that the persecution was directly instigated by Domitian himself, it does suggest that there was some persecution in some places during his reign.

Such a conclusion finds corroboration from the third piece of evidence, a letter written from Pliny the Younger, governor of Bithynia, to the emperor Trajan about the year A.D. 112. In this letter in which he asked the emperor what he should do with people accused of being Christians, Pliny noted that some of them claimed that they had ceased to be Christians, "some three years ago, some a good many years, and a few even twenty."[49] This final reference would tie in well with Christians surrendering their faith in the face of persecution in the wider area of modern-day Turkey in the time of Domitian. Together these three pieces of evidence suggest persecution of Christians by Domitian in Rome and by local authorities in modern-day Turkey.

One aspect that is unclear is the state's official attitude toward Christians at this time. Commonly it has been asserted that Roman law put religions into two categories, lawful (licita) and unlawful (illicita), and that Christianity was placed on the latter list. In part this view of a twofold classification is based on a reference in Tertullian's Apology to the Jewish religion being a lawful one.[50] We have no other evidence of such a clear systematic classification, and few scholars now accept that such a classification existed. One thing that is evident, however, is that authorities consistently seemed to assume the illegality of Christianity. It has been suggested that this flowed from Nero's oppression of the Christians in the mid 60s. However, Nero's persecution was ostensibly aimed only at arsonists, not at Christianity per se, although in practice the distinction was a fine, perhaps even practically nonexistent one.

It has been argued that in fact there was no law against Christians, that gover-

---

[47]For a fuller discussion of this argument see P. Keresztes, "The Jews, the Christians, and Emperor Domitian," Vigiliae Christianae 27 (1973): 1-28, see pp. 20-21.

[48]Irenaeus Against Heresies 5.30.3 (ANF 1:559-60).

[49]Pliny Letter 10.96.6 (in Stevenson, New Eusebius, p. 19).

[50]Tertullian Apology 21.2 (ANF 3:34).

nors simply acted on their general duty to preserve law and order *(coercitio)*, and suppress shameful actions *(flagitia)*.[51] This would include cannibalism and incest—scurrilous charges that were leveled against Christianity. Such a view suggests that persecution rested on the initiative or whim of individual governors to suppress specific crimes, initiative that was activated especially when pressured by mob opinion.

Pliny's letter discloses his uncertainty as to "whether punishment attaches to the mere name [Christian] apart from secret crimes, or to the secret crimes connected with the name."[52] Pliny proceeded, however, on the basis that the name alone was the offence, and the emperor's reply seemed to confirm this stance: "Whoso denies himself to be a Christian, and makes the fact plain by his action, that is, by worshipping our gods, shall obtain pardon on his repentance, however suspicious his past conduct may be."[53] The offence then was not what one had done, but what one was in the present time. Trajan added a cautionary note on this point: Christians were not to be sought out or prosecuted on anonymous complaint. This indicates that while Christians were a repressed class, imperial concern was at this stage minor, and there was no systematic attempt to eradicate the group entirely. Trajan's cautionary note was repeated by his successor Hadrian in about 125, particularly with regard to anonymous complaints.[54]

The martyrdom of Polycarp. Polycarp, bishop of Smyrna for much of the first half of the second century, seems to have been a major bridge from the first-century community to the second. Tradition from Irenaeus indicates that his life overlapped with the life of the apostle John.[55] Around 156, the very aged Polycarp was martyred. Immediately prior to this, several rank-and-file Christians perished in the arena. Mob hatred then craved the blood of the big fish, the bishop himself. A cry went up, "Away with the atheists; let Polycarp be sought out!" This sparked the governor to seek his arrest. The *Martyrdom of Polycarp* portrayed his outstanding courage under judicial examination:

And when he came near, the proconsul asked him whether he was Polycarp. On his confessing that he was, [the proconsul] sought to persuade him to deny [Christ], saying, "Have respect for your old age," and other similar things, according to their cus-

[51]A. N. Sherwin-White, "The Early Persecutions and Roman Law Again" and "Why Were the Early Christians Persecuted?—An Amendment," in *Church and State in the Early Church,* ed. E. Ferguson (New York: Garland, 1993), pp. 1-15 and 49-53 (these two articles were originally published in *Journal of Theological Studies* 3 (1952): 199-213; and *Past and Present* 27 (1964): 23-27, respectively).
[52]Pliny *Epistles* 10.96.
[53]Ibid., 10.97.
[54]*Rescript* of Hadrian to Caius Minucius Fundanus, Proconsul of Asia, c. 125, in Eusebius *Church History* 4.9 (*NPNF*[2] 1:182).
[55]Irenaeus *Against Heresies* 3.3.4 (*ANF* 1:416).

tom, [such as], "Swear by the fortune of Caesar; repent and say, Away with the atheists." But Polycarp, gazing with a stern countenance on all the multitude of the wicked heathen then in the stadium, and waving his hand towards them, while with groans he looked up to heaven, said, "Away with the atheists." Then, the proconsul urging him, and saying, "Swear, and I will set you at liberty, reproach Christ"; Polycarp declared, "Eighty and six years have I served him, and he never did me any injury; how then can I blaspheme my king and my saviour?"[56]

As the interrogation proceeded, Polycarp offered to explain the teachings of Christianity to the proconsul at a future date. The governor responded, "Persuade the people."[57] Evidently the crucial factor was the attitude of the populace. The mob response was to cry for the turning of a lion loose on Polycarp. Burning, however, was the method of execution. Jews were reportedly prominent in the mob response, even breaking their strictures against work on a sabbath to gather firewood for the bonfire.[58]

Pious additions have been added to the narrative of the martyrdom after its first recording. The text that follows may be one such addition. It is preceded by narrative indicating that though Polycarp was enveloped in flames he was not harmed. What then?

> At length, when those wicked men perceived that his body could not be consumed
> by the fire, they commanded an executioner to go near and pierce him through with
> a dagger. And on his doing this, there came forth a dove, and a great quantity of
> blood, so that the fire was extinguished.[59]

The moving, if embellished, story has significance not simply in its narration of courage, but in portraying Polycarp as an exemplar of martyrdom. This first extended Christian account of a saint's martyrdom became a model for the numerous similar accounts that were to follow. Not simply a story of heroism, it also offered a perspective on the significance of martyrs. As a class they were viewed as sharing an especially close communion with Christ: "Those holy martyrs of Christ, at the very time they suffered those torments, were absent from the body, or rather, that the Lord then stood by them, and communed with them."[60] Polycarp received this sort of communion as he entered the place of his trial: "There came to him a voice from heaven, saying, 'Be strong and show yourself a man, O Polycarp!'"[61]

---

[56]*Martyrdom of Polycarp* 9 (ANF 1:41).
[57]Ibid., 10.
[58]Ibid., 13; 17; 18; 21 (ANF 1:42-43).
[59]Ibid., 16.
[60]Ibid., 2.
[61]Ibid., 9.

Martyrs like Polycarp not only had close communion with God, but also were Christ figures. Polycarp "waited to be delivered up, even as the Lord had done."[62] His betrayers would "undergo the punishment of Judas himself."[63] The arresting law enforcement officer was named Herod.[64] At Polycarp's arrest, he prayed "for two full hours."[65] At his death "a great quantity of blood" came from his pierced body.[66] Enemy anxiety concerning the threat that his dead body posed (as a locus for cult worship) led to discussion on how to deal with the dead body.[67] All these features of Polycarp's death have parallels with the Gospel accounts of the death of Jesus. Allusion to martyrs as Christ figures came to be stock in trade even when the martyrs were women, as the next example shows.

The martyrs of Lyons and Vienne. Again it was mob violence that triggered attack on Christians, this time in the Rhone Valley in 177. The fourth-century Eusebius preserved an account of the events from a much earlier period:

> First of all, they endured nobly the injuries heaped upon them by the populace; clamors and blows and draggings and robberies and stonings and imprisonments, and all things which an infuriated mob delight in inflicting on enemies and adversaries. Then, being taken to the forum by the tribune and the authorities of the city, they were examined in the presence of the whole multitude, and having confessed, they were imprisoned until the arrival of the governor. . . . [A]fterwards, they were brought before him, and he treated us with the utmost cruelty.[68]

After prolonged imprisonment and torture, the Christians faced scurrilous charges of "Thyestean banquets and Oedipan incest,"[69] that is, cannibalism and sexual orgies. The charges were a sordid distortion of Christian beliefs and practices. The former charge arose from the Eucharist—eating and drinking the blood of Jesus. The latter charge arose out of the closeness of Christian community, where each was "brother" and "sister," and where the kiss of peace was shared. A generation later the Christian apologist Tertullian explained in colorful detail the common accusations:

> Monsters of wickedness, we are accused of observing a holy rite in which we kill a little child and then eat it; in which, after the feast, we practice incest, the dogs—our

---

[62]Ibid., 1.

[63]Ibid., 6.

[64]Ibid.

[65]Ibid., 7. Note the parallel between this reference and Jesus praying at Gethsemane.

[66]Ibid., 16.

[67]Ibid., 17; cf. Mt 27:62-66.

[68]Eusebius *Church History* 5.1.7-9 (*NPNF*[2] 1:212, English modernized).

[69]Ibid. For these very charges brought more generally against Christians, see Athenagoras of Athens, *A Plea for the Christians* 21, written about the time of the Lyons martyrdoms.

pimps no doubt—overturning the lights and providing us with the shamelessness of darkness for our impious lusts.[70]

Most of the Lyons martyrs died in prison under their unspeakably brutal treatment, but some faced public execution. Blandina emerged as their leader, a surprising choice given her double social impediment of being a woman and a slave. If social distinctions mattered to Christians, they ceased to do so in this extreme situation. What mattered now was charism—a godly life and the evident presence of the Holy Spirit. Though a woman, Blandina too became a Christ figure, providing inspiration for the suffering community. According to the narrative, her ability to suffer defeated all the powers of her torturers: "Blandina was filled with such power as to be delivered and raised above those who were torturing her by turns from morning till evening in every manner, so that they acknowledged that they were conquered, and could do nothing more to her."[71] The narrative of her subsequent treatment accentuated her Christ-type nature:

> Blandina was suspended on a stake, and exposed to be devoured by the wild beasts who should attack her. And because she appeared as if hanging on a cross, and because of her earnest prayers, she inspired the combatants with great zeal. For they looked on her in her conflict, and beheld with their outward eyes, in the form of their sister, him who was crucified for them, that he might persuade those who believe on him, that every one who suffers for the glory of Christ has fellowship always with the living God. As none of the wild beasts at that time touched her, she was taken down from the stake, and cast again into prison.[72]

Blandina subsequently faced repeated tossing by a bull. Even that did not finish her off. The narrative of her death concluded by noting that she was "sacrificed," presumably by a more direct sword or spear thrust. The fiery ordeal of the Christians seemed to die down almost as quickly as it had sprung up. At any rate the martyred bishop Pothinus had been succeeded within a year by Irenaeus, who appeared free to undertake his episcopal duties unhindered.

The martyrdom of Perpetua and Felicitas. In 202 the emperor Septimius Severus published an edict forbidding conversion to either Judaism or Christianity. The edict seems to have been provoked by Jewish disloyalty and revolt against the Roman Empire when Severus was fighting Parthia in 198-199, and to have been designed to confine Judaism to narrow national bounds. However, its effect fell largely on the Christian community. A group was arrested in the Roman prov-

[70]Tertullian Apology 7 (ANF 3:23, English modernized).
[71]Eusebius Church History 5.1.18 (NPNF² 1:214).
[72]Ibid., 5.1.41-42.

Figure 3.5. Ancient amphitheater ruins at Lyons (J. Du Sordet)

ince of Africa, among them Perpetua and Felicitas. The group members appear to have all been catechumens. They were, however, baptized a few days after their arrest.[73] The members of the arrested group were thus in the process of converting to Christianity in breach of the Severan edict. Again it was women, Perpetua and Felicitas, as well as the man Saturus, who were the most prominent members of the group. In this time of extremity the criterion for leadership was charism, not gender. Nor was class an issue, Felicitas being a slave to Perpetua. Revelations, courage and moral leadership were what counted.

Perpetua was single-minded, notwithstanding much family-relationship distress. Despite nursing an infant she remained steadfast, even though that meant separation from her child. The presence of a child without mention of a husband suggests she may have been married to a pagan, her marriage being another social relationship sacrificed for the cause of Christ. Her father likewise seems to have been a pagan. In persisting in her allegiance to Christ, Perpetua had to face his opposition, pleadings and suffering. In the time of trial, the narrator of her story depicts her as a Christ figure. Thus her father exhorted her at one point, "Behold your brothers; behold your mother and your aunt; look at your son who cannot

---

[73]*The Passion of Perpetua and Felicitas* 1.2 (ANF 3:700).

live without you."[74] This was a clear echo of the words of Jesus on the cross in John 19:26-27. Perpetua's tremendously elevated status was patent too at her death. When being tossed by a wild cow did not end her life, she faced the sword, placing "the wavering right hand of the youthful gladiator to her throat."[75] The narrator commented, "Possibly such a woman could not have been slain unless she herself willed it, because she was feared by the impure spirit."[76] Conquered martyrs such as Perpetua were actually indomitable conquerors—able to be slain only because they themselves laid down their own lives (cf. Jn 10:18).

Persecution under Decius. The mid third-century Roman Empire experienced pervasive crisis—repeated wars with barbarian forces breaking through into parts of the empire, rampant inflation, crushingly high taxes, plague, famine. Within weeks of taking power in A.D. 249, the emperor Decius launched a program of reform that for the first time involved an effective empire-wide persecution of Christians. It had two phases: first the arrest of higher clergy, then a few months later a universal order to offer sacrifice to the gods of the empire. This included pouring a libation (a drink offering to the gods) and tasting sacrificial meat. The Decian measures were not primarily a targeted attack on Christians. They were designed in the face of major crisis to strengthen the solidarity of the empire by calling all its members to return to traditional virtues and mores.[77] Christians who complied with the imperial requirement could apparently continue in their Christian faith.[78] Many Christians crumpled under the pressure. In some quarters a majority compromised their faith through sacrifice or through bribery to avoid sacrifice.

The aftermath of the persecution left major rifts in the church. What should the church do with those who had compromised under pressure? The ebb of persecution left two categories of sinners stranded on the outskirts of the church: those who had sacrificed to the gods (the *sacrificati*) and those who had not sacrificed but who had through bribery gained a certificate saying they had (the *libellatici*). (A third category, the *traditores*, those who had handed over Scriptures or other sacred church objects, appeared more as a problem in the "great persecution" at the beginning of the fourth century.) The issue of church response to the lapsed created less of a problem in the East where purchase of immunity and handing over of Scriptures do not appear to have been treated as sins. In the more rigorous West it brought much more heartache and division.

In Rome the issue of how to treat the lapsed became mixed up with the election

---

[74]Ibid., 2.1.
[75]Ibid., 6.4.
[76]Ibid.
[77]Frend, *Martyrdom and Persecution,* p. 405.
[78]J. P. Burns Jr., *Cyprian the Bishop* (London: Routledge, 2002), p. 1.

of a new bishop of Rome to replace the martyred Fabian. One candidate for the position, Novatian, argued that the lapsed should not be readmitted to the church. When the more tolerant Cornelius gained the episcopacy, Novatian was established as rival bishop, thus initiating the Novatian schism, which persisted for several centuries.

Complex developments took place in Carthage. Bishop Cyprian, who had fled to avoid seizure, saw the issue of the lapsed as a grave one, requiring judgment from the bishops of the church. He forbade presbyters to grant forgiveness and readmission to communion.[79] He also spoke against confessors who had granted God's forgiveness to the lapsed and had them readmitted to the church.[80] While the confessors at Lyons had earlier taken such action without any sense of controversy, Cyprian saw it as a grave weakening of church discipline. To forgive in such conditions involved danger to the community (admission despite the lack of deep public repentance), presumption (forgiving those who had denied Christ and whom Christ in Luke 9:26 had indicated he would reject) and usurpation of the episcopal role.[81] A tough line was taken when the council of bishops met at Carthage in 251 after the persecution had subsided. The *libellatici* (who had purchased certificates) were to face vigorous inquiry and to be readmitted after penances, but the *sacrificati* (those who had actually sacrificed) were to remain excluded from communion, and be readmitted only on their deathbeds. A fresh minor wave of persecution and the ravages of plague led to intense popular pressure for further relaxation—to die outside communion was a terrifying prospect. The pressure resulted in the African bishops agreeing to reinstate all who were fully penitent.

The Valerian persecution. Valerian, who became emperor in A.D. 253, left the church at peace for a few years. However, in 257 he renewed empire-wide persecution of Christianity. His motives are obscure but may be linked to crisis in the empire, particularly barbarian invasions and spiraling inflation (illustrated by the reduction of the silver in the main coinage from 40 percent to 2 percent in a few years).[82] Initially Valerian targeted the higher clergy, requiring them to worship the Roman gods, and banishing them when they did not comply. In addition, Christians were forbidden to hold assemblies and to visit burial areas. After this bloodless first stage, a second Valerian edict called for the execution of the clergy. In addition, it ordered the confiscation of the property of upper-class Christians,

---

[79]Cyprian *Letter* 9 (*ANF* 5:289).
[80]Cyprian *Letters* 10 and 17 (*ANF* 5:290, 296).
[81]Burns, *Cyprian*, pp. 81-85; Cyprian, *Letter* 11.2; *On the Lapsed* 20 (*ANF* 5:292, 443) .
[82]Frend, *Martyrdom and Persecution*, p. 422.

together with the death penalty if they persisted in their faith. Many Christians were executed in this year or two of persecution, including Cyprian, the famous bishop of Carthage. Valerian's ill-fated war against Parthia in 259 soon led to his defeat, capture and death. The accession of his son, Gallienus, to the imperial throne in 260 brought an immediate end to the persecution. The church then experienced forty-odd years of largely unbroken peace until the "great persecution." The period was described in glowing terms by the fourth-century historian Eusebius: Christians becoming governors, members of imperial households becoming Christians and openly practicing their faith, a great increase in the number of Christians, many new churches being built.[83]

The "great persecution." Though this broke out in A.D. 303, trouble had already been brewing for a few years. Its first manifestation appeared in the army, where Christians, contrary to their earlier general tendency to be pacifists, were now present. Their failure to participate in sacrifice led to a famous incident before the emperor Diocletian in 299 where the gods apparently would not reveal their will because of the presence of Christian soldiers. Diocletian's furious response led to a requirement that all soldiers sacrifice or face dismissal from the army. Subsequently a wave of edicts launched persecution against the Christians:

- All Scriptures were to be surrendered and destroyed, all churches were to be dismantled, Christian worship was to cease.

- The clergy were to be arrested (apparently implemented only in the East).

- The clergy were to be forced to sacrifice, then released. Enforcement led to a few recalcitrants being executed.

- In 304 a fourth edict ordered a general sacrifice throughout the empire (enforced only in the East and in North Africa).

This phase of persecution ended abruptly in the West when coemperors Diocletian and Maximian abdicated, and Constantius (father of Constantine), who had no personal inclination for persecution, was appointed as the new emperor in the West. In the East, bitter persecution persisted under Galerius. However, when struck by a fatal illness in 311, Galerius appears to have undergone a soul-searching in relation to his policies. As an outcome he issued an edict permitting Christian worship again. Persecution was now coming to an end in the Roman Empire, though Maximin, who had control of Egypt and the Asian part of the eastern empire, maintained bitter persecution for another year or two. Fundamentally, however, the accession of Constantine to the imperial throne in the West in 312

---

[83]Eusebius *Church History* 8.1.1-6 (*NPNF*[2] 1:323).

marked a new era. Constantine and Licinius (emperor of the East) met at Milan in 313 and issued a famous edict giving Christianity full legal status within the empire. From being a repressed religion, Christianity increasingly thereafter became a favored one, soon to become the only legitimate religion of the empire.

The Rationale for Persecuting Christians

The role of mobs in the persecuting process has already been stressed. With small upper and middle classes, most of the populace were of the desperately poor lower classes. The near-universal desire for esteem is commonly met by establishing that others hold an even lower rank than you. Nobodies of the Roman rabble could feel like somebodies by identifying other underdogs and kicking them. Christians provided a convenient target in the struggle for self-respect. From early days they constituted "a class hated for their abominations."[84]

The divisive influence of Christianity within many families also fuelled scapegoating passion. There seem to have been many more woman converts at first than men, and conversions within the larger family unit could easily drive a wedge into domestic relationships.[85] A story narrated by Justin Martyr highlights this aspect of persecution.[86] The wife of a dissolute resident of Rome converted to Christianity. Her husband's debauchery eventually led her to divorce him. The enraged husband, on finding his wife beyond judicial attack, turned on Ptolemy, the Christian who influenced her toward Christianity. He was put under judicial interrogation, to face one question only: was he a Christian? His affirmative answer led to a sentence of death. Two other Christians successively spoke up at the injustice of condemnation simply for being a Christian, with no other wrongdoing alleged. They too were delivered over to execution.

A major concern for non-Christians was the so-called atheism of the Christians. Popular understanding held that gods needed visible representations. Worship of an invisible god was virtually "atheism"—worship of no god at all. This impiety was particularly serious because of the sense of social solidarity and the need for society to behave in a way that would keep the divine powers happy—a vital concern because the gods controlled the events of this world. The world of the early church desperately needed power: for a regular supply of food (famine being not uncommon), for health (disease being rampant) and for peace (civil wars were not uncommon and "barbarians" threatened at the edges of the empire). Society looked to the gods for the needed power. Appropriately honored, they would

---

[84] Tacitus *Annals* 15.44.
[85] See, for example, Tertullian *Apology* 3 (*ANF* 3:20).
[86] Justin Martyr *Second Apology* 2 (*ANF* 1:188-89).

maintain the good order of the world (*pax deorum,* the right harmonious relationship between gods and humanity); dishonored, they would bring disaster. While standardization of belief was not expected, collective honor needed to be given to the gods. Its lack put society at risk. And that is what Christians did. Their disloyalty imperiled all.

A crucial problem was that Christians would not sacrifice. This created a greater dilemma than did the Jewish stance, for they at least used to have a sacrificial system. While Jews would not sacrifice to the gods, they would, prior to the temple's destruction in A.D. 70, offer sacrifice on behalf of the emperor (not to him), and this could be taken as appropriate religious behavior. Christians, however, would not sacrifice at all, as the sacrifice of Christ on the cross had superseded all sacrifices. In no way could they cooperate in any sacrifice.[87] Yet sacrifice was fundamental to first-century Mediterranean religion and piety. In the eyes of the general public, Christians were thus stupid, pig-headed and jeopardizers of society.

It was their stubborn exclusivity that endangered others. If only they would show tolerance and appropriate respect to the gods, they might well be able to keep their distinctive faith without persecution. Not only, however, did Christians cause offence by failing to sacrifice, they also openly broke with society, provocatively repudiating previous religious obligations in their baptismal pledge to renounce Satan and his pomp and his angels.[88] Christians were therefore to blame when the world went wrong. Tertullian mockingly portrayed pagan world-beliefs that demonized Christianity:

> [T]hey think the Christians the cause of every public disaster, of every affliction with which the people are visited. If the Tiber rises as high as the city walls, if the Nile does not send its waters up over the fields, if the heavens give no rain, if there is an earthquake, if there is famine or pestilence, straightway the cry is, "Away with the Christians to the lion!" What! Shall you give such multitudes to a single beast?[89]

Christianity presented a threat not only to social relationships but also to the well-being of the state itself. Emperors were never free of the possibility of coup, overthrow or assassination, and were therefore always nervous about permitting groups that might turn out to be subversive. Early in the second century, for example, the emperor Trajan was sufficiently jumpy to forbid the 150 firemen of the

---

[87]S. R. F. Price, *Rituals and Power,* pp. 220-21.
[88]This baptismal pledge first appears in Tertullian in the late second century: *On the Shows* 4; *On the Crown* 3 (ANF 3:81, 94). On this see O. Skarsaune, *In the Shadow of the Temple: Jewish Influences on Early Christianity* (Downers Grove, Ill.: InterVarsity Press, 2002), p. 60.
[89]Tertullian *Apology* 40.2 (ANF 3:47).

city of Nicomedia from forming a volunteer society.[90] In that climate, unsanctioned Christian meetings would appear as a risk to the state.

Persecution and lack of legal recognition forced Christianity to operate in semi-underground fashion in private homes. This fuelled suspicion as to the subversive nature of Christianity.[91] The movement was suspect from the start anyway, with its founder having been executed under Roman authority. Moreover, it circulated dangerous literature. The Book of Revelation in thinly disguised fashion identified Rome as a demonic beast and prophesied the city's overthrow. In place of the emperor Domitian's insistence on being addressed as "our Lord and God," the Book of Revelation portrayed another who was "our Lord and God," who would destroy all earthly powers and overthrow Rome itself.[92] By the end of the first century it had become conventional for emperors to be honored as gods in their lifetime. The irrational and mulish refusal of Christians to give this honor to the emperor seemed akin to treason.[93]

At first the church was just a flea bite on the sprawling back of the empire. It is significant that only as Christianity grew (though still a small minority) and became more prominent in the third century, did the empire make comprehensive efforts to suppress it. Since the church espoused peace and support for the empire, why did the emperors devote effort to its suppression? Part of the answer has already been explored: its failure to honor the gods, thereby risking divine wrath. Moreover, Christianity's suspicion of "the world" weakened the glue of social cohesion at a time when the empire's crises demanded social solidarity.

However, another dimension also appears: the solidarity of the church within itself. It had a highly cohesive organization with a vast social relief program administered by deacons. In the 250s in Rome, for example, there were "more than fifteen hundred widows and distressed persons," all of whom would have been on church support.[94] Cohesion was strengthened also through church leaders adjudicating most intra-Christian disputes (based on 1 Cor 6:1-8). Features such as these made the church almost a state within a state, and thus a perceived threat to the state itself.

---

[90]Pliny *Letters* 10.33.

[91]See the criticisms of Celsus that Christians separated themselves and stood aloof from all human society: Origen *Against Celsus* 8.2 (*ANF* 4:640).

[92]Rev 4:8; 17—19.

[93]Compare the difficulties faced by Christians in Japan in the first half of the twentieth century over the issue of emperor worship.

[94]Letter of Bishop Cornelius of Rome to Bishop Fabius of Antioch quoted in Eusebius *Church History* 6.43.11 (*NPNF*[2] 1:288).

At the beginning, persecution largely resulted from popular prejudice. Later it became an issue of the state's well-being. In both contexts there was a rational explanation for the persecution. The "atheism" of the Christians imperiled a society that held to a *pax deorum* (peace of the gods) worldview, and the solidarity of Christianity made it a threat to imperial rule.

The Impact of Persecution on Christianity

During those crucial first centuries, society rejected the church, and the church in turn rejected society. This impregnated the church with a sect-type mentality. The world was a hostile and evil place. For Christians it was "us against the world." Such a viewpoint fostered thinking like that advocated by Tertullian: Christians must avoid all "passionate excitement," not only gladiatorial contests but also events such as chariot racing and athletic competitions.[95]

This sect-type thinking greatly shaped the early theology of the church, significantly focusing it more on directly biblical thought forms and less on philosophical and speculative realms. Railing against Christian utilization of philosophy, Tertullian exclaimed:

> What indeed has Athens to do with Jerusalem? What concord is there between the Academy and the Church? What between heretics and Christians? Our instruction comes from "the porch of Solomon," who had himself taught that "the Lord should be sought in simplicity of heart." Away with all attempts to produce a Stoic, Platonic, and dialectic composition! We want no curious disputation after possessing Christ Jesus, no inquisition after enjoying the gospel! With our faith, we desire no further belief. For this is our primary faith, that there is nothing which we ought to believe besides.[96]

Such views of Tertullian were widely accepted. Persecution strengthened this perspective. Some of the second-century apologists, though, were much readier to affirm connections between philosophical thought and Christianity. Even while persecution persisted, some could articulate Christian doctrine in the language of the Greek Academy.[97] However, it was particularly after persecution ended and the church was becoming mainstream in society that it increasingly utilized the thought-forms of that society. In the process, the dominant flavor of Christian theology altered, leading to more and more sophistication and abstraction of thought. The new trend was particularly marked in the great theological debates of the fourth and fifth centuries.

---

[95]Tertullian *The Shows*, passim, particularly chap. 16 (*ANF* 3:86).
[96]Tertullian *Prescription Against Heretics* 7 (*ANF* 3:246).
[97]Origin is the most outstanding example of this broader approach.

The ongoing threat of martyrdom made becoming a Christian a risky matter. One needed to think twice about joining such a group, membership of which might ultimately result in execution. Consequently, conversion was more likely to have greater commitment and depth. Thus when Origen looked back around A.D. 240 on earlier times of persecution and martyrdom, he noted that while it meant that the faithful were fewer, it also meant that "they were truly faithful, advancing by the harsh and narrow way that leads to life."[98] This became much less the case in the post-Constantinian Christianization of the Roman Empire, with its many conversions of convenience. One's family, one's group, one's society was becoming Christian—so why not me?

Persecution and martyrdom may potentially have been a barrier to church growth, though not only because of social stigma, disadvantage and peril of death. In addition, the fact of persecution required that the church be careful about who came to their meetings, lest a spy come into their midst. Thus the *Didascalia Apostolorum (Teaching of the Apostles)* indicates that only the repentant were allowed in Christian gatherings (*Did. Ap.* 10.2.39), while the fourth-century *Testament of Our Lord* suggests that a deacon is to act as "ecclesiastical bouncer," investigating whether lambs or wolves are entering, to avoid the presence of spies.[99] Restricting entry in this way would likely also restrict church growth.

Tertullian expressed a contrary viewpoint: persecution actually fed church growth. "The oftener we are mown down by you the more in number we grow; the blood of the martyrs is seed."[100] In Tertullian's perspective the spectacle of martyrdoms had converting impact: "[W]ho that contemplates it, is not excited to inquire what is at the bottom of it? Who after inquiry does not embrace our doctrines?"[101] Certainly we have a number of examples of conversions directly springing from martyrdoms. Justin Martyr, for example, on observing the heroic death of Christians, concluded that theirs must be a noble faith, and this was a factor in his subsequent conversion.[102] The tendency of scholars, however, is not to attribute too large a converting role to the martyrdoms. MacMullen, for example, has given a far larger role to the performance of miracles, especially exorcism, than

---

[98]Origen *Homily on Jeremiah* 4.3 (trans. M. Dujarier, *A History of the Catechumenate: The First Six Centuries* [New York: Sadlier, 1979], p. 55).

[99]*Testament of Our Lord* 1.36, and see A. Kreider, *Worship and Evangelism in Pre-Christendom* (Cambridge: Grove Books, 1995), pp. 8-9.

[100]Tertullian *Apology* 50 (*ANF* 3:55).

[101]Ibid.

[102]Justin Martyr *Second Apology* 12 (*ANF* 1:192); but for a different account of his conversion see his *Dialogue with Trypho* 3—8 (*ANF* 1:195-99). The language used would suggest that the conversation with the old man was the primary factor, the witnessing of martyrdoms a secondary factor.

to martyrdom as a converting influence.[103] In addition, the powerful influence of the church's program of social welfare also needs to be considered.

We should note that the number of martyrs in those first centuries, while significant, was not massive. When Polycarp was martyred about A.D. 156, he was only the twelfth to be martyred at Smyrna.[104] Later, Origen, in rejecting the notion that Christians were a rebellious group in the empire, claimed that the martyrs comprised a relatively "few" individuals, who "can easily be numbered."[105] However, because of its purpose in giving a better image to Christians, this statement needs to be treated with caution. Eusebius recorded only 91 martyrdoms in Palestine in the ten years of the "great persecution" there.[106] Nonetheless, he also claimed that during that period of persecution in Egypt, for year after year, daily martyrdoms numbered ten or more, or even up to a hundred.[107] The data as a whole may suggest that over the 250 critical early years when the church faced the risk or actuality of martyrdoms, the total number of victims was likely in the thousands, but perhaps not in the tens of thousands. Frend, for example, on the basis of the skimpy data available, has suggested that maybe hundreds perished in the Decian persecution, and perhaps 3,000 to 3,500 in the "great persecution."[108] While martyrdoms may well have given many pagans their first awareness of Christianity,[109] it was not the key factor in the growth of the church.

A further legacy of the persecutions was a strengthened sense of linkage between the church and its past. Celebrating martyrs' days (the anniversary of their martyrdom), holding ceremonies at their burial places, treasuring relics from their persons, praying for their assistance, all gave the church a sense of solidarity with past generations. The role of relics in providing a sense of the living nature of martyrs is well preserved in Ambrose's account of the apparent discovery of the relics of saints Protasius and Gervasius in 386:

> Why should I use many words? God favoured us, for even the clergy were afraid who were bidden to clear away the earth from the spot before the chancel screen of SS. Felix and Nabor. I found the fitting signs, and on bringing in some on whom hands

[103]R. MacMullen, *Christianizing the Roman Empire (A.D. 100-400)* (New Haven, Conn.: Yale University Press, 1984), pp. 27-30. See also Irenaeus *Against Heresies* 2.32.4 (ANF 1:409); Tertullian *Apology* 23 (ANF 3:38).
[104]*The Martyrdom of Polycarp* 19 (ANF 1:43).
[105]Origen *Against Celsus* 3.8 (ANF 4:468).
[106]In R. M. Grant, *Early Christianity and Society* (San Francisco: Harper & Row, 1977), p. 5.
[107]Eusebius *Church History* 8.9.3 (NPNF² 1:330). It is likely that Eusebius's figures are here designed more for rhetorical purposes than to provide historical precision.
[108]Frend, *Martyrdom and Persecution,* pp. 413, 537.
[109]G. W. Bowersock, *Martyrdom and Rome* (Cambridge: Cambridge University Press, 1995), p. 66.

were to be laid, the power of the holy martyrs became so manifest, that even whilst I was still silent, one was seized and thrown prostrate at the holy burial-place. We found two men of marvellous stature, such as those of ancient days. All the bones were perfect, and there was much blood. During the whole of those two days there was an enormous concourse of people. Briefly we arranged the whole in order, and as evening was now coming on transferred them to the basilica of Fausta, where watch was kept during the night, and some received the laying on of hands. On the following day we translated the relics to the basilica called Ambrosian. During the translation a blind man was healed.[110]

The reburial under the altar of these martyrs, allegedly killed under Nero, gave the church added distinction through these newly discovered links with the ancient past and through having powerful protecting saints to guard the church.[111]

Figure 3.6. *The Martyrdom of St. Sebastian* painted by Antonio Pollaiuolo in 1475. The details of St. Sebastian's martyrdom are unknown, but Ambrose said that Sebastian was from Milan and that he had been martyred at Rome during Diocletian's persecution. The painting illustrates the way martyrdom provided a gripping image for the church in later centuries. (Alinari/Art Resource, NY)

---

[110]Ambrose *Letter* 22.2 (*NPNF*[2] 10:437).

[111]Ibid., 22.10. See also R. A. Markus, *The End of Ancient Christianity* (Cambridge: Cambridge University Press, 1990), pp. 143-45.

Figure 3.7. Daniel and his three friends in the fiery furnace of Babylon, from the Catacomb of Priscilla on the Via Salaria to the north of Rome. The church saw this scene as inspirational in relation to their own sufferings in persecutory times. (Scala/Art Resource, NY)

Ambrose's narrative highlights the fact that the significance of martyrdom did not end with the cessation of persecution early in the fourth century. Martyrdom continued to be the model par excellence of Christian perfection. When its attainment ceased to be possible, new avenues of "martyrdom," imbued with the same sort of reverential awe, arose to take its place.[112] We see this most markedly with the sprouting of monasticism. Though this phenomenon slightly predated the end of persecution, the impetus for its growth postdated that time. It was no accident that monasticism flourished when martyrdom ceased:

> The monastic life was a daily martyrdom of asceticism, a heroic substitute for the heroism of the martyr. "Let us not think," Jerome says in a homily addressed to his monks, "that there is martyrdom only in the shedding of blood. There is always martyrdom."[113]

---

[112]According to Ambrose, the death in self-imposed exile of Bishop Demetrius was an "honour higher even than [that of the] martyrs" (Ambrose *Letters* 63.70 [*NPNF*[2] 10:467]).

[113]B. Ramsey, *Beginning to Read the Fathers*, p. 133, quoting Jerome, *On the Persecution of Christians*.

Sulpicius Severus, hagiographer at the end of the fourth century, similarly saw the asceticism of St. Martin of Tours as akin to martyrdom:

> For although the character of our times could not ensure him the honour of martyrdom, yet he will not remain destitute of the glory of a martyr, because both by vow and virtues he was alike able and willing to be a martyr. . . . But although he did in fact suffer none of these things, yet he fully attained to the honour of martyrdom without shedding his blood. For what agonies of human sufferings did he not endure in behalf of the hope of eternal life, in hunger, in vigils, in nakedness, in fastings, in reproachings of the malignant, in persecutions of the wicked, in care for the sick, in anxiety for those in danger?[114]

Martyrdom left its mark on the early church. It was the environment in which the church survived and flourished. Even when martyrdom ceased, it remained significant—in memory, in miracle, in inspiring self-sacrificing commitment in the service of Christ. In shaping the ongoing life of the church, the blood of the martyrs was indeed seed.

For Further Reading

Barnard, L. W. *Studies in Church History and Patristics.* Thessalonica: Patriarchal Institute for Patristic Studies, 1978, especially pp. 131-80.

Bonner, G. "Martyrdom: Its Place in the Church." *Sobornist* 5, no. 2 (1983): 6-21.

Botha, P. J. J. "God, Emperor Worship and Society: Contemporary Experiences and the Book of Revelation." *Neotestamentica* 22 (1988): 87-102.

Bowersock, G. W. *Martyrdom and Rome.* Cambridge: Cambridge University Press, 1995.

Burns, J. P., Jr. *Cyprian the Bishop.* London: Routledge, 2002.

De Ste. Croix, G. E. M. "Why Were the Christians Persecuted?" *Past and Present* 26 (1963): 6-38.

Dodds, E. R. *Pagan and Christian in an Age of Anxiety.* Cambridge: Cambridge University Press, 1965 (esp. pp. 102-38).

Eusebius. *The History of the Church.* Translated by G. A. Williamson. Revised by A. Louth. London: Penguin Classics, 1989.

Ferguson, E., ed. *Church and State in the Early Church.* Studies in Early Christianity 7. New York: Garland, 1993.

Frend, W. H. C. *Martyrdom and Persecution in the Early Church: A Study of Conflict from the Maccabees to Donatus.* Oxford: Blackwell, 1965.

Grant, R. M. *Early Christianity and Society: Seven Studies.* San Francisco: Harper &

---

[114]*The Letters of Sulpicius Severus* 2 (NPNF² 11:20-21).

Row, 1977 (esp. pp. 13-43).

Keresztes, P. *Imperial Rome and the Christians.* Vols. 1-2. Lanham, Md.: University Press of America, 1989.

MacMullen, R. *Christianizing the Roman Empire (A.D. 100-400).* New Haven, Conn.: Yale University Press, 1984.

Markus, R. *The End of Ancient Christianity.* Cambridge: Cambridge University Press, 1990 (esp. pp. 85-155).

Ramsey, B. *Beginning to Read the Fathers.* London: SCM Press, 1993 (esp. pp. 122-48).

4

GETTING ORGANIZED
Ministry and Structure

The early church began with apparently high levels of spontaneity and lower levels of institutionalization. Later, institutionalization became much more dominant. Was this change a betrayal of the early Christian movement? Modern studies of social movements indicate that spontaneous groups tend to have a short shelf life unless they are welded into a stable organization.[1] To maintain coherence and impact on society, they need to develop centralized direction.[2] Though members often feel a deep nostalgia for the earlier, more spontaneous era, there needs to be a "routinization of communitas."[3] The problem, however, is to do this while maintaining the earlier vitality and vision—and in a more institutionalized context this is not easy. Thus, increasing institutionalization in the life of the early church was both necessary and problematic, good and bad.

The institutionalization of ministry and structure in the early church happened very much through an evolutionary process, which proceeded at different speeds in different regions. We must avoid sweeping statements and quickly acknowledge exceptions. Table 4.1 is intended to provide an overview prior to more detailed description. While the chart oversimplifies, it may nevertheless be useful in noting major developments that occurred in the period of our study.

The Church of the New Testament Period

The early church began as an evangelistic movement. Its goals were strikingly expansionist—to make disciples for Christ from all peoples (Mt 28:19). It also had markedly charismatic dimensions, welcoming ministry and leadership that apparently displayed personal qualities of divine gifting, even where proper processes of

---

[1] J. Freeman, "On the Origin of Social Movements," in *Social Movements of the Sixties and Seventies*, ed. J. Freeman (New York: Longman, 1983), pp. 8-30, see p. 26.
[2] A. N. Costain, "Representing Women: The Transition from Social Movement to Interest Group," in *Women, Power and Policy*, ed. E. Boneparth (New York: Pergamon, 1982), pp. 19-36, see pp. 21-22.
[3] P. Burke, *History and Social Theory* (Cambridge: Polity, 1992), pp. 89-90.

Table 4.1. The Institutionalization of Ministry and Structure in the Early Church

DATE (A.D.)	DOCUMENT, EVENT, PERSON, MOVEMENT	DEVELOPMENT OR SIGNIFICANCE
50-90	Most New Testament letters and Gospels	Itinerant ministry along with local settled ministry
60-120 (dating disputed)	Pastoral Epistles (1 Timothy, 2 Timothy, Titus)	Congregations led by bishops (= elders) and deacons
c. 96	*1 Clement*	Stress on duly appointed leadership; parallels drawn from Old Testament priesthood
c. 100	*Didache*	Major role of charismatic itinerant ministries
c. 110	Epistles of Ignatius	Stress on a ruling bishop, supported by presbyters and deacons
c. 170	Montanism	A movement claiming direct Spirit-inspiration, eventually rejected by the mainstream church
c. 190	Irenaeus	Stress on apostolic succession
c. 196-c. 212	Tertullian	Distinguishes between "clergy" and "laity," later supports Montanism
c. 220	*Apostolic Tradition* (attributed to Hippolytus)	Sets down a strong distinction between the ordained and not ordained
Third century		Increasing use of regional church councils
Third century		Metropolitan bishop viewed as senior to the other provincial bishops
c. 230-250	Origen	Shows important ongoing role of teacher, semi-independent of church hierarchy
250s	Cyprian	Bishops together rule the church and define its center
Third century		Bishop becomes leader of many churches. Presbyter then leads the local congregation
Third century		Rome increasingly has a leading role among the churches
325	Council of Nicea	Recognition of patriarchates as having a leading role
330s-373	Athanasius	Seeks to centralize authority in Egypt under the episcopal structure
Fourth-fifth centuries		Rome increasingly asserts primacy over all churches. This is less recognized in the East

appointment might be lacking. Both emissaries and ordinary members commonly spoke and acted with a sense of being Spirit-inspired. While patterns of due appointment and institutional structure developed, it remained the case that the church also looked for leaders emerging to meet needs as the Spirit initiated.[4] In addition, the spiritual atmosphere was charged with a strong sense of the imminent end (Rom 13:11-14; 1 Thess 4:13—5:11). The church's priority on preaching the gospel (2 Tim 4:1-2) meant that although matters of structure and organization were significant, it retained much ad hoc flexibility in its early life.

Ministry, therefore, was significantly a matter of function rather than appointment to office. People filled ministry roles through recognition of giftedness, a recognition of who had God's stamp and was effective in a role. This often meant a fluidity and flexibility in ministry, both in terms of who undertook the ministry and what the various tasks were. Examining the New Testament, one finds an array of ministries: overseers (bishops), elders, deacons, apostles, prophets, teachers, pastors and so forth. Certainly there was leadership, but no single determining template. The boundaries of specific leadership functions were not always clear, and there was often a lot of overlap. Much of the shape of ministry was ad hoc response to particular situations. From a systematic perspective, New Testament leadership looked messy, but it was dynamic. Those wanting to quarry for their particular model of leadership—episcopal, presbyterial or congregational—can find New Testament examples or precepts to fit their ecclesiology. Whether they have done justice to the totality of the data, however, is another matter.

A significant feature of congregational leadership in the New Testament was its plurality. At Antioch the church seems to have been led by "prophets and teachers" (Acts 13:1). Leadership of the churches first planted by Paul and Barnabas was given over to "elders," *presbyteroi* (Acts 14:23). Later, Paul addressed the leaders at Philippi as "bishops/overseers," *episkopoi,* and "deacons" (Phil 1:1). Acts 20:17, 28 suggests that for Luke and Paul "elders," *presbyteroi,* and "bishops/overseers," *episkopoi,* referred to the same group of people.

The pattern of plural leadership stood in tension with sole leadership. While there were plural local leaders of various titles, Paul felt that he had residual authority as an apostolic father of the churches he had founded (1 Cor 4:14-21; Gal 4:12-19). This authority on occasion might override local authority. Though it was sometimes contested, Paul had a *primus inter pares* (first among equals) role in the churches that he founded. Such a *primus inter pares* approach to leadership also

---

[4]K. Giles, *Patterns of Ministry Among the First Christians* (North Blackburn, Australia: HarperCollins, 1989), p. 8.

seems to have been the case in the early church at Jerusalem. That church had plural leaders, variously called "apostles" (Acts 2:42-43; 4:35; 5:12; 8:14; 9:27; 11:1) and "elders" (Acts 11:30; 21:18), the two terms likely involving much the same people (Acts 15:2, 4, 6, 22, 23; 16:4). However, James the brother of Jesus seems early to have been a recognized leader within this body of leaders (Acts 12:17; 15:13; 21:18; Gal 1:19; 2:9)—a possible model for later developments involving a bishop spearheading a team of presbyters.

The relationship between designated leaders and the rank-and-file congregation remained unclarified. There does not seem to have been a ministry of "word and sacraments" reserved for certain leaders alone. Paul did not, for example, address a single presiding leader of the Eucharist to sort out disordered aspects of the Corinthian Eucharist (1 Cor 11:17-34). Various spiritual gifts were not given to leaders alone (1 Cor 12:1-11). All might speak in turn as the Spirit led (1 Cor 14:26-33, 39-40). The whole congregation seems to have been responsible for church discipline (Mt 18:15-17; 1 Cor 5:1-5). Sometimes the congregation elected leaders (Acts 1:23; 6:5); at other times a single authority figure seems to have done so (Acts 14:23; Tit 1:5).

The Pastoral Epistles (1 and 2 Timothy and Titus) indicate a residential local church leadership.[5] A triad of terms is used: bishops/overseers, presbyters and deacons. Their distinctive roles are not articulated. Moreover, the term for elders seems to be used interchangeably with the term for overseers/bishops (Tit 1:5, 7), suggesting that the milieu of the Pastoral Epistles knew two main forms of leadership, that of deacons, and that of elders/bishops. It is, however, possible to argue that "elders" and "bishops" were partially or totally differentiated in the pastoral epistles, as the pastorals usually referred to "elders" in the plural, while the term "bishop" is always in the singular with a definite article.[6]

The situation is rather confusing (perhaps not surprising, given the fluid, flexible and functional nature of early ministry) and full clarity on the issue is not possible. The early subapostolic period may, however, shed some light. *First Clement* and the *Shepherd* of Hermas point to "elders" and "bishops" being interchangeable

---

[5]One should note that a majority of scholars hold that these epistles were written by a follower of Paul a generation or two after his death. I. H. Marshall, *The Pastoral Epistles* (Edinburgh: T & T Clark, 1999), discusses authorship and dating on pp. 57-92. He acknowledges both Pauline and non-Pauline dimensions to the writings and suggests the final form of the documents was set down soon after the death of Paul. His view is close to my own. Argument that the documents arose a generation or two later is possible, but the evidence is insufficient to make that claim strongly or to draw major conclusions on the basis of this alleged much later date.

[6]F. M. Young, "On EPISKOPOS and PRESBYTEROS," *Journal of Theological Studies* 45 (1994): 142-48, see p. 142; K. B. Steinhauser, "Authority in the Primitive Church," *Patristic and Byzantine Review* 3, nos. 1-2 (1984): 89-100, see pp. 92-93.

terms for the leaders of the congregation.[7] On the other hand, the letters of Ignatius witness to a leading bishop distinct from the elders.

Persisting charismatic features of the early church meant that other leadership patterns might cut across the two local ministries of bishops/elders and deacons. Especially was this the case with itinerant ministers who might drop in on local churches, especially apostles, prophets and teachers (who might also be local settled people).

Overall, the New Testament data does not allow for tidy classification of ministry in that period. Charismatic inspiration was often of greater significance than a designated role. Lines of authority blurred and overlapped. Ministry evolved and changed, shaped according to varying contexts. Crucial questions remained for the ongoing church: Was congregational leadership authority fundamentally singular or plural in nature? How should local congregational leadership relate to itinerant charismatic leadership?

Charismatic Ministry

A sense of direct Spirit inspiration persisted in the postapostolic church alongside increasing institutionalization. Earlier discussion in this book on the *Didache* highlights both the high standing of itinerant prophets and the difficulties created by their ministries. The movement of the church leaned more and more toward institutionalization. This meant that prophecy must increasingly find expression in the church under the umbrella of a presiding bishop and presbyters or not at all. The ultimately negative ruling of the mainstream of the church against late second-century prophetic Montanism strengthened that perspective.

Montanism began as a movement of prophetic inspiration about A.D. 170 in Phrygia in what is today inland Turkey. Three individuals especially were crucial in the emergence of the movement: a relatively new convert named Montanus, together with two women, Priscilla and Maximilla. The three claimed direct Spirit inspiration, with utterances such as, "I am the Lord God almighty dwelling at this moment in a man," and, "It is no angel that is here, nor a human spokesman, but the Lord God the Father." Their prophecies claimed to reveal new truths about matters such as fasting, remarriage after a spouse's death, and whether one should flee in time of persecution. In each case the new revelation called for greater rigor and self-sacrifice. Most dramatically, the present world order was about to end, with the coming down of the new Jerusalem at Pepuza (near Philadelphia).

---

[7]On "bishops": *1 Clement* 42.4 (*ANF* 1:16); Hermas *Visions* 3.5, 1; *Similitudes* 9.27 (*ANF* 2:14, 52); on "presbyters": *1 Clement* 1.3; 44.5; 47.6; 54.2; 57.1 (*ANF* 1:1, 17, 18, 19, 20); Hermas *Visions* 2.4.3; 3.1.8 (*ANF* 2:12, 13).

Despite its excesses and the clear failure of some of its predictions, the movement was not insignificant or ephemeral. Though a regional council of bishops eventually condemned Montanism, it remained the primary form of Christianity for the peasantry of Phrygia for several centuries. In addition, it spread to Rome, Gaul and North Africa. In the latter place it had sufficient credibility to win support from the great thinker and controversialist Tertullian. In fact, Tertullian claimed that the movement had initially gained support from the bishop of Rome, until Praxeas (viewed by Tertullian as heretical for his patripassian views) turned the bishop's ear against Montanist prophecy, and so "put to flight the Paraclete."[8]

In the end, mainstream church consensus went against the movement. There seem to have been two primary concerns about Montanist prophecy. One was the trance-like fashion (*a-mentia,* out of one's mind) in which the prophecies were typically received. The other concern involved its claim to provide new revelation that might clash with Scripture and tradition.[9] No doubt other factors were also involved. The prominence of its women prophets, for example, created a great deal of unease. And its independent lay utterance implied challenge to the institutional church and its bishops.

In opposing Montanism, the mainstream church acknowledged the continuing validity of prophecy.[10] Thus Irenaeus, in condemning Montanist excess, continued to accept the value of prophetic utterance in the congregation. Such utterance must not, however, add to or differ from "the Gospels of the Apostles,"[11] that is, Scripture and tradition. Such qualification meant that the prophet could not be a rival over against church officers who were the keepers of the apostolic teaching. Two or more centuries later Eusebius held a similar perspective. He explained the beginnings of the prophecy of Montanus as follows:

> He became beside himself, and being suddenly in a frenzy and an ecstasy, he raved, and began to babble and utter strange things, prophesying in a manner contrary to the constant custom of the church handed down by tradition from the beginning.[12]

Church leadership resolved the potential clash between charism (personal giftedness) and office (proper appointment) in favor of the latter. The bishops became the arbiters of charismata.

This resolution does not mean, however, that bishops had things all their own

---

[8]Tertullian *Against Praxeas* 1 (*ANF* 3:597).
[9]See examples of these two features in Tertullian (who eventually embraced Montanism): *Against Marcion* 4.22; 5.8; *On Modesty* 11; *On the Veiling of Virgins* 1 (*ANF* 3:383, 447; 4:85, 27-28). For concern about prophetic ecstasy or "involuntary madness" see Eusebius *Church History* 5.17.2 (*NPNF*[2] 1:234).
[10]See, for example, Novatian *On the Trinity* 29 (*ANF* 5:640-41).
[11]Irenaeus *Against Heresies* 3.11.9 (*ANF* 1:429).
[12]Eusebius *Church History* 5.16.7 (*NPNF*[2] 1:231).

Figure 4.1. Origen (Art Resource, NY)

way after the debate over Montanism. Apart from the prophet, another potential threat to the authority of the bishop came from the semi-independent teacher. Such teachers would prepare catechumens for baptism and also provide advanced instruction in the faith. Justin and Tatian provide examples of this role in the second century, Clement of Alexandria and Origen in the third. That such were not rare individuals seems indicated by Eusebius's reference to "the presbyters and teachers of the brethren in the villages" of Egypt in the third century.[13]

Origen held such prestige as a teacher that when Mammaea, the mother of the emperor, wanted to investigate Christianity while in Antioch, she approached not the bishop of the city, but Origen.[14] Gifted teachers might thus seem more important than institutional bishops. Origen had major difficulties with the bishop of Alexandria, where he resided, for much of his life. Perhaps his charismatic authority as a gifted teacher, threatening that of the bishop, explains much of the tangle of the conflict.[15]

---

[13]Ibid., 7.24.6 (NPNF[2] 1:309).
[14]Ibid., 6.21.3-4 (NPNF[2] 1:269).
[15]R. P. C. Hanson, *Studies in Christian Antiquity* (Edinburgh: T & T Clark, 1995), p. 139.

The semi-independent role of the charismatic teacher in Egypt persisted into the fourth century. David Brakke has shown how this shaped much of the politics of Athanasius in that period. He argues that Athanasius was not struggling simply against the heresy of the Arians. Rather, he was struggling to more greatly centralize the church in subordination to the bishop. Brakke argues that the early fourth-century church in Egypt was a loosely united confederation of structures, much of its life being relatively independent of the bishop.[16] A particular threat to centralizing episcopal authority was the teaching schools. Athanasius therefore used the rhetoric of anti-intellectualism to attack the role of the teacher.[17] The virgins, for example, should not heed human teachers: rather than listen to males, they should converse silently with their bridegroom, the Word of God.[18] Athanasius made the role of teacher, with its innovating dimensions, suspect: "For I have not written these things as if I were teaching, for I have not attained such a rank. . . . I have thus informed you of everything that I heard from my father [bishop Alexander]."[19] Brakke points out that the concern of bishops like Athanasius was not so much the teaching role per se, but rather the independence of the teacher: "he [Athanasius] adapted academic values to his cause by restricting teaching and learning to a carefully defined space in the public church that was under his control."[20] The teaching function thus increasingly became the prerogative of the bishop or at least subject to his scrutiny. Teachers as well as prophets were progressively domesticated and drawn into the episcopal domain.

We should not be surprised at the domestication of charismatic leadership. Sociologists have observed that ongoing charismatic legitimation of leadership in movements is typically transitory and unstable. A movement cannot sustain itself in the long run on charismatic validation of leadership alone; other forms of leadership legitimation must arise. In the long term, a process of some degree of institutionalization is inevitable.[21] And so it proved to be with the early church.

The Emergence of a Ruling Bishop

The primary organizational unit in the early church was the single congregation. While there was a network of relationships between churches, this remained

---

[16]D. Brakke, *Athanasius and the Politics of Asceticism* (Oxford: Clarendon, 1995), pp. 11, 58, 60 and passim.
[17]Ibid., p. 68.
[18]Athanasius *Letter to Virgins* 1.30, 45 (in Brakke, *Athanasius,* pp. 71-72).
[19]Athanasius *Easter Festival Letter* 39.21.11-12, 14-15 (in Brakke, *Athanasius,* p. 68).
[20]Brakke, *Athanasius,* p. 73.
[21]Giles, *Patterns of Ministry,* p. 196.

The roll of succession, according to Eleutherus, bishop of Rome c. A.D. 175-189:

The **blessed apostles** having founded and established the church, entrusted the office of the episcopate to **Linus**. Paul speaks of this Linus in his Epistles to Timothy. **Anencletus** succeeded him, and after Anencletus, in the third place from the apostles, **Clement** received the episcopate. He had seen and conversed with the blessed apostles, and their preaching was still sounding in his ears, and their tradition was still before his eyes. Nor was he alone in this, for many who had been taught by the apostles yet survived. . . . **Evarestus** succeeded Clement, and **Alexander**, Evarestus. Then **Xystus**, the sixth from the apostles, was appointed. After him **Telesphorus**, who suffered martyrdom gloriously; then **Hyginus**; then **Pius**; and after him **Anicetus**; **Soter** succeeded Anicetus; and now, in the twelfth place from the apostles, **Eleutherus** holds the office of bishop. In the same order and succession the tradition in the Church and the preaching of the truth has descended from the apostles unto us.[a] [Note that the earliest names in the list may be of uncertain historical reliability. Note also how strong the emphasis is on the link back to the apostles.]

---

[a]Eleutherus, preserved in Eusebius *Church History* 6.1-5 (*NPNF*[2] 1:221).

loose and informal for a couple of centuries. During the first century or more, the common pattern for leadership within the congregation involved a collegial team of presbyters. Such a pattern persisted in many places well into the second century. Hermas, for example, refers to "the presbyters who preside over the church."[22] In the second century, however, a single (monarchical) bishop seems also to have gradually emerged from within the presbyterate and become its leader. We see the first clear evidence for this pattern in the letters of Ignatius. That the monarchical bishop gradually emerged from the presbyterate is indicated by the fact that while Irenaeus recognized the mono-episcopate toward the end of the second century, he linked the preservation of the apostolic tradition

---

[22]Hermas *Visions* 2.4 (*ANF* 2:12).

with "the successions of presbyters in the churches."[23] Clement of Alexandria held similar views.[24] Their writings suggest that these two viewed the bishop as a chief elder or president of the presbytery rather than as a wholly distinct order.[25]

From the second half of the second century bishops were viewed as the apostles' successors. Such a perspective saw the first bishops as appointees of the apostles. These bishops then appointed others, leading to an unbroken chain from the apostles to the present. With the emergence of divergent and heretical forms of Christianity, apostolicity became an important criterion for distinguishing truth from error. From the mid second century we see a marked tendency to justify perspectives on the basis of apostolic connection.[26] Apostolic authorship became a primary criterion for determining New Testament Scripture; a rudimentary creed, which was felt to be rooted in the teaching of the apostles, was developed to guide the faithful in right belief; and bishops had authentication through their apostolic roots via a doctrine of apostolic succession.[27]

Advocates of ecclesial democracy and/or plural leadership may regret the emergence of a dominating mono-episcopate. The development was probably necessary, however, if the church was to remain strong and united, a major force in society. Without such unity it risked fragmenting into myriads of pieces because of diverging currents of doctrine, leadership and prophecy within the church. They needed leaders who had the last word, who could be foci of unity, who could guarantee adhesion to earliest Christianity. Celsus, penetrating critic of Christianity in the second half of the second century, gives witness to the fragmenting tendency of early Christian life:

> Christians at first were few in number, and held the same opinions; but when they grew to be a great multitude, they were divided and separated, each wishing to be his own individual party. . . . Being thus separated through their numbers, they confute one another, still having, so to speak, one name in common, if indeed they still retain it.[28]

Bishops provided a solution to that problem, as well as strengthening the faithful against the threats of pagan persecution. The emerging mono-episcopate pattern gradually pervaded church structures and was virtually universal by the end

---

[23]Irenaeus *Against Heresies* 3.2.2; cf. 4.26.2 (*ANF* 1:415, 497).
[24]Clement of Alexandria *Stromata or Miscellanies* 6.13 (*ANF* 2:504-5).
[25]Everett Ferguson, *Early Christians Speak*, 2nd ed. (Abilene, Tex.: ACU Press 1987), p. 175.
[26]Hanson, *Studies in Christian Antiquity*, p. 123.
[27]Hegesippus in Eusebius *History of the Church*, 3.11; 4.22 (*NPNF*[2] 1:146, 199); Irenaeus *Against Heresies* 3.3.2, 3; 3.4.2, 3 (*ANF* 1:415-16; 417); Tertullian *Prescription Against Heretics* 32 (*ANF* 3:258).
[28]Origen *Against Celsus* 3.10, 12 (*ANF* 4:468).

of the second century. At first the sole bishop was simply the senior presbyter, a point later argued by Jerome at the beginning of the fifth century: "When subsequently one presbyter was chosen to preside over the rest, this was done to remedy schism and to prevent each individual from rending the church of Christ by drawing it to himself."[29] Because the bishop came to be viewed as the preserver of the apostolic deposit, however, he came to inherit something of the status of the apostles. He became greater than mere mortals, larger than life.

The Emergence of a Concept of Clergy

At first, church ministry involved no sharp clergy-laity distinction because ministry operated significantly in terms of giftedness and function. However, at the end of the first century there arose an increasing sense of major ministries being permanent offices, to be exercised for a lifetime on the basis of proper appointment. *First Clement* is a primary witness to that development. That view naturally led to the primary church officers (bishop, presbyters, deacons) becoming separated off from the rank-and-file of the congregation, resulting in a sharp "clergy-laity" division by the third century. As early as the end of the first century, Clement showed the seeds of that distinction, asserting that "a layman is bound by the ordinances of the laity."[30] Ignatius soon pushed the view that certain functions, notably Eucharist and baptism, were reserved for the primary officers, especially the bishop. The fact that certain functions were the prerogative of certain officers alone led to a conceptual distinction between those officers and the rest—in a nutshell, between clergy and laity. In the long run, the distinction had enormous implications for the understanding and expression of Christian ministry.

Tertullian distinguished between "clergy," *ordo,* and "laity," *plebs,* at the end of the second century.[31] Such language proved very significant. In Roman thinking, people of any importance belonged to one *ordo* (class or rank) or another; the nobodies who had no *ordo* were *plebs.* As the church adopted this sort of language, it fostered the idea that lay Christians were *plebs*—nobodies. The Christians of significance were the clergy, designated as such by their solemn ordinations.

The concept of ordination made the clergy-laity distinction clear-cut. It was ordination—involving a special ceremony marking a lifetime appointment to a certain clerical position—that gave clerical authority.[32] *Ordinatio* was the process of consecration through which a Christian became a member of an *ordo* (= of-

---

[29]Jerome *Letter* 146 (*NPNF²* 6:288).
[30]*1 Clement* 40 (*ANF* 1:16).
[31]Tertullian *On Baptism* 17; *Exhortation to Chastity* 7; *On Monogamy* 12 (*ANF* 3:677; 4:54, 69).
[32]Cyprian *Epistle* 68.4 (*ANF* 5:373).

ficeholder/clergy). The ordination ceremony featured the laying on of hands for a special impartation of the Holy Spirit for the proper fulfillment of the office. The roots of the practice of laying on of hands for special setting apart and enabling for ministry lie in the New Testament (1 Tim 5:22; 2 Tim 1:6), though at that stage it was not necessarily an essential or regular practice. Later, laying on of hands was clear-cut with regard to such matters. The early third-century *Apostolic Tradition* carefully articulates which ministries are ordained and which are not, systematically linking this division with whether or not hands should be laid on the person. The identification of ordination with laying on of hands is most explicitly spelled out in relation to the ministry of widows:

> When a widow is appointed, she shall not be ordained but she shall be appointed by the name. . . . The widow shall be appointed by the word alone, and she shall be associated with the other widows; hands shall not be laid upon her because she does not offer the oblation nor has she a sacred ministry. Ordination is for the clergy on account of their ministry.[33]

In later early church perspective, ordination made the person different. By ordination, according to fourth-century Gregory of Nyssa, a priest was changed by an invisible power and gift into something better in his invisible soul.[34] Thus a sacralizing of the clergy took place. For Augustine ordination gave the recipient an irremovable imprint, just as baptism did to an uncomprehending infant.[35] The rank-and-file were therefore not to question the credentials of the clergy (thus the Donatist challenge to the validity of Catholic clergy was in error). Ordination remained valid irrespective of circumstances; hence enforced ordination could validly occur.[36]

With a developed theology of ordination, the clergy-laity distinction became even sharper: clergy were one thing and laity another. Tertullian criticized heretics for having ordinations that were "carelessly administered, capricious, changeable":

> At one time they put novices in office; at another time, men who are bound to some secular employment. . . . And so it comes to pass that today one man is their bishop, tomorrow another; today he is a deacon who tomorrow is a reader; today he is a pres-

[33]*Apostolic Tradition* 11 (in B. S. Easton, *The Apostolic Tradition of Hippolytus* [Cambridge: Cambridge University Press, 1934], p. 40).
[34]Cited in H. Von Campenhausen, *Tradition and Life in the Church,* trans. A. V. Littledale (Philadelphia: Fortress, 1968), pp. 228-29 (translating from *Patrologia Graeca,* ed. J.-P. Migne [Paris, 1857-1886], 46:581).
[35]Augustine *Against the Grammarian Cresconius* 2.13. On this point see C. A. Volz, "The Pastoral Office in the Early Church," *Word & World* 9, no. 4 (1989): 359-66, see pp. 365-66.
[36]Notable people, who were ordained against their wishes, included Ambrose, Augustine and Jerome's brother.

byter who tomorrow is a layman. For even on laymen do they impose the functions of priesthood.[37]

A trend toward salaried clergy in the third century accentuated the clergy-laity distinction. Some payments of church leaders occurred even within the New Testament era.[38] References to more definite salaries for clergy, however, first appear in two fragments from about A.D. 200 quoted by Eusebius.[39] In each instance the recipients belong to aberrant groups, and the receiving of these payments is described as if it were a mark against them. At the same time it indicates a more widespread trend toward the payment of clergy. The early third-century Syrian *Didascalia Apostolorum* evidences this trend. Drawing heavily from Old Testament injunctions to support the Levites with tithes and offerings, the manual asserts that the Levites and priests are now the bishops.[40] Thus the faithful are to give tithes and offerings to the bishops, who are to be "nourished and live from the revenues of the church."[41] The bishops are in turn to use these to support the needy, other clergy and themselves.[42] No longer is the criterion one of simple need: "How much (soever) is given to one of the widows, let the double be given to each of the deacons in honour of Christ; (but) twice twofold to the leader [the bishop] for the glory of the Almighty."[43]

The situation probably varied greatly in late antiquity, with many clergy receiving pay from the church but many remaining self-supporting. The mid fourth-century Basil of Caesarea provides evidence of the persistence of the latter situation, noting of his clergy that "the majority of them [were] plying sedentary crafts, whereby they get their daily bread."[44]

Another factor in the elevation of the clergy was their being viewed as priests. It was Tertullian who first explicitly applied the term "priest" to bishops and presbyters.[45] For Tertullian, clergy held a priestly office, a charge so solemn that normally clergy alone gave baptism, Eucharist and teaching in the life of the church.[46] While a full-blown equation of presbyters and bishops with priests occurred only

---

[37]Tertullian *Prescription Against Heretics* 41.6 (*ANF* 3:263).
[38]1 Cor 9:3-12; 1 Tim 5:17-18; also *Didache* 11—13.
[39]*Church History* 5.18.2 and 28.8-12 (*NPNF*[2] 1:235, 247).
[40]*Did. Ap.* 8.
[41]Ibid. (trans. R. H. Connolly [Oxford: Clarendon Press, 1929], p. 78).
[42]*Did. Ap.* 8 and 9. For other third-century reference to presbyters being paid from central church funds see Cyprian, *Letter* 33.5 (*ANF* 5:314).
[43]Ibid., 9 (trans. Connolly, p. 90).
[44]Basil *Letters* 198 (*NPNF*[2] 8:236).
[45]Von Campenhausen, *Tradition and Life,* p. 220. Tertullian, *Exhortation to Chastity* 7; *On Monogamy* 12 (*ANF* 4:54, 69).
[46]Tertullian *On Baptism* 17; *On the Veiling of Virgins* 9.1; (*ANF* 3:677; 4:33).

in the third century, a viewing of church officers in the light of the Old Testament priesthood, particularly in relation to the permanence of the role/status, began early. It is marked in 1 Clement. Parallels with the Old Testament also fostered the notion that some tasks were reserved for the clergy. As Clement said, each had their roles, the layman (laikos), for example, being "bound by the laws that pertain to laymen."[47] The implicit thought says that laypeople should stick to their designated functions and not attempt to meddle in church leadership. The sharp line between clergy and laity thus began very early in the history of the church.

The Power of the Clergy

According to mid third-century Cyprian, God ruled the church through the bishop. Part of the bishop's power was the result of his presiding at the Eucharist as pastor of the congregation. The early church strongly and increasingly centered its liturgical life on the Eucharist.[48] As the eucharistic elements were more and more viewed as essential to the nourishing of baptismal-initiated salvation, and as the bishop was increasingly seen as the priest of these sacraments, it elevated his position even more. Once the Eucharist was viewed unambiguously as a sacrifice, this intensified a view of the Christian ministry as paralleling that of the Old Testament priesthood. Sacrifice required an altar and a sacral minister to make the sacrificial offering.[49] In the view of John Chrysostom, the Eucharistic celebrant was an Elijah figure, "not bringing fire down from heaven, but the Holy Spirit" on the "sacrifice."[50]

The bishop's control over the Eucharist and his right to administer or to excommunicate, to retain sins or remit them, gave him the power of salvation or damnation. In their priestly role, bishops stood in the place of God. The third-century Syrian Didascalia Apostolorum heaps up words of honor, power and authority for the bishops: they are "high priests," "heads and governors," "chiefs," "kings."[51] The faithful are warned to do nothing apart from their bishop, to consider him as the mouth of God, never to speak of him in an evil manner.[52] Robin Lane Fox highlighted the power of the bishops:

> They could suspend a cleric or an ordinary Christian, ban him from church and damn him to eternal punishment. It was hard for a man to be open and humble

---

[47]1 Clement 40 (ANF 1:16).
[48]Hanson, Studies in Christian Antiquity, p. 129.
[49]J. Blenkinsopp, "Presbyter to Priest: Ministry in the Early Church," Worship 41, no. 7 (1967): 428-38, see pp. 433-34.
[50]John Chrysostom On the Priesthood 3.4 (NPNF[1] 9:47).
[51]Did. Ap. 9.
[52]Ibid.

when any slander against his person was said to be slander against God. "Love your bishop as a father: fear him as a king: honour him as God."[53]

Human nature being what it is, the status and power of the bishop fostered aspiration for the office, and foul as well as fair means might sometimes be part of one's electoral strategy. Thus Cyprian could commend Cornelius as legitimate bishop of Rome with the words: "he did not, as some do, use force to be made a bishop."[54] Power corrupts; and bishops from the third century onwards were increasingly at risk of being corrupted by their position. Around 270 Paul of Samosata was deposed for heresy. Criticisms of his episcopal role included acting more like a government official (which he also was) than like a bishop, being accompanied by bodyguards, acting violently and living in luxury and surfeiting.[55] Descriptions from opponents must be treated with caution, but most times smoke indicates some presence of fire. After Christianity became the favored and later the official religion in the post-Constantinian era, bishops increasingly ranked as officers of state, intensifying problems of wealth, prestige and power. The pagan but tolerant historian Ammianus Marcellinus articulated this change as follows:

> [The bishops] are well off, for they grow rich on the gifts of noble ladies. They ride in carriages, dressed in exquisite robes. They give such sumptuous dinners that their banquets rival those of kings.[56]

Constantine had effectively given the bishops certain state functions, so that in a sense they were now officers of state. In keeping with this, the state had logically to grant to the bishops the titles, insignia and privileges that corresponded to such status.[57] As the bishop of Rome thus had near-imperial dignity, it was natural for his portrait to hang in public buildings and his arrival to be greeted at church by a choir of singers. It seemed fitting for people to wait on him at his throne and at the altar with covered hands and to genuflect to him and kiss his foot.[58] To sum up the late fourth-century trend:

> The chasuble, dalmatic, stole, and maniple [items of episcopal garb] were borrowed

---

[53]R. Lane Fox, *Pagans and Christians* (New York: Knopf, 1986), p. 501; the final quotation used by Lane Fox is from the *Didascalia* 9.
[54]Cyprian *Letters* 51.8 (*ANF* 5:329).
[55]Eusebius *Church History* 7.30.6-16 (*NPNF*[2] 1:314-15).
[56]Ammianus Marcellinus *History* 27.3.14-15 (trans. Van der Meer, in E. Foley, *From Age to Age: How Christians Celebrated the Eucharist* [Chicago: Liturgy Training Publications, 1991], p. 44).
[57]T. Klauser, *A Short History of the Western Liturgy: An Account and Some Reflections* (London: Oxford University Press, 1969), p. 34.
[58]Ibid.

Qualifications for election as a bishop:

As the role of a bishop soared in importance, so the church developed more elaborate rules as to who could be chosen. This fourth-century extract is part of a much longer discussion on the qualities of a bishop:

> But concerning bishops, we have heard from our Lord, that a pastor who is to be ordained a bishop for the churches in every parish, must be unblameable, unreprovable, free from all kinds of wickedness common among men, not under fifty years of age; for such a one is in good part past youthful disorders, and the slanders of the heathen, as well as the reproaches which are sometimes cast upon many persons by some false brethren, who do not consider the word of God in the Gospel. . . . Let him therefore, *if it is possible,* be well educated; *but if he be unlettered, let him at any rate be* skilful in the word, and of competent age. But if in a small parish one advanced in years is not to be found, let some younger person, who has a good report among his neighbours, and is esteemed by them worthy of the office of a bishop—who has carried himself from his youth with meekness and regularity, like a much elder person—after examination, and a general good report, be ordained in peace. . . . Let examination also be made whether [the candidate for the episcopate] be unblameable as to the concerns of this life; for it is written: "Search diligently for all the faults of him who is to be ordained for the priesthood."[a]

[a]*Apostolic Constitutions* 2.1, 3 (*ANF* 7:396-97), italics in original.

directly from the Roman magistracy, and in every municipality where there had been a *flamen* [a priest of a particular deity] to supervise the worship of the emperor, there was now a bishop who inherited his privileges. These included an imperial salary, a seat on the city council, the right of direct access to the emperor, and rank second only to the provincial governor. Bishops were now becoming persons of great influence and office, accompanied by a retinue of servants bearing their insignia of office in processions, which instead of the Roman eagle was now the cross.[59]

Clerical power arose not only from secular models and practices but also from

[59]C. A. Volz, *Pastoral Life and Practice in the Early Church* (Minneapolis: Augsburg, 1990), p. 44.

spiritual argument. Starting with Cyprian in the 250s, we see the increasing assertion that outside the church there was no salvation.[60] And the bishops with their
supporting clergy constituted the essence of that church. Collectively the bishops
served as the glue holding the church together: "the episcopacy is one, each part
of which is held by each one for the whole."[61] Thus to flout such clergy was to
damn one's own soul.

Cyprian's teaching signaled a major shift. Whereas previously salvation had
been through faith and baptism in Christ or acceptance of teachings guaranteed
by the apostolate, now salvation also required submission to the bishop. One
could not separate faith and church relationships: "He can no longer have God for
his Father who does not have the Church for his mother."[62] On this basis Cyprian
could put the schismatic but otherwise orthodox Novatian beyond the pale:

> We ought not even to be inquisitive as to what he teaches, so long as he teaches out
> of the pale of unity. Whatever he may be, he who is not in the church of Christ is not
> a Christian. . . . He has cut himself off from the body of his fellow-bishops and from
> the unity of the church.[63]

A century and a half later, we see even more explicitly the bishops' tremendous
standing and power. John Chrysostom went so far as to assert that clerical power
to bind and loose bestowed authority on the cleric beyond even that of angels or
archangels. What folly then to despise the cleric:

> Away with such madness! For transparent madness it is to despise so great a dignity,
> without which it is not possible to obtain either our own salvation, or the good
> things which have been promised to us. . . . If all these things are accomplished only
> by means of those holy hands, I mean the hands of the priest, how will any one,
> without these, be able to escape the fire of hell, or to win those crowns which are
> reserved for the victorious?[64]

The Role and Pecking Order for Ministry Under the Bishops

For a century or so the elevation of a sole bishop tended to diminish the role of
the presbyters. The bishop did all that the presbyters did. Thus a tendency arose
for presbyters to exercise what became recognized as public clerical duties only in
the bishop's absence. The presbyters therefore served in the earlier period of the
mono-episcopate mainly as a council of advisers to the bishop and as his proxies.

---

[60]Cyprian *Letters* 72.21 (*ANF* 5:384).
[61]Cyprian *On the Unity of the Church* 5 (*ANF* 5:423).
[62]Ibid., 6.
[63]Cyprian *Epistles* 51.24 (*ANF* 5:333).
[64]John Chrysostom *On the Priesthood* 3.5 (*NPNF*[1] 9:47).

As a consequence they had a diminished status. A remarkable passage in Ignatius seems to indicate the relative status: the bishop presided "in the place of God," the deacons were "entrusted with the ministry of Jesus Christ," while the presbyters were simply compared to "the assembly of the apostles."[65]

Presbyters came into markedly increased status in the third century. In the first place they stood with the bishops as clerics and so shared in the increasingly sacerdotal perception of clerical office. In addition, the changing role of bishop led to a much greater role for presbyters. The earlier pattern had been for one bishop per town or center. This large number of bishops meant that, as a major part of the bishop's role, he served as pastor of the town congregation. The story goes that when Gregory Thaumaturgus (the "wonderworker") was appointed bishop of Neo-Caesarea in the middle of the third century, he had as few as nineteen Christians under his care. An early council in proconsular Asia, an area of about 2,500 square kilometers, was attended by 42 bishops, while third-century North Africa (the Roman province of Africa) had 470 episcopal towns.

Later in the third century, however, the church began to appoint presbyters rather than bishops to newly evangelized rural areas. In keeping with this, the Synod of Ancyra in Asia Minor about 315 forbade the ordination of bishops for small villages and prescribed that presbyters should be assigned to them. The Council of Sardica (modern Sofia) in 343 took a similar stance, justifying this "in order that the episcopal authority not be cheapened."

In addition, a centralized system of pastoral care under one bishop in growing churches in large cities was proving inadequate. Fabian, bishop of Rome, A.D. 236-250, is credited with assigning seven deacons and seven subdeacons to the regions of the city. Under a successor, Dionysius (260-269), Rome was organized into *tituli* or parishes, each with its own presbyter. By the end of the third century there were forty such parishes.[66] These changes led to a presbyter being pastor over one congregation, with the bishop supervising a number of churches. Having a distinct role and increasingly being the sacerdotal intermediary for the ordinary layperson, the presbyter—now priest—gained a distinct and strengthened role in the local setting.

Deacons' responsibilities originally were more practical. They assisted the bishop in matters of finance and worship. These matters involved caring for the sick and needy, distributing alms to the poor and, where the church had property, taking responsibility for its maintenance.[67] Justin also mentioned their role in distributing the elements at the Eucharist and carrying them to those who were ab-

---

[65]Ignatius *To the Magnesians* 6 (ANF 1:61).

[66]W. H. C. Frend, *The Rise of Christianity* (Philadelphia: Fortress, 1984), p. 401.

[67]Hermas *Similitudes* 9.26 (ANF 2:52); Hippolytus *Apostolic Tradition* 3.30.

sent.[68] Later the elevation of the presbyters' role meant a relative downplaying of the deacons' role. In the long run they became assistants to the local presbyters as well as to the bishops. However, their clearly defined role, subject to the bishop but not overlapping his function nearly as much as the early presbyters' did, gave the deacons great prestige at first.

Only with the emerging greater role of the presbyters did the deacons receive a dent to their standing. A decree of the Council of Nicea points to the changing situation:

> It has come to the knowledge of the holy and great Synod that, in some districts and cities, the deacons administer the Eucharist to the presbyters, whereas neither canon nor custom permits that they who have no right to offer should give the body of Christ to them that do offer. And this also has been made known, that certain deacons now touch the Eucharist even before the bishops. Let all such practices be utterly done away, and let the deacons remain within their own bounds, knowing that they are the ministers of the bishop and the inferiors of the presbyters.[69]

Gradually thereafter the diaconate receded in importance until it commonly became merely a preliminary and ceremonial step in clerical progression to the sacralized priesthood.[70]

An increasing hierarchy of layers mushroomed within the church. Minor orders, which were not treated as ordained clergy, came to be recognized by the middle of the third century. These included the offices of subdeacons, readers, acolytes, janitors and exorcists.[71] Above the minor orders stood the ordained clergy, those who were clergy by virtue of laying on of hands: bishop, priests and deacons. The trend was now to advance vertically through the church offices in a clerical career. Pope Siricius attempted to provide a regulatory framework to this pattern about 390.[72] One began as a lector at age six, later a subdeacon, followed by at least three years as a deacon before progressing to the presbyterate, eventually becoming bishop at about forty.[73]

The Development of Structure and Hierarchy in the Worldwide Church

In its beginnings the building blocks of the church were the local congregations. While there was a sense of the whole Christian church in all its locations, at the

---

[68]Justin Martyr *First Apology* 67 (*ANF* 1:186).
[69]Canon 18 of Nicea (*NPNF*[2] 14:38).
[70]Giles, *Patterns of Ministry,* p. 158.
[71]See the list of Bishop Cornelius of Rome to Bishop Fabius of Antioch in 252: Eusebius *Church History* 6.43.11 (*NPNF*[2] 1:288).
[72]Siricius *Letter* 1.9-10.
[73]W. H. C. Frend, *The Early Church* (London: Hodder & Stoughton, 1965), p. 250.

grassroots level the primary unit was the local church. This could easily have led to fundamental differences in doctrine and practice among the churches. One solution to this potential problem was informal networking between church leaders, seeking to keep the movement as a whole in step. For example, Bishop Polycarp of Smyrna visited Bishop Anicetus of Rome about 155 in an unsuccessful attempt to reconcile divergence between the Eastern and Western churches on how to calculate the date when Easter should be celebrated. This same sort of networking occurred a century later, with Cyprian of Carthage seeking to stay in close communication with Rome, when the church of North Africa was struggling with the vexed question of what to do about Christians who had lapsed in the recent persecution. Clearly it was important to the North African bishops that through such collaboration Rome and Carthage would have a common mind about the matter.

In addition, formal linkages increasingly occurred in the second half of the second century. This happened particularly through bishops meeting together in formal session in regional councils to develop a common mind on issues of doctrine and practice. By 325 this custom was sufficiently strong that the council of Nicea could legislate holding provincial synods twice a year.[74]

As a consequence of the provincial synods, hierarchy within the episcopate increased further. The bishop of the chief town (metropolis) of the province gradually came to have seniority and a supervisory role over the other bishops of the province. With that role came the title of "metropolitan." This development was more marked in the East than in the West, as bishops in the West often bypassed the metropolitan and appealed immediately to the pope for help and guidance.[75] Subjection to the metropolitan in the pre-Constantinian era must in some measure have been voluntary, as the church lacked the power to turn its rhetoric of hierarchy into reality.[76] In the fourth century, however, bishops worked much more to create a single "catholic" church, uniform in theology and hierarchical in structure. A synod at Antioch in the early 330s spelled out relationships between bishops and their metropolitans:

> It is fitting for the bishops in every province to acknowledge the bishop who presides in the metropolis and who has to take thought for the whole province; because all those with business come from every quarter to the metropolis. Therefore he shall have precedence in rank, and the other bishops shall do nothing without him, according to the canon already established in the time of our fathers, except what pertains to their own dioceses and the districts subject to them. For each bishop has

---

[74]Canon 5 (NPNF[2] 14:13).
[75]H. Chadwick, *The Early Church* (London: Penguin, 1967), p. 239.
[76]Brakke, *Athanasius*, p. 2.

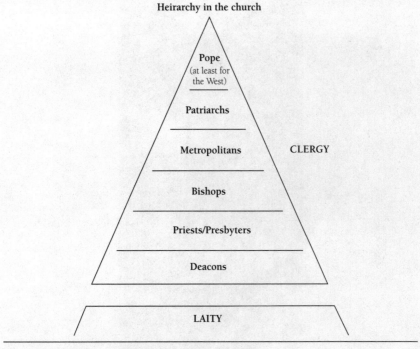

Figure 4.2. Hierarchy in the church

authority over that. . . . But let him undertake nothing further without the bishop of
the metropolis, nor the latter without the consent of the other bishops.[77]

The conclusion of this statement indicates a concern not just for regional unity
through hierarchy, but also for unity of the entire church through hierarchical relationships. This wider concern was significantly met in the fourth century by increasing recognition of the authority of the metropolitans of a few key cities over
the provinces. Thus developed the recognition of patriarchates. Nicea recognized
the leading role of Alexandria, Rome and Antioch. The Council of Constantinople
in 381 gave similar recognition to Constantinople, ranking that see after Rome because "Constantinople is New Rome." As Constantinople was a new city, it is clear
that this recognition had much more to do with its being the center of the eastern
empire rather than because of any ancient ecclesiastical significance. That per-
tained much more to Jerusalem, which was added as a fifth patriarchate at the
Council of Chalcedon in 451. Now the church had a hierarchy within both the lo-

---

[77]Canon of Antioch 9, reproduced in C. Markschies, *Between Two Worlds: Structures of Earliest Christianity,* trans. J. Bowden (London: SCM Press, 1999), p. 175.

Figure 4.3. Representation of St. Peter and St. Paul, traditionally regarded as founders of the church at Rome (Courtesy of Holy Transfiguration Monastery)

cal clergy and the clergy universal. Where, however, did Rome stand in relation to these developments?

Emergence of Papal Primacy at Rome

It is tempting but erroneous to read the present back into the past as if the two are identical. Early on this happened in relation to the authority of Rome's bishop in the church worldwide. The origins of the church at Rome are obscure. The New Testament and early tradition indicate that both Peter and Paul had associations with Rome, though not as its founders (Acts 28:11-31; Rom 15:32; 1 Pet 5:13).[78] Ignatius's letter to Rome early in the second century, while honoring Rome, shows no evidence of a perspective setting it on a pedestal unique among churches and deferring to its rule. Clement's slightly earlier letter from Rome to Corinth presents the church at Rome guiding the Corinthian church in its difficulties. However, the

---

[78]Also 1 Clement 5 (ANF 1:6).

letter gives no indication that the church at Rome feels that it can issue its fiat and the Corinthian church will fall into line. That letter devotes much careful argument to persuading the Corinthian church to adopt the position it advocated.

In all likelihood the early rise to prominence of the church at Rome was the result of the city's status in the empire—all roads lead to Rome. Had Peter and Paul died in an obscure village in inland Turkey, that village in all likelihood would have had little standing in the soon-to-emerge Catholic hierarchy. The status of the imperial city made all the difference. One can see this type of thinking in the fourth century with regard to Constantinople. Once it was founded and established as the capital of the eastern half of the Roman Empire, it soon became the second most significant see of the church as "new Rome" despite its patent lack of early apostolic connection.

A strengthening of Rome's standing came through writers such as Hegesippus in the middle of the second century, who set down Rome's lineage of bishops, tracing the line apparently right back to the apostle Peter.[79] As writings such as *1 Clement,* Ignatius and Hermas show no indication of one leading bishop at Rome around the beginning of the second century, this tradition is likely, in part at least, a projection of later developments back into a different and less clear situation.

The first clear indication of a sense of the seniority of the church at Rome came in the writings of Irenaeus late in the second century. In a famous passage he stated that "every church should agree with this church [Rome] on account of its preeminent authority."[80] What more could an advocate of Roman supremacy want than this text? There are, however, several cautions about so utilizing the text. In the first place, Irenaeus made this statement in the context of arguing for *general* episcopal authority on the basis of unbroken succession from the apostles. He then used Rome as a specific example of this, as it was "founded and organized . . . by the two most glorious apostles, Peter and Paul."[81] Irenaeus's point is more one of apostolic supremacy than of Petrine paramountcy. Further, the main statement being discussed includes phrases whose meaning is not altogether certain. The word translated "agree" is *convenire,* and this might simply mean "resort to," that is, "consult with." In addition, the words translated "pre-eminent authority" are *potiorem principalitatem* and these may simply mean "greater leadership." This may then suggest that Irenaeus indeed gave elevated status to Rome, but her role in Irenaeus's eyes was one simply of seniority and moral persuasiveness. In order to preserve unity, other churches should confer with Rome on difficult matters, respect-

---

[79]Eusebius *Church History* 3.21; 4.22.3 (*NPNF*[2] 1:149, 198-99).
[80]Irenaeus *Against Heresies* 3.3.2 (*ANF* 1:415-16).
[81]Ibid.

ing her bishop as leading bishop within the collective episcopate.[82] Irenaeus's own practice suggest that this was the intent behind his words.

A difference between Rome and the Eastern bishops had arisen earlier over the proper date to celebrate Easter. Each claimed apostolic sanction for their differing traditions. Who was right? The matter was not simply a technical or abstract one because many of the Roman Christians hailed from the East. Divergence on this point meant that people within the church at Rome celebrated Easter on different dates. In the 150s Polycarp had done what Irenaeus later indicated was proper and had resorted to Rome to try and straighten out the matter. No resolution was possible, but the two bishops parted on amicable terms, agreeing to disagree.[83] Toward the end of the century the matter flared up again. This time Bishop Victor of Rome attempted to resolve the issue by excommunicating the Asian churches. Other bishops protested this high-handed action, one of them being Irenaeus.[84] The incident shows two things: first, that Irenaeus did not view Rome's leading position as entitling her bishop to override other bishops by unilateral fiat; second, that Rome felt her position maybe entitled her to move in that direction.

The issue of unilateral fiat resurfaced half a century later. The African bishops had been careful to consult with Rome over difficult issues in the discipline of the lapsed after the Decian persecution. However, Bishop Cyprian of Carthage and his supporters had taken a stance denying the validity of baptisms performed by schismatics because of their view that the essence of the church lay in being in communion with legitimate bishops, united together through a succession that ran back to the apostles. In contrast, Bishop Stephen of Rome held that baptism in the triune name was valid, irrespective of the standing of the baptizer. In the stand-off that ensued, Stephen followed Victor's earlier precedent in excommunicating those of contrary opinion. Here, for the first time, we find the bishop of Rome appealing to his overriding authority as successor to Peter, to whom Jesus had given the keys of binding and loosing (Mt 16:19). The outcome remained a stalemate until the two main protagonists died a few years later. Subsequent irenicizing letters from Dionysius of Alexandria then seem to have left Rome and Carthage agreeing to disagree. Resolution finally came half a century later with the North African bishops dropping their position in the face of the Donatist schism. These developments portray a situation in which the

---

[82] For discussion of this point see further, J. N. D. Kelly, *Early Christian Doctrines,* 5th ed. (London: A & C Black, 1977), pp. 192-93.

[83] Eusebius *Church History* 5.24.16-17 (*NPNF*[2] 1:243-44).

[84] Ibid., 5.24.11-18 (*NPNF*[2] 1:243-44).

Figure 4.4. The pope as "the vicar of the city of Rome" (c. 400) (Victoria & Albert Museum, London/Art Resource, NY)

North African churches were prepared to respect Rome as a leading see but not to kowtow to any nonconsensus rulings.

The fourth and fifth centuries, when the church now enjoyed imperial patronage, saw marked development in Rome's claims to supreme authority. Julius I, for example, having welcomed the exiled Athanasius of Alexandria to Rome in 340, expressed displeasure at not being consulted on major matters of discipline:

Why was nothing said to us concerning the church of the Alexandrians in particular? Are you ignorant that the custom has been for word to be written first to us, and then for a just sentence to be passed from this place? If then any suspicion rested upon the bishop there, notice thereof ought to have been sent to the church of this place; whereas, after neglecting to inform us, and proceeding on their own authority as they pleased, now they desire to obtain our concurrence in their decisions, though we never condemned him.[85]

Despite claims from Rome to have final authority, the church as a whole never fully accepted such assertions. At times acceptance might appear complete; at other times we see marked rejection of Rome's stance or its right to rule. A lot depended on the direction of Rome's ruling. If it went your way, then of course the matter was finally resolved: Peter had spoken. If, however, Rome's ruling went against you, then that was not the last word; it was simply another opinion from a senior church figure in an ongoing process. Thus, in the early stages of the Donatist controversy soon after Constantine became emperor, neither the Donatists nor their Catholic opponents appear to have viewed the ruling of Rome on the matter as final.

Similarly, in the Nestorian controversy in the mid fifth century, while both sides appealed for support from Rome, neither was necessarily ready to accept Rome's opinion or ruling. Pope Leo's *Tome* eventually became the basis for the theological resolution of the debate at the Council of Chalcedon in 451 with the acclamation that "Peter has spoken." However, just two years previously, at an earlier stage in the controversy, the Council of Ephesus had ignored the *Tome*. Had the Eastern churches suddenly embraced papal supremacy? No. While respecting Rome's seniority, they never really accepted her jurisdictional claims. The crucial factor in resolving the matter was a change of emperor in 450. The new emperor, unlike the old, was sympathetic to the theological solution eventually adopted at Chalcedon. It was that change, rather than a kowtowing to Rome, that freed the theological logjam and led to a solution.

For its part, Rome became increasingly assertive in its claims. Leo, for example, forbade the bishops at Chalcedon to subject his *Tome* to the scrutiny of discussion. In keeping with developments of the previous century, Rome increasingly utilized its claim to legislate on the basis of holding the Petrine keys. In contrast to the Eastern churches, which tended to seek resolution of disputes through the consensus of councils, Rome tended more to seek simply to impose its will. From A.D. 385, the bishop of Rome increasingly began to send out its letters in the form of decretals, a form taken over by the Roman curia from the imperial chancery. The

---

[85]Letter of Julius to the Eusebians in Athanasius *Defense Against the Arians* 2.35 (*NPNF*[2] 4:118).

emperor had used it to give authoritative and binding answers to questions posed by lower-ranking officials.[86] Use of this form reveals the papal see's view of itself. Leo summed up Rome's view of hierarchical authority in a letter to Bishop Anastasius of Thessalonica in 446:

> Though they [priests] have a common dignity, yet they have not uniform rank; inasmuch as even among the blessed apostles, notwithstanding the similarity of their honourable estate, there was a certain distinction of power, and while the election of them all was equal, yet it was given to one to take the lead of the rest. From which model has arisen a distinction between bishops also, and by an important ordinance it has been provided that everyone should not claim everything for himself: but that there should be in every province one whose appointment should have the priority among the brethren: and again that certain whose appointment is in the greater cities should undertake a fuller responsibility, through whom the care of the universal church should converge towards Peter's one seat, and nothing anywhere should be separated from its head.[87]

Historically, hierarchy had progressively emerged from the ground up. Leo's perspective inverted that understanding of the authority having been granted from below: his top-down view meant that each bishop's position was a delegation of the plenitude of power that rested in Rome alone:

> We made you our deputy, beloved, on the understanding that you were engaged to share our responsibility, not to take plenary powers on yourself.[88]

A factor strengthening papal claims was the shaky state of the Roman Empire, especially in the West, with the onset of fresh Germanic wars and invasions in the fifth century. The empire looked to the papacy as a strong institution in a crumbling world. That Leo was used as a primary negotiator to get Attila the Hun to refrain from attacking Rome in 452 shows the significance of this factor. In seeking papal support, the empire also sought to reinforce the papal institution in this period. Valentinian III thus wrote in 445:

> It is certain that for us and our Empire the only defence is in the favour of the God of heaven; and to deserve it our first care is to support the Christian faith and its venerable religion. Inasmuch then as the primacy of the Apostolic See is assured by the merit of St. Peter, prince of the episcopal order, by the rank of the city of Rome, and also by the order of a sacred synod, lest presumption endeavour to attempt any unauthorized act contrary to the authority of that See, then at length will the peace of

---

[86]J. T. Lienhard, *Ministry,* Message of the Fathers of the Church 8 (Wilmington, Del.: Michael Glazier, 1984), pp. 171-72.
[87]Leo *Epistle* 14.12 (*NPNF*[2] 12:19).
[88]Ibid., 14.2 (*NPNF*[2] 12:17).

the churches be everywhere maintained, if the whole body acknowledges its ruler.[89]

Rome's self-perception of its overruling primacy among the churches was not universally held. Significantly rejected in the East, it was also not fully embraced in the West. Augustine's vision of the church, for example, looked at the church as a whole. The Donatists were not wrong because they were out of communion with Rome, but through lack of communion with the apostolic sees as a whole. While conceding precedence to Rome as symbolizing the universal church, Augustine did not regard Rome as having final jurisdictional or appellate status. The "power of the keys" did not belong to Rome alone. Church disputes should be resolved by councils—provincial and general—and not by Rome. Thus when Rome sought to override the North African church in its discipline of a priest named Apiarius in an affair dragging out for a number of years starting in 417, the African bishops finally sent a letter to Pope Celestine a few years later, bluntly rejecting such episcopal appeals to Rome:

> By no ordinance of the Fathers has the Church of Africa been deprived of this authority. . . . [The Fathers of Nicea] did not think that the grace of the Holy Spirit would be lacking to any province, by which the bishops of Christ may wisely discern and fairly maintain justice . . . unless it can be imagined that God can inspire a single individual with justice and refuse it to an innumerable multitude of bishops assembled in council.[90]

Rome clearly aspired to final decision-making rights over the church as a whole. Others saw that power as belonging to the church as whole and expressed through general councils. Struggle would intermittently occur in the West on such issues for the next thousand or more years until the Lutheran storm in the sixteenth century irrevocably shattered the unity of the Western church.

For Further Reading

Hansen, R. P. C. *Studies in Christian Antiquity.* Edinburgh: T & T Clark, 1985, especially chapter 8.

Hunt, D. "The Church as a Public Institution." In *The Cambridge Ancient History.* Vol. 13: *The Late Empire, A.D. 337-425,* edited by A. Cameron and P. Garnsey, pp. 238-76. Cambridge: Cambridge University Press, 1998.

Jay, E. G. "From Presbyter-Bishops to Bishops and Presbyters." *The Second Century* 1, no. 3 (1981): 125-62.

---

[89]Leo *Epistle* 11 (in J. Stevenson, ed., *Creeds, Councils and Controversies: Documents Illustrating the History of the Church, A.D. 337-461,* rev. ed. [London: SPCK, 1989], p. 328).

[90]Reported in R. B. Eno, "Authority and Conflict in the Early Church," *Église et Theologie* 7, no. 1 (1976): 59.

Lienhard, J. T. *Ministry.* Message of the Fathers of the Church 8. Wilmington, Del.: Michael Glazier, 1984.

Osborne, K. B. *Priesthood: A History of the Ordained Ministry in the Roman Catholic Church.* New York: Paulist, 1988.

Volz, C. A. *Pastoral Life and Practice in the Early Church.* Minneapolis: Augsburg, 1990.

———. "The Pastoral Office in the Early Church." *Word & World* 9, no 4 (1989): 359-66.

Wiles, M. F. "The Theological Legacy of St. Cyprian." *Journal of Ecclesiastical History* 14 (1963): 139-49.

5

GETTING RECOGNIZED
Emperor Constantine's Revolution

People often hold a "great man" view of history, explaining major developments in terms of a particular heroic figure. Frequently, however, that "great" person is simply the instrument of the tides of society. Without that person, the change would likely have occurred anyway.

Moreover, change often occurs more slowly than it appears. Take Christian conversion as an example. While conversion may be dramatic and sudden, there is still a measure of truth in the comment that it takes three generations to make a Christian—the statement highlighting the significance of generations in the formation of Christian character. These comments have a great deal of significance in relation to the "great man" Constantine. His "conversion" and policies have been held up in popular thought as a primary explanation for medieval church-state relations of centuries later. Opponents of a Christendom that intertwines church and state and makes each citizen an obligatory member of both have often blamed Constantine for this development.

Such a stance, however, grossly oversimplifies history and ignores both trends that were already occurring as well as post-Constantinian developments. Nevertheless, it is clear that Constantine had a very large impact on church development. At the time when Constantine embraced Christianity in 312, it was by no means certain that Christianity would eventually become the majority or favored religion of the empire. Lack of data obviously makes accurate statistics difficult to establish, but it is commonly estimated that at the time when Constantine converted, about ten percent of the empire was Christian. Would almost the entire population of the empire have eventually embraced the name *Christian* if Constantine or an imperial successor had not converted? Probably not. Alternatively, if Roman society were eventually to have embraced Christianity in some form despite a hostile ruler, it would have taken much longer than the 100-150 years that it actually took for most people within the Roman Empire to view themselves as

Christian. Constantine did in fact make an impressive contribution to Christianity. It should, however, be neither overvalued nor undervalued.

Constantine's Conversion

Constantine's conversion seems to have been sudden and dramatic: a sign in the sky on the eve of a crucial battle and immediately he was a Christian. That is a *Readers' Digest* condensed version. A long path, however, led up to that day. And a long converting process also followed, a process hardly begun in many facets of his person within his lifetime.

Constantine's father, Constantius, ruled Spain, Gaul and Britain as a senior emperor of the Roman Empire immediately prior to his death in 306. The "great persecution" of Christians had recently ceased in the West, though it raged for a few more years in the East. Ignoring protocols of dialogue over succession with the other three Roman emperors or caesars, Constantine had his soldiers proclaim him as "Augustus" in place of his just-deceased father. After consolidating his power, Constantine marched on Rome in 312. On the eve of the battle he adopted a Christian sign, the *labarum*, for his banners of battle; it was as a Christian that he went into the battle of Milvian Bridge, which would determine whether he would be emperor of the West or dead. Various later accounts relate what happened to produce this startling action. Some years after 312, Constantine himself swore on oath that he and his whole army had seen a light in the shape of a cross in the sky and the words "in this conquer." This was followed by a dream in which Christ appeared to him with the heavenly sign and the command to make standards for his army utilizing this symbol.[1] Regardless of dispute about details, Constantine evidently went into battle under a Christian symbol.

Did Constantine become a Christian? What is a Christian? Certainly much of Constantine's subsequent behavior seems sub-Christian. Cynics may view Constantine's delaying of his baptism until his deathbed in 337 as a case of having his cake and eating it. Constantine's completing his Christian conversion when he was fast losing the capacity to commit sin suggests a fine sense of Machiavellian judgment and timing—sin all you like and wash it all away right at the end. We should note, however, that end-of-life baptism was common in the fourth century. Baptism was a washing oncer; so why not tack it on to the end of one's life to ensure all sins were washed away?

Very disturbing to modern minds is Constantine's execution of his son Crispus for adultery in 326, and then his subsequent forcing of his second wife, Fausta, to commit suicide after he concluded that she had manipulated the situation to bring

---

[1] Eusebius *Life of Constantine* 1.28-29 (*NPNF*[2] 1:490).

Figure 5.1. The emperor Constantine (Timothy McCarthy/Art Resource, NY)

about her stepson's death. How could *"Christian"* Constantine do such things? Many Christians are "unevenly sanctified" and have huge blind spots in their apprehension of Christianity. Many otherwise fine Christians have, for example, given a blessing to bloody battles fought for far less-than-Christlike motives down to most of our own lifetimes. Can we then be too hard on Constantine for his blind spots?

Rather than ask, was Constantine "converted" according to our measures of Christianity, it may be better to ask, was Constantine changed by his Christianity? To that the answer must be yes.

This answer needs to take into account why Constantine may have embraced Christianity in the first place. Constantine was fundamentally an emperor, focused on imperial concerns. In identifying with a minority movement that was underrepresented in the powerful political and military sectors, it is unlikely that Constantine was attempting to gain the support of Christians as a vehicle to power.

Thus, his motives were better than pragmatic expediency. However, Constantine's concern in becoming a Christian was probably less the salvation of his own soul and more the well-being of the empire.[2] For him Christianity was less a religion of love or humility and more a religion of power.[3] The Christian God did indeed rule. It was therefore vital to obtain the support of this supreme ruler of the universe in his battles for power, and in the subsequent administration and defense of the empire. Constantine, in line with his predecessors, wanted to maintain the *pax deorum* (the "peace of the gods")—the blessing of heaven crucial for good outcomes on earth. In contrast with his predecessors, however, Constantine looked to a new divinity to achieve this purpose.

In some ways the conversion was clear-cut. Constantine's subsequent twenty-five years as emperor show a great deal of consistency in his favoring of Christianity. His Milvian Bridge victory, celebrated in a triumphal arch, attributed his success, not to pagan gods, but to the "Divinity"—though that term was ambiguous, probably designed not to be offensive to pagans.[4] In a more explicit Christian affirmation, however, Constantine had his own statue, in which he held a cross in his right hand, erected soon after the Milvian Bridge victory.[5]

Nevertheless, in other ways Constantine's conversion initially seemed muddled, with years to elapse before the light of the gospel began to penetrate aspects of his non-Christian fog. He celebrated his victory at Milvian Bridge by issuing a medallion attributing victory to the Sun. For some years prior to the march on Rome, Constantine had been monotheistic, worshipping the Unconquered Sun. Was the medallion a syncretistic blending of his past and present? Roman coins continued to feature traditional pagan gods until 317 and the Unconquered Sun until 319/20.[6] Was this also syncretism, or was it political astuteness, substantially maintaining continuity with the past so as not to alarm his subjects with too sudden a change? There was certainly some mixing of religious systems together. For example, Constantine continued to follow his imperial predecessors in serving as *pontifex maximus*, head in name at least of the pagan religious system.

The ambiguous character of Constantine's Christianity was perhaps inherent in the nature of his Milvian Bridge conversion. What happened on that day was not so much an ethical turning or the embracing of a new belief system, but rather the adopting of a symbol, the sign of the cross. Magic loomed large in popular belief.

---

[2]J. H. W. G. Liebeschuetz, *Continuity and Change in Roman Religion* (Oxford: Clarendon, 1979), p. 292.
[3]M. Grant, *Constantine: The Man and His Times* (New York: History Book Club, 1993, 2000), p. 222.
[4]A. H. M. Jones, *Constantine and the Conversion of Europe* (London: English Universities Press, 1948), p. 90.
[5]Eusebius *Church History* 9.9.10 (*NPNF*[2] 1:364).
[6]Grant, *Constantine,* p. 134.

Figure 5.2. The arch of Constantine (Scala/Art Resource, NY)

Constantine faced victory or death. He stood in dire need of divine favor or luck. The right ritual or symbol might well do the trick. Divine revelation showed him the symbol to use. And it worked. The magical aspect of Constantine's worldview was patent some years later when his mother Helena sent him relics of the true cross. He had splinters of the precious wood embedded in a statue of himself in Constantinople as a talisman for the eternal protection of that city.[7] Apparently he also took the nails by which Christ had been fastened to the cross (also supplied by his mother) and made them into bridle bits and a helmet for use in military expeditions.[8] Constantine's Christianity clearly had a "lucky-rabbit's-foot" dimension.

Who can tell the strength or truth of Constantine's Christianity? It would seem that in his earliest postconversion years he retained vestiges of his old belief system and lacked full understanding of the exclusive claims of Christianity. The muddle of his story is typical of many converts to Christianity. The difference is that his role was so public that it left his inconsistencies of faith and practice exposed to armchair critique down to the present. While Constantine's personal inner life, be-

[7]Socrates *Ecclesiastical History* 1.17 (NPNF[2] 2:21).
[8]Ibid.

liefs and motivations may be questionable, he must at least be credited with brilliant statecraft in giving standing to Christianity in the Roman Empire. His religious changes took place largely unchallenged, leading to the creation of a consensus in favor of a broadly inclusive monotheism under which both Christians and most pagans lived in harmony.[9]

The Favoring of Christianity

Prior to Constantine, Christianity had no secure place in society or in the law. Tolerated at best, faced with pogrom and state execution at worst, the standing of Christians had been precarious for nearly three centuries. Constantine's accession quickly and irreversibly changed that. Constantine met his coemperor Licinius, emperor of the East, at Milan in 313. Whether the "Edict of Milan" initiated or simply confirmed Christian protection and legal status is a matter of debate.[10] Irrespective of detail, however, from the beginnings of Constantine's reign Christianity had not only solid imperial protection, but also imperial favor for the first time. Christianity was still not, however, the state religion. That step did not occur until Theodosius decisively banned pagan worship in 391. Constantine himself may have been moving in that direction, as a subsequent law of his sons ineffectually abolishing "the madness of sacrifices" refers to their father's previous ban.[11] Such earlier measures were, however, half-hearted and ineffective. At most, Constantine's direct measures against paganism were effectively limited to despoiling some pagan temples for their wealth and shutting a few of the more notoriously depraved pagan shrines.[12]

More significant were measures not so much against paganism but *for* Christianity, for example, giving state significance to Sunday, the Christian day of worship, as a day of rest. In 321 Constantine decreed the closure of the courts on "the Day of the Sun" and also urged the cessation of unnecessary work on that day.[13] In addition, he required his soldiers to pray on Sundays to "the supreme God."[14] Even more significant was Constantine's early decision to channel state relief to the poor through Christian charitable endeavors.[15] It etched into popular consciousness the notion that church was a primary source of practical succor for those in

---

[9]H. A. Drake, "Constantine and Consensus," *Church History* 64, no. 1 (1995): 1-15, see p. 15.

[10]See Eusebius *Church History* 10.5.4 (*NPNF*[2] 1:379). For modern discussion, see T. D. Barnes, *Constantine and Eusebius* (Cambridge, Mass.: Harvard University Press, 1981), p. 318n. 4.

[11]Eusebius *Life of Constantine* 4.25 (*NPNF*[2] 1:546); Drake, "Constantine and Consensus," pp. 5-6.

[12]Jones, *Constantine and the Conversion*, p. 214; Socrates *Church History* 1.18 (*NPNF*[2] 2:22).

[13]Eusebius *Life of Constantine* 4.18 (*NPNF*[2] 1:544).

[14]Ibid., 4.19-20 (*NPNF*[2] 1:545).

[15]Ibid., 4.28.

desperate material circumstances. Prior to Constantine the church had already developed an impressive system of poor relief. Most of this, however, was in-house, for the relief of needy Christians. Receiving a boost of much greater resources through state contribution made the church a more significant benefactor to society at large. Half a century later, the pagan emperor Julian clearly recognized the challenge that church aid meant to paganism:

> While there are no persons in need among the Jews, and while the impious Galileans provide not only for their own party who are in want, but also for those who hold with us, it would indeed be disgraceful if we were to allow our own people to suffer from poverty.[16]

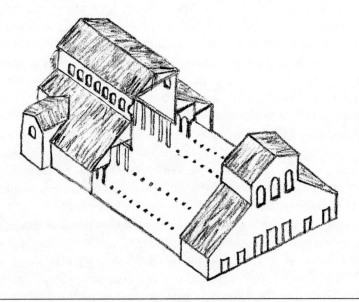

Figure 5.3. Sketch of the church of San Giovanni, Lateran, begun in A.D. 313 (length c. 98 m) (Line drawing by William Caulton)

The state also funded the erection of grand church basilicas. Basilicas were rectangular buildings of prestige, used as royal audience halls, law courts, business offices and a variety of other civic offices.[17] The fact that churches were commonly now meeting in such structures demonstrates the changed, more prestigious standing of Christianity in society. Seven such basilicas were erected in Rome alone. A

---

[16]Sozomen, *Ecclesiastical History* 5.16 (*NPNF*[2] 2:338).
[17]E. Foley, *From Age to Age: How Christians Celebrated the Eucharist* (Chicago: Liturgy Training Publications, 1991), p. 45.

letter from Constantine to Eusebius of Caesarea urged the repair and expansion of existing church buildings and the construction where necessary of new ones, and he encouraged the bishops "to demand what is needful for the work, both from the provincial governors and from the praetorian prefect."[18] Eusebius indicated that a copy of the letter went throughout all the provinces to the bishops of the various churches, that the provincial governors received instructions accordingly, and thus "the imperial edict was speedily carried into effect."[19] This indicates a great deal of state funding of much grander church buildings than ever before.

In addition to prestigious buildings, fiscal favor also meant prestigious furnishings. As a result of Constantine's gifts, St. Peter's had a shrine for the apostle made of precious marbles and gold, a great cross of solid gold, a silver-gilt altar set with 400 precious stones and a golden dish to receive the offertory of the people's breads, to name the most notable items.[20]

Such imperial favor and lavishness greatly fostered the standing of the church in society at large. Was this wealth and grandeur, however, also a threat, a source of corruption? Hilary of Poitiers, in a statement quoted above, certainly thought so: "What an evil it is, this love of building that possesses you."[21]

State favor clearly accelerated mass conversion to Christianity. Much of this mass movement was no doubt superficial, arising from all sorts of motivations. The port city of Majuma in Gaza, for example, was able to win a new and improved charter by informing Constantine that it was now completely Christian.[22] A century after Constantine, Augustine suggested that entry standards had commonly been lowered a great deal to make the transition into Christianity much easier. Augustine's comments arose in the context of his seeking to correct drunken revelry associated with the celebration of a saint's day. In response to the objection that such behavior had been permitted in the past, Augustine gave the following answer:

> I explained to them the circumstances out of which this custom seems to have arisen in the church—namely that when in the peace which came after such numerous and violent persecutions, crowds of heathen who wished to assume the Christian religion were kept back, because, having been accustomed to celebrate the feasts connected with their worship of idols in revelling and drunkenness, they could not easily refrain from pleasures so hurtful and habitual, it had seemed good to our ancestors, making for a time a concession to this infirmity, to permit them to celebrate, instead

---

[18]Eusebius *Life of Constantine* 2.46 (*NPNF*² 1:511).
[19]Ibid.
[20]D. G. Dix, *The Shape of the Liturgy* (Glasgow: University Press, 1945), p. 310.
[21]Hilary of Poitiers *Against Auxentius* 3 (quoted in P. Rousseau, *Ascetics, Authority, and the Church in the Age of Jerome and Cassian* [Oxford: Oxford University Press, 1978], p. 3).
[22]Sozomen *Ecclesiastical History* 2.5 (*NPNF*² 2:262).

of the festivals which they renounced, other feasts in honour of the holy martyrs, which were observed, not as before with a profane design, but with similar indulgence. I added that now upon them, as persons bound together in the name of Christ, and submissive to the yoke of his august authority, the wholesome restraints of sobriety were laid—restraints with which the honour and fear due to him who appointed them should move them to comply—and that therefore the time had now come in which all who did not dare to cast off the Christian profession should begin to walk according to Christ's will; and being now confirmed Christians, should reject those concessions to infirmity which were made only for a time in order to their becoming such.[23]

State sympathy commonly meant burgeoning congregations. While one may make derogatory comments about quantity at the expense of quality, the influx created enormous potential for church influence in society and in individual hearts and lives where there was good catechetical-type instruction and able church leadership. The situation at Hippo described above, with the world flooding into the church, illustrates the scope for influence of a bishop like Augustine. Basil could similarly use his influence in an expanded church in the late 360s to stir consciences for the relief of suffering when Cappadocia experienced a dreadful famine:

> Why are you rich and another poor? Surely it is that you may win the reward of charitableness and faithful stewardship, and he the noble prizes of patience? And yet you store up everything in the pockets of insatiable covetousness and think you wrong no one when you are defrauding many. Who is the covetous man? One for whom plenty is not enough! Who is the defrauder? One who takes away what belongs to everyone. And are you not covetous, are you not a defrauder, when you keep for private use what you were given for distribution? When someone strips a man of his clothes we call him a thief. And one who might clothe the naked and does not—should not he be given the same name? The bread in your board belongs to the hungry; the cloak in your wardrobe belongs to the naked; the shoes you let rot belong to the barefoot; the money in your vaults belongs to the destitute. All you might help and do not—to all these you are doing wrong.[24]

Societal influence could, however, be a two-edged weapon. Would the church convert the world that now lived much more in its midst? Or would the world in the church convert the church? The challenge was that church success was also potentially corrupting. Becoming a Christian was increasingly becoming a socially and politically wise move. Motives for conversion are commonly mixed at the best

---

[23]Augustine *Letter* 29.9 (*NPNF*[1] 1:255-56).
[24]Basil of Caesarea *Homily on "I Will Pull down My Barns"* 7 (in P. C. Phan, *Social Thought,* Message of the Fathers 20 [Wilmington, Del.: Michael Glazier, 1984], p. 117).

of times. How much more so in the fourth-century Roman Empire. For most of the fourth century, wealthy Roman senators were significant holdouts in the conversion process. However, with their wives and families increasingly adhering to Christianity, and with Theodosius's measures clearly putting paganism out of favor, conversion became advisable. So much of the senatorial class did convert in the decade or two around the beginning of the fifth century. But what sort of conversions would they turn out to be? Would such converts bring unconverted values of the world into the church? Would, for example, class structures replace the equality of Christian brotherhood and sisterhood? Gregory of Nazianzus expressed this concern in 381:

> Do not disdain to be baptized with a poor man, if you are rich; or if you are noble, with one who is lowborn; or if you are a master, with one who is up to the present time your slave.[25]

Worldly values had always carried some influence in the church; now they were increasingly prominent. Through state subsidies, donations and bequests, the church was fast becoming a wealthy institution. Bishops began to live in high style. Their senior representatives would even dine with Constantine and his successors on occasion.[26] A factor in John Chrysostom's difficulties as bishop of Constantinople involved his maintaining an ascetic lifestyle. This resulted in his failing to provide the now-expected lavish hospitality of a bishop.[27] Christians have commonly been endangered by seductive influences in the spheres of money, sex and power. Jerome warned the virgin Eustochium about the first two of those dangers in the clergy themselves:

> The very clergy, who ought to inspire them [widows] with respect by their teaching and authority, kiss these ladies on the forehead, and putting forth their hands (so that, if you knew no better, you might suppose them in the act of blessing), take wages for their visits.[28]
>
> There are others—I speak of those of my own order—who seek the presbyterate and the diaconate simply that they may be able to see women with less restraint. Such men think of nothing but their dress; they use perfumes freely—and see that there are no creases in their leather shoes. Their curling hair shows traces of the tongs; their fingers glisten with rings; they walk on tiptoe across a damp road, not to splash their feet. When you see men acting in this way, think of them rather as bridegrooms than as clergy. Certain persons have devoted the whole of their ener-

---

[25]Gregory of Nazianzus *Oration on Holy Baptism* (*Oration 40*) 40.27 (NPNF[2] 7:369).
[26]Eusebius *Life of Constantine* 3.15 (NPNF[2] 1:524); Sozomen *Ecclesiastical History* 1.25 (NPNF[2] 2:257).
[27]Sozomen *Ecclesiastical History* 8.9 (NPNF[2] 2:405).
[28]Jerome *Letter* 22.16 (NPNF[2] 6:28).

gies and life to the single object of knowing the names, houses, and characters of married ladies.[29]

Wealth complicated clerical calling and function. Early in his reign Constantine declared Christian clergy exempt from taxation and from the burdens of public office. Here Constantine merely accorded to the Christian clergy the same right that heathen priests and certain professions had enjoyed for many years.[30] Being a *decurion* (an inherited town council leadership position) by this time commonly involved making large payments to make up the shortfall in taxation levies. Thus Constantine's declaration offered an opportunity for decurions to escape such burdens by seeking ordination. Constantine twice sought to legislate to block that escape route (in 326 and 329).

Financial attractions could clearly taint the motivation for ordination. So attractive was the wealthy lifestyle of Damasus, bishop of Rome, 366-384, that the rich aristocrat Praetextus, priest in the cult of many deities, used to joke with Damasus: "Make me bishop of Rome and I will become a Christian."[31] Damasus himself was known as "the ladies' ear-tickler" for his ability to charm wealthy Christian women to give money to the church.[32] In addition to greater temptations in the areas of sex and wealth, power was an even more subtle danger. Damasus seems to have felt that lure also. Rival aspirations for the papacy in 366 led to a bitterly contested election that Damasus ultimately won. In the process, however, there was a riot in which 137 men were killed. Clearly there was now a markedly different spirit between the ambitions and lifestyle of some of these vicars of Christ and their master.

Bishops as Judicial Officers

Paul had urged the Christian community at Corinth to utilize its own wise counselors to arbitrate disputes between Christians rather than bringing them before heathen judges (1 Cor 6:1-8). Paul was most likely concerned about fairness, as powerful members of society commonly triumphed over the weak in the "bent" system of Roman justice.[33] Whatever Paul's reason, his injunction became a rule for Christians to follow; Constantine enshrined it in imperial law.[34] Where two

---

[29]Ibid., 22.28 (*NPNF*[2] 6:34).

[30]E. A. Johnson, "Constantine the Great: Imperial Benefactor of the Early Christian Church," *Journal of the Ecclesiastical Theological Society* 22, no. 2 (1979): 161-69, see p. 165.

[31]H. Chadwick, *The Early Church* (London: Penguin, 1967), p. 161.

[32]Ibid.

[33]A. C. Mitchell, "Rich and Poor in the Courts of Corinth: Litigiousness and Status in 1 Corinthians 6.1-11," *New Testament Studies* 39, no. 4 (1993): 562-86.

[34]The innovatory law has been lost, but is inferred from two subsequent laws: see Barnes, *Constantine and Eusebius*, p. 51.

Christians were engaged in a legal dispute, either one could have the case transferred from the hearing of a state magistrate to the binding arbitration of a bishop
(the famous *audientia episcopalis*). This gave enormous influence, but also expanded workload, to the bishops. This especially became the case as the empire as
a whole gradually turned Christian, leading to very large numbers of cases having
the potential to be transferred to the bishops' jurisdiction. A consequence was that
Augustine, for example, spent all his mornings as a bishop adjudicating in law-
suits.[35] The same was probably true of Ambrose. At least Augustine complained
how it was almost impossible to speak with Ambrose in the daytime, being "de-
barred . . . by crowds of busy people whose infirmities he devoted himself to."[36]
Not only was the bishop's judicial role enormously time consuming, it also made
the bishop a powerful judge, and so shaped his perception of himself and of the
episcopal role. The *audientia episcopalis* role was another factor that contributed to
the rapidly expanding power of the bishop. Lord Acton's famous dictum expressed
the danger: "Power tends to corrupt and absolute power corrupts absolutely."

State Involvement in Church Affairs

Overlap between the two systems of church and state was a likely development
from the outset of Constantine's reign. Whereas the twenty-first-century West may
sharply delineate the spheres of religion and state, society was then a much more
integrated whole. With good religious practice considered a key to the state's well-
being, the state had a major interest in religious issues. Third-century pagan Rome
had shown marked concern to determine the will of the gods by divination and to
observe the proper religious rites. Thus Constantine inherited a situation where religion was very much a state concern, where state involvement in religious affairs
was normal. The role of emperors to supervise religious life as *pontifex maximus*
exemplifies this.

Though we may not agree with Constantine's understandings and motivations
as a Christian, we must acknowledge that he took his faith seriously and displayed
a great deal of interest in religious affairs. Apparently he once even stated that he
was a bishop, saying to a gathering of bishops, "You are bishops whose jurisdiction
is within the church; I also am a bishop, ordained by God to overlook what is external to the church."[37] Constantine's remark suggests that he did not view his religious powers as untrammeled: he was not to interfere with the internal life of the
church, but simply to concern himself with those aspects that were matters of

---

[35]P. Brown, *Augustine of Hippo: A Biography* (London: Faber & Faber, 1967), pp. 195-96, 226.
[36]Augustine *Confessions* 6.3.3 (*NPNF*[1] 1:91).
[37]Eusebius *Life of Constantine* 4.24 (*NPNF*[2] 1:546).

state, outside of internal church life. However, sooner or later there was bound to be a conflict between his claim to decide what measures should be taken to ensure God's favor for the empire and the claim of the church to decide what Christians must believe and do.[38]

Constantine saw himself as having a divine mission, especially in foreign policy, to use his political and military power to foster Christianity and protect Christians.[39] Thus, his policies fostered the spread of Christianity. He took an interest in providing protection to Christians in Persia. His defeat of the Goths in 331 could be interpreted as a statement of the power of the Christian God. And his insisting on religious clauses in the subsequent peace treaty were likely contributing factors to the success of the missionary evangelizing of the Goths by Ulfilas a decade later.[40]

Imperial Involvement in the Donatist Schism

Church-state relations presented problems when they dealt with matters much more internal to the life of the church. Even Constantine's apparently innocent decision to channel state relief to the poor through the church led to major involvement in church issues in North Africa. There a schism had occurred following the "great persecution." Beyond issues of rigor or flexibility in the face of state terror lay a complex of other matters, including socio-economic and ethnic issues.[41] The outcome was that, when Constantine came to power, rival Catholic and Donatist churches both existed. Thus, his state support policy immediately faced the question of which was the legitimate church in Africa through which to channel state subsidies. Along with this came another question, "Does church property confiscated in the great persecution belong to the Catholics or to the Donatists, and to whom should it be restored in accordance with imperial decrees?"[42] Constantine quickly backed the Catholic bishop, Caecilian. When the Donatist clergy appealed to Constantine in 313, he referred the matter to a council of bishops at Rome. Subsequently, he referred an appeal to the Council of Arles in 314. In both cases the ruling went against the Donatists. Complications and appeals caused the issue to drag on, with the state enmeshed in the process. In the end Constantine had had enough. Among his repressive measures, starting in 317, were the exiling of Don-

---

[38]Jones, *Constantine and the Conversion*, p. 251.
[39]Eusebius *Life of Constantine* 4.8 (*NPNF*[2] 1:542); Barnes, *Constantine and Eusebius*, p. 258.
[40]Eusebius *Life of Constantine* 4.5 (*NPNF*[2] 1:541-42); Barnes, *Constantine and Eusebius*, p. 258; Jones, *Constantine and the Conversion*, p. 205.
[41]See W. H. C. Frend, *The Donatist Church* (Oxford: Clarendon, 1952), pp. 24, 143, 319ff.
[42]L. W. Barnard, "Church-State Relations, A.D. 313-337," *Journal of Church and State* 24, no. 2 (1982): 337-55, see p. 342.

atist leaders and an order for the confiscation of their churches.[43] State repression led to several people, including two Donatist bishops, being killed in a skirmish between military forces and Donatist supporters. Dangerous precedents were being set in the tortuous process of dealing with the Donatist issue. Henceforward, the church routinely expected the state to enforce the decisions of its councils, especially in relation to the deposing of bishops. The once-persecuted church was starting to become a persecutor.

State enforcement reached a new level in 385 when Maximus, the usurping emperor of the West, sanctioned the execution of the theologically suspect Priscillian, bishop of Avila, on a charge of witchcraft. While a horrified church, including Martin of Tours, Ambrose of Milan and Pope Siricius, condemned the action, a new precedent had been set: execution might now be deemed appropriate in the name of Christ. The voluntary nature of faith came increasingly under threat.

In the 390s imperial legislation against paganism was widened to coerce heretical and schismatic Christians also. In 405 an "Edict of Unity" was passed against the Donatists. They were declared heretics and ordered to disband. Augustine of Hippo had earlier opposed coercive measures to resolve the Donatist schism for pragmatic reasons: it would produce only "pretend" Catholics.[44] The effects of the edict changed his mind, again for pragmatic reasons—coercion worked: "my own town . . . was brought over to the Catholic unity by fear of the imperial edicts."[45]

There is no need here to trace the subsequent convoluted process that led to total suppression of the Donatists—only to see their resurgence a generation later when Roman authority broke under the weight of barbarian invasion. The point is that force was again justified in matters of church faith and organization. Augustine saw force largely as economic pressure, the imposing of disabilities on property owners (though recalcitrant rustic laborers could receive a beating to bring them into line).[46] He opposed the execution of Donatists, but was powerless to stop some that did occur.[47] At the same time his views led to the firming of a principle: it was legitimate to "compel them to come in."[48] It is not therefore altogether outrageous to suggest that the saintly Augustine may be "the first theorist of the Inquisition," even though Augustine would have been horrified at what developed

---

[43]Augustine *Letter* 88.3 (*NPNF*[1] 1:370).
[44]Augustine *Letter* 93.5.17 (*NPNF*[1] 1:388).
[45]Ibid.
[46]Augustine *Letters* 93.3.10; 93.5.18; 111.2 (*NPNF*[1] 1:385, 388, 433); H. Chadwick, *Augustine* (Oxford: Oxford University Press, 1986), p. 82.
[47]Augustine *Letter* 100.2 (*NPNF*[1] 1:412).
[48]A misuse of Lk 14:23.

under that regime.[49] We are now a long way both from the spirit of the gospel and the rule of Constantine. However, the temper of the age and the precedent-setting early actions of Constantine against the Donatists blazed a trail that the medieval church eventually utilized in sometimes-devilish ways.

Imperial Involvement in Theological Disputes

Concerns of state shaped Constantine's view of the church: he needed a united church as part of his goal of a united empire. Fractiousness within the church frustrated that desire. More serious even than the Donatist schism was the Arian dispute that raged in many parts of the empire from the 320s onwards. The theological issues will be explored in chapter eleven, but in a nutshell, they concerned the relationship of the Son to the Father. Arius's view that the Son had a beginning made the Son a divine intermediary and not really God. A theological issue with huge implications was at stake. Constantine's concern for unity probably caused him to intervene on theological ground where angels themselves might fear to tread. Arius, presbyter in Alexandria, expounded his views about 318. Archbishop Alexander soon excommunicated him. The issue soon polarized much of the Eastern church. Constantine's concern for unity led to his writing a letter to the two chief protagonists in 324. Both were in error, Alexander for asking a presbyterial gathering for their theological views that led to Arius expounding his controversial views, and Arius for replying. Such sublime, abstruse and subtle issues should not be nailed down in definitive statements. The primary error, according to Constantine, was not false belief, but dividing the church with "profane disunion," for they were scrapping over "small and very insignificant questions."[50]

Constantine followed up his letter in highly interventionist manner, calling together the Council of Nicea in 325. He arranged public conveyance for the 300 or so bishops who attended and provided for their living expenses.[51] Significantly, Constantine himself chaired this august church council in its deliberations on a theological matter that was both crucial and complex. Constantine's role clearly affected the outcome. The council adopted the term *homoousios*, "same substance," to explain the relationship of the Son to the Father. While the term may be very appropriate, it is difficult to see how the council apart from Constantine's pressure would have appropriated it, given its usage in a different context by the heretic Paul of Samosata half a century earlier. Constantine's adviser, Hosius, bishop of Cordova, likely proposed the term, but it was Constantine's intimidating presence

---

[49]Brown, *Augustine of Hippo*, p. 240.
[50]Eusebius *Life of Constantine* 2.71 (NPNF² 1:517).
[51]Ibid., 3.6, 9 (NPNF² 1:521, 522).

that coerced the council into adopting the suspect word. Constantine's flatterer, Eusebius of Caesarea, was impressed with Constantine's role:

> By the affability of his address to all, and his use of the Greek language, with which he was not altogether unacquainted, he appeared in a truly attractive light, persuading some, convincing others by his reasonings, praising those who spoke well, and urging all to unity of sentiment, until at last he succeeded in bringing them to one mind and judgment respecting every disputed question.[52]

Though Eustathius of Antioch was on the winning side at Nicea, he held a different view of Constantine's influence, muttering that unnamed persons put forward the name of peace and thereby reduced to silence those who normally spoke best.[53] Either way, Constantine's efforts proved to be a papering over the cracks. Controversy flared afresh, with Arianism, now aided by imperial sympathy, apparently starting to gain the upper hand in the next decade. Constantine came to depend on Eusebius of Nicomedia as his close adviser, even receiving baptism from him at the end of his life, despite the Arian-leaning Eusebius having been deposed for a time after Nicea. Constantine's theological shift suggests that issues of state influenced his perspective more than did issues of theological truth. His concern was more for unity than for theology. A happy state needed a united church.[54] Consequently, Constantine set his sails according to his sense of mainstream opinion, even though theologically this might mean running with the hares and hunting with the hounds.

All these developments highlight the increasing intertwining of theology and politics. It is significant that final resolution of the Arian controversy again came through imperial influence. When Theodosius became emperor of the East in 379, his support for Nicea was soon patent. Following Constantine's precedent, he initiated the calling of an ecumenical council at Constantinople in 381 that endorsed the Nicene position. Similarly, when dispute arose later over the relationship of the divine and human natures of Christ, again a new emperor's influence led to the Council of Chalcedon and its decision in 451. What we now call trinitarian orthodoxy significantly emerged through imperial influence. We may applaud the conclusion while disputing the process. Was imperial influence appropriate? Was it a dangerous precedent for the future? Constantine initiated a direction that treated church discipline, dogma and unity as matters of public policy.[55]

---

[52]Ibid., 3.13 (NPNF^2 1:523).

[53]Theodoret *Ecclesiastical History* 1.7 (NPNF^2 3:44); Barnes, *Constantine and Eusebius*, p. 216.

[54]Ø. Norderval, "The Emperor Constantine and Arius: Unity in the Church and Unity in the Empire," *Studia Theologica* 42, no. 2 (1988): 113-50, see p. 138.

[55]N. Brox, *A History of the Church,* trans. J. Bowden (London: SCM Press, 1994), p. 57.

Church-State Relations in the Aftermath of Constantine's Rule

Nowhere in the empire did a complete ongoing kowtowing to imperial will on
church matters take place. In the 350s the emperor began pressuring the church
in a more Arian direction, particularly in seeking condemnation of the anti-Arian
Athanasius. At the Council of Milan (355) the West appeared to fall into line on
the matter in response to the browbeating of Constantius: "I am the accuser of
Athanasius. . . . Let my will serve as a canon as it does with the Syrian bishops."[56]
Both Arianism and caesaropapism (state dominance of church affairs) seemed tri-
umphant. However, a few months later the aged Hosius sent a stinging response
to Constantius:

> Intrude not yourself into ecclesiastical matters, neither give commands unto us con-
> cerning them; but learn from us. God has put into your hands the kingdom; to us
> he has entrusted the affairs of his church; and as he who would steal the empire from
> you would resist the ordinance of God, so likewise fear on your part lest by taking
> upon yourself the government of the church, you become guilty of a great offence.[57]

The imperial will did not render the churches totally docile. The Eastern
church, however, tended to be much more subservient than the church in the
West. Increasingly the Eastern pattern followed imperial domination, with the
church effectively becoming the religious department of the state. In the West the
pattern shows a much more even balance, partly perhaps because of the outspo-
ken stance of Ambrose, discussed below. The West came to have a clearer view of
church and state as two separate spheres, overlapping, but each with their own jurisdiction. Thus church and state stood in dynamic tension, each from time to time
seeking to expand its influence at the expense of the other. Who prevailed over the
next millennium—pope or king—depended significantly on strength of particular
personalities, context, and other historical developments.

Ambrose's Claims for the Church over Against the State

The most influential reaction in the fourth century against state meddling in
church affairs and also the greatest meddling by church in state affairs came from
Ambrose of Milan. Significantly, this stance did not come from the bishop of Rome,
but from a bishop lower in the hierarchy. This is partly explained by the fact that
the Western court was now not normally located at Rome but at Milan. Moreover,
Ambrose was a man born to rule. He was the son of a prefect of Gaul, and Ambrose
himself had been governor of Aemilia-Liguria, which included Milan, prior to his

---

[56]Athanasius *History of the Arians* 4.33 (*NPNF²* 4:281), in W. H. C. Frend, *The Early Church* (London:
Hodder & Stoughton, 1965), p. 165.
[57]Athanasius *History of the Arians*, 6.44 (*NPNF²* 4:286).

Figure 5.4. Image of Ambrose of Milan (Scala/Art Resource, NY)

being press-ganged into the episcopate. An imperious man, he proved a match for imperial power.

Ambrose had three especially significant confrontations with imperial authority. The first related to a disputed basilica in Milan. In 385-386, the influence of Justina, mother of the emperor, led to the imperial court requiring the church to hand over a basilica for the use of the sizeable Arian minority at Milan. From Justina's point of view, it was a reasonable requirement, an expression of tolerance in relation to a building that had no doubt been built partly at least with state funds. Ambrose, however, was implacably anti-Arian. He argued that God's things were not subject to imperial decree, and that a "temple of God" was one such thing:

> Do not, O Emperor, lay on yourself the burden of such a thought as that you have any imperial power over those things which belong to God. Exalt not yourself, but if you desire to reign long, submit yourself to God. It is written, "The things which are God's to God, those which are Caesar's to Caesar." The palaces belong to the emperor, the churches to the bishop.[58]

---

[58]Ambrose *Letter* 20.19 (*NPNF*[2] 10:425).

Theodoret's imaginative recreation half a century later of the encounter between Ambrose and Theodosius after the latter had been excommunicated for eight months for his role in the Thessalonica massacre:

The archbishop was seated in the audience hall and there the emperor approached him and besought that his bonds might be loosed.

'Your coming," said Ambrose, "is the coming of a tyrant. You are raging against God; you are trampling on his laws." "No," said Theodosius, "I do not attack laws laid down, I do not seek wrongfully to cross the sacred threshold; but I ask you to loose my bond, to take into account the mercy of our common Lord, and not to shut against me a door which our master has opened for all them that repent." The archbishop replied, "What repentance have you shown since your tremendous crime? You have inflicted wounds right hard to heal; what medicine have you applied?" "Yours," said the emperor, "is the duty alike of pointing out and of mixing the salve. It is for me to receive what is given me." Then said blessed Ambrose, "You let your rage minister justice, your anger, not your reason, gives judgment. Put forth therefore an edict which shall make the sentence of your anger null and void; let the sentences which have been published inflicting death or confiscation be suspended for thirty days awaiting the judgment of reason. When the days shall have elapsed, let them that wrote the sentences exhibit their orders, and then, and not till then, when passion has calmed down, reason acting as sole judge shall examine the sentences and will see whether they be right or wrong. If it find them wrong it will cancel the deeds; if they be righteous it will confirm them, and the interval of time will inflict no wrong on them that have been rightly condemned."

This suggestion the emperor accepted and thought it admirable. He ordered the edict to be put out forthwith and gave it the authority of his sign manual. On this, blessed Ambrose loosed the bond.

Now the very faithful emperor came boldly within the holy temple but did not pray to his Lord standing, or even on his knees, but lying prone upon the ground he tittered David's cry, "My soul cleaves to the dust, revive me according to your word." He plucked out his hair; he smote his head; he sprinkled the ground with drops of tears and prayed for pardon. When the time came for him to bring his offering to the holy table, weeping all the while, he stood up and approached the sanctuary.[a]

---

[a]Theodoret *Church History* 5.17 (*NPNF*[2] 3:144, English modernized).

To block the transfer of the building, Ambrose organized a sit-in. Direct defiance of imperial rule nearly resulted in military action and bloodshed. Ambrose's steel nerves eventually won the day. Though one may justify his actions in that incident, one can do so much less in the second episode.

This related to the Callinicum synagogue incident in 387. At the instigation of the bishop at Callinicum on the Euphrates, a mob had destroyed the local synagogue. Theodosius ordered the rebuilding of the synagogue by the bishop and the punishment of the rioters. Ambrose objected to God's patrimony being used for the building of a place of worship for Jewish unbelievers. After writing to the emperor, he preached in his presence, applying the Nathan and David story to the current situation. The emperor charged Ambrose with preaching against him. Ambrose responded by alluding to the Callinicum affair and implying that communion might be withheld if the emperor did not come into line with Ambrose's viewpoint. He extracted a promise from the emperor to do as Ambrose sought. Ambrose recorded his own response: "I went to the altar whither I should not have gone unless he had given me a distinct promise. . . . And so everything was done as I wished."[59]

Further confrontation occurred a couple of years later. Theodosius's actions in responding to the murder of an army officer in Thessalonica led to the massacre of 7,000 of its citizens. Ambrose wrote a masterly sensitive letter to the emperor, calling him to repentance and again making an implicit threat of excommunication: "I dare not offer the sacrifice if you intend to be present."[60] Ambrose's stance produced imperial penitence expressed in acts of public penance.[61] Ambrose thus practiced brinkmanship at its best. His encounters thereby established the precedent that the emperor was also a layman and subject to church discipline for acts of wickedness. Moral order stood above the will of the emperor, and the church could call him to account. Ambrose exercised courageous leadership in relation to the Thessalonica massacre. The church was now a check on unbridled imperial power.

No sharp line separated political and church issues in the fourth century. The church at times spoke into "state affairs" and the state into "church affairs." There could never be precise definition of those boundary lines, nor clear rules for whether or not speaking into the affairs of the other institution was justified. Constantine's conversion and religious interventions left a legacy of overlap, confusion, clash and struggle that was to persist for a millennium and more.

---

[59]Ambrose *Letter* 41.28 (*NPNF*[2] 10:450).
[60]Ambrose *Letter* 51.13 (*NPNF*[2] 10:452).
[61]Sozomen *Ecclesiastical History* 7.25 (*NPNF*[2] 2:394).

For Further Reading

Barnard, L. W. "Church-State Relations, A.D. 313-337." *Journal of Church and State* 24, no. 2 (1982): 337-55.

Barnes, T. D. *Constantine and Eusebius.* Cambridge, Mass.: Harvard University Press, 1981.

Drake, H. A. "Constantine and Consensus." *Church History* 64, no. 1 (1995): 1-15.

Grant, M. *Constantine: The Man and His Times.* New York: History Book Club, 1993, 2000.

Jones, A. H. M. *Constantine and the Conversion of Europe.* London: English Universities Press, 1948.

MacMullen, R. "Constantine and the Miraculous." *Greek, Roman and Byzantine Studies* 9 (1968): 81-96. Repr. pp. 155-70 in *Conversion, Catechumenate, and Baptism in the Early Church.* Studies in Early Christianity 11. Edited by E. Ferguson. New York: Garland, 1993.

Norderval, Ø. "The Emperor Constantine and Arius: Unity in the Church and Unity in the Empire." *Studia Theologica* 42 (1988): 113-50.

Rahner, H. *Church and State in Early Christianity.* Translated by L. D. Davis. San Francisco: St. Ignatius, 1992.

6

RADICAL DISCIPLESHIP
Asceticism and Monasticism

Early monastic practices could be bizarre in the extreme: people living on small platforms on top of poles, incredible feats of fasting, solitaries living for years on their own in the desert. Over against this image, we must recognize that such behavior was exceptional rather than normal—it is the sensational that often gets recorded. For a comprehensive perspective we need to consider the more ordinary lives of the more ordinary ascetics and monks, as well as the lives of the more bizarre. Moreover, we need to be cautious about using the label "bizarre." Bizarre by whose standards? We are often too ready to label that which is odd from our particular cultural perspective, without first entering into the cultural world and context of that practice and understanding the phenomenon from within. Only then should we use the word *bizarre*—and then we will seldom if ever use it.

Monasticism was a complex and varied phenomenon. Although we may categorize it into solitary, communal and semicommunal forms, within and beyond these paradigms considerable variation appears. This makes it important to recognize diversity and not view monasticism in too rigid a fashion. Moreover, monasticism evolved over many centuries, only gradually assuming certain forms after trial and error. We run the danger of reading early monasticism too much through its later developments. We need to recognize that early monasticism and even earlier, disciplined, ascetic lifestyles lie along a continuum without any sharp line between them. We cannot say that certain ascetic practices and theology developed in the church and that these developments suddenly mutated de novo into fourth-century monasticism. The initially blurry monastic identity emerged only gradually. Thus the term *monakoi* (monks) covered not only hermits and coenobites (communal monks), "but also fervent Christians who, while still moving around *in the world*, were striving to live a life as far as possible detached from it, focused wholly on God."[1]

---

[1] J. N. D. Kelly, *Golden Mouth: The Story of John Chrysostom—Ascetic, Preacher, Bishop* (New York: Cornell University Press, 1995), p. 20, emphasis added.

The novel aspect of the fourth-century development that we now label "monasticism" typically involved "monks" changing their residence—dropping out of ordinary society for the sake of their heavenly citizenship.[2] Even this apparently new phenomenon, however, existed prior to the fourth century and prior to Saint Antony. It simply was less visible and less frequent. But ascetic communities and isolated hermits separated from the world did predate Antony. Certainly a huge shift occurred in Christianity in relation to monasticism in the fourth century, but it should not be looked at in all-or-nothing fashion, as if it emerged at one point without existing at all in earlier times.

A further danger in studying monasticism is to view it through the life and practice of Saint Antony. Most of what we know about this figure has come through his *Life* by Bishop Athanasius of Alexandria. Athanasius faced constant entanglement and controversy in ecclesiastical and state politics throughout his life. Parties and positions to be challenged and defeated always confronted him. The *Life* is not simply a life as it was, but rather a life as Athanasius wanted it to be. While informative with regard to Antony, his work was also a propaganda tool. Among its dangers, the *Life* causes one to focus too much on solitary monastic practice and too much on the desert as the location of monasticism.

Women and men both feature prominently in the story of monasticism. The ascetic movement, with its emphasis on celibacy and the perils of sexual temptation, fostered sharp separation between male and female asceticism. To some extent monastic developments moved along different paths for each of the two sexes. Yet much common development also occurred. Moreover, male and female ascetics often found themselves to be kindred spirits of each other. This led to strong friendships between leaders such as Jerome and Paula and between John Chrysostom and Olympias. Only a wall, for example, separated Chrysostom's residence from that of Olympias and her 250 nuns, and she washed his clothes and sent him a meal each day. In acknowledging female asceticism, we should note that it also played a part in the story of women in general and their treatment in the church. For this reason, the major focus on female asceticism and monasticism will come in the following chapter on women, with this chapter focusing more on developments among men.

The Roots of Monasticism

A striking feature of Christian monasticism is that it did not mesh with pagan practice of that time. In particular, paganism regarded a long-term lifestyle of sexual

---

[2]E. A. Judge, "The Earliest Use of *Monachos* for 'Monk' (P. Coll. Youtie 77) and the Origins of Monasticism," *Jahrbuch für Antike und Christentum* 20 (1977): 72-89, see pp. 76-78.

abstinence as abnormal, being limited to a very small number of persons whose lives were dedicated to the services of the gods, for example, the Vestal Virgins. While pagan influences (particularly its dualistic thought) may have contributed to Christian perspectives that led to monasticism, no major direct borrowing from pagan practice occurred.

Monasticism was to some degree alien to Jewish practice also. Judaism was basically life affirming, in contrast to extremes of world denial in some expressions of monasticism. However, some first-century groups within Judaism practiced communal living in a context of withdrawal from the world. These included Essene communities, the best known of which was that at Qumran associated with the Dead Sea scrolls. Another was the *Therapeutae* referred to by Philo of Alexandria around the time of Christ. Such strands within Judaism may have influenced Christian monasticism, but this connection cannot completely explain the Christian phenomenon.

In seeking to understand later developments in asceticism and monasticism, the best starting point is probably the New Testament communities themselves. We need to begin with Christianity's founder, Jesus. Though he ate and drank freely, there were also markedly ascetic dimensions to Jesus' life: his associating with the poor, his sometimes being a homeless wanderer, his embracing a life of suffering, and his remaining an unmarried celibate throughout his life (Lk 6:24; 9:22; 9:58). Jesus' disciples were called to pattern their lives on his (Lk 9:23). Later Christians often sought to imitate Jesus as literally as possible. This could easily include an imitation of his lifelong celibacy.

Also fostering an ascetic lifestyle was the fact that Paul, the most influential Christian in the first generation of the early church, was single and expressed a preference for the single state (1 Cor 7:7-9, 32-35). In addition, early church interpretation commonly viewed 1 Corinthians 7:1b—"it is well for a man not to touch a woman"—as a statement of Paul rather than a statement of Paul's opponents that he intended to rebut. As a consequence, Paul was misread as having a very negative view of marital relationships.[3] Tertullian articulated such a perspective on 1 Corinthians 7:1b: "It follows that it is evil to have contact with a woman; for nothing is contrary to good except evil."[4] While scholarship now generally regards this interpretation of Paul's thought as erroneous, it powerfully influenced the church for a number of centuries.

Furthermore, the opening chapters of Acts show the early church modeling as-

---

[3]For this early church interpretation see W. E. Phipps, "Is Paul's Attitude Toward Sexual Relations Contained in 1 Cor. 7.1?" *New Testament Studies* 28 (1982): 125-31.
[4]Tertullian *On Monogamy* 3 (*ANF* 4:60).

pects of ascetic living: community, radical sharing and divestiture of property. This meant that when structured monasticism emerged, it did not necessarily see itself as innovative, but rather as returning to primitive Christianity. In the early fifth century John Cassian claimed that communal monastic practice "took its rise in the days of the preaching of the apostles," that church coldness led to the dying away of the practice, and that recent monastic practice "maintained the fervour of the apostles."[5]

Asceticism gained prominence early on, particularly in Syrian Christianity. Several strands of Luke's Gospel show striking affinities with the earliest shape of Syrian asceticism.[6] These include a radical stance on poverty, strong emphasis on prayer and the importance of the Holy Spirit. As Luke's Gospel is traditionally associated with the West Syria region, this may point to this Gospel's influence on early asceticism in Syria. Christian Encratites (from the Greek word *enkrateia,* "self-control") flourished in Syria in the second century.[7] These strict ascetic movements rejected the use of meat and wine, and often marriage itself.[8] One such ascetic, Tatian, who compiled the *Diatessaron,* a harmony of the four Gospels, in the second half of the second century, was based in Syria. His work skewed the Gospels in an ascetic direction in relation to food, possessions and marriage. An example of his skewing of the biblical text is his altering John 15:1 so that it does not mention wine ("I am the true vine" became "I am the tree of the fruit of life"). Another example is his version of Luke 2:36 such that Anna did not experience marital relationship (she "remained seven years *as a virgin* with her husband").[9] The *Diatessaron,* being the primary Gospel text in Syria until the end of the fourth century, significantly fostered asceticism in that region. Thus, from a very early date Syrian Christianity included celibate ascetics. Known as "sons [and daughters] of the covenant," such persons were an elite within the Christian community, having embraced a covenant of perpetual celibacy at their baptism.[10]

In addition to New Testament influences on later asceticism, we should also be

---

[5]John Cassian *Conferences* 18.5 (*NPNF*[2] 11:480-81).

[6]G. Winkler, "The Origins and Idiosyncrasies of the Earliest Form of Asceticism," in *The Continuing Quest for God: Monastic Spirituality in Tradition and Transition,* ed. W. M. Skudlarek (Collegeville, Minn.: Liturgical Press, 1982), pp. 9-43, see pp. 16-17.

[7]Ibid., p. 11.

[8]For early church references to encratite movements, see Irenaeus *Against Heresies* 1.28 (*ANF* 1:353); Hippolytus *Refutation of All Heresies* 8.13 (*ANF* 5:124).

[9]V. Desprez, "Christian Asceticism between the New Testament and the Beginning of Monasticism: The Second Century," *American Benedictine Review* 42, no. 2 (1991): 163-78, see p. 174.

[10]For an in-depth discussion on this, see G. Nedungatt, "The Covenanters of the Early Syrian-Speaking Church," *Orientalia Christiana Periodica* 39 (1973): 191-215, 419-44.

aware of the possible influence of Gnosticism (and also Manichaeism), especially through the second-century *Gospel of Thomas,* which likely originated in Syria. Gnosticism was a polymorphous movement arising in that century, often drawing on a mixture of Jewish, Christian and pagan elements. At its core, Gnosticism was fundamentally dualistic, denying the value of the material world and seeking a return to the realm of pure spirit through esoteric knowledge. Gnosticism came to be seen as fundamentally anti-Christian, turning Christianity's rootedness in history into a timeless myth. However, Gnosticism commonly drew heavily on Christian material, and its ideas significantly penetrated the life of the church. We can see a connection, for example, in a leading Gnostic exponent, Valentinus, having apparently been an unsuccessful candidate for the bishopric of Rome prior to his separation from the church.[11] Such connections mean that we should be aware not only of disjunction but also of possible influence arising from Christian and Gnostic interactions.

The Gnostic *Gospel of Thomas* includes stress on living as ascetic exiles on earth in preparation for a return to a nonsexual paradise. The ascetic "solitaries" are the saved ones: "Many are standing at the door, but the solitary *(monachos)* are the ones who will enter the bridal chamber."[12] The Syrian provenance of the book again highlights the significance of Syria in early Christian asceticism. Early Syrian asceticism played an important role in the later emergence of monasticism. In addition, the roots of monasticism were nourished by Gospel texts, some of which were written at the same time that ascetic practice was starting to flourish in communities of that area.

Early Ascetic Practice

From an early period, certain Christians were convinced that they should be committed to lifetime abstention from marriage and sexual relationships. The second-century pagan doctor Galen noted this practice among Christians: "Their contempt for death is patent to us every day, and likewise their restraint from intercourse. For they include not only men but also women who refrain from intercourse all their lives."[13] Writing about the same time, the Christian apologist Athenagoras also noted this practice:

> You would find many among us, both men and women, growing old unmarried, in

---

[11]Tertullian *Against the Valentinians* 4 (*ANF* 3:505).

[12]*Gospel of Thomas,* logia 75. See translation by A. Guillaumont (Leiden: Brill, 1959). While the work was preserved only in a Coptic translation, it preserves the Greek *monachos* for "solitary." The term *monachos* later became the descriptor for participants in the monastic movement in the fourth century.

[13]Cited in P. Brown, *The Body and Society: Men, Women, and Sexual Renunciation in Early Christianity* (New York: Columbia University Press, 1988), p. 33.

hope of living in closer communion with God. . . . Remaining in virginity and in the state of an eunuch brings nearer to God, while the indulgence of carnal thought and desire leads away from him.[14]

For some, this practice was a private matter, but for others the position was adopted in the context of collective church life, supported and guided by the church. Thus Ignatius, in writing to his fellow bishop Polycarp at the beginning of the second century, urged that those continuing in celibacy out of spiritual devotion should do so without boasting, being known only to the bishop.[15] This implies that such practice was known to and supported by the church. It is not clear whether a vow was taken at this time, as it later came to be taken in fourth- and fifth-century Christianity. Once formal vows of chastity started to be taken, however, it soon became a locked-in decision. Thus, forsaking one's vows for the sake of marriage was, in John Chrysostom's eyes, adultery.[16]

Tertullian provides evidence that as early as the start of the third century some virgins at least took a vow (votum) in relation to celibacy.[17] A half-century later again, Cyprian indicated that this was a common phenomenon in his church. He referred to the church that "abundantly flourishes" in its virgins, and explicitly noted that they had "vowed themselves to God."[18] Cyprian highlighted the eschatological focus of virgins:

> Hold fast, O virgins! Hold fast what you have begun to be; hold fast what you shall be. . . . That which we shall be, you have already begun to be. You possess already in this world the glory of the resurrection. You pass through the world without the contagion of the world; in that you continue chaste and virgins, you are equal to the angels of God.[19]

To Cyprian perpetual virginity was a heroic state, "second in grace" only to that of martyrdom: "The first-fruit of the martyrs is a hundred-fold; the second is yours, sixty-fold. As with the martyrs, there is no thought of the flesh and of the world."[20]

Some virgins and male celibates practiced asceticism as individuals in a normal household; others expressed their lifestyle in household communities of ascetics. In the third century, at least in Rome, there were groups of people in urban homes

---

[14]Athenagoras A Plea for Christians 33 (ANF 2:146). Similarly, Justin Martyr First Apology 15.1-5 (ANF 1:167).

[15]Ignatius To Polycarp 5 (ANF 1:95).

[16]John Chrysostom Letters to the Fallen Theodore 2.3 (NPNF[1] 9:113).

[17]Tertullian On Prayer 22.9 (ANF 3:688); On the Veiling of Virgins 11.4 (ANF 4:34).

[18]Cyprian On the Dress of Virgins 3—4 (ANF 5:431).

[19]Ibid., 22 (p. 436).

[20]Ibid., 21.

living lives of chastity and prayer.[21] Such practices did not cease when more institutionalized monasticism emerged. Jerome, that great advocate of monasticism
and the ascetic life at the end of the fourth century, counseled Eustochium to "find
in the busy city the desert of the monks" through household asceticism.[22] The purpose of such practices was the seeking of God, and this could be sought through
personal asceticism as well as through increasingly socially constructed roles.

For most people, a radically ascetic life needs to be maintained through community with like-minded people. Did one's fellows need to be of the same gender?
Or could they be of the opposite sex? There is a complementarity to the sexes, and
the society of the first centuries was very gender-stereotyped. If the community
was all male, who would wash the clothes? And if an all-female community, who
would chop the firewood? A mixed community might seem best. Those supporting such a community asserted that one need not worry about the risk of sexual
misconduct. After all, the ascetics had renounced the use of the body and were
now living as quasi-angels. So why not live in a mutually beneficial "brother-sister"
relationship? That was the argument of the *subintroductae,* the couples who lived
together in "spiritual marriage."

This phenomenon arose very early. Virgins in the second-century *Shepherd* said
to Hermas, "You will sleep with us as a brother and not as a husband; for you are
our brother, and for the time to come we intend to abide with you, for we love you
dearly."[23] Tertullian appeared similarly to commend the practice, suggesting that a
widower should take a "spiritual wife" or wives, to provide a "consort in domestic
duties" and to assuage loneliness, rather than enter into what in Tertullian's eyes
was a shameful state, namely, a second marriage.[24]

Overall, however, the church waged a centuries-long war against the practice,
both for the sake of reputation and also with realism about the desires and weak-
nesses of human nature. Second-century Irenaeus denounced certain Gnostic
groups in this regard:

> Others of them, again, who pretend at first, to live in all modesty with them as sis-
> ters, have in course of time been revealed in their true colours, when the sister has
> been found with child by her brother.[25]

Numerous church councils and writers of the fourth century, including the

---

[21]P. Rousseau, *Ascetics, Authority, and the Church in the Age of Jerome and Cassian* (Oxford: Oxford University Press, 1978), p. 81.
[22]Ibid., p. 109; Jerome *Letter* 22.25 (NPNF[2] 6:32-33).
[23]Hermas *Similitudes* 9.11 (ANF 2:47).
[24]Tertullian *Exhortation to Chastity* 12; *On Monogamy* 16 (ANF 4:56-57, 71-72).
[25]Irenaeus *Against Heresies* 1.6.3 (ANF 1:324).

Council of Nicea, and Basil, Jerome and John Chrysostom, vigorously opposed "spiritual marriage" because of its perils.[26] The repeated expression of opposition to the practice indicates its persistence and frequency. Basil offered a harsh and simple solution for the woman in such a domestic relationship: "place her in a monastery."[27] Thus by the later fourth century an alternative to household asceticism existed for many women: the female monastery.

The Development of Ascetic Thought in Early Christianity

While lifetime celibacy was not a normal part of Greco-Roman life, Greek thought often fostered a dualistic worldview that could lead to suppressing or punishing the body. Greek dualism evoked disdain for the material world as contaminated with evil; in contrast, spirit was good. Not all Greek thought, however, was so thoroughly dualistic. Some perspectives saw the soul and the body as intertwined. Clement of Alexandria reflected such thinking in describing the body as "the soul's consort and ally."[28] As a consequence, one should live very carefully in the body so as to enhance and not deaden the soul.[29] Christians needed to "regulate the body," to "use food and drink for sustenance, not for pleasure," for "by keeping pleasures under command we prevent lusts."[30] For Clement, care of the body involved a myriad of concerns: hair styles, sneezing, hiccups, digestion, deportment, sexual relations, and so on. All these were ethical and spiritual concerns. The body really did matter. Only through careful and controlled living could one have a Christian life characterized by "composure, tranquillity, calmness and peace."[31] Meat and wine, for example, should be avoided, as they fostered sensuality.[32]

Whether Greek thought was dualistic or not, we frequently find the sense that the body has an influence on the soul—in a downward direction. It was a weight, an impediment to the higher life of the spirit.[33] Plotinus, the third-century founder of Neo-Platonic thought, took this view to such an extreme that his biographer,

---

[26]E. A. Clark, *Ascetic Piety and Women's Faith: Essays in Late Ancient Christianity* (Lewiston: Edwin Mellen, 1986), pp. 265-90; Basil *Letter* 55 (*NPNF*[2] 8:158); Jerome *Letter* 22.14 (*NPNF*[2] 6:27); John Chrysostom *Against Julianus 1*, 1ff.; *Retractions 2*, 62, 1.

[27]Basil *Letter* 55 (*NPNF*[2] 8:158).

[28]Clement of Alexandria *Instructor* 1.13 (*ANF* 2:235).

[29]Clement's views parallel much emphasis among a number of Roman intellectuals in the first two centuries A.D. on the need to take care and cultivate the self. On this Roman thought, see Michel Foucault, *The Care of the Self*, vol. 3 of *The History of Sexuality*, trans. R. Hurley (New York: Pantheon Books, 1986).

[30]Clement of Alexandria *Instructor* 2.1 (*ANF* 2:239).

[31]Ibid., 2.7 (*ANF* 2:253).

[32]Clement of Alexandria *Stromata or Miscellanies* 7.6 (*ANF* 2:532).

[33]For Jerome, for example, this physical life was a "burden" for the life of the spirit: *Letter* 39.1 (*NPNF*[2] 6:49).

Porphyry, claimed that Plotinus was ashamed to have a body at all.[34] Influence from such views helped intensify Christian thinking about asceticism. Thus in Clement of Alexandria's thinking, truly advanced Christians (in his conceptual framework "Gnostics") avoided bodily indulgence, not simply to restrain passion, but rather to separate themselves from it, successfully eliminating it from their lives.[35]

Tertullian, in the late second and early third century, was one of the first Christian writers to explore ascetic issues to a major degree. The prophetic second-century Montanist movement strongly influenced his views. That movement featured rigorism on ascetic issues, particularly in relation to fasting, marriage and flight from persecution. Though Tertullian could express himself positively in relation to marriage,[36] a deep rigorism also made him fear the lure of women and decry the marital relationship as an enemy of spiritual development:

> How different a man feels himself when he chances to be deprived of his wife. He savours spiritually. If he is making prayer to the Lord, he is near heaven. If he is bending over the Scriptures, he is "wholly in them." If he is singing a psalm, he satisfies himself. If he is adjuring a demon, he is confident in himself. Accordingly, the apostle added (the recommendation of) a temporary abstinence for the sake of adding an efficacy to prayers, that we might know that what is profitable "for a time" should be always be practised by us, that it may be always profitable. Daily, every moment, prayer is necessary to men; of course continence (is so) too, since prayer is necessary. Prayer proceeds from the conscience. If the conscience blushes, prayer blushes.[37]

From such a perspective Tertullian argued that marriage was a legitimized form of "fornication" given as a "concession" to "concupiscence."[38] The weak might engage in marriage once, but second marriages should not be entered.[39]

Tertullian sharply distinguished between "soulish" or "psychic" Christians, who were preoccupied with material pleasure, and spiritual Christians, who were totally given to seeking the Lord and his will. In Tertullian's view, fasting was essential to spiritual development. Thus he was highly critical of "psychics" who failed to fast, or failed to fast with the sort of rigor that Tertullian and other Montanists advocated. In his view those who failed to fast were gluttons, obsessed with food. Their desire for food was the doorway to sexual lust.[40] Such greedy nonfasters were idolaters:

---

[34]*Life of Plotinus* 1. See E. R. Dodds, *Pagan and Christian in an Age of Anxiety* (Cambridge: Cambridge University Press, 1965), p. 29.

[35]Clement of Alexandria *Stromata or Miscellanies* 7.12 (ANF 2:543).

[36]Tertullian *To His Wife* 2.8 (ANF 4:48).

[37]Tertullian *Exhortation to Chastity* 10 (ANF 4:56).

[38]Ibid., 9.

[39]Ibid., 8—13; *On Monogamy* 2—3 (ANF 4:54-58, 59-61).

[40]Tertullian *On Fasting* 6 (ANF 4:105).

For to you your belly is god, and your lungs a temple, and your paunch a sacrificial altar, and your cook the priest, and your fragrant smell the Holy Spirit, and your condiments spiritual gifts, and your belching prophecy.[41]

Tetullian's position on asceticism and especially on second marriage was a minority voice in the wider church. Nevertheless, his razor-sharp thought and biting words became powerful weapons for later advocates of the ascetic life.

Origen's perspectives also provided significant support for that cause. Deeply influenced by Neo-Platonism, Origen viewed spirit as the key aspect of personhood. He believed the body needed to be transformed for the life of the spirit to become fully manifest. At present the frame of the body limited the spirit. Marital intercourse dulled the spirit's true capacity for joy.[42] Celibacy then was the higher way for those who could receive it: "God has allowed us to marry because not all are fit for the higher, that is, the perfectly pure life."[43] Perhaps the greatest thinker of the church until Augustine a century and a half later, Origen deeply influenced the ascetic movement, especially his perspective on the crucial role of celibacy in encouraging the human spirit to aspire to God and to purity. Not all, however, could attain to that way. This dichotomy influenced Christians to see their fellows as one of two classes: ordinary Christians or heroic Christians aspiring to perfection through renunciation of sexual relations and possessions.

As a sharp distinction now separated clergy and laity, it was natural to apply the higher standard of perfection (i.e., celibacy and the foregoing of marriage) to the clergy. On the basis of 1 Timothy 3:2, widowers who had remarried were ineligible to become clergy within the first century or two of the founding of the church, and clergy who were widowers were forbidden to remarry.[44] By the fourth century the question was arising as to whether clergy could have even a first marriage. Thus the regional Council of Elvira in southern Spain laid down about 305 that married clergy should abstain from their wives and not father children, or else forfeit their ministry.[45] The regional Council of Neocaesarea in Cappadocia (northern Turkey) expressed a similar view c. 314-315: married priests were to be excluded from the priesthood. Expressing similar concern, the Canons of Ancyra c. 314-319 specified that deacons could marry after their ordination only if they indicated at the time of their ordination that they would later do so. If they did not give that indi-

---

[41]Ibid., 16 (ANF 4:113).

[42]On this see Brown, The Body and Society, p. 173.

[43]Origen Against Celsus 8.55 (ANF 4:660).

[44]Tertullian Exhortation to Chastity 7 (ANF 4:54).

[45]Council of Elvira, Canon 33 (in J. Stevenson, ed., A New Eusebius: Documents Illustrating the History of the Church to A.D. 337, rev. ed. by W. H. C. Frend [London: SPCK, 1987], p. 292).

cation and subsequently married, their ministry was to be terminated.[46]

At this stage no universal ruling prohibited married clergy. In the end, the East never came to that position, except for bishops. The West did finally take that stand, but that process took several more centuries before it became an absolute blanket rule (which even then was commonly ignored at the local level). The discussion shows, however, the church's largely negative view of sex, such that it strongly encouraged those aspiring to a higher spiritual life to adopt lifelong celibacy. And this is what the emerging fourth-century monks did.

The Life of Antony

Antony has commonly been seen as the pioneer of monasticism. I have already indicated, however, that monastic (or ascetic) renunciation already existed prior to Antony. Antony's *Life* provided a new and dramatic way of viewing such practices. As Peter Brown said of Antony, "The constellation of renunciations had come together in a single organizing myth—the myth of the desert."[47] In Brown's words, "The effect of the myth of the desert was to heighten the dramatic impact of renunciations that had long been practised by devout Christians in the settled land."[48]

Antony's life spanned more than a century (c. 251-356). As an orphaned youth, he was moved to give away everything he owned. The trigger for this radical action was hearing two Scriptures read in church: Matthew 19:21 ("If you wish to be perfect, go, sell your possessions, and give the money to the poor") and Matthew 6:34 ("do not worry about tomorrow"). Although popular opinion holds Antony to be the first known monk, the *Life* itself shows this was not the case. A "virgin's house" (*parthenon*) existed, to which Antony could entrust his sister when he started his life of asceticism.[49] Moreover, when Antony began his ascetic life near his village, he placed himself under the guidance of "an old man who had lived the life of a hermit from his youth up" and other ascetic mentors.[50] Thus we should not hold a "big bang" theory of a sudden emergence of monasticism starting with Antony.[51]

Antony's uniqueness lies not so much in his developing solitary monasticism as in his developing that monasticism in the depths of the desert. After his first years of ascetic lifestyle, Antony was driven to seek increasing solitude, moving further

---

[46]Canons of Ancyra 10, quoted in Stevenson, *New Eusebius,* p. 314.

[47]Peter Brown, "Asceticism: Pagan and Christian," in *The Cambridge Ancient History,* vol. 13: *The Late Empire, A.D. 337-425,* ed. A. Cameron and P. Garnsey (Cambridge: Cambridge University Press, 1998), pp. 601-30, quote p. 614.

[48]Ibid., p. 615.

[49]Athanasius *Life of Antony* 3 (NPNF² 4:196).

[50]Ibid.

[51]J. E. Goehring, *Ascetics, Society, and the Desert: Studies in Early Egyptian Monasticism* (Harrisburg, Penn.: Trinity Press, 1999), p. 5.

Figure 6.1. Modern icon of Saint Antony (Courtesy of Holy Transfiguration Monastery)

and further into the desert. Eventually he walled himself inside a disused fort for twenty years. During this time, the narrative indicates that he practiced extremes of asceticism, having virtually no human contact and living on bread and water, frequently battling with demonic forces. In the end, concerned friends broke down the fort door. Antony emerged as a living saint with perfect self-control, completely impassive to emotion or desire:

> Antony, as from a shrine, came forth initiated in the mysteries and filled with the Spirit of God. . . . And again his soul was free from blemish, for it was neither contracted as if by grief, nor relaxed by pleasure, nor possessed by laughter or dejection, for he was not troubled when he beheld the crowd, not overjoyed at being saluted by so many. But he was altogether even as being guided by reason, and abiding in a natural state.[52]

Antony's elevated state drew many to seek him out for help and counsel, so that in the end, "the desert was colonized by monks."[53] Feeling rather claustrophobic at the crowds interrupting his solitude, Antony eventually retreated even further into solitary desert wastes, taking up his abode at the "Inner Mountain" toward the Red Sea. However, his spiritual stature was such that he still served as a kind of guru to seekers and imitators until his death in 356.

Antony himself was clearly a heroic figure. However, what made Antony so sig-

---

[52]Athanasius *Life of Antony* 14 (*NPNF*² 4:200).
[53]Ibid.

nificant in church history was not so much his life, as his *Life*. Despite some uncertainty regarding the authorship of the *Life of Antony*, it was probably written by Athanasius within a year or two of Antony's death. Athanasius, bishop of Alexandria between 328 and 373, was an intensely political figure, not averse to buttressing his power by organizing an "ecclesiastical mafia" to instigate a riot or prevent the orderly administration of his city.[54] Athanasius often came under intense pressure because of his role in spearheading resistance to Arian teaching. His stance led to his being exiled or forced into hiding on five occasions, involving seventeen years of dislodgment from Alexandria. Athanasius's political temperament in that extremely tense and turbulent period encourages one to read the *Life* with caution. As Goehring said, "The image of Antony as the father of Christian monasticism is dependent less on the historical undertaking of Antony than on the literary success of the *Life of Antony*."[55] While much of that *Life* has its roots in history, much is also shaped by the ecclesiastical goals of Athanasius.

Some of the opposition to Athanasius in his struggle for ecclesiastical control of Alexandria and for a unity based on his Catholic Church came from urban ascetics. A good way of diminishing the authority of those urban ascetic opponents was to encourage emulation of a solitary monk, whose location in the desert could not create difficulty in the city.[56] Thus in the *Life* the true ascetics were desert ascetics.[57] Athanasius's ascetic opponents often engaged in a learned teaching ministry not fully under church control. Contrast the true wise man Antony, who, according to Athanasius, had "not learned letters."[58] However, seven letters attributed to Antony reveal a far more educated Antony—one familiar with Platonic philosophy and Origenist thought.[59] Even in the *Life* we see evidence of an Antony who supports and is involved in reading and writing.[60] The complex data indicates that the Antony of the *Life* is very much the construct of Athanasius rather than a reliable biography.

The *Life* portrayed Antony as very loyal to church authorities, observing "the rule of the church most rigidly" and even bequeathing his cloak and sheepskin blanket to Athanasius at his death.[61] This paralleled Elijah's cloak passing to Elisha and legitimated Athanasius's leadership (as a kind of successor to Antony). Ac-

---

[54]T. Barnes, *Constantine and Eusebius* (Cambridge, Mass.: Harvard University Press, 1981), p. 230.

[55]Goehring, *Ascetics, Society*, p. 19.

[56]See the introductory comments in the *Life of Antony* encouraging emulation of his life.

[57]J. E. Goehring, "Withdrawing from the Desert: Pachomius and the Development of Village Monasticism in Upper Egypt," *Harvard Theological Review* 89, no 3 (1996): 267-85, see p. 270.

[58]Athanasius *Life of Antony* 72 (*NPNF*[2] 4:215).

[59]D. Brakke, *Athanasius and the Politics of Asceticism* (Oxford: Clarendon, 1995), p. 214.

[60]On reading: Athanasius *Life of Antony* 25 (*NPNF*[2] 4:203); on writing: ibid., 55, 81, 86 (*NPNF*[2] 4:211, 217, 219).

[61]Athanasius *Life of Antony* 67, 91 (*NPNF*[2] 4:214, 220).

cording to the *Life,* Antony "loathed the heresy of the Arians" and "never held communion with the Meletian schismatics,"[62] a policy exactly coinciding with that of Athanasius. Antony's life greatly inspired later generations, but much of that influence came from the Antony reworked by Athanasius.

The Emergence of Semieremitic Monasticism

While the solitary eremitic life was the ideal, a purely eremitic life was rare. Even the solitary Antony could not altogether get away from others. A semieremitic pattern emerged as the more common practice. This commonly involved living on one's own, but intentionally gathering at times with one's fellows who lived close by for instruction and/or the Eucharist. Such a pattern of monasticism involved no fixed rule of life and a bare minimum of organization. Eventually three forms of monasticism came to be recognized: the eremitic (solitary, anchoritic), the semieremitic (largely solitary, but with some communal interaction), and the coenobitic (involving full community).[63]

The semieremitic pattern included the development of mentors. Their authority was largely personal, based on their recognized quality of spiritual wisdom. The earliest desert fathers commonly honed their spirituality by years of rigor and isolation. Disciples formed around such ascetic masters, to be near them, to receive their words of wisdom and to model themselves on their lives.[64] As a saying of the desert fathers expressed it, "An old man said, 'Be like a camel, bearing your sins and following, bridled, someone who knows the way of God.'"[65] For some, following others came to be of the essence of the ascetic life:

> The old men used to say that if someone has faith in someone else, and makes himself subject to him, he does not need to apply himself to the commandments of God, but only to give up his will to his father, and he will not suffer reproach from God; for God requires nothing more from beginners than the labour which comes through obedience.[66]

Increasingly focus shifted from individual humility (as in Antony) to an emphasis on submission to others. Abba John the Dwarf was outstanding in this regard:

> It was said of Abba John the Dwarf that he withdrew and lived in the desert at Scetis with an old man of Thebes. His abba, taking a piece of dry wood, planted it and said

---

[62]Ibid., 68 (*NPNF*[2] 4:214).
[63]Jerome *Letters* 22.34-36 (*NPNF*[2] 6:37-38); John Cassian, *Conferences* 18.4 (*NPNF*[2] 11:480).
[64]Rousseau, *Ascetics, Authority,* p. 20.
[65]The Greek anonymous series of *Apophthegmata Patrum* 436 (quoted in G. Gould, *The Desert Fathers on Monastic Community* [Oxford: Clarendon, 1993], p. 29).
[66]*Apophthegmata Patrum* 290 (in Gould, *The Desert Fathers,* p. 27).

to him, "Water it every day with a bottle of water, until it bears fruit." Now the water was so far away that he had to leave in the evening and return the following morning. At the end of three years the wood came to life and bore fruit. Then the old man took some of the fruit and carried it to the church, saying to the brethren, "Take and eat the fruit of obedience."[67]

The Abbas (fathers) stressed rumination on Scripture in order to interiorize it and live it out.[68] Devotees looked also, however, for the living word of the master. When Antony sought to turn seekers toward the Scriptures, they still pressed him: "We want to hear from you too, Father."[69] The words of the masters had charismatic power. Even their presence might be felt to bring God's presence:

> Three Fathers used to go and visit blessed Anthony every year and two of them used to discuss their thoughts and the salvation of their souls with him, but the third always remained silent and did not ask him anything. After a long time, Abba Anthony said to him, "You often come here to see me, but you never ask anything," and the other replied, "It is enough for me to see you, Father."[70]

Eventually the charismatic immediacy of the first generation or two faded. Rather than receiving fresh revelation via the living holy man, people began to look back to the past, to sayings and rules of the masters of before. Written texts came to replace oral revelation.[71]

Rigor in Early Monasticism, Especially in the Life of the Solitaries

Antony's own life was extreme. But other eremitic or semieremitic monks sometimes displayed and even exceeded that same extremism. The goal was to break free of the limiting demonic powers and enter into full communion with God. The desires of the body were Satan's doorway to the control of the soul. The body must therefore be subjugated. As one desert father expressed the matter: "I am killing it because it is killing me."[72] These ascetics sought to master the body in various ways:

Fasting. All forms of monasticism commonly limited food intake. Fasting frightened the devil and brought one close to God.[73] Occasionally this could lead

---

[67]In B. Ward, trans., *The Sayings of the Desert Fathers* (Kalamazoo, Mich.: Cistercian Publications, 1975), pp. 85-86.

[68]D. Burton-Christie, "'The Word in the Desert': The Biblical Spirituality of Early Christian Monasticism," *American Baptist Quarterly* 16 (1997): 69-80, see p. 69.

[69]Quoted in Ward, *Sayings of the Desert Fathers,* p. 5.

[70]Ibid., p. 7.

[71]Rousseau, *Ascetics, Authority,* pp. 36, 70.

[72]*Heraclidis Paradeisos* 1, quoted in Dodds, *Pagan and Christian,* p. 30.

[73]Athanasius *Life of Antony* 30 asserts that demons "dread ascetics for their fasting."

to dangerous extremes: Paula's daughter Blaesilla died in Rome as an anorexic because of her excessive fasting. The practice of eating food only once every two days was common.[74] Extremism could be moderated in community monasticism, but solitaries had no brake on their heroics, apart from their own judgment and the advice of a mentor. Cold food was the order of the day for Jerome: "to eat one's food cooked is looked upon as self-indulgence."[75] Limited and basic food was seen as a key in the suppression of bodily desire. Abba Evagrius commented: "Certain of the fathers used to say that a dry and even diet combined with loving-kindness shall speedily bring the monk into the harbour of invulnerability."[76]

Sleep deprivation. Another way for monks to discipline themselves was by sleeping sitting up. Abba Bessarion said, "For fourteen years I have never lain down, but have always slept sitting or standing."[77] Macarius of Alexandria once attempted to go without sleep for twenty nights.[78] Arsenius was reported as saying that an hour of sleep a night was enough for a monk if he was "a good fighter."[79] The same report indicated that Arsenius himself would go most of the night without sleep until compelled to do so by weariness. He would then say to sleep, "Come here, wicked servant," snatch a little sleep in sitting position, and soon reawaken.[80] In Cassian's view, failure to limit sleep would produce not only laziness but also "a sluggish torpor," a dulling of vigor, a doorway for Satan.[81]

Deprivation from people (solitude). This state was prized by Antony: "He who wishes to live in solitude in the desert is delivered from three conflicts: hearing, speech, and sight; there is only one conflict for him and that is fornication."[82] Antony urged the continual seeking of solitude:

> Just as fish die if they stay too long out of water, so the monks who loiter outside their cells or pass their time with men of the world lose the intensity of inner peace. So like a fish going towards the sea, we must hurry to reach our cell, for fear that if we delay outside we will lose our interior watchfulness.[83]

---

[74]A. Rouselle, *Porneia: On Desire and the Body in Antiquity,* trans. F. Pheasant (Oxford: Blackwell, 1988), p. 168.

[75]Jerome *Letters* 22.7 (*NPNF*[2] 6:25). See, similarly, Palladius *Luasiac History* 18.1 regarding Macarius of Alexandria, who ate no cooked food for seven years at a stretch.

[76]In H. Waddell, trans., *The Desert Fathers* (New York: Vintage Books, 1998), p. 68.

[77]Ward, *Sayings of the Desert Fathers,* p. 42.

[78]Palladius *Luasiac History* 18.3.

[79]In Ward, *Sayings of the Desert Fathers,* p. 11.

[80]Ibid.

[81]John Cassian *Institutes* 2.13 (*NPNF*[2] 11:210-11).

[82]In Ward, *Sayings of the Desert Fathers,* p. 3.

[83]Ibid.

When Arsenius prayed to know the way of salvation, "a voice came saying to him, 'Arsenius, flee from men and you will be saved.'"[84] Solitude could, however, be practiced even within monastic groups. As coenobitic monasticism increasingly became the norm, the focus became the "cell of the heart," an interior solitude even in the midst of others, fostered by such things as the Pachomian practice of not talking at mealtime.[85]

Hard work. Egyptian asceticism believed that hard work could aid the development of one's spiritual life.[86] Although some high-born individuals entered Egyptian monasticism, most monks were simple, often illiterate, peasants, used to hard work. The great Arsenius, formerly of senatorial rank prior to his embracing radical asceticism, was questioned:

> "How is it that we, with all our education and our wide knowledge get nowhere, while these Egyptian peasants acquire so many virtues?" Abba Arsenius said to him, "We indeed get nothing from our secular education, but these Egyptian peasants acquire the virtues by hard work."[87]

These monks prized an alternating rhythm of work and prayer. The sayings record Antony receiving a vision at a time when he was feeling depressed, harassed by evil thoughts and abandoned:

> Antony saw a man like himself sitting at his work, getting up from his work to pray, then sitting down to plait a rope, then getting up again to pray. It was an angel of the Lord sent to correct and reassure him. He heard the angel saying to him, "Do this and you will be saved." At these words, Antony was filled with joy and courage. He did this, and he was saved.[88]

The goal of all these various practices was a "transformational asceticism," a cutting of links with one's lower nature and moving to a more spiritual plane of existence.[89] While some of these practices may seem to our society both bizarre and extreme, they were based on ancient understandings of the body. The views of the second-century pagan medical doctor Galen dominated medical understanding into the fourth century. For Galen, as for earlier thinkers, the body was affected by four elements (fire, earth, air and water), four qualities, (warm, cold, dry and moist) and four main bodily humors or fluids (blood, black bile, yellow

---

[84]Ibid., p. 9.
[85]Rousseau, *Ascetics, Authority*, pp. 45-49.
[86]Ibid., p. 26.
[87]Ward, *Sayings of the Desert Fathers*, p. 10.
[88]Ibid., p. 2.
[89]M. Dunn, *The Emergence of Monasticism: From the Desert Fathers to the Middle Ages* (Oxford: Blackwell, 2000), pp. 4, 7.

Jerome's advice to the widow Furia on dietary regulation:

I do not . . . condemn food which God created to be enjoyed with thanksgiving, but I seek to remove from youths and girls what are incentives to sensual pleasure. Neither the fiery Etna nor the country of Vulcan, nor Vesuvius, nor Olympus, burns with such violent heat as the youthful marrow of those who are flushed with wine and filled with food. . . . Physicians and others who have written on the nature of the human body, and particularly Galen in his books entitled *On matters of health,* say that the bodies of boys and of young men and of full grown men and women glow with an interior heat and consequently that for persons of these ages all food is injurious which tends to promote this heat: while on the other hand it is highly conducive to health in eating and in drinking to take things cold and cooling. . . . In the first place then, till you have passed the years of early womanhood, take only water to drink, for this is by nature of all drinks the most cooling. . . . Then as regards your food you must avoid all heating dishes. I do not speak of flesh dishes only . . . but of vegetables as well. Everything provocative or indigestible is to be refused. . . . If I am to say what I think, there is nothing which so much heats the body and inflames the passions as undigested food and breathing broken with hiccoughs. As for you, my daughter, I would rather wound your modesty than endanger my case by understatement. Regard everything as poison which bears within it the seeds of sensual pleasure. A meagre diet which leaves the appetite always unsatisfied is to be preferred to fasts three days long.[a]

---

[a]Jerome *Letter* 54.9, 10 (*NPNF*[2] 6:105-6).

bile and phlegm), and it was important that these be mixed in the right proportions.[90] Diet had a crucial role in getting the balance right. In Galen's judgment, "the character of the soul is corrupted by poor habits in food, drink, exercise,

---

[90]T. M. Shaw, *The Burden of the Flesh: Fasting and Sexuality in Early Christianity* (Minneapolis: Fortress, 1998), p. 53.

sounds and all the arts."[91] This then called for careful living. Extreme monastic practices make more sense when considered in the light of this sort of thinking.

Particularly problematical for fourth-century monks was the matter of sexual desire. The problem was intensified when the body was "warm" and "moist." The best foods were those that were "light" and "dry."[92] Ascetic views commonly asserted that a meager diet, based particularly on uncooked dry vegetables and bread, provided a vital key for avoiding sexual desire. In contrast, meat and wine were especially dangerous. Drawing from a description from John Cassian of a meal of only about 1000 calories and his comment that having food intake of two loaves a day would lead a novice to perfect chastity within six months, Aline Rouselle has argued that Egyptian ascetics reduced their sexual impulses through a harsh diet of undernutrition and a strictly controlled lifestyle.[93] In fact, Jerome claimed that an empty stomach was "indispensable as means to the preservation of chastity."[94] Fasting could potentially recover the paradise that was lost through lust for food.[95] Yet for all his theory and rigor, Jerome, when in the dietary rigor of a solitary, often found himself not in paradise but rather, in his fantasies, "amid bevies of girls."[96]

The Significance of Pachomius

Solitary and semieremitic monasticism could easily be charged with extremism and excessive individualism. Their observances involved dangerous spiritual heights for the inexperienced ascetic mountaineer. One ventured too much on one's own. A framework was needed within which individuals could fit, a pattern they could follow, a community in which they could live. After all, relationship with others is fundamental to Christianity (Mt 22:34-40; 25:31-46).

Though not a total innovator, Pachomius helped configure monasticism as something primarily expressed in community, in structured relationships, under direction. With regard to the three great vows that eventually became a hallmark of monasticism, the influence of the Pachomian approach led to the addition of obedience to poverty and chastity.

Pachomius was born of a pagan family. He was conscripted into the army and taken down the Nile as a semiprisoner, locked up with others at night to prevent escape. While in this state, Christians at Thebes brought him food. This kindness

---

[91]*De Sanitate Tuenda* 1.8 (in Shaw, *Burden of the Flesh,* p. 48).
[92]John Cassian *Institutes* 4.22 (NPNF² 11:226); Jerome *Letter* 22.7 (NPNF² 6:25).
[93]Rouselle, *Porneia: On Desire and the Body,* pp. 175-77.
[94]Jerome *Letter* 22.11 (NPNF² 6:26).
[95]Ibid., 22.10.
[96]Ibid., 22.7 (NPNF² 6:25).

led Pachomius to convert to Christianity. After discharge from the army in about 314, Pachomius soon joined other solitaries in practicing a semieremitic lifestyle, linking himself particularly with one, Palamon, as his mentor. Convinced that Christianity included a sense of obligation to others, Pachomius came to the conclusion that asceticism was best expressed in community. His convictions were strengthened by a vision: "Stay here and make a monastery, for many will come to you to become monks." This led him in 323 to start a community in the deserted village of Tabennesi, located in a fertile area adjacent to the Upper Nile. Because the history of monasticism has commonly been read so strongly through the lens of Antony, many have the impression that Pachomius's monasteries were in the desert away from village life. This was not the case.

It is possible that Tabennesi was only relatively and not totally deserted when Pachomius's community took it over. Certainly the village returned to life, with many villagers living there again. Pachomius's life seemed to have a quality that attracted people to live with him wherever he settled, because he was good to them.[97] In addition, people revered Pachomius as one in direct communion with God. For example, on one occasion he had an inspired awareness that, contrary to the rules, monks were talking while at work in the bakehouse.[98]

Pachomius's monastery eventually became a walled structure, giving control over who entered and left the community. However, the monastery did not exist in isolation from the village community. Pachomius's monks built and attended a church in the village until growth in their own numbers led them to build a church for themselves within the monastery.[99] Interaction with society also occurred while farming, gathering reeds for basket making, trading or navigating the Nile in a monastery-owned boat. The Pachomian communities were socially integrated centers, not shut off from wider society.

Pachomius's success led to his planting five other monasteries. In addition, at least three other existing communities came under the Pachomian umbrella. These three other communities show that something akin to community monasticism already existed prior to Pachomius. Pachomius did not initiate coenobitic (community) monasticism, but rather he developed a common rule for the life of the monks and a system of affiliated coenobitic monasteries.[100] That was his innova-

---

[97]A. Veilleux, "The Origins of Egyptian Monasticism," in *The Continuing Quest for God: Monastic Spirituality in Tradition and Transition,* ed. W. M. Skudlarek (Collegeville, Minn.: Liturgical Press, 1982), pp. 44-50, see p. 49.

[98]SBo 77 (in A. Veilleux, *Pachomian Koinonia,* vol. 1, *The Life of Saint Pachomius and His Disciples* [Kalamazoo, Mich.: Cistercian Publications, 1980], p. 100).

[99]Goehring, "Withdrawing from the Desert," pp. 276-77.

[100]Goehring, *Ascetics, Society,* pp. 26-28.

tion. Perhaps Pachomius's military background explains this imposition of order. However, we should note that the Tabennesi monastery at first lacked a systematic rules structure. Love was felt to be the key to community, and Pachomius set an example in seeking to become the servant of others in all things.[101] After this approach failed, rules were imposed in order to achieve the goal of mutual service. There were set times of prayer, day and night, with the Eucharist being celebrated twice a week. There were two meals a day, though the evening one was optional. Monks consumed their food in enforced silence. Standardized clothing also expressed the uniformity of life: a brown habit, a sleeveless tunic, a mantle of goatskin, a girdle and a stick. The monasteries themselves were made up of houses embracing about twenty people (often those having the same occupation), each in their own cell, each under the superior of the house.

It would be misleading to think of the evolving Pachomian rule as being comprehensive and excessively rigorous. Much depended on the personal charism of Pachomius, with a minimum of regulations.[102] The goal of discipline was not external conformity but restoration and forgiveness. Generally then, warnings came before imposition of punishments. Six warnings were to be given for bad-temperedness, for example, prior to the imposition of any punishment. Expulsion was rare and was usually associated with the need to preserve sexual discipline within the community.[103]

Life for a Pachomian monk consisted of a rhythm of work, study and prayer. The illiterate were required to learn to read. Each had to learn considerable portions of Scripture by heart,[104] to be recited at all times—sitting in one's cell, working in the fields, walking in the monastery, keeping vigils at night—so fulfilling Paul's injunction to pray at all times.[105] The shaping of Scripture was one of the principal elements in the formation of a young monk.[106]

Pachomius was a born community-builder. His disciplined approach to the organization of monastic life, both for the individual monastery and for the interlinking of monasteries, left a significant legacy, for Pachomian monasteries as well

---

[101]Veilleux, "Origins of Egyptian Monasticism," p. 49.

[102]Ibid., p. 50.

[103]P. Rousseau, *Pachomius: The Making of a Community in Fourth-Century Egypt* (Berkeley: University of California Press, 1985), pp. 93-97.

[104]*The Rules of Pachomius—Precepts* Pr. 140 (in A. Veilleux, ed., *Pachomian Koinonia*, vol. 2: *Pachomian Chronicles and Rules* [Kalamazoo, Mich.: Cistercian Publications, 1981], p. 166).

[105]D. J. Chitty, *The Desert a City* (Oxford: Blackwell, 1966), p. 27; A. Veilleux, "Prayer in the Pachomian Koinonia," in *The Continuing Quest for God: Monastic Spirituality in Tradition and Transition*, ed. W. M. Skudlarek (Collegeville, Minn.: Liturgical Press, 1982), pp. 61-66, see pp. 62-63.

[106]V. Desprez, "Pachomian Cenobitism: II," *American Benedictine Review* 43, no. 4 (1992): 358-94, see p. 380.

as for other monasteries influenced by his pioneering example. Though not the originator of communal monasticism, he became a fundamental reference point for that ascetic lifestyle.[107]

The Multiplication of Monasticism in the Fourth Century

I have already indicated that monasticism did not suddenly emerge from nothing in the fourth century. It had its roots in earlier life forms. But the question still arises, Why did it multiply so rapidly in the fourth-century world? The fact that it multiplied so soon after persecution ceased is probably no accident. The threat and reality of martyrdom had shaped Christians to stand over against the world and to give themselves in total self-sacrifice. When persecution ended, the heroism of martyrdom ceased to be an option. The heroism of radical asceticism became an alternative for those wanting to be perfect. In addition, state favor for Christianity after persecution ended led to the church being inundated with converts—many, however, with mixed motives. Soon the church was less marked by purity over against the world, becoming more mixed and contaminated with the world. Monastic withdrawal thus provided a purer environment to continue the dream of perfection and communion with God.

Developments in society also played their part. Roman government was an increasingly costly burden to sustain. The second half of the third century had seen hyper-inflation (1000% between the years 258 and 275), massive increases in taxation and regular forced deliveries for the army.[108] One way to escape this pressure was to retreat beyond administrative control: "*Anachoresis* was in the air in the third century in Egypt—men, sometimes whole communities, withdrawing into deserts or swamps to escape the intolerable burden of taxation and the public liturgies [the oppressive system of collective obligations]."[109] This existing phenomenon of withdrawal thus made monastic withdrawal less of an odd occurrence. Moreover, for many of the Egyptian peasants who made up the bulk of the monastic company, the structure of community and the greater certainty of food may have made the monastic option attractive.[110]

For wealthier people, monasticism's parallel with the "philosophic life" presented another attraction. Epicurean teaching advocated the avoidance of public responsi-

---

[107]V. Desprez, "Pachomian Cenobitism: I," *American Benedictine Review* 43, no. 3 (1992): 233-49, see p. 233.

[108]M. Grant, *History of Rome* (London: Weidenfeld & Nicholson, 1978), pp. 286-88.

[109]Chitty, *The Desert a City*, p. 7. Contrast Marilyn Dunn, who suggests that many of those who fled may simply have gone to a neighboring village (*The Emergence of Monasticism: From the Desert Fathers to the Early Middle Ages* [Oxford: Blackwell, 2000], p. 6).

[110]H. Chadwick, *History and Thought of the Early Church* (London: Variorum Reprints, 1982), 14:22.

bilities in favor of withdrawal, reflection, ease and friendship. A famous statement from the first-century-B.C. Roman writer Lucretius exemplifies such ideas:

> But this is the greatest joy of all: to stand aloof in a quiet citadel, stoutly fortified by the teachings of the wise, and to gaze down from that elevation on others wandering aimlessly in a vain search for the way of life, pitting their wits against another, disputing for precedence, struggling night and day to scale the pinnacles of wealth and power.[111]

The concept of a "philosophic life," where one could live a quiet reflective life meshed easily with such Epicurean concepts. The notion of a philosophic life flowed like a significant tributary into the fourth-century river of monasticism.[112] While educated people were very much a minority in early monasticism, as the monastic phenomenon developed it could easily attract those drawn to a philosophic life. One such person was Basil of Caesarea.

The Significance of Basil of Caesarea for Monasticism

Basil (c. 329-379) was significant for the monastic movement in at least three ways:

- in fostering more moderate forms of monastic discipline;
- in encouraging monastic communities to focus on service in society;
- in facilitating a monasticism that came much more under the umbrella and control of the church.

Basil was born of a Christian family. After a literary education that included university-type studies at Athens, he turned toward an ascetic lifestyle, first visiting monastic settlements in Syria, Palestine and Egypt, before establishing an ascetic community with family and friends on the family estates in Pontus. A few years later he was called to leave his seclusion, becoming a presbyter in 362 and then bishop of Caesarea in 370.

Along with other great preachers of that era, Basil felt a deep concern for the abject plight of the poor. Famine in the region in 369 led him to preach powerful sermons challenging the rich to distribute their largesse. He himself became involved in poverty relief. Basil encouraged the setting up of monastic communities, most notably the "new city"—so called by his friend Gregory of Nazianzus,[113] but

---

[111]Lucretius *On the Nature of the Universe* 90 (quoted in J. N. Jordan, *Western Philosophy from Antiquity to the Middle Ages* [New York: Macmillan, 1987], pp. 193-94).

[112]R. A. Markus, *The End of Ancient Christianity* (Cambridge: Cambridge University Press, 1990), pp. 72-74.

[113]Gregory of Nazianzus *Orations* 43.63 (*NPNF*² 7:416).

Figure 6.2. Modern icon of St. Basil (Courtesy of Holy Transfiguration Monastery)

later named the *Basileias* in his honor—on the outskirts of Caesarea. The "new city" was both a place of relief for the poor and a hospital, especially in the care of lepers. It stored and distributed surpluses, giving out basins of soup and meat to relieve the deprivations of famine. Beyond that grand development, however, Basil also sought to sprinkle the Christian landscape of Cappadocia and Pontus with carefully organized ascetic "brotherhoods."[114] Some of the "brotherhoods" were little cottages on the edges of villages, while others were larger converted country houses. However, each was to be an ideal Christian household, giving its surpluses for the aid of the poor. Thus Basil's dream was for communities interacting with society and ministering to its needs. At the heart of ascetic Christianity should be love both for God and for one's neighbor.[115] Basil saw human beings as social and not solitary; thus perfection must be sought in the common life.[116] According to his great friend, Gregory of Nazianzus, Basil sought to integrate the eremitic and the coenobitic lifestyles "in order that the contemplative spirit might not be cut off from society, nor the active life be uninfluenced by the contemplative."[117]

Basil's thinking on his "brotherhoods" evolved gradually. At the center of his as-

---

[114]Brown, *The Body and Society,* p. 289.

[115]P. Rousseau, *Basil of Caesarea* (Berkeley: University of California Press, 1994), p. 205.

[116]W. H. C. Frend, *The Rise of Christianity* (Philadelphia: Fortress, 1984), p. 631.

[117]Gregory of Nazianzus *Oration* 43.62 (NPNF[2] 7:416).

cetic vision, however, lay a clearly recognizable group of ascetics, distinct in identity from clergy and laity, living with at least a minimum of structure, though with much variation. The communities were gradually shaped by Basil's emerging "rules," which, however, achieved fixity only well after his death.[118] The rules were not systematic, but rather consisted of short answers to specific questions. Rousseau has rightly noted that in genre they are closer to the *Sayings of the Fathers* than, say, the *Rule* of Benedict.[119]

A feature of the "brotherhoods" involved the personal supervision of Basil himself. Because Basil was both ascetically oriented and also bishop of the region, he fostered a far greater integration of church and monastery than was normal at that time. The leadership of people like Basil increasingly drew the monastic life into the orbit and supervision of institutional church life. Earlier, the ascetic movement developed markedly outside of the control of the church. While not defiant of the church, earlier ascetics had been suspicious of the movement being captured and neutralized by the church. John Cassian, for example, preserved a much earlier saying of the Fathers: "A monk ought by all means to fly from women and bishops."[120] Arsenius refused even to speak with Archbishop Theophilus when the latter called on him.[121] Pachomius discouraged his monks from accepting ordination.[122] There is some debate as to whether Pachomius himself underwent ordination, though one account notes that when Athanasius sought out Pachomius for ordination, he "hid from the pope among the brothers until he had passed by."[123] A generation later the story is narrated of an attempt in the 380s to consecrate Ammonius, one of the "Tall Brothers," as bishop:

> But when they came to arrest him for consecration, he cut off his left ear and told them no mutilated man could be bishop. When they said that was a bit of Judaism, and should not stand in the way, he threatened to cut out his tongue.[124]

Not only were monks suspicious of the church; in some contexts the church was suspicious of the monks. This was particularly the case where they lived in urban areas without external discipline. Church authorities repeatedly deprecated urban monasticism as unruly and undesirable.[125] This does not mean urban mo-

[118]Rousseau, *Basil*, pp. 76, 192-96.
[119]Ibid., p. 354.
[120]John Cassian *Institutes* 11.18 (*NPNF*[2] 11:279).
[121]Ward, *Sayings of the Desert Fathers*, p. 10.
[122]Rousseau, *Ascetics, Authority*, p. 57.
[123]Rousseau, *Pachomius*, p. 162.
[124]Palladius *Lausiac History* 11 (trans. in Chitty, *The Desert a City*, p. 53).
[125]Jerome *Letters* 22.28 (*NPNF*[2] 6:34); in relation to John Chrysostom's attitude, see also Sozomen *Ecclesiastical History* 8.9 (*NPNF*[2] 2:405).

nasticism was uncommon. A report on the Theban city of Oxyrhynchus in A.D. 394-395 indicated that monks within its walls numbered 5,000 and were "almost the majority over the secular inhabitants."[126] If monks were to interrelate with the city, it made a strong argument for their being under ecclesiastical control. Basil's close relationships with his monks provided a model for the future. Eventually informal ecclesiastical influence became ecclesiastical rule at the Council of Chalcedon (A.D. 451):

> Domestic oratories and monasteries are not to be erected contrary to the judgment of the bishop. Every monk must be subject to his bishop and must not leave his house except at his suggestion.[127]

The Significance of Augustine of Hippo for Monasticism

After his famous conversion in 387, Augustine was drawn to a life of ascetic reflection. Enticed into clerical life, first as priest at Hippo, and then as its bishop, Augustine fostered community that reflected the ideal Christian life of Acts 2. He envisioned a community that had all things in common and had "one soul and heart in the Lord."[128] Thus community life had value in its own right. Augustine founded a monastery on the church grounds once he became a priest, living there in regulated community. After he became bishop of Hippo, Augustine made communal ascetic life a requirement for all his clergy. Augustine thus viewed community as closely linked to the mainstream of church life. Unlike John Cassian, who stressed obedience for its own sake as necessary for perfection, Augustine stressed obedience only for the sake of preservation of the community. Augustine's scheme replaced the formative relationship of monk to abbot by the relationship of monk to community. Now the community took center stage.[129] The stress on ascetic practice shifted more toward the values of renewed relationships through communal living.[130] Augustine's community structure was loose and adaptable, which made it a very suitable model for "secular" clergy (those living in the *saeculum*, in the world, and therefore not living under a strict rule). Consequently, in the eleventh century when secular clergy were encouraged to become part of a monastic lifestyle, they looked to Augustine for inspiration and became known either as "Regular" canons (those living under a *regula*, a rule) or as "Augustinian" canons.

---

[126]In Goehring, *Ascetics, Society,* p. 21.
[127]Council of Chalcedon, Canon 4 (*NPNF*[2] 14:270).
[128]Augustine *Of the Work of Monks* 17 (*NPNF*[1] 3:513).
[129]R. Maas and G. O'Donnell, *Spiritual Traditions for the Contemporary Church* (Nashville: Abingdon, 1990), p. 62.
[130]Markus, *End of Ancient Christianity,* pp. 78-80.

Figure 6.3. Fresco of St. Augustine of Hippo, in Chiesa di Ognissanti, Florence, Italy (Scala/Art Resource, NY)

The Significance of John Cassian for Monasticism

Born in what is now Romania, John Cassian (c. 360-c. 435) participated in Eastern monasticism in Palestine, Egypt and Constantinople for a number of years before establishing a monastic community at Marseilles. Cassian's writings significantly influenced Western monasticism. A century later, Benedict of Nursia, for example, directed that Cassian's *Conferences/Collationes* be read by his monks before compline (the last of the seven daily prayers, i.e., at bedtime). While Cassian's earlier views favored solitary monasticism over communal, he came to see that most people needed the protection, encouragement and discipline that community life offered.[131] Cassian stressed the growth of holiness (especially humility) rather than a focus on miracles.[132] Cassian was highly critical of an undisciplined life that ig-

---

[131]See, for example, *Conferences* 19.9 (*NPNF*[2] 11:493) where he seems to value community as a place of meritorious trials. See also T. Kardong, "John Cassian's Evaluation of Monastic Practices," *American Benedictine Review* 43, no. 1 (1992): 82-105, see p. 95.

[132]John Cassian *Conferences* 15 (*NPNF*[2] 11:445-49).

nored traditional monastic rules.[133] Regular manual labor by all members of the community was one of the keys to the success of monastic life.[134] Overall, Cassian seemed clearly to be advocating an Eastern regulated model of the monastic life, in contrast to the more free-form indigenous model then common in Gaul. Thus he seems to have been reacting against the native monastic tradition of Gaul, especially that associated with Martin of Tours.[135]

Cassian saw close links between his monastery on the one hand, and church and society on the other. He founded his monastery under the patronage of the bishop of Marseilles. It was to be a model for society, "that we should gain the greatest good from the conversion of many, who were to be turned to the way of salvation by our example and instructions."[136] Monastic contemplation would thus lead into a teaching ministry for outsiders.[137] The strength of monasteries such as those of John Cassian in fifth-century Gaul led to many of Gaul's great church leaders increasingly being drawn from the ranks of the monks. Ascetic ideology thus increasingly moved from the fringes of society to its center.[138] The image of the ascetic holy man began to merge with the image of the holy bishop, with personal sanctity being harnessed to the life of the church.[139]

Some monks viewed fornication as *the* sin, that which loomed larger than all the others. Cassian held a different view. Fornication was simply one of the "eight principal faults which attack mankind" (the eight deadly sins),[140] and was not the first one. Cassian listed these in order as gluttony, fornication, avarice, anger, dejection, low spirits, vainglory and pride. In Cassian's judgment, the eight faults were linked: succumbing to the first exposing one to the allure of the second, and so forth.[141] Thus sexual desire was not the fundamental problem but rather a footprint betraying the presence of heavier beasts within the soul: anger, greed, avarice and vainglory.[142] At heart the root problem was self-centered egotism.[143] One needed not only to break the grip of the lure of the world and of egotism, but also to have a pure heart filled with love.[144] The passions needed to be disciplined and subdued to the point where they no longer constituted an impediment to union

---

[133]John Cassian *Institutes* 2.3; 4.16 (*NPNF*[2] 11:205-6, 223-24).
[134]Ibid., 10.22-23 (*NPNF*[2] 11:274).
[135]C. Stewart, *Cassian the Monk* (New York: Oxford University Press, 1998), p. 17.
[136]John Cassian *Conferences* 24.1 (*NPNF*[2] 11:532).
[137]Markus, *End of Ancient Christianity*, p. 194.
[138]Ibid., p. 214.
[139]Ibid., p. 201.
[140]John Cassian *Conferences* 5.2 (*NPNF*[2] 11:339).
[141]Ibid., 5.10 (*NPNF*[2] 11:343).
[142]Ibid., 1.22; 5.10 (*NPNF*[2] 11:306, 343); Brown, *The Body and Society*, p. 422.
[143]P. Munz, "John Cassian," *Journal of Ecclesiastical History* 11 (1960): 1-22, see pp. 4-6.
[144]Ibid., p. 7; *Conferences* 5.25; 11.8 (*NPNF*[2] 11:350, 418).

with God.[145] Wealth presented a significant peril. By Cassian's time, many monasteries were well established, with some on the way to becoming rich and powerful.[146] Cassian thus put heavy stress on the need of his monasteries to give money away.

The Significance of Simeon Stylites for Monasticism

Living up a sixty foot pole on a six-foot-square platform seems bizarre. Yet that is what Simeon (c. 390-459) did in Syria for 36 years. He began with a platform only six feet off the ground. Then he went to a higher one, finally ascending the sixty-foot version. What was he doing? We have two main versions of his life, one written by Theodoret during his lifetime, and the other written by Simeon's disciples about eleven years after his death. Both are hagiographic, full of praise for this wonderful saint. On the question of motive(s), the accounts disagree. Theodoret presents Simeon as ascending the pole because he found the crowds too exhausting. In that case we should view his approach as another experiment in withdrawal and solitude. In the account of his Syrian disciples, however, Simeon is a man of visions, particularly influenced by the models of Moses and Elijah, the latter giving him the culminating directive to climb the pillar. In that case Simeon's call was not to disengage from the world, but rather to be a prophetic leader of his people—preaching, mediating and advising.

In deciding between these views, we should also note that Simeon and his imitators clearly did not altogether cut themselves off from their communities. Peter Brown has written a crucial study of the function of the holy man in the fifth and sixth centuries in late Roman society.[147] Brown notes the crucial role of the good patron in Syrian village life, a "hinge-man" who, belonging to the outside world and therefore not caught up in the struggles of local factions, could place his knowledge and power at the disposal of the villagers as arbitrator in settling of disputes and so forth. Brown observes that with the breaking up of the great estates, the presence of such patrons declined, leading to a crisis of leadership. The holy man, including the stylite, came to fill this void, making a crucial contribution to the smooth running of village relationships. While up a pole, the stylite drew vil-

---

[145]Kardong, "John Cassian's Evaluation," p. 94.

[146]The problems of monastic communities becoming wealthy occurred very early in their development. A much earlier expression of concern comes from Theodore, a mid fourth-century successor of Pachomius: *The Bohairic Life of Pachomius*, SBo 197-98; *The First Greek Life of Pachomius*, G[1]146 (in Veilleux, *Pachomian Koinonia*, 1:243-46, 403).

[147]P. Brown, "The Rise and Function of the Holy Man in Late Antiquity," *Journal of Roman Studies* 61 (1971): 80-101; repr. in P. Brown, *Society and the Holy in Late Antiquity* (London: Faber, 1982), pp. 103-51.

Figure 6.4. Simeon Stylites on his pillar (Werner Foreman/Art Resource, NY)

lagers to him, exercising a strong preaching ministry to the crowds below. In addition, he exercised a mediating role, sorting out disputes between villagers. Simeon seems to have had that sort of role.

In understanding Simeon's motives and role, we should also note the perspective of David Frankfurter.[148] He points out that in the second century A.D., Lucian noted the existence of a cult of the goddess Atargatis at Hieropolis only one hundred kilometers from the location of Simeon's pillar. Twice a year a devotee of Atargatis would ascend a pillar for a seven-day period to commune with the gods. While there is no direct evidence for the persistence of this practice into Simeon's time, Franfurter felt that the parallel practice in an adjacent location could not be accidental. He suggests that rather than being bizarre behavior, Simeon's act was a very natural development in Late Antique Syria, fitting within traditional modes of religious expression. Consequently Simeon's stylite lifestyle wittingly or unwittingly tapped into traditional roots. It was a successful act of

---

[148]D. T. M. Frankfurter, "Stylites and *Phallobates:* Pillar Religions in Late Antique Syria," *Vigiliae Christianae* 44 (1990): 168-98.

evangelism, as Simeon's local popularity and magnetism testify.[149]

The ideas of both Frankfurter and Brown tend to support the version of Simeon's disciples. He took up residence atop a pillar for mission, for engagement with the world. As Frankfurter argues:

> Are we to believe Theodoret's suggestion that Symeon climbed a pillar to get away from people? And if so, how could Symeon have expected solitude when he placed the pillar on a mountain top in full view of the major Syrian trade routes and of a substantial village below? What could a six-foot column (its first approximate height) have done but focus attention on him?[150]

Indeed, there was method in the stylite "madness." Rather than retreat from society, it arose as a dramatically structured engagement with it. The phenomenon did not take root in the West, being limited to the Eastern Roman Empire (the Near East and Greece). Practitioners of the unusual lifestyle persisted until the nineteenth century.[151]

Conclusion

Monasticism certainly included the heroic and the bizarre. It also, however, included the ordinary. While the spectacular attracts attention, we should take note of ordinary men and women who lived their lives in a routine of prayer, work and study. We have seen the very charismatic nature of much early monasticism, how it involved people who seemed to be stamped with a strong sense of direct communion with God. Nevertheless, the heady first wine soon mellowed. Monasticism became increasingly subject to rule, structure and obedience to superiors. This was not altogether a disaster. In the process, monasticism became of greater service to both church and society. Historian Ramsay MacMullen was not convinced that the Christianization of the Roman Empire made much difference to the quality of society in that empire.[152] However, he qualified that conclusion, noting the ultimately enormous influence of monasticism on manners and morals.[153] When the empire in the West plunged into disorder, destruction and darkness from the mid fifth century, it was the monks who eventually became forces for stabilization and the transmission of education and knowledge. The later church

---

[149]Ibid., pp. 189-91.

[150]Ibid., p. 189.

[151]S. A. Harvey, "The Sense of a Stylite: Perspectives on Simeon the Elder," *Vigiliae Christianae* 42 (1988): 376-94, see p. 377.

[152]R. MacMullen, "What Difference Did Christianity Make?" *Historia* 35 (1986): 322-43. MacMullen examined the areas of sexual norms, slavery, gladiatorial shows, judicial penalties and corruption in coming to his conclusion.

[153]Ibid., p. 343.

owes a huge debt to those daring pioneers of new forms of spirituality.

For Further Reading

Brakke, D. *Athanasius and the Politics of Asceticism.* Oxford: Clarendon Press, 1995.

Brock, S. P. "Early Christian Asceticism," *Numen* 20, no. 1 (1973): 1-19.

Brown, P. *The Body and Society.* New York: Columbia University Press, 1988.

Burton-Christie, D. "'The Word in the Desert': The Biblical Spirituality of Early Christian Monasticism." *American Baptist Quarterly* 16 (1997): 69-80.

Chitty, D. J. *The Desert a City.* Oxford: Blackwell, 1966.

Corrington, G. P. "The Defense of the Body and the Discourse of Appetite: Continence and Control in the Greco-Roman World." *Semeia* 57 (1992): 65-74.

Desprez, V. "Christian Asceticism between the New Testament and the Beginning of Monasticism II: Africa in the Third Century (A.D. 180-310)." *American Benedictine Review* 42, no. 3 (1991): 334-44.

———. "The Origins of Western Monasticism II: Africa and Spain." *American Benedictine Review* 41, no. 2 (1990): 167-91.

———. "Pachomian Cenobitism I." *American Benedictine Review* 43, no. 3 (1992): 233-49.

Dunn, M. *The Emergence of Monasticism: From the Desert Fathers to the Middle Ages.* Oxford: Blackwell, 2000 (esp. pp. 1-81).

Goehring, J. E. *Ascetics, Society, and the Desert: Studies in Early Egyptian Monasticism.* Harrisburg, Penn.: Trinity Press, 1999.

———. "Withdrawing from the Desert: Pachomius and the Development of Village Monasticism in Upper Egypt." *Harvard Theological Review* 89, no. 3 (1996): 267-85.

Meyer R. T., trans. *St. Athanasius: The Life of St. Anthony.* New York: Newman Press, 1978.

Rousseau, P. *Ascetics, Authority, and the Church in the Age of Jerome and Cassian.* Oxford: Oxford University Press, 1978.

———. *Pachomius: The Making of a Community in Fourth-Century Egypt.* Berkeley: University of California Press, 1985.

Shaw, T. M. *The Burden of the Flesh: Fasting and Sexuality in Early Christianity.* Minneapolis: Fortress, 1998.

Skudlarek, W. M., ed. *The Continuing Quest for God: Monastic Spirituality in Tradition and Transition.* Collegeville, Minn.: Liturgical Press, 1982.

Waddell, H., trans. *The Desert Fathers.* New York: Vintage Books, 1998.

Ward, B., trans. *The Sayings of the Desert Fathers.* Kalamazoo, Mich.: Cistercian Publications, 1975.

7

WOMEN IN THE EARLY CHURCH
Liberated or Confined?

The impact of feminism in the last half century has led Christians eagerly to quarry early Christian writings to unearth the status and ministry of women in the early church. The men, however, held most of the levers of recognized power and public discourse two millennia ago. Men were the historians and bishops. It is therefore not surprising to find a male-focused bias in so much of the historical data. Women were seen and heard much less than men in the historical records. As a consequence, it is much more difficult to recover the story of women from that early past because of a relative lack of material compared with the data for men. And sometimes (for men too) we simply do not know the answers to our questions: we do not have the data. Thus studies relating to women in the early church often face greater difficulty because of paucity of material and because it is often skewed by its male-dominated context.

Today's intense focus on women's issues and women's rights can easily run the danger of reading history through a twenty-first-century Western lens, from the context of modern feminism. Doing so means failing to understand the data within its own context, which is a fundamental prerequisite for good history.

A further danger is the temptation to quarry for the material that one hopes to find, ignoring other data. The great diversity within the development of the early church and the frequent ambiguity of the data means that one can nearly always succeed in finding what one sets out to find. But has one found the main riverbed, or simply a minor tributary?

Yet another, contrasting danger is to take all the texts at face value in what they assert about women. Men wrote the texts, which may therefore project what men wanted to happen rather than what always did happen. This is not to dismiss the texts. They may still indicate what happened most of the time. In addition, the texts shaped later thinking, so that they influenced the actual world to line up more with their ideal world. Despite the texts being male-dominated, they do, in part at least, indicate reality. We must carefully seek to determine the degree to which any given text indicates the whole reality.

In wrestling with the historical evidence, it is important that we recognize our likely modern biases and seek to divest ourselves as much as possible from them. First let the data speak, and only then let us draw our conclusions. To begin with, however, we need to consider the role of women in the Mediterranean world of the early centuries, for much of the role of women in the emerging church will either reflect that cultural perspective or be a conscious challenge to it.

Women in Classical Antiquity

One cannot easily make statements on this topic that apply across the board. Social and religious experience ran across a huge range, from noble-women to slave-women, from Roman women to Jewish women. We should proceed with this caution in mind.

Women in Greco-Roman society. Marked diversity appears within this category. One legacy of classical Greece largely kept Eastern women veiled and in the home, without formal education.[1] The tendency for women to remain in the home had become much more relaxed, however, by the time of the early church. Many women remained veiled, but many others, especially from the upper class, were starting to go about unveiled.[2] In some ways, rural and lower class women were freer in their movements than urban and upper class women, for example, in drawing water and trading in the marketplace.[3] On the other hand, high-status women, Greek and Roman alike, might sometimes transcend gender in determination of social role. So occasionally, women owned brick factories, became philosophers and acted as barristers.[4] A few achieved public prominence, but they seldom filled roles that would require their speaking in public.[5]

The Roman world restricted women's movements within the wider society less than did Hellenistic society, and wealthier women had access to education up to age twelve or so.[6] At the same time, women might sometimes hold public office in

---

[1]S. B. Pomeroy, *Goddesses, Whores, Wives, and Slaves: Women in Classical Antiquity* (New York: Schocken, 1975), pp. 188-89; B. Witherington, *Women in the Earliest Churches* (Cambridge: Cambridge University Press, 1988), pp. 5, 16.

[2]R. MacMullen, "Woman in Public in the Roman Empire," *Historia* 29, no. 2 (1980): 208-18, see pp. 217-18.

[3]J. M. Arlandson, *Women, Class, and Society in Early Christianity: Models from Luke-Acts* (Peabody, Mass.: Hendrickson, 1997), p. 7; C. C. Kroeger, "Women," in *Dictionary of New Testament Background*, ed. C. A. Evans and S. E. Porter (Downers Grove, Ill.: InterVarsity Press, 2000), pp. 1276-80, see p. 1276.

[4]C. Osiek and D. L. Balch, *Families in the New Testament World: Households and House Churches* (Louisville, Ky.: Westminster John Knox, 1997), p. 58.

[5]MacMullen, "Woman in Public," p. 213.

[6]Witherington, *Women in the Earliest Churches*, pp. 16-18.

the East, Cleopatra being an obvious example. This was not so in the Roman West, where they could not vote or hold public office; at most they could act as the power behind the throne.[7]

Though variations existed, the overall structure of society was patriarchal. Men dominated. Apart from exceptions such as the Vestal virgins and the Sibylline prophetesses, women basically had no leadership roles in Greco-Roman religion.[8] A sharp distinction between the public and the private spheres of life enforced the separate roles: the man's sphere was the public place, the woman's the private place. Women were created for domesticity.

With regard to marriage, until recently historians agreed that women in the Mediterranean world normally entered marriage somewhere around ages twelve to fifteen.[9] More recently B. D. Shaw has persuasively argued that this conclusion comes from faulty interpretation of the data and that women in both halves of the empire typically married in their late teens.[10] Shaw's perspective still indicates, however, that women married at a young age, a factor that would encourage submission to their older husbands. Moreover, even if a majority of women married in their late teens, quite a number married earlier. In the Christian community, Melania the Elder was married at fourteen, Melania the Younger at twelve, and Macrina was engaged at age eleven.[11]

Roman culture (though not Greek culture) viewed women as under the tutelage of men. The father held unlimited power over his household, even that of life and death.[12] At marriage the daughter usually passed from the hand (manus) of her father to that of her husband. This practice reinforced a sense of women's inferior nature. Devaluing of women can also be seen in the common practice of infanticide, which typically meant the exposure of female infants. This was justified on the basis of an alleged law stemming from Romulus, requiring a father to raise all male children, but only the first-born daughter.[13] This resulted in a great gender imbalance, with perhaps one-third more men than women.[14] A study of 600 fam-

---

[7]Ibid., pp. 18, 23; Pomeroy, Goddesses, Whores, p. 189.

[8]H. C. Kee, "The Changing Role of Women in the Early Church World," Theology Today 49 (1992): 225-38, see p. 226.

[9]Pomeroy, Goddesses, Whores, p. 164.

[10]B. D. Shaw, "The Age of Roman Girls at Marriage: Some Reconsiderations," Journal of Roman Studies 77 (1987): 30-46; Osiek and Balch, Families in the New Testament World, p. 62.

[11]G. Cloke, "This Female Man of God": Women and Spiritual Power in the Patristic Age, A.D. 350-450 (London: Routledge, 1995), p. 51.

[12]Pomeroy, Goddesses, Whores, p. 150.

[13]Ibid., p. 164.

[14]Stark quoted J. C. Russell's figures estimating the ratio in Rome between male and female as 131 to 100, and the ratio in Italy, Asia Minor and North Africa as 140 to 100 (R. Stark, "Reconstructing the Rise of Christianity: The Role of Women," Sociology of Religion 56, no. 3 [1995]: 222-44, see p. 231).

ilies based on inscriptions at Delphi has shown that only six of these families had raised more than one daughter.[15]

The hierarchical nature of Roman society and the low status it gave to women is likely evident in Trajan's food distribution programs for children in Italy in the early second century. According to inscriptions of Veleia (Elea), a town in southern Italy, the monthly allowance was sixteen sesterces for boys, twelve for girls, twelve for illegitimate boys and ten for illegitimate girls. Of the 300 recipients only 36 were girls.[16] This sort of data points to a perception of women as inferior, of less value, subject to a dominant man, and with no public role in life. Exceptions occasionally occurred—through wealth, through connections, through outstanding strength of personality—but they were exceptions. It was fundamentally a man's world.

Women in Judaism. Though details differed, the lot of Jewish women overall was not unlike that of their Gentile neighbors. They had no public role.[17] As the first-century Jewish writer Philo explained:

> Market places, and council chambers, and courts of justice, and large companies and assemblies of numerous crowds, and a life in the open air of actions relating to war and peace, are suited to men; but taking care of the house and remaining at home are the proper duties of women; the virgins having their apartments in the centre of the house within the innermost doors, and the full-grown women not going beyond the vestibule and outer courts; for there are two kinds of states, the greater and the smaller. And the larger ones are really called cities; but the smaller ones are called houses. And the superintendence and management of these is allotted to the two sexes separately; the men having the government of the greater, which government is called a polity; and the women that of the smaller, which is called oeconomy [household management].[18]

Along with the rest of the Mediterranean world, Jewish girls married in their teenage years.[19] Marriage may have had greater honor among Jews, but divorce was not uncommon. In addition, in contrast to Roman law, Jewish law vested the right of divorce in men only.[20]

---

[15]R. Stark, *The Rise of Christianity* (San Francisco: HarperCollins, 1997), p. 97.

[16]Pomeroy, *Goddesses, Whores,* p. 203.

[17]J. Jeremias, *Jerusalem in the Time of Jesus* (London: SCM Press, 1969), pp. 359-63.

[18]Philo *On the Special Laws* 3.169-70 (in *The Works of Philo,* trans. D. Yonge [Peabody, Mass.: Hendrickson, 1993], p. 611).

[19]Jeremias indicated twelve as the normal age of betrothal for a Jewish girl, with marriage taking place a year later (*Jerusalem in the Time,* pp. 365, 368). However, Tai Ilan queried whether marriage normally occurred as young as twelve, but accepted that it was commonly at a relatively early age for both sexes (Tai Ilan, *Women in Greco-Roman Palestine: An Inquiry into Image and Status* [Peabody, Mass.: Hendrickson, 1995], pp. 65-69).

[20]Jeremias, *Jerusalem in the Time,* pp. 370-71.

Women had no significant role in public worship.[21] While women were subject to the negative commands of the law (the "thou shalt nots" in the Torah), they were not subject to its positive commands (keeping the festivals, reciting the *Shema*, prayers at meals, etc.).[22] Most pronouncements on the matter asserted that women were not to be taught the Torah (though other statements indicated that it did happen—rhetoric and reality often differed in relation to women).[23] About A.D. 90, Rabbi Eliezer asserted, "If a man gives his daughter a knowledge of the law, it is as though he taught her obscenity."[24] In praising God for the opportunity to learn the law, a male pray-er in Rabbinic Judaism expressed the sorry plight of women: "Praised be God that he has not made me a gentile; praised be God that he has not made me a woman; praised be God that he has not created me an ignorant man."[25]

Regulations concerning access to the great temple at Jerusalem limited women to the Gentiles' court and the women's court.[26] Their insignificance in worship is indicated in the fact that they could not be counted as part of the quorum of ten necessary to form a worshipping synagogue congregation.[27]

Pervasive negativity toward women can also be seen in the way Jewish sources regularly viewed the birth of a daughter as a disappointment.[28] Several Talmudic sayings mark this perspective: "It is well for those whose children are male, but ill for those whose children are female"; "at the birth of a boy all are joyful, but at the birth of a girl all are sad"; "when a boy comes into the world, peace comes into the world; when a girl comes, nothing comes."[29] The diminished value of women stands out starkly in the fact that they were commonly not acceptable witnesses in court proceedings.[30] Josephus urged, "Let not the testimony of women be admitted because of the levity and boldness of their sex."[31] Jewish women shared the low status of women generally in the pervasively patriarchal Mediterranean world. Within such a world Christianity began.

---

[21]R. Gryson, *The Ministry of Women in the Early Church*, trans. J. LaPorte and M. L. Hall (Collegeville, Minn.: Liturgical Press, 1976), p. 1.

[22]*m. Qiddushin* 1:7; *m. Berekhot* 3:3 (in Jeremias, *Jerusalem in the Time*, pp. 372-73).

[23]Ilan, *Women in Greco-Roman Palestine*, pp. 34, 190-91.

[24]*m. Sotah* 3:4 (in Jeremias, *Jerusalem in the Time*, p. 373).

[25]*t. Berakhot* 7.8 (in L. Swidler, *Biblical Affirmations of Women* [Philadelphia: Westminster Press, 1979], pp. 154-55).

[26]Josephus *Antiquities* 15.418-19; *Wars of the Jews* 5.199.

[27]*m. Avot* 3:6 (in Swidler, *Biblical Affirmations*, p. 156).

[28]Ilan, *Women in Greco-Roman Palestine*, p. 46.

[29]*t. b. Qiddushin* 82b; *t. b. Niddah* 31b. In Swidler, *Biblical Affirmations*, p. 157.

[30]See, however, exceptions in Ilan, *Women in Greco-Roman Palestine*, pp. 163-65, showing that this was not an absolute rule.

[31]Josephus *Antiquities* 4.219; see also *m. Shabbat* 4:1.

Women in the New Testament

The Gospels. Against the backdrop of Mediterranean culture, we find Jesus re-
markably free of gender stereotypes. He seemed to relate to women with little concern for gender constraints. This stands out in the way Jesus ennobled women, often in situations where they stood in contrast to male religious leadership.
Examples of women to whom he gave dignity and honor include the poor widow
who gave her all in the temple (Mk 12:41-4), the sinful woman who gate-crashed
the dinner party (Lk 7:36-50) and the faith-filled woman who touched him as he
was on his way to heal unbelieving Jairus's daughter (Lk 8:40-56). In allowing the
hemorrhaging woman to touch him, Jesus broke gender taboos. Contrary to his
usual sensitivity, he embarrassed this publicity-shy, "unclean" woman by causing
her to identify herself. Swidler comments:

> It seems clear that Jesus wanted to call attention to the fact that he did not shrink
> from the ritual uncleanness incurred by being touched by the "unclean" woman, and
> by immediate implication that he rejected the concept of the "uncleanness" of a
> woman who had a flow of blood. Jesus apparently placed a greater importance on
> the dramatic making of this point, both to the afflicted woman herself and to the
> crowd, than he did on avoiding the temporary psychological discomfort of the em-
> barrassed woman, which in the light of Jesus' extraordinary concern to alleviate the
> pain of the afflicted meant he placed a great weight on the teaching of this lesson
> about the dignity of women.[32]

The Synoptic Gospels commonly depict the women and other "little people"—
the nobodies—as exemplars of faith and devotion (Mt 15:28; Lk 1:45; 10:42).
Notwithstanding its scandalous potential, women traveled with Jesus and his disciples, providing vital financial resources (Lk 8:1-3). Women followers were outstanding in staying with Jesus to the end when the (male) disciples fled (Mk 15:40;
cf. Mk 14:50). Given the strong prejudice against women witnesses, it is remarkable that the Gospels record that women were the first witnesses of the risen Jesus.

Through the centuries, invisibility has been a common problem for women—
they have been simply ignored. In that context the Gospels give surprising prominence to women. This is especially so with Luke, who commonly presents paired
stories dealing with both men and women. Consider the following:

• Simeon and Anna both praise God for the birth of Jesus (Lk 2:25-38)

• Healing, first of the male demoniac, then of Peter's mother-in-law (Lk 4:31-39)

• Healings in response to the centurion and to the widow of Nain (Lk 7:1-17)

---

[32]Swidler, *Biblical Affirmations,* pp. 180-81.

Figure 7.1. Roman catacomb painting of Jesus and the woman at the well (Scala/Art Resource, NY)

- Simon the Pharisee and the sinful woman (Lk 7:36-50)
- A man with mustard seed and a woman with yeast (Lk 13:18-21)
- A shepherd with a lost sheep and a woman with a lost coin (Lk 15:4-10)
- An importunate widow and a penitent tax-collector (Lk 18:1-14)
- Women at the tomb and the Emmaus disciples (Lk 24:1-35)[33]

    The story of the lost coin is striking. It is the second of three parables justifying Jesus' fellowship with sinners on the basis of how God seeks out the lost. The primary figure in each of the parables represents God. In the second parable the primary figure is a woman. A woman representative of God! Given the cultural context of that time, such an image is remarkable.

    John's Gospel has a striking story of Jesus' encounter with a Samaritan woman (Jn 4:1-42). He engages with a person who is a sinner, a Samaritan and a woman—three categories that a good Jew would avoid. Jose b. Johannan of Jerusalem (c.

---

[33]Further on this point, see B. Witherington, *Women in the Earliest Churches* (Cambridge: Cambridge University Press, 1988), p. 129.

150 B.C.) urged, "Talk not much with a woman," to which was added, "They said this of a man's own wife: how much more of his fellow's wife!"[34] Rules of propriety forbade a man to be alone with a woman, or even to give her a greeting.[35] No wonder then that Jesus' disciples were astonished that he was talking with a woman (Jn 4:27). Jesus not only talked with her, but also disclosed his Messiahship to her and acknowledged her role as a proto-evangelist to her people (Jn 4:37-38).[36]

Very little gender-focused teaching appears in the Gospels. Yet the stories and the way they are narrated demonstrate a respect for women that was revolutionary for that period. Nevertheless, one component seems to be missing: women being counted within the inner Twelve. We can note, however, the absence also of non-Jews among the Twelve.[37] Why the omission of both groups? Surely the issue of cultural appropriateness must be considered. Jesus' ministry was to the Jews. At that point in their cultural perspective, inclusion of members from either group—women or Gentiles—would have blocked the reception of Jesus' message among his target audience. The Gospels bear witness to the principle of gender equality. Practice, however, might not fully express this equality because of cultural sensitivities. One may draw a parallel with Paul's stress on cultural sensitivity with regard to women being veiled or wearing their hair in a certain manner, while also providing comment on women's equality and authority in 1 Corinthians 11. Thus the Gospels remain a witness to Paul's point in Galatians 3:28, that there is neither male nor female in Christ.

Pauline teaching. We should begin by looking at what happened in practice in Pauline circles.[38] Most striking is the list of Paul's colleagues in Romans 16:1-16. In a list of twenty-eight people, nine are women. One, Phoebe, is a *diakonos,* "deacon" (Rom 16:1). The word used is not the feminized "deaconess," but rather the regular term for deacon. Phoebe was clearly a person of position as a *prostatis,* "patron" (Rom 16:2). In a world of huge inequality, where many poor survived through dependence on the rich in a patron-client relationship, she had a powerful role in society. Another important person was Prisca (or Priscilla) whom Scripture

---

[34]*m. Avot* 1:5; Jeremias, *Jerusalem in the Time,* p. 360.

[35]*m. Qiddushin* 4:12; *b. Qiddushin* 81a; *b. Qiddushin* 70a-b; Jeremias, *Jerusalem in the Time,* p. 360; Ilan, *Women in Greco-Roman Palestine,* pp. 126-27.

[36]For further discussion on this, see R. E. Brown, "Roles of Women in the Fourth Gospel," *Theological Studies* 36 (1975): 688-99, see pp. 691-92.

[37]E. Stagg and F. Stagg, *Women in the World of Jesus* (Philadelphia: Westminster Press, 1978), pp. 123-25.

[38]We should note that many scholars dispute the authorship of some of the writings attributed to Paul. I hold a conservative view on this matter, though recognizing that Paul's use of an amanuensis may have resulted in his scribes' views also being part of the text, especially in the Pastoral Epistles (1 and 2 Timothy and Titus).

regularly mentions ahead of her husband, Aquilla (Rom 16:3). This may suggest that she operated as the primary leader. Here the two are introduced as coworkers of Paul and joint leaders of a house church. Elsewhere the couple is represented as teachers, skilled in doctrinal understanding (Acts 18:26).

Most remarkable is the reference to Junia (now clearly understood to be a woman), who, with Andronicus, is an *apostolos*, "apostle" (Rom 16:7).[39] The term *apostolos* had a narrower and a broader reference in the New Testament. In its narrower sense it meant one of the Twelve who had accompanied Jesus during his earthly life and who had witnessed his resurrection (Lk 6:13; Acts 1:21-26). In its broader sense it might include other church leaders, especially those who had a pioneering church-planting missionary role (Acts 14:1-4). As an *apostolos* Junia clearly had a very significant church role in ministry and leadership.

Other major evidence for a public role for women in Pauline churches comes from 1 Corinthians 11:2-16. This is a very difficult passage to interpret. However, certain features stand out:

- The passage takes for granted that women pray and prophesy in public meetings (1 Cor 11:5; see also Acts 2:18; 21:9; Rev 2:20 in regard to women prophets).

- In a complex discussion Paul notes that women have *exousia*, "authority" (1 Cor 11:10). The text makes this statement; not a statement that women should show their submission by having a "sign of authority" on their heads, as the New Revised Standard Version may imply. In verse 10 the head covering is a sign of authority, not of submission. Considerations regarding female submission in the New Testament must be exercised in the context of this text.

- The passage as a whole shows a great deal of parallelism in relation to men and women. It is not a one-sided passage dealing with one gender alone. There is a sense of mutuality, especially in 1 Corinthians 11:11-12. Note the parallel with 1 Corinthians 7 where Paul is also careful to write in a balanced way to both sexes.

- There is discussion of headship, but it parallels the relationship of Christ and God (1 Cor 11:3). This parallel may suggest role differentiation rather than subordination in a hierarchical sense.

- The overall tenor of the passage does contain aspects of subordination. In this regard we need to note that Paul here (1 Cor 11:13), as elsewhere (1 Cor 5:1; 14:23), is very concerned with the reputation of the church. His theology and practice is shaped by the need to commend the gospel to outsiders and to build up the fledgling community (1 Cor 9:19-23; 10:31-33; 14:1-5). Thus Paul's the-

[39]S. Heine, *Women and Early Christianity: A Reappraisal* (Minneapolis: Augsburg, 1988), p. 42.

ology includes a cultural dimension, which may accept a measure of what we now call sexism because of the cultural context of that time.

The picture that emerges from this complex matter shows that Paul's discussions of women in ministry have two poles. There is the gospel principle that affirms the equal value of women and men: "neither male nor female" (Gal 3:28). There is also gospel practice of adjusting somewhat to culture for the sake of commending the gospel (1 Cor 9:19-23; 10:31-33). Paul's teaching embraces both poles, even though that stance may not seem satisfactory to all modern minds.[40]

Paul's theology is pastoral; he was responding to particular contexts and crises in his churches rather than writing systematic theology divorced from specific situations. Thus the context is crucial both in assessing the meaning of his teaching and in deciding whether it is context-specific or of universal application. This issue must be considered when weighing his injunction in 1 Corinthians 14:34-35 for women not to teach in church but to be silent. Taken at face value, it attempts to silence women altogether in public church life. This would be at odds with his earlier teaching in chapter 11. The matter is best resolved by looking at the context of the passage. It falls within a section on Christian worship where Paul is concerned with disruption and disorder. He has already silenced overly enthusiastic tongues-speakers and prophets who override others (1 Cor 14:27-33). While verse 34 could be taken to address all women generally, verse 35 may suggest that it applies only to those who have husbands (i.e., wives). A possible context, then, suggests that women were calling out to their spouses (they were separated from them in gender-segregated seating) and over-riding them when they were prophesying or teaching: "What are you saying?" "I don't agree!" and so on. Paul says this behavior is disgraceful and should be talked through at home.[41] Public worship should not be subject to this sort of disruption.

The 1 Timothy 2:11-15 passage, which also urges that women learn in silence and not teach, is more problematic. It may be taken at face value as the renewed dominance of cultural values, muzzling women from any public speaking role. If we understand the material to come from a Pauline interpreter, writing maybe decades after Paul's death, it enhances this perspective. Alternatively, we can note that the overriding concern in the Pastoral Epistles is heretical teaching (1 Tim 1:3-4;

---

[40]On the tension between missiology and gender equality, see also R. A. Tucker and W. Liefeld, *Daughters of the Church: Women and Ministry from New Testament Times to the Present* (Grand Rapids, Mich.: Zondervan, 1987), pp. 78-79.

[41]For this sort of interpretation of both 1 Cor 14 and 1 Tim 2 see R. J. Karris, "Women in the Pauline Assembly: To Prophesy, but not to Speak?" in *Women Priests: A Catholic Commentary on the Vatican Declaration,* ed. L. Swidler and A. Swidler (New York: Paulist, 1977), pp. 305-8. See also T. Paige, "The Social Matrix of Women's Speech at Corinth: The Context and Meaning of the Command to Silence in 1 Corinthians 14:33b-36," *Bulletin for Biblical Research* 12, no. 2 (2002): 217-42.

2 Tim 2:17-18), probably of a pre-Gnostic type. This teaching involved fanciful speculation (1 Tim 1:4; 2 Tim 4:3) and a sharp dualism between body and spirit, which downplayed the body (1 Tim 4:3-4; Tit 1:15). Such teaching particularly influenced women who took a leading role in its propagation (2 Tim 3:6). This explains the reference to the deception of Eve, as well as the positive value placed on normal domestic life, including the bearing and raising of children (1 Tim 2:13-15). In this context, suppression of teaching is not aimed at women generally, but rather at women exponents of this sort of erroneous teaching.[42]

We find further material relating to women in letters under Paul's name in the "household code" teaching in Colossians 3:18-19 and Ephesians 5:21-33. This material reflects societal concern for order in relationships, especially within the household. Such teaching clearly embodies a "love-patriarchalism" that involves elements of authority and subordination.[43] In short,

> The early Christian codes, despite their distinctive motivations, turn out in practice to be in line with the variety within the consistent patriarchal pattern throughout Greco-Roman society, where subordination of wives to husbands, children to parents, and slaves to masters was the overarching norm.[44]

In recognizing this cultural and hierarchical perspective, we also need to notice the following:

- Ephesians 5:21 sets a context of general Christian submission. The teaching thus exhorts mutuality as well as submission.

- Ephesians 5:25 calls the husband to self-sacrificing love exemplified by Christ himself. The passage develops this theme at far greater length than it does the call to submission. Furthermore, the call for wives to submit (Eph 5:22-24) should never be separated from the husband's call to love (Eph 5:25-33).

- Ephesians 5:28, with its call for the husband to love his wife as his own body, stresses the unity, the one-flesh nature, of the marriage relationship.

- Ephesians 5:32 elevates marital relationships to the highest possible level. They present the best earthly picture of the relationship between Christ and his believing community. Marriage then "participates in and reflects the new reality of grace which is at the heart of salvation."[45]

---

[42]As an example of this sort of contextual interpretation, see I. H. Marshall, *The Pastoral Epistles,* International Critical Commentary (Edinburgh: T & T Clark, 1999), pp. 452-71.

[43]Linkage of Paul with "love-patriarchalism" is found in G. Theissen, *The Social Setting of Pauline Christianity* (Edinburgh: T & T Clark, 1982), p. 107 and passim.

[44]A. T. Lincoln, *Ephesians,* Word Commentary (Dallas: Word, 1990), p. 359.

[45]Ibid., p. 363.

This brief discussion of women in the New Testament shows a remarkable honoring and dignifying of women in the Gospels. The epistles also provide a great deal of evidence for women exercising teaching and other roles within the Christian church. This is in keeping with the charismatic strand to ministry in the New Testament. When the Spirit was poured out on all flesh (Acts 2:17-18)—and that included women—how could the church nay-say that inspiration (cf. Acts 15:8-12)? This provides a pointer in relation to future developments. When the church weighed ministry strongly in terms of inspiration it found much scope for women's ministry. When, however, the focus became more on institutionalized office, cultural perceptions soon raised insurmountable barriers to many roles for women in the church. While the ferment of gospel new wine made for gender equality in the new communities, this stood in tension with cultural perceptions, from within the church and without, limiting the role of women to what was "decent" and "proper." In the New Testament, to varying degrees, revolutionary principle and pragmatic accommodation remained in tension. In the centuries after the New Testament period, cultural pressures increasingly diminished the earlier Christian ennobling of women.

Perspectives on Women in the Post New Testament Church

Egalitarian sentiments might still find occasional expression in the decades immediately following the New Testament period. Early second-century Ignatius, for example, exhorts *both* husbands and wives to love each other.[46] However, culture capture meant that the church progressively overlooked Jesus' ennoblement of women, reflecting rather the pervasive patriarchal perspectives of society. Male gender superiority was both assumed and asserted. For early third-century Clement of Alexandria, physical characteristics of the two sexes made this patent:

> Thus the beard is the mark of the man. By this he is seen to be a man . . . and is the token of the superior nature. In this God deemed it right that he should excel, and dispersed hair over man's whole body. God removed whatever smoothness and softness was in man when he formed the woman Eve from his side, physically receptive, his partner in parentage, his help in household management, while he (for he had parted with all smoothness) remained a man, and shows himself man. And to him has been assigned action, as to her suffering; for what is shaggy is drier and warmer than what is smooth. Thus males have both more hair and more heat than females.[47]

Male superiority meant female inferiority, commonly attributed to the original

---

[46]Ignatius *To Polycarp* 5 (ANF 1:100).
[47]Clement of Alexandria *Instructor* 3.3 (ANF 2:276, English modernized).

sin of Eve.[48] That sin led to the contamination of all marital activity, because, according to Augustine, it now involved inappropriate passion, and it was the vehicle for the transmission of original sin.[49] From a man's point of view women were thus a dangerous gender, pulling men into sin:

> In pains and in anxieties dost thou bear (children), woman; and toward thine husband (is) thy inclination, and he lords it over thee." And do you not know that you are (each) an Eve? The sentence of God on this sex of yours lives in this age: the guilt must of necessity live too. You are the devil's gateway; you are the unsealer of that (forbidden) tree; you are the first deserter of the divine law: you are she who persuaded him whom the devil was not valiant enough to attack. You destroyed so easily God's image, man. On account of your desertion—that is, death—even the Son of God had to die.[50]

This perspective, articulated in colorful and abrasive language here by Tertullian, was not peculiar to him. His view of woman as Eve the temptress was commonplace perspective in the church. Augustine, for example, wrote to a young man oppressed with his mother: "What is the difference? Whether it is in a wife or a mother, it is still Eve (the temptress) that we must beware of in any woman."[51] The tempting nature of women held back men from spiritual development. Thus Jerome wrote:

> I will just say now that the apostle bids us pray without ceasing, and that he who in the married state renders his wife her due cannot so pray. Either we pray always and are virgins, or we cease to pray that we may fulfil the claims of marriage.[52]

Women should not put temptation in the way of men. How appropriate it was, therefore, for their life largely to be centered on the home. The good woman, according to Clement of Alexandria, avoids the public arena in favor of the domestic one, "avoiding frequent departures from the house, and shutting herself up as far as possible from the view of all not related to her, and deeming housekeeping of more consequence than impertinent trifling."[53]

Given the increasingly negative view of women as seductive sexual beings,

---

[48]E.g., John Chrysostom *Homily 26 on 1 Cor 2* (*NPNF*[1] 12:150-51).

[49]Augustine *On Marriage and Concupiscence* 1.7-8, 27 (*NPNF*[1] 5:266-67, 274-75); *On Forgiveness of Sins and Baptism* 1.20 (*NPNF*[1] 5:22).

[50]Tertullian *On the Apparel of Women* 1.1 (*ANF* 4:14, English modernized). One should note that elsewhere Tertullian attributed the fall to gluttony (*On Fasting* 3.2, *ANF* 4:103), to Adam (*Against Marcion* 2.8, *ANF* 3:303-4) and to the devil (*Against Marcion* 2.8, *ANF* 3:303-4).

[51]Augustine *Epistle* 243.10 (in P. Brown, *Augustine of Hippo: A Biography* [London: Faber & Faber, 1967], p. 63).

[52]Jerome *Letter* 22.22 (*NPNF*[2] 6:31); also *Epistle* 48.15 (*NPNF*[2] 6:75).

[53]Clement of Alexandria *Stromata or Miscellanies* 2.23 (*ANF* 2:379).

women sometimes held surprisingly significant roles in the early postapostolic church. They persisted as prophetesses, for example, into the third century.[54] Tertullian discussed in detail the ministry of a woman prophet.[55] It is perhaps significant, however, that she did not declare her prophecies directly to the gathered church but rather shared them privately with church leaders at the conclusion of the service. The fourth-century historian Eusebius expressed no embarrassment about a list of women prophets.[56]

While we lack much direct evidence, women probably exercised a fair amount of leadership in the house churches of the first two or three centuries. In doing so they would be continuing the role exercised by women such as John Mark's mother Mary (Acts 12:12), Lydia (Acts 16:15, 40) and Phoebe (Rom 16:1) in the New Testament. It would have been natural for wealthier women to assume functions within the house church that they already exercised in their own households.[57] It is likely, however, that societal pressures and progressive church institutionalization would increasingly make such leadership the exception rather than the rule.

Two factors appear to be involved in women's continuing to have ongoing leadership and speaking roles. The first is the more charismatic and less institutional nature of the early church. Initially the church was more open to surprise, to exception, and readier to welcome that which came from God, irrespective of the instrument of communication. Great honor attached to those close to God, whether confessors or women prophets, even though their roles may have cut across institutional understandings of ministry and authority. Only as ministry and leadership became more and more defined in institutional fashion were women increasingly squeezed out of previously accepted ministry roles.

The second factor involved in female ministry was the church's typical location into the third century in private homes. In the distinction between public and private gender roles, women's particular role was in the home, and this was where the church gathered (Acts 12:12; 16:40; Rom 16:3-5; 1 Cor 16:19; Col 4:15). It would not be surprising then, for a wealthy woman to exercise some degree of leadership when the church met in her home. The shift from private home to public place of worship in the later third century, and especially the fourth century, likely speedily excluded any public leadership and teaching function of women within the congregation as a whole.

Archaeological evidence exists that may suggest a leading role for women in at least some contexts in the early church. Several inscriptions have been located re-

---

[54]On female prophets in the second century, see Justin Martyr *Dialogue with Trypho* 88.1 (*ANF* 1:243).
[55]Tertullian *Treatise on the Soul* 9 (*ANF* 3:188).
[56]Eusebius *History of the Church* 5.17.3 (*NPNF*[2] 1:234).
[57]K. Torjesen, "The Early Controversies over Female Leadership," *Christian History* 8, no. 1 (1988): 20-24, see p. 24.

ferring to a woman as "presbyter" or "bishop" (using a feminine form of the word).[58] The rarity of such inscriptions, their brevity, and the fact that they may be used in a nontechnical sense or with a view to indicating the woman not as, say, bishop, but as mother to the male bishop, makes their evidential value uncertain. We should heed the apt comment: "It is difficult to know with any certainty what these titles mean in regard to any of the women but it is worth considering that they mean what they say."[59]

In addition to textual evidence, fragments of evidence may be located in a few works of art. One most commonly appealed to is a fresco from the catacombs of the early third century that is apparently a eucharistic scene in which women have right hands outstretched over what may be eucharistic elements.[60] As with the inscriptions, it is difficult to weigh the evidential value of this fresco:

Figure 7.2. Meal scene in the Capella Greca in the Catacomb of Priscilla (2nd-century Rome) (Scala/Art Resource, NY)

The fresco poses the question: does a picture of seven women breaking bread together mean that there were women priests who celebrated eucharist in the early church? Arguments in the affirmative suffer from anachronism, assuming a more de-

---

[58]D. Irvin, "The Ministry of Women in the Early Church: The Archaeological Evidence," *Duke Divinity School Review* 45, no. 2 (1980): 76-86, see pp. 80-81; U. E. Eisen, *Women Officeholders in Early Christianity: Epigraphical and Literary Studies,* trans. L. M Maloney (Collegeville, Minn.: Michael Glazier, 2000), p. 224 and passim. For a good discussion on the limited weight of Eisen's evidence, see Paul McKechnie, *The First Christian Centuries: Perspectives on the Early Church* (Leicester, U.K.: Apollos, 2001), pp. 204-8.
[59]F. Cardman, "Women, Ministry, and Church Order in Early Christianity," in *Women & Christian Origins,* ed. R. S. Kraemer and M. R. D'Angelo (New York: Oxford University Press, 1999), pp. 300-329, quote p. 321.
[60]Irvin, "Ministry of Women," pp. 81-84.

veloped practice and theology of both priesthood (ordination) and eucharist than
were the case in the early third century. They also sidestep the difficulty of discerning
whether a meal scene in the context of the catacombs indicates an agape meal (love-
feast), a eucharist, or a funeral banquet (refrigerium).[61]

At most, archaeology indicates that occasionally women may have exercised
what came to be regarded as clerical roles or may have held what came to be
viewed as clerical titles. The evidence on this point is ambiguous. Either way, the
official (and male) church voice came consistently to emphasize that such practices should not occur. Whether from early times or somewhat later, the growing
power of the church increasingly led to silencing the voice of women.

Justification for forbidding women from any public teaching or leadership role
was buttressed by Scripture, with particular emphasis on 1 Timothy 2:12.[62] The
private-public distinction significantly strengthened this understanding:

> Our life is customarily organized into two spheres: Public affairs and private matters,
> both of which were determined by God. To woman is assigned the presidency of the
> household; to man, all the business of state, the marketplace, the administration of
> justice, government, the military, and all other such enterprises. A woman is not able
> to hurl a spear or shoot an arrow, but she can grasp the distaff, weave at the loom;
> she correctly disposes of all such tasks that pertain to the household. She cannot ex-
> press her opinion in a legislative assembly, but she can express it at home, and often
> she is more shrewd about household matters than her husband. She cannot handle
> state business well, but she can raise children correctly, and children are our princi-
> pal wealth. . . . God maintained the order of each sex by dividing the business of hu-
> man life into two parts and assigned the more necessary and beneficial aspects to the
> man and the less important, inferior aspects to the woman.[63]

Another factor in women not having a public role lay in the desire of the church
to distance itself from heretical and fringe church groups that allowed that public
role. In Montanism, for example, the prophetesses Maximilla and Priscilla had
equal prestige with Montanus himself.[64] At least some expressions of Gnosticism
gave women liberty in public ministry—prophetic and priestly.[65] Such expressions
were all the more reason to condemn the errors of these groups. Thus Tertullian

---

[61]Cardman, "Women, Ministry," pp. 321-22.

[62]For example, John Chrysostom *On the Priesthood* 3.9 (*NPNF*[1] 9:49); *Homily 9 on 1 Timothy* (*NPNF*[1]
13:435).

[63]John Chrysostom *The Kind of Women Who Ought to Be Taken as Wives* (in Elizabeth A. Clark, *Women
in the Early Church* [Wilmington, Del.: Michael Glazier, 1983], pp. 36-37).

[64]Gryson, *Ministry of Women*, p. 16; C. Trevett, "Gender, Authority and Church History: A Case Study
of Montanism," *Feminist Theology* 17 (1998): 9-24, see pp. 11-13.

[65]Irenaeus *Against Heresies* 1.13 (*ANF* 1:334-36); Hippolytus *The Refutation of All Heresies* 6.35 (*ANF*
5:92).

fulminated, "The very women of these heretics, how wanton they are! For they are bold enough to teach, to dispute, to enact exorcisms, to undertake cures—it may be even to baptize."[66] Women were viewed as particularly prone to error and to heresy.[67] All the more reason not to allow them to teach.

Tertullian argued both from Scripture and from distinct male/female roles for denying women any teaching or priestly role: "It is not permitted to a woman to speak in the church; but neither (is it permitted her) to teach, nor to baptize, nor to offer, nor to claim to herself a lot in any manly function, not to say (in any) sacerdotal office."[68] The allusion to prohibition from priestly office or function is significant. In the New Testament period we see no sharp sense of what we might now call ordination, but rather a sense of call and commission for mission and ministry.[69] However, a concept of Christian ministry paralleling Jewish priestly ministry began to emerge from the end of the first century.[70] The perception of priestly function as being a manly role—something Tertullian reflected—thus denied public ministry to women.

The *Didascalia* sets out a similar early third-century prohibition against women teachers: "It is not required nor necessary that women should be teachers, especially about the name of the Christ and about salvation by his passion; women were not appointed to teach, especially not a widow, but that they should make prayer and supplication to the Lord God."[71] The presence of such a prohibition suggests that some were teaching or inclined to teach. Women engaged in teaching would, however, be the exception. The weight of the church voice largely silenced women's public voices in church.

All this may suggest that Christianity provided no social advancement to women in the early post-New Testament church. However, despite its departure from its more radical beginnings, Christianity still provided significant benefit to women. It lifted their domestic status by giving to women greater honor as bearing the image of God.[72] However, even here we can see some cultural erosion of this principle. Sometimes at least, the church fathers display a sense of women partic-

---

[66]Tertullian *Prescription Against Heretics* 41 (*ANF* 3:263). It is ironic, however, that Tertullian himself later became a Montanist.

[67]Jerome *Letter* 133.4 (*NPNF*[2] 6:275).

[68]Tertullian *On the Veiling of Virgins* 9 (*ANF* 4:33).

[69]J. L. McKenzie, "St. Paul's Attitude to Women," in *Women Priests: A Catholic Commentary on the Vatican Declaration*, ed. L. Swidler and A. Swidler (New York: Paulist, 1977), pp. 212-15, see p. 213; B. B. Thurston, *The Widows: A Woman's Ministry in the Early Church* (Minneapolis: Fortress, 1989), pp. 18-19.

[70]*The First Epistle of Clement* 40 (*ANF* 1:16); *Didache* 13.3.

[71]*Did. Ap.* 15 (trans. M. D. Gibson, *The Didascalia in English* [London: Cambridge University Press, 1903], p. 72); see also the late fourth-century *Apostolic Constitutions* 3.6 (*ANF* 7:427).

[72]H. Chadwick, *The Early Church* (London: Penguin, 1967), p. 59. On this see Augustine, *On the Trinity* 12.7 (*NPNF*[1] 3:158-60).

Figure 7.3. Praying woman (from the cubiculum of Velatia in the Priscilla Catacomb in Rome, mid-3rd century) (Scala/Art Resource, NY)

ipating imperfectly in the image of God. Whereas man was made directly by God (Gen 2:7), women participated derivatively—through man (Gen 2:22; 1 Cor 11:7). Women then had a more tenuous link with the divine, lacking some essential quality that men shared with the Godhead.[73] Augustine's extended discussion on this matter in *On the Trinity* markedly presents this idea: men on their own reflected the image of God, but women did not. Only as co-joined with her husband did a woman bear the image of God. Such views left a question mark over the standing of the female sex: she was in the image of God, but only through her standing with her husband.[74]

Other aspects of Christian teaching did more to enhance unequivocally the place of women in society. Condemnation of divorce, incest, infanticide and adultery all strengthened the position of women.[75] A high view of widowhood, their care within the community, and the lack of pressure on them to remarry—in sharp contrast to Augustus's edict fining widows who had not remarried within two years of their husband's death—all commended Christianity further to women.[76]

---

[73]Cloke, *"Female Man of God,"* pp. 26-27.
[74]Augustine *On the Trinity* 12.7 (*NPNF*[1] 3:158-60).
[75]R. Stark, "Reconstructing the Rise of Christianity: The Role of Women," *Sociology of Religion* 56, no. 3 (1995): 222-44, see p. 235.
[76]Ibid., p. 236.

Augustine's nuanced stance on women as being in the image of God:

According to that which I have said already, when I was treating of the nature of the human mind, that the woman together with her own husband is the image of God, so that that whole substance may be one image; but when she is referred separately to her quality of *help-meet*, which regards the woman herself alone, then she is not the image of God; but as regards the man alone, he is the image of God as fully and completely as when the woman too is joined with him in one.[a]

[a]Augustine *On the Trinity* 12.7 (NPNF[1] 3:159).

These features made Christianity attractive to inquiring pagan women.[77]

Christianity also gave the highest honor to women when they entered into exceptional roles. The only catch was that these roles typically required death. By this I mean the elevated status given to women martyrs (see chapter three on persecution and martyrdom). The elevated status, however, was also given to those who died to themselves in asceticism. To this theme we now turn.

Women and Asceticism

The previous chapter in this book focused on the emergence of Christian asceticism and monasticism, and the following material must be read in that wider context. However, at a number of points ascetic and monastic practice carried a different significance for a woman than it did for a man, and the particular significance of these practices for women needs to be emphasized.

Asceticism and virginity, features that seem to have been more prevalent among women, were quickly honored in the early church. The New Testament narrative honored godly women who set themselves apart for God and the Christian community (Lk 2:36-38; Acts 9:36; also 1 Tim 5:3-5, 9-10). This sort of practice soon led to a pattern of household asceticism in which women (and men) abstained from marriage and practiced piety within domestic arrangements. Thus Ignatius wrote very early in the second century, "If any one can continue in a state of purity, to the honour of Him who is Lord of the flesh, let him so remain without boasting."[78] Further evidence of women renouncing marriage for the sake of the gospel can be seen in his letter to Smyrna: "I salute the families of my brethren, with their

---

[77]Ibid., p. 231.
[78]Ignatius *To Polycarp* 5.2 (ANF 1:95).

wives and the children, and the virgins who are called widows."[79]

In those early centuries the increasing practice was for Christian women to live in their own homes, observing household asceticism under the general supervision of a bishop. Such women also pioneered ascetic communities long before institutionalized monasticism emerged.[80] The earlier stages often tended toward extremes of ascetic rigor. In the case of Blaesilla, daughter of Paula, the rigors of fasting likely contributed to her death in the late fourth century. Jerome sang the praises of Lea, recently deceased, for her ascetic practices: "She was careless of her dress, neglected her hair, and ate only the coarsest food."[81] Not all ascetic lifestyle involved such a degree of abandonment. Elizabeth Clark has drawn attention to wealthy fourth- and fifth-century Roman women whose ascetic renunciation left them with servants and a comfortable lifestyle on their rural estates with very little self-sacrifice.[82] Similarly, when Jerome wrote to the highborn Demetrias, who had recently embraced the vocation of virginity, he assumed that she would continue to have servants.[83]

A major feature of vocational asceticism was the renunciation of sexual relationship. While a sex-charged, twenty-first-century perspective might view this as an unnatural deprivation, for many women it may have been a relief, an escape from an early, imposed and commonly unhappy marriage, and from the perils of pregnancy and childbirth. In Greco-Roman times it was extremely unusual for a woman not to marry. Thus Christian asceticism was very innovative in offering women an alternative to marriage.[84] Sexual renunciation gave ascetic practitioners a very elevated status, as Jerome indicated:

> Virginity is to marriage what fruit is to the tree, or grain to the straw. Although the hundred-fold, the sixty-fold, and the thirty-fold spring from one earth and from one sowing, yet there is a great difference in respect of number. The thirty-fold has reference to marriage. . . . The sixty-fold applies to widows . . . while one hundred-fold . . . expresses the crown of virginity.[85]

Consecrated virgins were commonly treated as different, as transcending their

[79]Ignatius *To the Smyrnaeans* 12.2 (*ANF* 1:92).
[80]J. Simpson, "Women and Asceticism in the Fourth Century: A Question of Interpretation," *Journal of Religious History* 15, no. 1 (1988): 38-60, see p. 42 (repr. in *Women in Early Christianity*, ed. D. M. Scholer [New York: Garland, 1993], pp. 296-318, see p. 300).
[81]Jerome *Letter* 23.2 (*NPNF*[2] 6:42).
[82]Elizabeth A. Clark, "Ascetic Renunciation and Feminine Advance," *Theological Review* 63, no. 3 (1981): 240-57.
[83]Jerome *Letter* 130.13 (*NPNF*[2] 6:267); also 108.2 (*NPNF*[2] 6:196); 123.14 (*NPNF*[2] 6:235).
[84]A. D. Lee, *Pagans and Christians in Late Antiquity: A Sourcebook* (London: Routledge, 2000), p. 261.
[85]Jerome *Against Jovinian* 1.3 (*NPNF*[2] 6:347, English modernized). For Augustine's prizing of virginity above marriage see *On Faith and Works* 4.5. For earlier elevation of virgins, in comparison with other women, see Tertullian *Exhortation to Chastity* 1 (*ANF* 4:50); Cyprian *On the Dress of Virgins* 21 (*ANF* 5:436).

gender. In the words of Elizabeth Clark, "Most of the Fathers believed that women who renounced the sexual life were elevated above their natural abject condition to the degree that they almost constituted a "third sex", so much did they differ from females still in the thrall of Eve's birth pains and submission to husbands."[86] Ambrose saw the believing woman as becoming a perfect man (Eph 4:13), such that "she dispenses with her worldly label, with the sex of her body."[87] To the fifth century historian, Palladius, heroic female ascetics had transcended their sex and become like men—they were "manly women" (*gynaikai andreiai*).[88] One such was the female ascetic Melania the Elder, whom Palladius described as "a man of God" (*anthrōpos tou Theou*).[89] Such language expresses a "sanctified androgyny."[90]

Transcending sex might give consecrated celibate women liberties not normally permitted to other women. One such liberty was travel, something not normally possible for a woman unless in the company of her husband or father. Of course it could not be travel for travel's sake. There must be a spiritual purpose; it must be a pilgrimage.[91] Jerome recorded the freedom grasped by Paula in this transcending of gender:

> Need I speak of the Macarii, Arsenius, Serapion, or other pillars of Christ! Was there any cell she did not enter? Or any man at whose feet she did not throw herself? In each of his saints she believed that she saw Christ himself; and whatever she bestowed upon them she rejoiced to feel that she had bestowed it upon the Lord. Her enthusiasm was wonderful and her endurance scarcely credible in a woman. Forgetful of her sex and of her weakness she even desired to make her abode, together with the girls who accompanied her, among these thousands of monks.[92]

The experience of Melania the Younger was similar, monks being ready to receive her into their monasteries as though she were a man, "for she had gone beyond the limits of her sex and acquired a virile mentality, or rather a celestial one."[93] The problem with all this, as Gillian Cloke has pointed out, is that when

---

[86]Elizabeth A. Clark, *Women in the Early Church* (Wilmington, Del.: Michael Glazier, 1983), p. 17.

[87]Ambrose, *On Saint Luke* 10.161 (quoted by J. K. Coyle, "The Fathers on Women," in *Women in Early Christianity*, ed. D. M. Scholer [New York: Garland, 1993], pp. 117-67, quote p. 126.

[88]Palladius *Luasiac History* 41; also preface 1 and 5; also Jerome *Letter* 71.3 (NPNF[2] 6:153). See also S. Elm, *"Virgins of God": The Making of Asceticism in Late Antiquity* (Oxford: Oxford University Press, 1994), p. 330.

[89]Palladius *Luasiac History* 41.

[90]Cloke, *"Female Man of God,"* p. 127.

[91]Clark, "Ascetic Renunciation," p. 251.

[92]Jerome *Letters* 108.14 (NPNF[2] 6:202).

[93]*Life of Saint Melania* 20 (quoted in J. A. McNamara, "Sexual Equality and the Cult of Virginity in Early Christian Thought," in *Women in Early Christianity,* ed. D. M. Scholer [New York: Garland, 1993], pp. 219-32, quote p. 228).

the fathers praised women for virtue such as this, they commonly made particular reference to their sex, only then to set them apart from it. For Cloke it had echoes of Dr. Johnson's famous aphorism about a woman preacher being like a dog standing on its hind legs—it was startling for a woman to be like this. The fathers paid them the ultimate compliment of being "manly." The outstanding nature of such women was comprehensible only by their being viewed as raised to the level of men or by leaving their sex behind altogether. In Cloke's view this created the perspective that such women surpassed their sex, rather than elevating expectations concerning women.[94]

Those women who entered the monastic cloister did not necessarily view it as restrictive. They lived in a secure, female-directed environment, in some cases with the possibility of further personal development beyond that provided by their elementary schooling. While the prospect of monasticism has fewer attractions in the modern West, for ascetic women in the early church the role might seem more attractive than any others commonly expected of them.

In some cases, however, monasticism was not a woman's choice but that of her patriarchal household. Some households made that decision to avoid the expense of marriage dowry. As Basil of Caesarea wrote, "Many girls are brought forward by their parents and brothers and other kinsfolk, before they are of full age, and have no inner impulse towards a celibate life. The object of the friends is simply to provide for themselves."[95]

Many of the roles of these early women began as roles of function, as something one did. However, with the increasing institutionalization of the church, the status of women undertaking such roles came into question. Into what category did they fall? Were they a rank? Were they clergy? To such questions we now turn.

Recognized Orders of Women

Widows. While we may think of widows simply as women whose husbands had died, their status was somewhat more complex in the New Testament period. Continued Old Testament perspectives commonly saw them as vulnerable, poor, in need of protection (Acts 6:1; 1 Tim 5:16; Jas 1:27). They were also frequently viewed as particularly inclined to piety (Mk 12:41-44; Lk 2:36-38; Acts 9:36). First Timothy shows that in the situation of that epistle at least, the term "widow" had now acquired a more technical meaning. A "widow" was one who was formally registered in the church records as such (1 Tim 5:9). Not all widows in the ordinary sense could have that role—age and character qualifications applied. The

---

[94]Cloke, "Female Man of God," pp. 213-15.
[95]Basil Letter 199.18 (NPNF[2] 8:237).

lives of such "widows" were marked by piety and they forswore future marriage.

In the second century such widows were increasingly seen as having a role of prayer and charitable deeds. In Polycarp's view they were to display holy living appropriate to being "the altar of God."[96] The third-century Syrian document *Didascalia Apostolorum (Teaching of the Apostles)* stressed the intercessory role of such women:

> The widow who wishes to please God sits within her house, and meditates in the Lord by day and by night, without ceasing, at all times offering prayer and supplication, praying purely before the Lord. And she receives whatever she asks, because all her mind is set upon this."[97]

The elevated status of widows made their rank commonly associated with that of the major clergy of the church. Thus Clement of Alexandria could write: "Innumerable commands such as these are written in the holy Bible appertaining to chosen persons, some to presbyters, some to bishops, some to deacons, others to widows."[98]

The honor attributed to such women invited the question: were they ordained clergy? The *Didascalia Apostolorum* left the question open, simply acknowledging they had a special call from God and occupied a "place" or "rank" apart from laypeople.[99] Hippolytus, however, writing in Rome about the same period of time, decisively opposed any suggestion of ordination:

> When a widow is appointed, she shall not be ordained but she shall be appointed by the name. . . . The widow shall be appointed by the word alone and let her be associated with the other widows; hands shall not be laid upon her because she does not offer the oblation nor has she a sacred ministry. But the widow is appointed for prayer, and prayer is the duty of all.[100]

Hippolytus saw the laying on of hands as central to ordination, and this should not be given to women, but only to those administering the Eucharist (and baptism). The *Apostolic Constitutions* similarly restrict women. The *Constitutions* reflect modifications of and additions to the *Didascalia* a century and a half later. They slam shut any doors potentially left open by the *Didascalia* to the ordination of widows. They are not "ordained" but only admitted to the "order" of widows.[101] The *Constitutions* omits the *Didascalia's* references to the widows praying, fasting

---

[96]Polycarp *Epistle to the Philippians* 4 (ANF 1:34).

[97]*Did. Ap.* 15 (trans. M. D. Gibson, *Didascalia in English,* English modernized).

[98]Clement of Alexandria *Instructor* 3.12 (ANF 2:294).

[99]*Did. Ap.* 3 and 15. See also Gryson, *Ministry of Women,* pp. 38-39.

[100]*Apostolic Tradition* 11 (trans. B. S. Easton, *The Apostolic Tradition of Hippolytus* [Cambridge: Cambridge University Press, 1934]).

[101]*Apostolic Constitutions* 8.3.25 (ANF 7:493).

and laying hands on the sick; drops any reference to their power of blessing; and fails to mention them after the bishop, presbyter and deacon. In so doing, the *Constitutions* shut any loopholes that may have suggested an ecclesiastical function in the *Didascalia.*[102]

The *Constitutions* signal a redefining of the role of widow, moving it closer to that of virgin: "By insisting on the promise of continence attached to admission to the order of widows, on perpetual prayer more than on prayer for benefactors, on vigils, fasting, and other exercises of piety; by presenting widows as 'consecrated to God'; and by associating them systematically with virgins, the *Constitutions* strongly accentuate the ascetic character of the ideal of widowhood."[103] The *Constitutions* point to commonality and overlap between widows and virgins. As an expression of this association, widows were commonly looked to as role models and supervisors of virgins. Ambrose articulates this association: "I ought not to leave them [the widows] without honour, nor to separate them from the commendation belonging to virgins, since the voice of the Apostle has joined them to virgins."[104] Later fusion of the two orders within the cloister was a natural outcome of this close linkage.

Virgins. Consecrated widows and consecrated virgins both took vows of abstinence from sexual relationships. While the former were once married and the latter never married, the distinction between the two categories was not always sharp. The *Constitutions* themselves are evidence for this in their close association of the two groupings of women, though clearly they do not merge—the virgins take priority over both widows and the general laity in receiving the Eucharist.[105] Much earlier, Ignatius, at the start of the second century, illustrated the blurring that sometimes existed between widows and virgins. "I salute," he wrote, "the families of my brethren, with their wives and children, and the virgins who are called widows."[106]

The intentionality and seriousness of being a "widow" or virgin was apparent early in church history. A vow seems to have been involved. Thus in 1 Timothy 5:11-12 an enrolled remarrying "widow" incurs condemnation for having set aside her first "faith," *pistis.* The harshness of the judgment and its link with fundamental matters of faith suggest that a woman made a solemn promise not to marry. The

---

[102]Gryson, *Ministry of Women,* p. 59.

[103]Ibid.

[104]Ambrose *Concerning Widows* 1.1 (*NPNF*[2] 10:391).

[105]*Apostolic Constitutions* 2.7.57 (*ANF* 7:421).

[106]Ignatius *To the Smyrnaeans* 12.2 (*ANF* 1:92). For another example of blurring between virgins and widows, see Tertullian's instance of a twenty-year-old virgin who was enrolled as a widow: *On the Veiling of Virgins* 9 (*ANF* 4:33).

vow was a matter for the church as well as the individual, as Ignatius's stress on
the supervisory function of the bishop in relation to virgins indicates: "If anyone
remains in chastity in honour of the body of the Lord, let it be done without boasting, for if they boast of it they are lost; only the bishop should know, otherwise it
is spoiled."[107]

While vows were an early feature of consecrated virginity, only about the fourth
century did virgins come to be described as an "order," as in, for example, the
above-quoted fourth-century material of the *Constitutions*.[108] The Council of Elvira
in 306 underscored the seriousness of the virginal vow:

> It has been decided that virgins who dedicated themselves to God must not be given
> communion, not even on their death-bed, if they have broken their promise (*pac-
> tum*) of virginity, and have given in to their desire, not being aware of what they
> were losing.[109]

The quasi-legal language of contract (*pactum*) suggests that a promise of virginity was a very serious lifetime commitment.[110] Through the vow, the virgin became
a "bride" of Christ,[111] and her veil was a "bridal-veil."[112] While a life of virginity
was expressed in one's own household within those first centuries, communities
of virgins emerged even before monasticism became widespread. Thus when Antony became a solitary he first provided for his sister by placing her in a *parthenon*
(a house of virgins).[113] As structured female monasticism increasingly took hold,
this more and more became the arrangement within which to express consecrated
virginity. This led in the early Middle Ages to the categories of "virgin" and
"widow" increasingly being subsumed under that of "nun."

Deaconesses. We have already noted references to female deacons in the New
Testament, similar to that of male deacons (Rom 16:1; 1 Tim 3:11). While argument may be mounted that such women were not a regular diaconate but simply
certain women exercising a serving function,[114] "deacons" in general were a defined body in both Philippians 1:2 and 1 Timothy 3:8. This suggests that when
Paul called Phoebe a *diakonos* she had a defined and recognized role. Several other
important points regarding 1 Timothy 3:8-13 support the argument that the

---

[107]Ignatius *To Polycarp* 5.2 (ANF 1:95).
[108]J. LaPorte, *The Role of Women in Early Christianity* (Lewiston: Edwin Mellen, 1982), p. 70.
[109]Canon 13 of the Council of Elvira (quoted in Elm, "*Virgins of God,*" p. 26).
[110]Elm, "*Virgins of God,*" p. 26. See also Elm's discussion of sanctions imposed at the Council of Ancyra,
314, against virgins who broke their vows. Ibid.
[111]Tertullian *On Prayer* 22 (ANF 3:689).
[112]Jerome *Letters* 130.2 and 147.6 (NPNF[2] 6:261, 292).
[113]*Life of Antony* 3 (NPNF[2] 4:196).
[114]For example, Gryson, *Ministry of Women,* p. 109.

women were women deacons and not simply deacons' wives:

- If they were wives, one would expect discussion also of the qualities of the more important bishops'/elders' wives.

- If the passage refers to wives, one would expect reference to "the/their women/wives" instead of "women/wives" without any article or possessive pronoun.

- Use of the term "likewise" implies a group in parallel with the male *diakanoi* who have just been discussed.[115]

The upshot of these arguments is that the Pastoral Epistles seem to indicate the presence of a recognized group of women deacons.

What developed in the immediately post-New Testament period is not clear, though Pliny's reference to "two maid-servants who were called deaconesses *[ministrae]*" suggests an ongoing Christian pattern of recognized female ministry.[116] Such ministry persisted in the East in succeeding centuries, though it never seems to have become established in the West. In the East deaconesses were an order, clearly distinct from that of widows in the third century. They had an honored place, as the following material from the *Didascalia* indicates:

> The bishop sits for you in the place of Almighty God. But the deacon stands in the place of Christ. You should love him; but let the deaconesses be honoured by you in the likeness of the Holy Spirit. Moreover, let the elders be to you in the likeness of the apostles.[117]

The high status of the fourth-century deaconess of the East is also reflected in her entering the role through an ordination involving prayer and the laying on of hands.[118] Her role focused on ministry to women. The *Apostolic Constitutions* stressed the mediatory role of the woman deacon between clergy and lay women (no doubt for the sake of propriety): "Let not any woman address herself to the deacon or bishop without the deaconess."[119] One duty of the deaconess was anointing the entire body of women after their baptism, something obviously inappropriate for men to undertake.[120] The role of deaconess persisted in the East into the Middle Ages, eventually also to be absorbed into the one clearly accepted religious role for women—that of nun.

---

[115]K. Giles, *Patterns of Ministry among the First Christians* (North Blackburn, VIC: HarperCollins, 1989), p. 61.

[116]Pliny *Epistle* 10.96.8.

[117]*Did. Ap.* 9 (trans. M. D. Gibson, *The Didascalia in English* [London: Cambridge University Press, 1903], p. 48).

[118]*Apostolic Constitutions* 8.3.19-20 (*ANF* 7:492); Council of Chalcedon, canon 15 (*NPNF*[2] 14:279).

[119]*Apostolic Constitutions* 2.4.26 (*ANF* 7:410).

[120]Ibid., 3.2.15 (*ANF* 7:431).

Conclusion

The church that arose after the radical and women-affirming ministry of Jesus soon faced the pervasive cultural attitudes that women should not teach, be leaders of men or otherwise have a public religious role. In commending the gospel within society, the church soon reflected cultural perspectives more than the example of Jesus with regard to women. Thereafter women's public ministry became increasingly problematic. The location of churches in homes—the private sphere—kept the door open to a limited extent for a couple of centuries, but as the church moved more into public view and became more institutionalized, it progressively shut down loopholes allowing women's public leadership and ministry. A recognized place in social work and in woman-to-woman ministry persisted in the East in the role of deaconess, but it was clearly specified that this did not mean a teaching or sacramental role. Gospel and society always stand in tension. On the issue of women, the early church lost the tension. It gradually restricted female religious vocation, which increasingly became limited to that of the veiled nun.

For Further Reading

Bailey, K. E. "Women in the New Testament: A Middle Eastern Cultural View." *Anvil* 11, no. 1 (1994): 7-24.

Brown, R. E. "Roles of Women in the Fourth Gospel." *Theological Studies* 36 (1975): 688-99.

Clark, E. A. "Ascetic Renunciation and Feminine Advance." *Anglican Theological Review* 63, no. 3 (1981): 240-57.

———. *Women in the Early Church*. Wilmington, Del.: Michael Glazier, 1983.

Cloke, G. *"This Female Man of God": Women and Spiritual Power in the Patristic Age, A.D. 350-450.* London: Routledge, 1995.

Eisen, U. E. *Women Officeholders in Early Christianity: Epigraphical and Literary Studies.* Translated by L. M. Maloney. Collegeville, Minn.: Liturgical Press, 2000.

Elm, S. *"Virgins of God": The Making of Asceticism in Late Antiquity.* Oxford: Oxford University Press, 1994.

Gryson, R. *The Ministry of Women in the Early Church.* Translated by J. LaPorte and M. L. Hall. Collegeville, Minn.: Liturgical Press, 1976.

Ilan, T. *Women in Greco-Roman Palestine: An Inquiry into Image and Status.* Peabody, Mass.: Hendrickson, 1995.

Irvin, D. "The Ministry of Women in the Early Church: The Archaeological Evidence." *Duke Divinity School Review* 45, no. 2 (1980): 76-86.

Jeremias, J. *Jerusalem in the Time of Jesus.* Chap. 18: "Appendix: The Social Position of Women." London: SCM Press, 1969.

Lang, J. *Ministers of Grace: Women in the Early Church.* Middlegreen, U.K.: St. Paul
    Publications, 1989.

LaPorte, J. *The Role of Women in Early Christianity.* Lewiston: Edwin Mellen, 1982.

Scholer, D. M., ed. *Women in Early Christianity.* New York: Garland, 1993.

Torjesen, K. "The Early Controversies over Female Leadership." *Christian History*
    7, no, 1 (1988): 20-24.

Witherington, B. *Women in the Earliest Churches.* Cambridge: Cambridge University Press, 1988.

8

THE EMERGING SHAPE OF WORSHIP
Eucharist and Liturgy

Christian worship underwent tremendous evolution in its earliest centuries. The changes were not uniform, however: practices commonly varied, not only from century to century, but also from region to region. In seeking a clear picture of that worship we need to remain alert to its complexity and variety. This requires caution in generalizing about the worship of the early church.

The Roots of Early Christian Worship

Charismatic inspiration. The early church began with a strong sense of direct inspiration: the Spirit had been poured out on them and was actively inspiring them in utterance (Mk 13:11; Acts 2:4, 17-18; 1 Cor 12:4-11; 14:26-33). Spirit-inspired enunciation abounds in the New Testament.[1] Its most extensive discussion of worship comes in 1 Corinthians 12—14. In that epistle Paul seeks to restrain enthusiastic excess while not devaluing Spirit-inspired worship. He rather assumes a Spirit-led dimension to worship (1 Cor 14:1, 24-26, 39-40). Alongside this component, early Christian worship also made significant use of set forms. Paul himself appears to incorporate material in his letters that likely stems from community liturgical use (e.g., Rom 1:3-4; Phil 2:6-11).[2] Spontaneity or loose structure, however, was also to the fore. Ralph Martin commented, "Much of the descriptive data [of New Testament worship] gives the appearance of being *ad hoc,* especially in 1 Cor 12—14 where Christian worship practices are most fully set

---

[1]Obvious examples include Lk 1:67; 2:27-32; 10:21; Acts 4:8; 7:55; 13:9; 21:11. Less obvious references include Rom 8:15-16; 1 Cor 12:3; Gal 4:6. On this see J. D. G. Dunn, *Romans 1—8,* Word Biblical Commentary (Dallas: Word, 1988), p. 453.

[2]Scholars commonly conclude that such material is traditional, rather than composed by Paul himself, because of features such as words not normally used by Paul and/or the poetic/liturgical forms of expression.

forth."[3] The already-discussed locus of worship in the house-congregation for the first two or more centuries of Christianity fostered this informal and participatory worship. We must keep spontaneity and inspiration in view as we consider traditional influences that also shaped early Christian worship.

The Jewish matrix. Christianity began in a Jewish environment. While critical of aspects of current religious practice, Jesus continued in Jewish religious observances, attending synagogue and temple (Lk 4:16-30; Jn 2:23; 7:14). His postresurrection followers did the same (Acts 2:46; 6:9; 9:2; 13:5, 14; 14:1; 17:1-2, 10; 18:4; 21:26). Christian communities broke from Judaism at different times but it wasn't a common practice until a generation after Christianity began. Even then some contact and influence remained; the Eastern church, for example, largely continuing to observe Easter on the day when the Jews "put away the leaven" at Passover.[4] The need to keep their date of observance in line with Jewish calculations points to Christian interaction with Jews. Examples like this suggest that early Christian worship was significantly influenced by Judaism, both before and after A.D. 70. Before 70, Jewish-Christian worship used the same centers for worship as did other Jews: temple, synagogue and home.[5] The Jewish matrix of early worship influenced the shape and nature of Christian worship.[6] As a consequence, Christianity followed Judaism in having regular weekly worship (in contrast to paganism) and expounding readings from authoritative writings.[7]

Corporate worship was located primarily in homes for the first two or more centuries. Such location probably stems from the exigencies of persecution and also the influence of Judaism—originally its synagogues were commonly house gatherings.[8] A home location made worship and fellowship closely intertwined realities. The fellowship dimension permeates New Testament worship in its use of "one another" language. The believers were to "teach and admonish one another," "consider how

[3]R. P. Martin, "Patterns of Worship in New Testament Churches," *Journal for the Study of the New Testament* 37 (1989): 59-85, quote p. 61. See also his comments on the felt presence of the Holy Spirit in worship on p. 68.
[4]Bishop Polycrates of Ephesus, late second century, quoted in Eusebius *Church History* 5.24.6 (*NPNF*[2] 1:242).
[5]R. T. Beckwith, "The Daily and Weekly Worship of the Primitive Church: Part II," *Evangelical Quarterly* 56, no 3 (1984): 139-58, see p. 139.
[6]For examples of this see T. Klauser, *A Short History of the Western Liturgy: An Account and Some Reflections* (London: Oxford University Press, 1969), pp. 4-6.
[7]G. Stanton, "Aspects of Early Christian and Jewish Worship: Pliny and the *Kerygma Petrou*," in *Worship, Theology and Ministry in the Early Church: Essays in Honor of Ralph P. Martin,* ed. M. J. Wilkens and T. Paige (Sheffield: JSOT Press, 1992), pp. 84-98, see p. 87.
[8]Excavated synagogues from as early as the first century A.D. are rare: J. T. Burtchaell, *From Synagogue to Church: Public Services and Offices in the Earliest Christian Communities* (Cambridge: Cambridge University Press, 1992), p. 226.

to provoke one another to love and good deeds," and "confess [their] sins to one another and pray for one another" (Col 3:16; Heb 10:24; Jas 5:16). Early church life, including early church worship, was steeped in close bonds of fellowship.

One expression of this fellowship was the holy kiss. Kissing in the first centuries could have a variety of meanings, including the erotic. The New Testament contains several exhortations to kiss one another (Rom 16:16; 1 Cor 16:20; 2 Cor 13:12; 1 Thess 5:26; 1 Pet 5:14). The fact that the kiss is in the context of greeting and that it is to be a "holy kiss" indicates that the kiss was essentially an expression of warmth and fellowship. The kiss remained an element of a more formal liturgy well into the medieval period.[9]

The Components of Christian Worship

To understand early church worship we need to examine its undergirding theology as well as its practice. Acknowledging that worship practices differed significantly in different locations and periods of time, we can identify several dimensions that seem to have been standard in Christian worship.

Eucharist. Clearly the Eucharist had prominence in the New Testament period. We have evidence in the focus given to Jesus' Last Supper, as well as direct references to the communion meal.[10] However, the prominence is not overly great, as direct discussion of the Eucharist occurs in only a few places in the New Testament. This suggests that the Eucharist may have then had lesser prominence than it did later in church history. The evidence we have indicates that the meal was understood to be a "remembering" of Jesus' Last Supper, which itself pointed to Jesus' death (1 Cor 11:24). It also functioned as a rite of participation in the events that were remembered—the word *anamnesis* (remembrance) involves "an action whereby the object is re-presented in memory."[11] There was a sense then, of Christ's death—the sacrifice of his life—being re-expressed in the meal (1 Cor 10:16). The early church had a sense that the matter re-presented was presently operative in its effects. This concept of the present effectiveness of the re-presentation of Christ's death easily led to the sense that the Eucharist was a sacrifice, because it re-presented the original sacrifice.[12]

---

[9]Examples of the kiss as part of the liturgy can be seen in Justin Martyr *First Apology* 65 (*ANF* 1:185); Hippolytus *Apostolic Tradition* 4.1; 18.3-4; 22.6; *Apostolic Constitutions* 2.7.57; 8.2.11; (*ANF* 7:422, 486); *The Divine Liturgy of James* 2 (*ANF* 7:541); *The Liturgy of the Blessed Apostles* 10 (*ANF* 7:563).

[10]For example, 1 Cor 5:8; 10:16-21; 11:20-34. One can also note the apparently eucharistically related references to "breaking of bread" (Acts 2:42, 46; 20:7) and to "love feasts," meals originally associated with the Eucharist (Jude 12).

[11]J. Behm, "Anamnesis," in *Theological Dictionary of the New Testament*, ed. G. Kittel, trans. G. W. Bromiley (Grand Rapids, Mich.: Eerdmans, 1964), 1:348; also 1 Cor 10:16-22; also D. G. Dix, *The Shape of the Liturgy* (Glasgow: University Press, 1945), pp. 243, 245.

[12]Dix, *Shape of the Liturgy,* pp. 245-46.

The Eucharist, though connected with the Jewish Passover, was not simply a Christian repetition of that rite. The fact is that the rite of the paschal meal was too complicated for frequent repetition.[13] Furthermore, one can sense likely echoes of a Jewish fellowship meal, the *chaburah* (used to inaugurate the sabbath and used on other occasions when friends gathered), in the Eucharist (cf. 1 Cor 11:17-22, 33-34).[14] Yet another possible influence is the Greco-Roman *eranos* or potluck meal, where invitees contributed to the meal (cf. 1 Cor 11:17-22, 33-34).[15] Thus while its connection with the Jewish Passover certainly shaped the Eucharist, other influences contributed to its shape as well.

By the end of the first century the Eucharist was clearly a prominent feature of worship. The *Didache* indicates the centrality of the Eucharist to worship in that community (*Did.* 9; 10; 14). It strongly associated the rite with thanksgiving (*eucharistia*) (*Did.* 9.1, 2, 3; 10.1, 2, 3, 4, 7; 14.1), and accordingly called the rite by that name (*Did.* 9.1, 5). This was the name thereafter commonly given to the meal. Half a century earlier, Paul had not spelled out the appropriate participants in the rite, although he had expressed a concern that participants not eat "in an unworthy manner" (1 Cor 11:27). The *Didache*, however, clarifies who may participate. Only those "baptized in the name of the Lord" were to partake (*Did.* 9.5). As a result, in the early church the weekly gathering came to have two parts, first the *synaxis,* a general worship meeting open to all, then the *Eucharist* proper for the baptized (the nonbaptized being dismissed before this was held).[16] Limiting the Eucharist to the baptized became the standard view of the church. Half a century later, Justin articulated this carefully:

> And this food is called among us *Eucharistia* [the Eucharist], of which no one is allowed to partake but the man who believes that the things which we teach are true, and who has been washed with the washing that is for the remission of sins, and unto regeneration, and who is so living as Christ has enjoined.[17]

One reason for defining participants in the Eucharist more closely was the high view of the significance of the meal. According to second-century Justin Martyr, the elements had ceased to be "common bread and drink." In his words, "the food which is blessed by the prayer of his word . . . is the flesh and blood of that Jesus who was made flesh."[18]

---

[13]J. A. Jungmann, *The Early Liturgy: To the Time of Gregory the Great* (London: Darton, Longman & Todd, 1959), p. 31.

[14]Ibid.

[15]P. Lampe, "The Eucharist: Identifying with Christ on the Cross," *Interpretation* 48 (1994): 36-49, see pp. 38-39. The *chaburah* meal could, however, also have this potluck dimension.

[16]Dix, *Shape of the Liturgy,* p. 36.

[17]Justin Martyr *First Apology* 66 (*ANF* 1:185).

[18]Ibid.

The Eucharist began in the context of a full meal (1 Cor 11:17-34). Fairly quickly, however, the substantial meal (*agapē* or love feast) became separated from the Eucharist proper. Problems linked with the love feast (e.g., gluttony) may have caused its separation from the Eucharist—that problem had appeared as early as the time of 1 Corinthians. Alternatively, increasing formalization of the eucharistic ritual may have made the love feast seem out of place in a eucharistic setting.

The *Didache,* with its reference to the giving of thanks "after being filled" at the Eucharist, suggests that the two meals still occurred together (*Did.* 10.1). However, in about A.D. 112, when Governor Pliny of Bithynia wrote to the Roman emperor, describing, among other things, the worship of Christians, he seemed to be describing two separate meals and meetings. The first, before daybreak, probably involved the Eucharist. While not spelled out, it does refer to the Christians binding themselves with an oath at this meal, which may reflect the solemnity of the Eucharist. The letter then refers to a second meeting, apparently in the evening, "to take food, but ordinary and harmless food," probably the love feast.[19] A century later, both Tertullian and Minucius Felix in North Africa provide evidence of the love feast being held at nighttime.[20] Justin Martyr's mid second-century description of the Eucharist makes no mention of a love feast at all. Collectively this data points to the second-century church increasingly holding its Eucharist on Sunday mornings, and its love feast as a separate occasion in the evening.[21] Tertullian himself nevertheless still appeared to connect the two, referring to "the sacrament of the Eucharist, which the Lord . . . commanded to be eaten at meal-times."[22] Gradually the love feast largely disappeared from view, though it was still significant enough to need regulation by canon 74 of the Quinisect Council in 692.[23]

At its beginnings the Eucharist was fundamentally a memorial to or thanksgiving for the death of Christ. This understanding persisted in the early third-century *Apostolic Tradition* of Hippolytus: "Having in memory, therefore, his death and resurrection, we offer you the bread and the cup, giving you thanks because you counted us worthy to stand before you and minister to you."[24] However, the early church also viewed the elements as the embodiment of Christ. In Ignatius's words,

---

[19]Pliny *Letter* 10.96.

[20]Tertullian *Apology* 39 (ANF 3:47); Minucius Felix *Octavius* 9 (ANF 4:178).

[21]Tertullian *On the Crown* 3 (ANF 3:94).

[22]Ibid.

[23]Beckwith, "Daily and Weekly Worship," p. 148.

[24]*Apostolic Tradition* 4.11 (trans. B. S. Easton, *The Apostolic Tradition of Hippolytus* [Cambridge: Cambridge University Press, 1934]).

Figure 8.1. Eucharistic loaves and fish. While this third-century picture from the cemetery of Domitilla in Rome depicts the miracle of the loaves and fishes, it also carries overtones of the Eucharistic meal. (Scala/Art Resource, NY)

"The Eucharist is the flesh of our Savior Jesus Christ."[25] In making this statement, Ignatius was refuting the Docetists who argued that Jesus was not really a man. Ignatius's stress that Jesus really was flesh and blood indicates that Ignatius was not speaking of the elements of the Eucharist in metaphorical fashion, but believed them really to be the body and blood of Jesus. Ignatius does not, however, articulate a theory on the matter, apart from connecting the eucharistic bread with the body of Christ.[26]

In these earlier centuries we do not see total consistency and clarity concerning the nature of the eucharistic elements. Tertullian generally took a literalistic approach: the bread was the body of Jesus because Jesus said so. Thus he could decry unworthy celebrants causing scandal to the Lord's body, and he expressed deep concern if any of the bread or wine should fall to the ground by carelessness.[27] Nevertheless, in one place Tertullian described the elements simply as a

[25]Ignatius To the Smyrnaeans 7.2 (ANF 1:89, English modernized).
[26]C. C. Richardson, The Christianity of Ignatius (New York: AMS Press, 1967), p. 56.
[27]Tertullian On Idolatry 7; On the Crown 3 (ANF 3:64, 94).

"figure" of the body and blood of Jesus.[28] This may suggest that people like Tertullian did not have a tightly consistent theology on this matter, but wrote in varied ways to fit the varying issues they were addressing. However, Tertullian's use of the term "figure" may indicate a belief that the bread and wine were body and blood only in the sense that they were authorized and effective representations of the realities they symbolized.[29]

Overall the early church tended to view the eucharistic elements as having become objectively different through their consecration. Thus the early third-century *Apostolic Tradition* expressed deep concern lest a mouse or some other creature have access to dropped crumbs or spilled wine.[30] To treat an element of the Eucharist lightly was to "despise it and become guilty of the Blood of Christ."[31]

We find an increasing consensus that the eucharistic elements were indeed the body and blood of Jesus.[32] One way of coming to this conclusion was to recognize the spiritual presence of Christ in the elements. Clement of Alexandria, Origen and Augustine all reflect this perspective, based on the Platonic worldview that behind the visible world lay a spiritual world that showed itself in the material elements (such as bread and wine).[33] The elements thus "showed" the deeper reality though they were not directly this reality.[34] However, a new and growing tendency in the fourth and fifth centuries explained the Eucharist as an actual change in the bread and the wine (even though the doctrine of transubstantiation itself did not formally become church dogma in the West until 1215). To quote fourth-century Cyril of Jerusalem:

> The bread and wine of the eucharist before the invocation of the holy and adorable Trinity were simple bread and wine . . . after the invocation the bread becomes the body of Christ, and the wine the blood of Christ.[35]

---

[28]Tertullian *Against Marcion* 4.40 (*ANF* 3:419).

[29]H. B. Swete, "Eucharistic Belief in the Second and Third Centuries," *Journal of Theological Studies* 3 (1902): 161-77, see p. 173 (repr. in *Worship in Early Christianity,* ed. E. Ferguson, Studies in Early Christianity 15 [New York: Garland, 1993], pp. 109-25, see p. 121).

[30]*Apostolic Tradition* 32.2-3. Origen (in *Homily on Exodus* 13.3) likewise spoke of the way Christians guarded carefully "the body of the Lord . . . lest the least crumb of it should fall to the ground, lest anything should be lost of the hallowed gift" (in H. Bettenson, trans., *The Early Christian Fathers* [London: Oxford University Press, 1956], p. 344).

[31]*Apostolic Tradition* 32.3.

[32]See, for example, fourth-century John Chrysostom, who refers to partaking of Christ in the sacrament: *Homilies on Hebrews* 20.3 (*NPNF*[1] 14:458); similarly Gregory of Nyssa, *The Great Catechism* 37 (*NPNF*[2] 5:505-6).

[33]Clement of Alexandria *Instructor* 1.6 (*ANF* 2:220); Origen, *Commentary on the Gospel of Matthew* (on Mt 26:26-28, in D. J. Sheerin, *The Eucharist,* Message of the Fathers of the Church 7 [Wilmington, Del.: Michael Glazier, 1986], pp. 187-91); Augustine, *Commentary on Psalm 99,* 8.

[34]On this point see N. Brox, *The Early Church* (London: SCM Press, 1994), p. 103.

[35]Cyril *Catechetical Lectures* 19.7 (*NPNF*[2] 7:145-46).

How did this change in the elements occur? Again East and West differ. Cyril reflected the general Eastern view, which tended to focus on change occurring through the Holy Spirit acting on the elements:

> We beseech the merciful God to send forth His Holy Spirit upon the gifts lying before Him; that He may make the bread the body of Christ, and the wine the blood of Christ; for whatsoever the Holy Ghost has touched, is surely sanctified and changed.[36]

The Western church placed more focus on the words of consecration effecting a change in the elements. Ambrose illustrates this view:

> For that sacrament which you receive is made what it is by the word of Christ. . . . The Lord Jesus himself proclaims: "This is my body." Before the blessing of the heavenly words another nature is spoken of, after the consecration the body is signified. He himself speaks of his blood. Before the consecration it has another name, after it is called blood.[37]

The increasing sense that Jesus was really present in the elements brought a perception that the Eucharist itself was a fresh sacrifice of Christ to God. While not the first to use the language of sacrifice in relation to the Eucharist, third-century Cyprian was an early exponent of the view that this sacrifice was a reenactment of Christ's sacrifice:

> That priest truly discharges the office of Christ, who imitates what Christ did; and he then offers a true and full sacrifice in the church to God the father when he proceeds to offer it according to what he sees Christ himself to have offered.[38]

Language of "sacrifice" became associated with the eucharistic meal very early, the first reference being in *Didache* 14.2.[39] However, that usage appears to have been metaphorical, a simple echoing of Malachi 1:11. In context, the sacrifice in the *Didache* was a sacrifice of thanksgiving rather than a sacrifice of atonement.[40] This is not the case with Cyprian. He views the Eucharist as having an objective efficacy such that it has benefits for others, and perhaps even for the dead.[41] Cyprian marks a major shift away from "thanksgiving" and toward "sacrifice" as the dominant motif of the Eucharist.[42]

---

[36]Ibid., 23.7 (*NPNF²* 7:154).
[37]Ambrose *On the Mysteries* 9.52, 54 (*NPNF²* 10:324-25).
[38]Cyprian *Letter* 62.14 (*ANF* 5:362).
[39]For other usages indicating that the Eucharist is a "sacrifice," see Ignatius, *To the Philadelphians* 4 (*ANF* 1:81); Justin Martyr, *Dialogue with Trypho* 117.1 (*ANF* 1:257).
[40]Oskar Skarsaune, *In the Shadow of the Temple: Jewish Influences on Early Christianity* (Downers Grove, Ill.: InterVarsity Press, 2002), p. 420.
[41]Cyprian *Letters* 15.1; 65.2 (*ANF* 5:295, 367).
[42]D. R. Lindsay, "*Todah* and Eucharist: The Celebration of the Lord's Supper as a 'Thanksgiving' in the Early Church," *Restoration Quarterly* 39, no. 2 (1997): 83-100, see p. 97.

John Chrysostom also expresses a "sacrifice" theology with regard to the Eucharist: when he refers to Christians having "enjoyed the sacrifice," he explains it as referring to "as many as have partaken of the immortal table."[43] Chrysostom may have felt, nevertheless, that identifying the Eucharist with Christ's sacrifice was a little too bold and lacking in scriptural support. His qualification in the following statement suggests hesitancy or uneasiness on this point: "It is not another sacrifice, as the high priest, but we offer always the same, *or rather we perform a remembrance of a sacrifice.*"[44]

The potency of the Eucharist gave it salvific value. Increasingly it became the chief means of union with Christ when received by faith. Hilary of Poitiers reflected this view in the fourth century:

> For if in truth the Word has been made flesh and we in very truth receive the Word made flesh as food from the Lord, are we not bound to believe that He abides in us naturally, who, born as a man, has assumed the nature of our flesh now inseparable from Himself, and has conjoined the nature of His own flesh to the nature of the eternal Godhead in the sacrament by which His flesh is communicated to us? For so are we all one, because the Father is in Christ and Christ in us.[45]

Emerging views about the Eucharist were now moving the church toward an *ex opere operato* ("by the work performed") view of both Eucharist and baptism—the view that the sacraments automatically impart the grace they signify. The Eucharist soon came to be regarded as having potency for those not physically present and partaking, most particularly in relation to the dead. Cyril of Jerusalem provides a good example of this emerging belief:

> Then, after the spiritual sacrifice, the bloodless service, is completed, over that sacrifice of propitiation we entreat God for the common peace of the Churches. . . . Then we commemorate also those who have fallen asleep before us . . . believing that it will be a very great benefit to the souls, for whom the supplication is put up, while that holy and most awful sacrifice is set forth. . . . In the same way we . . . offer up Christ sacrificed for our sins, propitiating our merciful God.[46]

A marked feature of the Eucharist from the fourth century onward is a deliberate focus on its evoking awe and dread.[47] Various factors have been suggested to

---

[43]John Chrysostom *Homilies on Hebrews* 13.9 (*NPNF*[1] 14:431).
[44]Ibid., 17.6 (*NPNF*[1] 14:449, emphasis added).
[45]Hilary of Poitiers *On the Trinity* 8.13 (*NPNF*[2] 9:141).
[46]Cyril *Catechetical Lectures* 23.8-10 (*NPNF*[2] 7:154).
[47]On this see J. G. Davies, "The Introduction of the Numinous into the Liturgy: An Historical Note," *Studia Liturgica* 8 (1971-72): 216-23; P. Bradshaw, "The Effects of the Coming of Christendom on Early Christian Worship," in *The Origins of Christendom in the West*, ed. A. Kreider (Edinburgh: T & T Clark, 2001), pp. 269-86.

explain this change. One is the influence of paganism. As Christian buildings became more elaborate, they came to be seen as akin to pagan temples—centers of the numinous. Part of this influence no doubt took place at a subconscious level. However, there may well have also been an intentional missiological motive: creating a greater sense of awe and mystery would make new converts from paganism more at home in Christian worship and would make Christianity more attractive to potential converts.

The downside of the tremendous potency and awe felt in Christian worship was that many Christians from about the fourth century, particularly in the East, came to feel unworthy of participation in the Eucharist. When Chrysostom spoke of the eucharistic elements as "fearful and full of awe" and "charged with terror" he must have made people think twice about partaking of the sacred meal.[48] This sort of emphasis often resulted in far less frequent reception of communion, even only once or twice a year, particularly at Easter. To counter this, Chrysostom had to exhort the pure to "draw near continually."[49] The effect of non-communicating attendance at the Eucharist was to sever the act of communion from the rest of the eucharistic action, making it possible to see the Eucharist as complete without partaking of the elements, and thus furthering the idea that the liturgy was something that the clergy did on behalf of a passive laity.[50]

This section has highlighted the way the Eucharist quickly became the central focus of early church worship. Potency was attributed to the Eucharist on the basis that it embodied the reality of Jesus Christ himself and was a repeated sacrifice bringing afresh the benefits of Christ's great sacrifice on the cross. Having explored the significance of the Eucharist proper in early church worship, we now turn to other elements of that worship.

Ministry of the word. The Scriptures of the earliest church were those of the Jews—basically the Old Testament. However, New Testament writings soon gained widespread circulation as authoritative documents, though clarification of the status of a few books on the edge of the emerging canon (the official list of authoritative writings) took several centuries. The mid second-century Justin Martyr provides the first witness to the reading and exposition of New Testament writings in worship:

> On the day called Sunday, all who live in cities or in the country gather together to one place, and the memoirs of the apostles [writings of the New Testament] or the writings of the prophets [the Old Testament] are read, as long as time permits; then,

---

[48]John Chrysostom *On the Priesthood* 3.4 (*NPNF*[1] 9:46-47).
[49]John Chrysostom *Homilies on Hebrews* 17.7 (*NPNF*[1] 14:449).
[50]Bradshaw, "Effects of the Coming of Christendom," p. 278.

when the reader has ceased, the president verbally instructs, and exhorts to the imitation of these good things.[51]

This public reading of Scripture was crucial to the life of the early church. If ordinary members in the early church were to become familiar with the contents of Scripture, it had to be read publicly:

> Reading from a first century manuscript was not as straightforward as we might think, for manuscripts were written entirely in capital letters, there was practically no punctuation, there were no spaces between words, and there were quite a few abbreviations. . . . Most people could not read for themselves (and would not have been able to afford manuscripts if they could) so public reading was very important.[52]

Scripture was formative for the young faith, expounded by great (and not so great) preachers and memorized by monks. Reading and exposition made up regular aspects of the early church liturgy. The great number and high quality of preserved sermons of the church fathers demonstrates the vital continuing role of preaching in the first centuries of the church.

Prayer. Early liturgies highlight the importance of prayer. While early worship included extempore prayer, we have clear evidence that set prayers were being crafted within the period of New Testament formation. The primitive oral version of the Lord's Prayer recorded in Luke 11:2-4 became a polished liturgical prayer in Matthew 6:9-13 through community shaping processes. The slightly later *Didache* displays further shaping, with the addition to the Lord's Prayer of the doxology: "for yours is the power and glory forever" (*Did.* 8.2). This addition is now an integral part of the Lord's Prayer despite its post-New Testament origin.

Given the low percentage of educated people in the largely plebeian Christian movement, one could anticipate that worship leaders would need prayer templates. While the *Didache* prescribes prayers at the Eucharist, they were not rigidly fixed—prayer was to be uttered "after this manner" (*Did.* 9.1; 10.1). Moreover, the standard prayers could be set aside because of Spirit inspiration: "allow the prophets to give thanks in such terms as they wish" (*Did.* 10.7). This suggests that set prayers were developed and used on a pragmatic basis; they were helpful for the less articulate and the less inspired, but were not essential.

---

[51]Justin Martyr *First Apology* 67 (*ANF* 1:186).
[52]L. Morris, "The Saints and the Synagogue," in *Worship, Theology and Ministry in the Early Church: Essays in Honor of Ralph P. Martin,* ed. M. J. Wilkens and T. Paige (Sheffield: JSOT Press, 1992), pp. 39-52, quote p. 47.

A blend of free and fixed forms of prayer seems to have persisted for another century or two.[53] Mid second-century Justin Martyr suggests as much by saying the president offers "prayers and thanksgivings" over the Eucharistic elements "according to his ability."[54] Tertullian boasts of heartfelt extempore prayer for the emperor:

> Thither we lift our eyes, with hands outstretched, because free from sin; with head uncovered, because we have nothing whereof to be ashamed; finally without a monitor, because it is from the heart we supplicate.[55]

While the slightly later *Apostolic Tradition* abounds in prayers for various occasions, flexibility persists:

> The bishop shall give thanks as we have prescribed. It is not, to be sure necessary for anyone to recite the exact words that we have prescribed, by learning to say them by heart in his thanksgiving to God; but let each one pray according to his ability. If, indeed, he is able to pray competently with an elevated prayer, it is well. But even if he is only moderately able to pray and give praise, no one may forbid him; only let him pray sound in the faith.[56]

The fact that the document felt the need to clarify that flexibility remained an option suggests that in popular practice it was in fact disappearing. Further, the final qualification that the prayers must be orthodox also points to the prayers increasingly becoming stereotyped. From the fourth century, residual flexibility fast evaporated. The transition "from freedom to formula" was for the most part completed.[57] Set forms of worship became a prescribed treasure, not to be altered—a dimension fundamental in the Orthodox Church to the present.[58]

A primary motif in Christian prayer was joy—rejoicing over the gift of life in creation and of new life in Christ.[59] This may be linked with the joy of Christ's presence among them, particularly expressed in the Eucharist. The common posture of standing symbolized that joy.[60]

Hymn singing. Singing hymns to the Divine formed part of first-century Jewish

---

[53]R. P. C. Hanson, "The Liberty of the Bishop to Improvise Prayer in the Eucharist," in *Vigiliae Christianae* 15 (1961): 173-76, see p. 176 (repr. in *Worship in Early Christianity,* ed. E. Ferguson, Studies in Early Christianity 15 [New York: Garland, 1993], pp. 83-86, see p. 86).

[54]Justin Martyr *First Apology* 67 (ANF 1:186).

[55]Tertullian *Apology* 30 (ANF 3:42).

[56]*Apostolic Tradition* 10.3 (trans. B. S. Easton).

[57]C. Markschies, *Between Two Worlds: Structures of Earliest Christianity,* trans. J. Bowden (London: SCM Press, 1999), p. 163.

[58]T. Ware, *The Orthodox Church* (Baltimore, Md.: Penguin, 1963), pp. 203-4.

[59]Justin Martyr, *First Apology* 13 (ANF 1:166).

[60]Ibid., 67 (ANF 1:186); Tertullian *On the Crown* 3; *On Prayer* 23 (ANF 3:94, 689).

Figure 8.2. Standing before God in prayer (from a third-century fresco in Rome's Catacomb of Priscilla) (Scala/Art Resource, NY)

as well as pagan worship.[61] It is not surprising then to find hymn singing in the New Testament (Mk 14:26; Acts 16:25; 1 Cor 14:15; Eph 5:19; Col 3:16; Jas 5:13; Rev 5:9-10). Luke appears to have hymns embedded in his Gospel narrative (most obviously the Benedictus, Lk 1:67-79; the Magnificat, Lk 1:46-55; and the Nunc Dimittis, Lk 2:29-32). The fact that these are not distinctively Christian hymns, but are fully appropriate to mainstream Jewish worship most likely points to their Jewish origin. The "singing," being Near Eastern, would be more akin to chanting than to the more melodious Western tunes of later times. The Jewish roots of this singing/chanting can be seen in Tertullian's identifying the singing/chanting of psalms as at the center of Christian worship, alongside the reading of Scripture, preaching and praying.[62]

While community singing by its very nature needs a large if not complete degree of fixity, the early church also seemed to have free Spirit-inspired songs, sung

---

[61]R. Lane Fox, *Pagans and Christians* (New York: Knopf, 1986), pp. 114-16; R. P. Martin, "Hymns in the New Testament: An Evolving Pattern of Worship Responses," *Ex Auditu* 8 (1982): 33-44, see p. 35.
[62]Tertullian *On the Soul* 9.4 (ANF 3:188).

presumably by individuals. References to "spiritual songs" in Ephesians 5:19 and Colossians 3:16 may point in this direction. Paul's reference to singing with the spirit as well as with the mind (1 Cor 14:15) more certainly indicates such a phenomenon. At the end of the second century something of this phenomenon persisted, with Tertullian noting that individuals worshiping at the love feast would bring a hymn to God, "either one from the Scriptures *or one of his own composing*."[63]

Increasingly, however, set songs displaying richness of thought and expression predominated. At the beginning of the second century Pliny appears to refer to the emergence of antiphonal singing: "by turns."[64] In the latter part of the fourth century we find the development of large choirs leading antiphonal singing. Greater sophistication of performance thus accompanied increasing sophistication in hymn singing.

As early as the beginning of the second century, though, the suggestion of Ignatius that the Romans can jointly sing praise that God has deemed Ignatius worthy of martyrdom presupposes a common congregational song.[65] The first surviving Christian hymn in Greek versification appears at the conclusion of the *Paedagogus* or *Instructor* by Clement of Alexandria (end of the second century).[66] While Clement positively affirmed singing, he spoke negatively about instruments accompanying such singing as being too stirring of base emotions, as being "warlike, inflaming to lusts, or kindling up amours, or rousing wrath."[67] For a long time the church remained wary of the emotional dimensions of music as a vehicle for worship.

Increasing sophistication in hymn singing was accompanied by greater sophistication of performance in the latter part of the fourth century, with the development of large choirs leading antiphonal singing. Communal singing can both unite a group and also express the deep feelings of the heart. A demonstrative emotional dimension persisted in early church worship, despite worship becoming more formal. On one occasion John Chrysostom thought congregational members were getting too carried away in contorting their bodies and twisting their raised arms while chanting, and he rebuked them for their behavior.[68]

The North African church had some disagreement over the appropriateness of using music in worship. Augustine, while acknowledging that the persuasive power of singing could lead astray, nevertheless affirmed its use in worship, that

[63]Tertullian *Apology* 39 (ANF 3:47, emphasis added).

[64]Pliny *Letter* 10.96; see also Stanton, "Aspects of Early Christian," p. 85.

[65]Ignatius *To the Romans* 2.2 (ANF 1:74).

[66]Clement of Alexandria *Instructor* 3.12 (ANF 2:295-96). See also G. Kittel and G. Friedrich, eds., *Theological Dictionary of the New Testament*, trans. G. W. Bromiley (Grand Rapids, Mich.: Eerdmans, 1972), 8:502.

[67]Clement of Alexandria *Instructor* 2.4 (ANF 2:248).

[68]J. H. W. G. Liebeschuetz, *Barbarians and Bishops: Army, Church and State in the Age of Arcadius and Chrysostom* (Oxford: Clarendon Press, 1990), p. 183, citing Chrysostom *In illud: Vidi Dominum* Hom. 1.

Clement's *Hymn to Christ the Savior* (verse 1 only):

Bridle of colts untamed,
Over our wills presiding;
Wing of unwandering birds,
Our flight securely guiding.
Rudder of youth unbending,
Firm against adverse shock;
Shepherd, with wisdom tending
Lambs of the royal flock:
Thy simple children bring
In one, that they may sing
In solemn lays
Their hymns of praise
With guileless lips to Christ their King.[a]

---

[a]Clement of Alexandria *Instructor* 3.12 (*ANF* 2:295-96).

"through the delights of the ear the weaker mind may rise up towards the devotion of worship."[69] The benefit applied not only to the "weaker mind" but also to Augustine himself:

> When I remember the tears which I poured out at the time when I was first recovering my faith, and that now I am moved not by the chant but by the words being sung, when they are sung with a clear voice and entirely appropriate modulation, then again I recognize the great utility of music in worship.[70]

Offering. From the beginning, Christians' strong sense of communal identity included a call to assist the weak and vulnerable members of the community (Mt 25:31-46; Acts 2:44-45; 4:32-35; 6:1-6; 11:27-30; 20:35; 2 Cor 8—9; Gal 2:10; 1 Tim 5:16; Jas 1:27; 1 Jn 3:16). Justin Martyr, having described the baptismal and eucharistic practices of his Christian community, prefaced his description of the weekly worship with these words: "the wealthy among us help the weak."[71] Thus

---

[69]Augustine *Confessions* 10.33.50 (trans. H. Chadwick, *Augustine* [Oxford: Oxford University Press, 1991], p. 208).
[70]Ibid.
[71]Justin Martyr *First Apology* 67 (*ANF* 1:186).

liturgy and life belonged together.[72] This sense persisted strongly into the third century, and was urged as a Christian duty by the great preachers of the fourth century. John Chrysostom asked the rich this biting question: "Do you pay such honor to your excrements as to receive them in a silver chamber pot when another man made in the image of God is perishing of cold?"[73]

Back in the second century, Justin Martyr claimed that with conversion, "we who valued above all things else the acquisition of wealth and possessions, now bring what we have into a common stock, and hand over to everyone in need."[74] Fifty years later Tertullian made the boast that Christians had everything in common except their wives.[75] Clearly Tertullian employed rhetorical exaggeration here because he also noted that the giving was voluntary and that donors could make a small donation if they so desired. At the same time, repeated testimony of practical giving and distribution to the needy points to reality rather than mere rhetoric alone. Giving might be in kind or in cash. In the *Didache* it was produce (*Did.* 13). In Justin Martyr and in Tertullian it appears to have been in cash.[76]

While we find strong exhortations to give, according to several of the early sources the giving was voluntary.[77] Tithing was sometimes mentioned, but the stress was rather on radical generosity. Increasingly, however, tithing became a goad to spur on Christians to give at least to that level. This perspective was strong in Augustine:

> Cut off then and prune off some fixed sum; a tenth if you choose, though that is but little. For it is said that the Pharisees gave a tenth. . . . And what says the Lord? "Unless your righteousness exceed the righteousness of the Scribes and Pharisees, you shall not enter into the kingdom of heaven." He whose righteousness you ought to exceed gives a tenth: you do not even give a thousandth. How will you surpass him whom you do not match?[78]

An even stronger goad linked giving with salvation. As early as the writing of the *Didache* we find a sense that giving provided "a ransom for your sins" (*Did.* 4.6). A century later Clement of Alexandria more boldly asserted of almsgiving, "One purchases immortality for money; and by giving the perishing things of the

---

[72]E. Ferguson, "Justin Martyr and the Liturgy," *Restoration Quarterly* 36, no. 4 (1994): 267-78, see p. 269.

[73]John Chrysostom *Homilies on Colossians* 7.5 (*NPNF*[1] 13:292, English modernized).

[74]Justin Martyr *First Apology* 14 (*ANF* 1:167) English modernized.

[75]Tertullian *Apology* 39 (*ANF* 3:46).

[76]Justin Martyr *First Apology* 67 (*ANF* 1:186); Tertullian, *Apology* 39 (*ANF* 3:46).

[77]Tertullian *Apology* 39 (*ANF* 3:46).

[78]*Exposition on the Psalms* 147.13 (*NPNF*[1] 8:668, English modernized). On one tenth being at least a recommended minimum, see also John Chrysostom *Homilies on 1 Corinthians*, 43 (*NPNF*[1] 12:262).

world, receives in exchange for these an eternal mansion in the heavens!"[79] Ambrose made the point with bluntness: "You have money; redeem your sin."[80] The desperate plight of the poor was undoubtedly a factor in Christian teaching moving in this direction. However, giving, which at the birth of the church, was primarily recipient-centered, focusing on the others' needs, at the end of the period under study, stood in danger of being subverted, becoming donor-centered, focusing on the donor's need for salvation.

We should note that while clergy needed financial support from the laity, the early church exhortation to give did not focus primarily on clergy need but rather on relieving the need and suffering of the poor. How the giving was received and distributed is not altogether clear. Certainly one channel of the giving was through the Sunday worship gathering. Thus Paul in 1 Corinthians 16:2 seems to indicate that the church met weekly and that regular offerings were to be received at its gatherings. A century later Justin Martyr indicated that the church at Rome followed this pattern:

> They who are well to do and willing, give what each thinks fit; and what is collected is deposited with the president who succours the orphans and widows, and those who through sickness or any other cause are in want, and those who are in bonds, and the strangers sojourning among us, and in a word takes care of all who are in need.[81]

At the end of the second century Tertullian noted a regular collection for similar purposes, though his discussion indicates that the offering to alleviate social distress occurred at the monthly love feast.[82] That such giving was a regular practice in church gatherings in North Africa seems to be indicated by Cyprian who, in the context of a discussion on almsgiving, rebuked rich Christians who came to the Lord's Supper unconcerned for the poor: "not at all considering the offering . . . without a sacrifice."[83] The presence in third-century North Africa of many churches with storehouses for corn and oil attached demonstrates the remarkable levels of Christian concern for the poor at that time.[84]

The fact that offerings to aid the poor occurred in the context of worship is significant. Worship was not simply vertical (toward God) but also horizontal (to-

---

[79]Clement of Alexandria *Who Is the Rich Man that Shall Be Saved?* 32 (*ANF* 2:600).

[80]Ambrose *On Elijah and Fasting* 20.76 (quoted in B. Ramsay, "Almsgiving in the Latin Church: The Late Fourth and Early Fifth Centuries," *Theological Studies* 43 [1982]: 226-59, quote p. 242).

[81]Justin Martyr *First Apology* 67 (*ANF* 1:186).

[82]Tertullian *Apology* 39 (*ANF* 3:46-47).

[83]Cyprian *Treatise 8: On Works and Alms* 15 (*ANF* 5:480).

[84]A. Ehrhardt, "The Adoption of Christianity in the Roman Empire," *Bulletin of the John Rylands Library* 45 (1962): 97-114, see p. 109 (repr. in *Conversion, Catechumenate and Baptism in the Early Church,* ed. E. Ferguson, Studies in Early Christianity 11 [New York: Garland, 1993], pp. 125-42, see p. 137).

ward fellow-Christians). We should not be surprised at such a breadth in worship, given the strong early church focus on *koinonia* and given that the church held a worldview in which the sacred and the secular formed a unified whole.

Offering was not limited to helping the clergy or the needy; it also involved contributing to the elements of the Eucharist. Thus each communicant brought along a little bread and wine as an "oblation" to be "eucharistized" as the bread and wine of the Eucharist.[85] This gave each baptized worshiper a deep sense of personal participation. In the East the later custom was for the worshippers to bring their oblations for the Eucharist to the sacristy or to a special table before the service began; in the West the laity brought these offerings to the chancel rail at the start of the Eucharist proper.[86] Dix aptly noted the significance of this dimension of worship:

> Each communicant . . . gave *himself* under the forms of bread and wine to God, as God gives himself to them under the same forms.[87]

Sacred Time

We have looked at the regular gatherings of the Christian community. We shall now look at the way time generally was made Christian: each day, each week, and each year.

Daily household prayer. Worship took place not only in congregations but also in the home. Tertullian, in movingly articulating the spiritual oneness of husband and wife, seemed to be referring at least in part to family devotions: "Together they pray, together prostrate themselves, together perform their fasts. . . . Between the two echo psalms and hymns; and they mutually challenge each other, which shall better chant to their Lord."[88] Private prayer was encouraged from early times either twice or, more likely, three times a day. This apparently continued the Jewish custom, which in the first century seems to have held to one or other of those patterns.[89] The *Didache* urged the use of the Lord's Prayer three times a day (*Did.* 8.2). Other early writers also urged thrice-daily prayer.[90] Gradually, the two patterns of thrice-daily prayer (third, sixth and ninth hours) and twice-daily prayer (morning and night) fused into a fivefold pattern of prayer, a practice which both Tertullian

---

[85]*Apostolic Tradition* 4.2; elements offered by a catechumen were not to be received: *Testament of Our Lord* 1.23.
[86]Dix, *Shape of the Liturgy*, p. 120.
[87]Ibid. p. 110, emphasis original.
[88]Tertullian *To His Wife* 2.8 (ANF 4:48).
[89]For thrice-daily prayer, see Daniel 6:10; Psalm 55:17. For twice-daily temple sacrifice, see Josephus *Antiquities of the Jews* 3.10.1; 14.4.3.
[90]Clement of Alexandria *Stromata or Miscellanies* 7.7 (ANF 2:534); Tertullian *On Prayer* 25 (ANF 3:689-90); Cyprian *Treatise 4: On the Lord's Prayer* 34.34 (ANF 5:456).

and Cyprian noted.[91] In the *Apostolic Tradition* of Hippolytus the pattern was supplemented by further prayer at midnight and at cockcrow, thus bathing the day in sevenfold prayer.[92] This part of the *Apostolic Tradition* seems to have a wider focus than clergy only, being specifically addressed to "all the faithful." The fourth-century *Apostolic Constitutions* refers to prayers six times a day, and the document appears to acknowledge that these prayers may be held in the church or at home.[93] That same document also indicates the practice of daily morning and evening prayers in the church for all Christians.[94] Increasing expression of the divine office in a round of daily services of the church probably stemmed in part at least from the monastic vision of sanctifying time through corporate worship. In this regard monasticism was leavening the church as a whole.[95]

One can discern in all this material significant variations, depending on location geographically and chronologically. It is evident, however, that for the pious at least, prayers at set times shaped and pervaded the day. These prayers would likely include recitation of the Lord's Prayer, perhaps some psalms, spontaneous prayer and a hymn.[96]

The Christian week. A significant marker for the rhythms of the week was the general Christian practice of fasting on Wednesdays and Fridays.[97] Tradition explained Wednesday as the day the Jewish council plotted to kill Jesus (Mt 26:2-5) and Friday as the day he was crucified.[98] The custom appears, however, to have had its original inspiration in Jewish practice of twice-weekly fasting (on Mondays and Thursdays), even though the *Didache* argues for the Christian practice as standing in contrast to the days observed by Judaism (*Did.* 8.1). Fasting appeared to be largely voluntary in the earlier centuries, but the fourth-century *Apostolic Constitutions* declares the practice to be mandatory.[99] Regular general fasting appears typically to have lasted only till mid-afternoon of the fast day and to have been a restriction from certain foods only.[100] Despite its limited nature, such fasting brought God into the everyday time of the fasting believer.

The other regular rhythm of the week was the worship gathering. Originally on

---

[91]Tertullian *On Prayer* 25 (ANF 3:689-90); Cyprian *Treatise 4: On the Lord's Prayer* 35 (ANF 5:457).
[92]*Apostolic Tradition* 35—36. For rising to pray at night see also Tertullian *To His Wife* 2.5 (ANF 4:46).
[93]*Apostolic Constitutions* 8.34 (ANF 7:496).
[94]Ibid., 2.7.59; 8.4.35-41 (ANF 7:423, 496-98).
[95]Dix, *Shape of the Liturgy*, p. 329.
[96]B. Ramsey, *Beginning to Read the Fathers* (London: SCM Press, 1993), p. 165.
[97]For example, Tertullian *On Fasting* 2; 14 (ANF 4:103, 112); Augustine *Letter* 36.13.30 (NPNF[1] 1:269).
[98]*Apostolic Constitutions* 5.3.15 (ANF 7:445); Augustine *Letters* 36.13.30 (NPNF[1] 1:269).
[99]*Apostolic Constitutions* 5.3.15 (ANF 7:445).
[100]Tertullian *On Fasting* passim. (ANF 4:102-14).

the Jewish sabbath, it quickly shifted to Sunday (the first day of the week). Hints
of this shift appear in the New Testament itself and find confirmation in early second-century church history data. The New Testament demonstrates that some
meetings at least were held on a Sunday (Acts 20:7), that it appeared to be the regular day of worship for the Corinthian church because Paul enjoined them to hold
their offertory collection on that day (1 Cor 16:2), and that a day was known as
"the Lord's Day" (Rev 1:10). While the first-century data on the Christian day of
worship may not be totally clear, that of the second century is. The *Didache* indicates that the regular day of Christian meeting was "the Lord's Day" (*Did.* 14.1).
Ignatius also provides evidence, speaking of those who "have come to the possession of a new hope, no longer observing the sabbath, but living in observance of
the Lord's Day."[101] Justin Martyr also confirms the change of worship day from that
observed by the Jews, referring to the collective Christian gathering "on the day
called Sunday."[102] The evidence as a whole indicates that the early church soon
held its primary collective worship on a Sunday, a custom to which the three New
Testament references above probably witness.

Not everyone automatically came to divine service each Sunday. The urging of
"not neglecting to meet together" in the New Testament itself evidences this (Heb
10:25). As time went on, nonattendance likely became more of a problem, both
from danger (when persecution threatened) and apathy. As a consequence the
Council of Elvira in 305 set down excommunication as the penalty for a Christian
resident in a town who did not attend worship on three successive Sundays.[103]

Was the Christian Sunday a sabbath held on a different day? The writings of
Paul and other early Christian leaders point to a common Christian conviction, at
least in the Gentile wing of the church, that the sabbath was abrogated (Rom 14:5;
Col 2:16-17).[104] Moreover, Sunday was an ordinary workday in the Roman Empire, making it unlikely that Christians could observe it as a full day of rest even if
they had wanted to (especially if they were slaves). Clearly, sabbath teaching did
have some pull on Christian thinking, especially with the ongoing presence of
Jewish-Christian communities who continued to keep the sabbath. Constantine's
motives for decreeing in 321 that all work except that of farmers should cease "on
the most honourable day of the Sun" remain obscure. The effect, however, was not

---

[101]Ignatius *To the Magnesians* 9 (*ANF* 1:63).
[102]Justin Martyr *First Apology* 67 (*ANF* 1:186).
[103]In Jungmann, *Early Liturgy*, p. 173.
[104]For the common post-apostolic view that the sabbath commandment called for perpetual holiness
   rather than physical rest, see R. J. Bauckham, "Sabbath and Sunday in the Post-apostolic Church,"
   in *From Sabbath to Lord's Day: A Biblical, Historical and Theological Investigation*, ed. D. A. Carson
   (Grand Rapids, Mich.: Zondervan, 1982), pp. 251-98, see pp. 259-61, 265-68.

to move worship to Sunday (that had been done centuries before) but rather to move toward a Sabbatarianism (viewing the Christian Sunday through the lens of the fourth commandment).[105] Significantly, the first Christian writer to suggest that the sabbath had been transferred to Sunday is Eusebius of Caesarea (post 330). Eusebius did not focus, however, on the cessation of work but rather on devoting the day to the service of God.[106]

Many still did not regard work as taboo on Sunday. The fourth-century Pachomian monks were prohibited from washing their clothes on any day other than Sunday.[107] Similarly, nuns in Paula's monasteries in Palestine in the fifth century made garments on Sunday after worship.[108] As late as 523, Benedict's Rule (48.23) laid down that a monk who would not study or read on Sunday should "be given some work to do, so that he may not be idle." There were very few attempts to prohibit Sunday work by ecclesiastical regulation before the sixth century. Thus Sabbatarianism was a medieval, not a patristic, development.[109] At the same time the strong emphasis on Sunday as a worshiping day was a further significant contribution to the Christian sacralizing of time.

The Christian Year

Easter. Through its connection with the Jewish Passover, the observance of Easter began early. Retaining this connection when celebrating Easter tied the Christian observance to the Jewish calendar. One wing of the church (the Quartodecimans) did this precisely, the crucifixion being remembered during the night from 14 to 15 Nisan even though this did not commonly fall on a Friday. Other Christians, while linking Easter to Passover, insisted that the Easter feast should be held on the Sunday after Passover. After controversy in the second century, the views of the second position ultimately prevailed, being officially confirmed at the Council of Nicea in 325.[110] Until the fourth century Easter celebrations were not split between Good Friday and Easter Sunday, but the whole of the Easter story was celebrated on what we would now consider the eve of Easter.[111] The practice of fasting on Easter Saturday emerged in the second century. By the third century Syrian Christians had extended this fast to cover six days prior to

[105]Dix, *Shape of the Liturgy*, p. 336.
[106]Eusebius *Life of Constantine* 4.18 (*NPNF*[2] 1:544).
[107]*The Rules of Pachomius—Precepts* Pr. 67 (in A. Veilleux, ed., *Pachomian Koinonia*, vol. 2: *Pachomian Chronicles and Rules* [Kalamazoo, Mich.: Cistercian Publications, 1981], p. 157).
[108]Jerome *Letter* 108.20 (*NPNF*[2] 6:206).
[109]Bauckham, "Sabbath and Sunday," pp. 282-87.
[110]Indicated in Constantine's letter after Nicea: Eusebius *Life of Constantine* 3.18-20 (*NPNF*[2] 1:524-25).
[111]K. W. Noakes, "From New Testament Times until St Cyprian," in *The Study of Liturgy*, ed. C. Jones, G. Wainwright and E. Yarnold (London: SPCK, 1978), pp. 80-94, see p. 91.

Easter sermon of Gregory of Nazianzus (note how Gregory relives the great events in the past, so that they become present experiences in his life):

Yesterday the Lamb was slain and the door-posts were anointed, and Egypt bewailed her Firstborn, and the Destroyer passed us over, and the Seal was dreadful and reverend, and we were walled in with the Precious Blood. To-day we have clean escaped from Egypt and from Pharaoh; and there is none to hinder us from keeping a Feast to the Lord our God—the Feast of our Departure; or from celebrating that Feast, not in the old leaven of malice and wickedness, but in the unleavened bread of sincerity and truth, carrying with us nothing of ungodly and Egyptian leaven. Yesterday I was crucified with Him; to-day I am glorified with Him; yesterday I died with Him; to-day I am quickened with Him; yesterday I was buried with Him; to-day I rise with Him.

---

[a]Gregory of Nazianzus *Oration* 1:3-4 (*NPNF*[2] 7:203).

Easter Sunday.[112] Around this time baptisms were being held on Easter Sunday, preceded by forty days of instruction. The fusion of the baptising and fasting traditions in the fourth century created a pre-Easter Lent, involving forty days of fasting for all the faithful. This fast involved taking only one meal, the *coena*, in the evening, and totally abstaining from wine and meat during Lent.[113]

Pentecost. By the end of the second century, fifty days of post-Easter rejoicing marked the period of Pentecost.[114] By the fifth century, the Pentecost period was broken by the increasingly universal celebration of Ascension on the fortieth day.

Christmas and Epiphany. The earliest evidence for the celebration of the Nativity on December 25 stems from the middle of the fourth century. The reasons for choosing that date remain unclear. Some scholars argue that it was a Christianizing of the birthday of the sun on that date; others assert that there was a belief that Jesus' life lasted an exact number of years, and that as his death was on March

---

[112]*Didascalia Apostolorum* 21.

[113]Jungmann, *Early Liturgy*, p. 255.

[114]Tertullian *On Idolatry* 14 (*ANF* 3:70); *On Fasting* 14 (*ANF* 4:112); and see also *Apostolic Constitutions* 5.3.20 (*ANF* 7:449).

25, his conception must have been on that date also, resulting in Jesus' birth being on December 25.[115] In other places the birth was celebrated on January 6. Other traditions, such as the epiphany (manifestation) of Jesus to the Magi and the baptism of Jesus, also attached to that day. Eventually the church amalgamated the various traditions and marked both December 25 and January 6 as special days.[116]

Saints' days. We have already seen that the church honored martyrs on the anniversaries of their death from an early period. Multiplication of the number of saints remembered in this way meant an increasing number of holy days and thus an increasingly sacralized year. By the fifth century the calendar was crowded with saints' days: "Hardly a day can be found in the circle of the year on which martyrs are not somewhere crowned," claimed Augustine, who went on to assert that the church had to space out the celebrations to avoid the tedium of habit.[117]

Concluding Comments on the Development of Worship

Two developments particularly stand out in the evolution of Christian worship. One is the increasing number of hours and days that became special. Time was increasingly baptized as "Christian time," a repeating cycle with all sorts of markers reminding the faithful that all of life was God's life, to be lived in awareness of him. The other is the increasing elaboration and formalization of Christian worship, especially from the fourth century. Ceremonial actions, distinctive clothing, processions and music all combined to create a marked sense of the grandeur and otherness of God, who was yet present in Christ in the mystery of the Eucharist.[118]

For Further Reading

Bradshaw, P. *Early Christian Worship: A Basic Introduction.* London: SPCK, 1996.

———. "The Effects of the Coming of Christendom on Early Christian Worship." In *The Origins of Christendom in the West,* pp. 269-86. Edited by A. Kreider. Edinburgh: T & T Clark, 2001.

———. *The Search for the Origins of Christian Worship.* London: SPCK, 1992.

Dix, D. G. *The Shape of the Liturgy.* Glasgow: University Press, 1945.

Ferguson, E. "Justin Martyr and the Liturgy." *Restoration Quarterly* 36, no. 4 (1994): 267-78.

---

[115]On this see P. Bradshaw, *The Search for the Origins of Christian Worship* (London: SPCK, 1992), pp. 202-4.

[116]Ibid. Also P. Bradshaw, *Early Christian Worship: A Basic Introduction to Ideas and Practice* (London: SPCK, 1996), pp. 86-89.

[117]Augustine *Sermon on Denis* 13.1 (in R. A. Markus, *The End of Ancient Christianity* [Cambridge: Cambridge University Press, 1990], p. 99).

[118]Bradshaw, *Early Christian Worship,* p. 64.

Ferguson, E., ed. *Worship in Early Christianity.* Studies in Early Christianity 15. New York: Garland, 1993.

Jones, C. W., G. Wainwright and E. Yarnold, eds. *The Study of Liturgy.* London: SPCK, 1978.

Martin, R. P. "Patterns of Worship in New Testament Churches." *Journal for the Study of the New Testament* 37 (1989): 59-85.

Weinrich, W. C. "Cyprian, Donatism, Augustine, and Augustana VIII: Remarks of the Church and the Validity of Sacraments." *Concordia Theological Quarterly* 55, no. 4 (1991): 267-96.

Wilkens, M. J., and T. Paige, eds. *Worship Theology and Ministry in the Early Church: Essays in Honor of Ralph P. Martin.* Sheffield: JSOT Press, 1992.

9

GETTING IN AND STAYING IN
Baptism and Penance

A fundamental question for any Christian is how to connect with God and receive his grace. Increasingly the early church answer moved in the direction of the sacraments, especially baptism and the Eucharist. A sacrament is commonly viewed as a religious ceremony or act that is an outward and visible sign of inward and spiritual grace. It is a vehicle for encounter with the Divine. Denominations are divided over a precise understanding of the nature of a sacrament and which rites (if any) are sacraments. Part of this confusion stems from early church usage, which itself had no sharp definition or identification of sacraments. Various acts were called a *sacramentum* (Latin) or *mysterium* (Greek). Of the seven rites declared to be sacraments in the medieval Catholic Church, only three rituals seem to have had such significance in the early church that they may be called sacraments: Eucharist, baptism and penance. Here we will focus on the latter two rituals.

Baptism

Baptism clearly and powerfully symbolizes cleansing and renewal. There was major variation of rite and custom depending on time period and location. Nevertheless, our discussion can provide an overview and highlight major features that tended to occur in the complex baptismal process.

The centrality of baptism within Christianity. Christian baptism has its roots in the baptismal practices of John the Baptist. Why John adopted it in the first place is unclear. He may have been drawing from a Jewish practice of baptizing proselytes.[1] However, we have no certain evidence that Jewish proselyte practice

---

[1]J. Jeremias, *Infant Baptism in the First Four Centuries* (London: SCM Press, 1958), pp. 28-40; also T. F. Torrance, "Proselyte Baptism," *New Testament Studies* 1 (1954): 150-54; J. P. Hyatt, "The Origin and Meaning of Christian Baptism," *Encounter* 21, no. 3 (1960): 255-68; K. Pusey, "Jewish Proselyte Baptism," *Expository Times* 95, no. 5 (1984): 141-45.

occurred as early as the first century of the Christian era.[2] Nevertheless, it would be odd if Christians began an initiatory or proselyte baptism and the Jews subsequently took on a similar practice at a time of animosity with Christians.[3] Therefore an arguable case can still be made for Christian baptism having links with already-existing Jewish proselyte baptism. In addition, Christian baptism may have been influenced in some measure by the repeated Essene ritual washings practiced in the Dead Sea area (which may have had influence on John the Baptist who spent some time in that general location).[4] The fact, however, that the Essene washings were daily and related to ritual purity, whereas John's washing was initiatory and apparently a once-and-for-all rite, makes significant connection between John's baptism and the washings of the Essenes unlikely.[5]

Another matter for debate is whether baptism was central in all expressions of New Testament theology. The story of the disciples at Ephesus (Acts 19:1-7) whose baptism was incomplete and needed rectification suggests that Luke and Paul considered baptism as a crucial matter. Other Pauline material also witnesses to baptism's centrality, for example, Romans 6:1-11; Galatians 3:25-27; Colossians 2:12. It should be noted, however, that each of these references links baptism to faith, thus indicating that baptism should not be studied in isolation. Christian initiation in the New Testament was a complex matter involving repentance, faith, baptism, reception of the Holy Spirit and joining with the faith community. Baptism was the locus of this initiation, the place where faith and change were expressed bodily in physical washing and where the Holy Spirit was received.

While Paul emphasized baptism, at times he also somewhat downplayed its role. On one occasion he thanked God that he baptized only a few of the Corinthians, probably saying this to distance himself from the factionalism that had emerged subsequent to his ministry among them (1 Cor 1:14-17). He also cautioned the Corinthian church against relying on baptism if they persisted in evil (1 Cor 10:1-12). Although Paul had a high view of baptism, he did not elevate it in such a way that it overshadowed other dimensions of Christian faith and life (1 Cor 1:12-17). Nor did he have an *ex opere operato* view of baptism—that it automatically worked, irrespective of the inward state of the baptizer or baptized (see

---

[2]J. A. Fitzmyer, *The Gospel According to Luke I—IX*, Anchor Bible (New York: Doubleday, 1979), p. 460; T. M. Taylor, "The Beginnings of Jewish Baptism," *New Testament Studies* 2 (1956): 193-98; D. Smith, "Jewish Proselyte Baptism and the Baptism of John," *Restoration Quarterly* 25, no. 1 (1982): 13-32; A. Y. Collins, "The Origin of Christian Baptism," *Studia Liturgica* 19 (1989): 28-46, see pp. 32-35.
[3]On this and other points supporting Jewish practice of proselyte baptism before the time of Christ see P. E. Harrell, "Jewish Proselyte Baptism," *Restoration Quarterly* 1, no. 4 (1957): 159-65, see p. 160.
[4]Ibid.
[5]Collins, "Origin of Christian Baptism," pp. 31-32.

1 Cor 10:1-5). First Peter also attests to a high view of baptism, with the explicit statement that it "now saves you," but with a recognition that the inner person must correspond to the outer rite, that it should be undertaken by those with a "good conscience" (1 Pet 3:21).

In many ways Christian baptism built on the Jewish understanding of the human person as a whole entity. Although such thought could distinguish inward and outward aspects, it did not do so in a way that separated the two. Jews did not isolate what happened to the body from what happened to the soul. What affected the body could therefore also have spiritual effects.[6] Baptism was thus inextricably intertwined with faith, as the body side of believing. It was a symbolic action paralleling prophetic actions such as that of Isaiah's going naked (Is 20:2-3) or Jeremiah's wearing a yoke (Jer 27:2-7) in order to portray the future. Baptism was similarly an acted parable, setting forces in motion to accomplish what it symbolized.[7] Such a mindset made baptism a crucial rite, though recognizing repentance and faith as coessential.[8]

Thus in the post-New Testament era baptism was clearly the central and culminating rite of Christian initiation. Both mid second-century Justin Martyr and the slightly later Clement of Alexandria noted that baptism was called "enlightenment"—the place where the lights came on.[9] While linking baptism with repentance and faith, Justin explained that in the baptismal rite believers were "regenerated in the same manner in which we were ourselves regenerated."[10] Similarly Hermas was informed that his life had been and would be saved through water.[11] Likewise John Chrysostom in the fourth century saw baptism as the locus of grace. In his view, "we must repent beforehand . . . and so come forward *for grace* [in baptism]."[12] Human response thus only made a preparation for grace, the reception of which came in baptism. It is "the laver [which] causes the sins to disappear."[13] Thus baptism did something: it imparted grace. As the legendary late second-century Thecla was reported as saying: "Only give me the seal in Christ, and temptation shall not touch me."[14] For Ambrose the absolute necessity for baptism was patent:

---

[6]Pusey, "Jewish Proselyte Baptism," p. 143; Hyatt, "Origin and Meaning," p. 265.

[7]Hyatt, "Origin and Meaning," p. 266.

[8]So argued by Augustine at the beginning of the fifth century in *On Faith and Works.*

[9]Justin Martyr *First Apology* 61 (*ANF* 1:183); Clement of Alexandria *Instructor* 1.6 (*ANF* 2:215).

[10]Justin Martyr *First Apology* 61 (*ANF* 1:183); also *Dialogue with Trypho* 13.1; 14.1 (*ANF* 1:200, 201). For similar views on repentance, faith and baptism see Clement of Alexandria, *Instructor* 1.6 (*ANF* 2:217).

[11]Hermas *Visions* 3.3 (*ANF* 2:14).

[12]John Chrysostom *Instructions to Catechumens* 2.3 (*NPNF*[1] 9:167, emphasis added).

[13]Ibid.

[14]*Acts of Paul and Thecla* (*ANF* 8:489).

Even the catechumen believes in the cross of the Lord Jesus, wherewith he too is signed; but unless he be baptized in the name of the Father, and of the Son, and of the Holy Spirit, he cannot receive remission of sins nor gain the gift of spiritual grace.[15]

Though Christian initiation developed in a complex manner, baptism was the locus of rebirth. Faith, however, was not ignored. Justin, for example, saw a trilogy of "water and faith and wood [i.e., the cross]" as the means of salvation.[16] Likewise Basil in the fourth century spoke of the interdependence of faith and baptism: "Faith and baptism are two kindred and inseparable ways of salvation: faith is perfected through baptism, baptism is established through faith."[17]

At the same time, however, faith increasingly became faith as expressed by the creed. It became less an interior matter, less faith-as-trust, and more something to be memorized and recited. Such a perspective facilitated the development of the concept of proxy faith, a looking to the faith of the community when the faith of the baptized individual might be lacking, as with infant baptism.[18]

Baptism had such centrality that increasingly the view emerged that without baptism there is no salvation. This powerful view later spurred the church toward an eventually universal practice of infant baptism. The view that there was no salvation without baptism posed a problem, however, in relation to the righteous saints of the Old Testament. Tertullian had sufficient theological nimbleness to scramble around this problem: faith without baptism was enough for the earlier era, but for the later era now, the fuller revelation of Christ required baptism.[19] Hermas lacked that nimbleness: in his view the Old Testament saints of necessity received after-death baptism in order to obtain life.[20]

The view that baptism was essential for salvation also created a dilemma in relation to catechumens who were martyred prior to completing their initiation in baptism. This difficulty was resolved by the view that such persons were in fact baptized—in their own blood.[21] Another difficulty related to the fact that baptism itself was regarded as the mechanism by which sins were removed, and that it dealt with sins only up to the date of baptism. Initially this suggested that there may be no cleansing for serious postbaptismal sin—no second chance.

Such a quandary led to the emergence of the ritual process of penance as a "sec-

---

[15]Ambrose On the Mysteries 4.20 (NPNF[2] 10:319).

[16]Justin Martyr Dialogue with Trypho 138 (ANF 1:268).

[17]Basil On the Holy Spirit 12.28 (NPNF[2] 8:18).

[18]See, for example, Augustine On Baptism 4.24.32 (NPNF[1] 4:461-62).

[19]Tertullian On Baptism 13 (ANF 3:676).

[20]Hermas Similitudes 9.16 (ANF 2:49).

[21]For example, Tertullian On Baptism 16 (ANF 3:677); Hippolytus Apostolic Tradition 19.

ond baptism" to deal with postbaptismal sin. Another development, especially in the fourth century, was the delaying of baptism, lest subsequent sin negate its efficaciousness. Augustine, for example, desired baptism as a boy at a time of dangerous illness. His mother, however, stopped this from happening because, in Augustine's words, "the guilt of my future sins would be both greater and more dangerous after baptism."[22] Some believers delayed their baptism as long as possible, even till death's door, so that when the ritual occurred, it might cleanse an entire lifetime of sinning. This approach required great skill and calculation: delaying baptism as long as possible, but making sure baptism occurred before death intervened. The emperor Constantine displayed excellent judgment in this regard, being baptized at the end of his life and dying just a few days later.

The conundrum of nakedness in baptism. Baptism, understood in the most profound way, was a "washing . . . for the remission of sins and unto regeneration,"[23] a "spiritual circumcision,"[24] a rebirth. As a new creation, it was commonly paralleled with that of Adam. John Chrysostom, for example, said of the "laver of regeneration," that "it creates and fashions us anew, not forming us again out of earth, but creating us out of another element, namely, of the nature of water."[25] Cyril of Jerusalem stressed the naked dimension of this new creation, paralleling not only the nakedness of Christ on the cross, but also the nakedness "of the first-formed Adam who was naked in the garden and was not ashamed."[26] This most radical understanding of baptism as a new creation most likely explains the practice of "naked" baptism of both men and women, despite the extreme modesty of the early church in relation to the public covering of the body.[27] Baptism was so radical a rite of passage that it used the language of "tomb" (death) and "womb" (birth) to explain its nature.[28] In the same way that a baby emerged naked in physical birth, only nakedness in baptism could adequately depict the new birth process. Baptism's radical nature called for dramatic representation that appeared to flout the basic modesty of the early church.

Nakedness in baptism raises a conundrum, however: given the church's strict-

---

[22]Augustine *Confessions* 1.11 (trans. T. Matthew and D. R. Hudleston [London: Collins, 1923]).

[23]Justin Martyr *First Apology* 61 (*ANF* 1:183).

[24]John Chrysostom *Homily 6 on Col* 2.6, 7 (*NPNF*[1] 13:285).

[25]John Chrysostom *Instructions to Catechumens* 1.3 (*NPNF*[1] 9:162).

[26]Cyril of Jerusalem *Catechetical Lectures* 20.1 (*NPNF*[2] 7:147).

[27]For a fuller discussion of the baptism of women by male clergy see later in this chapter.

[28]On the language of tomb and womb see John Chrysostom *Baptismal Instruction* 10.8, and *In Principium Actorum* 6; Ambrose *Concerning the Sacraments* 3.11; 4.21 (*NPNF*[2] 10:318, 319); Narsai *Homily 21 on Baptism*; Augustine *Homilies on the First Epistle of John*, Homily 1.5 (*NPNF*[1] 7:463); Theodore of Mopsuestia *On Baptism* 4; T. M Finn, *From Death to Rebirth: Ritual and Conversion in Antiquity* (New York: Paulist, 1997), pp. 254-56.

ness and emphasis on modesty in sexual matters, how could it have male clergy baptizing naked female candidates? One possibility is that in fact female deaconesses baptized female candidates, with no males present. Tertullian, however, at the beginning of the third century, emphatically denied the right of women to baptize.[29] In no way should a woman exercise "any masculine function, still less to the priestly office."[30] Half a century later, Firmilian, bishop of Caesarea, denounced a woman who baptized as being the agent of a "most wicked demon."[31] The vehemence and frequency of such language against women baptizing suggests that in mainstream Christian circles women could not have commonly been permitted to baptize other women, issues of modesty not withstanding.[32]

One document giving some degree of comprehensive discussion of the matter is the third-century Syrian *Didascalia Apostolorum*. That document contains discussion of the need to have deaconesses provide full body anointing for women at their baptism, for "it is not fitting that women should be seen by men."[33] At the same time the document makes clear that the deaconesses' role is simply to anoint; the baptism itself is clearly to be done by bishop, presbyters or deacons.

The acknowledgment that it was not fitting for a man to see a woman's body suggests a second solution to the conundrum: the nakedness was not absolute. The Greek term *gymnos*, translated "nakedness," might simply indicate the absence of outer garments, without which a decent person did not appear in public.[34] John Chrysostom seems to support such an understanding in referring to the about-to-be-baptized as disrobing after catechetical instruction and then being conducted to the exorcizers (the final major process prior to baptism) as follows: "removing your shoes and raiment, unclad and unshod, with but one garment on."[35] This seems to indicate that in Chrysostom's view the baptized, though "naked," still had a basic covering.

A third possibility is that male clergy did baptize women who were indeed na-

---

[29]Tertullian *On the Veiling of Virgins* 9 (ANF 4:33); *Refutation of Heresies* 41 (ANF 3:263); *On Baptism* 17 (ANF 3:677).

[30]Tertullian *On the Veiling of Virgins* 9 (ANF 4:33).

[31]In Cyprian *Letters* 74.11 (ANF 5:393); see also *Apostolic Constitutions* 3.1.9 (ANF 7:429).

[32]Contrast E. J. Christensen, "Women and Baptism," *Studia Theologica* 35 (1981): 1-8.

[33]*Did. Ap.* 16.3.12 (trans. R. H. Connolly, *Didascalia Apostolorum* [Oxford: Clarendon, 1929], p. 146). For an almost identical ruling over a century later see *Apostolic Constitutions* 3.2.15-16.

[34]For such a possible meaning of *gymnos*, see W. F. Arndt and F. W. Gingrich, *A Greek-English Lexicon of the New Testament and Other Early Christian Literature*, 2nd ed. of the translation of the 4th revised and augmented ed. of Walter Bauer's *Griechisch-Deutsches Wörterbuch* (Chicago: University of Chicago Press, 1979), p. 167.

[35]John Chrysostom *Instructions to Catechumens* 1.2 (NPNF[1] 9:160). See also Theodore of Mopsuestia *Instructions to Candidates for Baptism*, Part 2, Sermons 2-4, for similar references to removal of *outer* garments.

Figure 9.1. The epitaph of Aquila

ked. There is evidence that this may have happened, at least in some situations. We have one example on the Epitaph of Aquila from the fourth century, which clearly depicts a naked girl (probably preadolescent) being baptized by two men, one of whom is wearing priestly robes.[36]

Incorporating all the data into one coherent explanation is difficult. Overall, however, it seems that male clergy regularly undertook baptism of adult female candidates. In a few situations at least, the female candidates may have been stark naked. Most commonly, however, the situation described by John Chrysostom was the norm: the disrobing left the catechumen covered by one basic garment only.[37]

Description of baptism as "nakedness" highlights baptism's importance in the early church. It was such a radical new beginning—it really was a new birth—that only the language of nakedness adequately described this rite of passage, and only

---

[36]H. Leclercq, "Nudité Baptismale," in *Dictionnaire D'Archeologie Chretienne et de Liturgie,* vol. 12, ed. F. Cabrol, H. Leclerq and H. I. Marrou (Paris, Letouzey et Anbe, 1936), pp. 1801-5, see p. 1803.
[37]For a fuller discussion of this topic, see my article, "Naked Baptism in the Early Church: The Rhetoric and the Reality," *Journal of Religious History* 27, no. 2 (2003): 133-42.

some level of nakedness was appropriate for this rebirth drama.

The early practice of baptism. We can be fairly sure that early baptism was not normally by sprinkling. Other possible alternatives were pouring (affusion) and immersion. Probably immersion was the norm. A number of factors point in this direction. First the wider usage of the word *baptizō* generally has the sense of dipping or immersing, for example, the dyeing of cloth. Second, John's location at Salim, because "there was much water there," suggests a practice that used a lot of water (Jn 3:23). Third, immersion better expresses the radical notion of rebirth, of dying and rising again, that is central to baptismal theology (Jn 3:3-6; Rom 6:1-11; Tit 3:5). Fourth, the continuing practice of the Orthodox Church is to immerse (babies). One can imagine a shift in practice toward sprinkling in the West after infant baptism became the norm. It is difficult to imagine a shift in the East toward immersion after infant baptism became the norm. Finally, the concession of the *Didache* in allowing pouring where factors made the normal mode of baptism problematic also points toward baptism by immersion (*Did.* 7.3). The church took the mode of baptism seriously, with immersion a normal requirement, though not an absolute one. This can be seen in Cyprian's response to persons who were troubled about the validity of affusion or sprinkling where the baptized was sick. Cyprian traversed the matter carefully, but stressed that the act of God and the faith of the recipient, not the amount of water, was the vital matter.[38]

On the other hand, shortage of water may well, to some extent, have led to pouring instead of immersion. This might particularly be the case when baptisteries were built, some scholars asserting that archaeological evidence indicates that baptistries commonly lacked the depth for full immersion.[39] For example, the depth of the baptistery in the earliest church that was no longer utilized as a house but rather as a church—the church at Dura-Europos in the mid third century—is only 0.955 meters. However, thigh-deep water is sufficient for immersion, and commonly used language of going down into or being plunged into or being covered with water points in the direction of immersion.[40] Nevertheless, numerous baptisteries have a depth even less than the one at Dura-Europos, and those therefore tend to rule out full immersion (though allowing for affusion or for the im-

---

[38]Cyprian *Letters* 75.12-17 (*ANF* 5:400-402).

[39]On this argument, see C. E. Pocknee, "The Archaeology of Baptism," *Theology* 74 (1971): 309-11; J. E. Taylor, *John the Baptist within Second Temple Judaism: A Historical Study* (London: SPCK, 1997), p. 53; C. F. Rogers, "Baptism and Christian Archaeology," in *Studia Biblica et Ecclesiastica: Essays Chiefly in Biblical and Patristic Criticism* (Oxford: Clarendon, 1903), pp. 239-58.

[40]On this see W. N. Cote, *The Archaeology of Baptism* (London: Yates & Alexander, 1876), pp. 16, 19, 22, 134 and passim. See also Tertullian *On Baptism* 2 (*ANF* 3:669); Cyril of Jerusalem *Catechetical Lectures* 17.14 (*NPNF*[2] 7:127).

Figure 9.2. The baptistery of the house church at Dura-Europos, mid-third century (Christian Baptistery [reconstruction] Dura-Europos Collection)

mersion of the head without the immersion of the whole body).[41] The church most likely practiced full immersion, partial immersion and affusion at various times and places in the early centuries, with sprinkling being practiced rarely (and probably only for medical reasons) during that time period.

The earliest Christian baptisms were probably administered "in the name of Jesus" (Acts 2:38; 8:16; 19:5). However, baptism in the threefold trinitarian name was also a very early alternative practice (Mt 28:19). This then led to threefold immersion, a practice that persists in the Orthodox Church to the present. Ambrose bore witness to such practice in Milan in the fourth century:

> You were asked: "Do you believe in God the Father almighty?" You said: "I do believe," and you dipped, that is you were buried. Again you were asked: "Do you believe in our Lord Jesus Christ and his cross?" You said: "I do believe," and you dipped. So you were also buried together with Christ. For who is buried with Christ rises again with Christ. A third time you were asked: "Do you believe also in the Holy

---

[41]On this see J. G. Davies, *The Architectural Setting of Baptism* (London: Barrie and Rockliff, 1962), pp. 23-26.

Spirit?" You said: "I do believe," and you dipped a third time, so that the threefold confession absolved the multiple lapse of the higher life.[42]

Early baptism lacked the complex richness of ritual that emerged later. The New Testament reveals no standard process or ritual beyond the plunging of the baptized under water. Most likely, "Christian baptism at first dispensed with catechesis," and "it was spontaneous, unprepared and, indeed, wholesale."[43] While the narratives in the Gospels and in the Acts of the Apostles may be too brief to argue the point with certainty, they certainly point in this direction.

If there was in fact no prebaptismal catechesis, that situation did not last long. The end-of-first-century *Didache* seems to indicate prebaptismal instruction and one or two days of prebaptismal fasting. Half a century later, Justin Martyr indicated that baptism was preceded by instruction, and followed by prayers, the kiss of peace and communion, but he did not indicate other elaboration.[44] One can note that Justin contains no reference to a formally structured catechumenate, no indication that baptism was restricted to a time such as Easter, no allusion to exorcism or other prebaptismal ceremonies, and no mention of postbaptismal prayer with laying on of hands and anointing.[45] By the end of the second century, at least in the West, however, Tertullian and Hippolytus indicate a much richer and more elaborate process was emerging.

Tertullian describes more of a staged baptismal process. Immediately prior to the baptism apparently came a heightened time of spiritual preparation: "repeated prayers, fasts, bending of the knees, vigils all night through, and with the confession of all bygone sins."[46] In Tertullian's view, baptism itself was not the actual locus for receipt of the Holy Spirit but rather the preparation for it.[47] In his judgment the Holy Spirit was given in the anointing of the body with oil after baptism, accompanied by the laying on of hands.[48] Baptism was normally administered by the bishop, or by a presbyter or deacon as the bishop's delegate, though baptism by a layperson was theoretically possible.[49] While baptism could be administered at any time, the most suitable time was Passover (Easter), with Pentecost as second preference.[50]

---

[42]Ambrose *On the Sacraments* 2.20 (trans. T. M. Finn, *Early Christian Baptism and the Catechumenate: Italy, North Africa, and Egypt,* Message of the Fathers of the Church 6 [Collegeville, Minn.: Liturgical Press, 1992], p. 71).
[43]J. J. Z. Werblowsky, "On the Baptismal Rite According to St. Hippolytus," *Studia Patristica* 2 (1957): 93-105, quote p. 94.
[44]Justin Martyr *First Apology* 61; 65 (*ANF* 1:183, 185).
[45]P. Bradshaw, *The Search for the Origins of Christian Worship* (London: SPCK, 1992), p. 174.
[46]Tertullian *On Baptism* 20 (*ANF* 3:678-79).
[47]Ibid., 6 (*ANF* 3:672).
[48]Ibid., 7; 8 (*ANF* 3:672-73).
[49]Ibid., 17 (*ANF* 3:677).
[50]Ibid., 19 (*ANF* 3:678).

We see even more complexity within baptism in the *Apostolic Tradition* of Hippolytus at the end of the second century.[51] This document sets out four facets of baptism: preparation as a catechumen, penultimate preparation, baptism proper and postbaptismal rites. Each of these will now be explored, first in the *Apostolic Tradition* and then in later developments and variations.

Baptism in the Apostolic Tradition *of Hippolytus*

Preparation as a catechumen in the Apostolic Tradition. The scheme of Hippolytus presents a three-year apprenticeship of training and instruction as the norm.[52] Hippolytus calls catechumens "hearers of the word." The catechumenate was a serious period of "engagement" to Christianity prior to the "marriage" of baptism. It was for "new converts," but inquiry must first be made and testimony heard as to their competence to "hear the word." A long list of restrictions stopped certain classes of people from being enrolled: actors, charioteers, soldiers who might kill people, civic magistrates, eunuchs, diviners, men with concubines and others. The document displayed marked concern about the maintenance of social and sexual order: particular inquiry was to be made on whether the candidate was a slave or was single. Slaves of believers needed their masters' approval, while other slaves needed to live pleasingly for their masters. Single men were to be warned to abstain from impurity, either by marrying or by maintaining celibacy. Only after passing this investigative screening did applicants become catechumens and enter the church's instructional process.

Penultimate preparation in the Apostolic Tradition. At the close of the more general period of instruction, those to be baptized entered a more intensive process. They first needed final approval for baptism, which focused on a life of goodness, expressive of the gospel: "whether they have honoured the widows, whether they have visited the sick, whether they have been active in well-doing."[53] Screening for baptism was a serious matter: sponsors needed to confirm the quality of the candidate's life prior to final selection. Clearly the primary factor in assessing whether or not conversion had taken place was changed behavior. The select group judged ready for baptism then underwent exorcism daily, with a concluding exorcism from the bishop close to the date of baptism. Then final private bathing came on the last

---

[51]One should note that authorship of the *Apostolic Tradition* is a complex issue. The document is unlikely to have originated fully with Hippolytus, though it has been traditionally associated with him.

[52]For directions on the catechumenate, see *Apostolic Tradition* 16—17.

[53]*Apostolic Tradition* 20 (trans. B. S. Easton, *The Apostolic Tradition of Hippolytus* [Cambridge: Cambridge University Press, 1934]). Even though the catechizing process was much shortened later on, screening of candidates to ensure a good moral life persisted: see, for example, a description of the practice of the fourth-century Cyril of Jerusalem in *Egeria's Travels* 45.1-20.

Thursday, followed by fasting on Friday. On Saturday (which does not seem in Hippolytus to be restricted to the Easter season) there would be a final exorcism:

> The bishop shall assemble them and command them to kneel in prayer. And laying his hand upon them, he shall exorcize all evil spirits to flee away and never to return; when he has done this he shall breathe in their faces, seal their foreheads, ears and noses, and then raise them up.[54]

The prominence given to exorcism in Hippolytus and elsewhere, in association with baptism, appears remarkable to twenty-first-century Western eyes. It was, however, consistent with worldviews of that time. Exorcism drew from a dualistic understanding of reality. Everyone was subject to spiritual forces, of God or of the Devil. There was no neutral state in between. This worldview led to a heightened sense of the demonic in the early church. Thus prebaptismal exorcism was vital in order to dislodge the forces or spirits of evil so that a home could be created for the Holy Spirit at baptism.[55] Consequently, the baptismal preparation involved symbolic violence and struggle. Significantly, John Chrysostom paralleled the prebaptismal anointing with that of "wrestlers about to enter the lists."[56] In baptism then, the candidate broke free of the devil's grip, but only after wrestling with "principalities and powers."

In Hippolytus, after the solemn exorcism and sealing of the orifices (so that the expelled demons would not re-enter), the baptismal candidates were to spend the night in vigil, listening to reading and instruction.

Baptism proper in the Apostolic Tradition. The waters in the baptismal tank were consecrated "at cockcrow." The baptized removed their clothing, being baptized "naked." Perhaps because of the "nakedness," children, men and women were baptized successively, presumably with no group viewing the other (to preserve propriety).

Consecration of the "oil of exorcism" and "oil of thanksgiving" came after consecration of the water. Demons were dealt a final blow. As each candidate entered the water they uttered the words, "I renounce you Satan, and all your servants and all your works." This was followed by anointing with the consecrated oil of exorcism, accompanied by words of banishment: "Let all spirits depart far from you." The presbyter, assisted by a deacon, then administered a threefold baptism, after the candidate successively affirmed credal declarations in relation to the Father, the Son and the Holy Spirit. The baptism concluded with a final anointing, this time with the oil of thanksgiving.

---

[54]*Apostolic Tradition* 20 (trans. B. S. Easton).
[55]On this point see Werblowsky, "On the Baptismal Rite," passim.
[56]John Chrysostom *Homilies on Colossians* 6 (*NPNF*[1] 13:287).

***Postbaptismal rites in the* Apostolic Tradition.** Procedures had not yet grown as elaborate as they would later. However, after drying, reclothing and reentering the church, the candidate had prayer with the laying on of hands from the bishop, followed by a further anointing and "signing" (making the sign of the cross) on the forehead with the oil of thanksgiving. At this point, full fellowship with the congregation was expressed by giving "the kiss of peace," something in which catechumens could not participate because "their kiss is not yet pure."[57] Then followed a celebration of the Eucharist. Two extra cups were added to this postbaptismal Eucharist, one with water to symbolize the inward washing that had taken place, the other with a mixture of milk and honey as a token of entry into the promised land.[58] Each of the three cups was tasted three times, a total of nine sips in all, successively in the name of the Father and of the Son and of the Holy Spirit. Already we find a hint that postbaptismal instruction may also be needed:

> If there is any other thing that ought to be told, let the bishop impart it to them privately after their baptism; let not unbelievers know it until they are baptized. This is the white stone which John said: "There is upon it a new name written, which no one knows except the one who receives the stone."[59]

The *Apostolic Tradition* cannot be used to explain the theology and practice of the early church as a whole throughout its first centuries of existence. It simply gives a snapshot of baptism in the church at Rome at the end of the second century. We can, however, note an increasing complexity of ritual before, during and after baptism. The effect on many believers must have been overwhelming. In baptism believers did not go through a minor or brief ceremony. It was a once-in-a-lifetime event, the marker and locus of passage from death to life. As such the church increasingly ritualized the event so that the believer experienced and felt its meaning deeply. The fact that baptism was a complex process involving substantial teaching, rigorous testing and elaborate ritual must be underscored. Herman Wegman aptly concluded, "What is clear is that for Hippolytus, baptism was no one-shot affair, but a way of conversion that was ritually expressed and supported."[60]

The various strands in the complex baptismal ritual drew on biblical texts for justification. It has been ably argued, however, that the real roots of much of the ritual lie elsewhere.[61] The following can be noted:

---

[57]*Apostolic Tradition* 22.6; 18.3.
[58]Also Tertullian *On the Crown* 3; *Against Marcion* 1.14 (ANF 3:94, 281).
[59]*Apostolic Tradition* 23.14.
[60]Herman Wegman, *Worship in East and West: A Study Guide to Liturgical History,* trans. G. W. Lathrop (New York: Pueblo Publishing, 1985), p. 35.
[61]A. J. Chupungco, "Baptism in the Early Church and in Its Cultural Settings," in *Worship and Culture in Dialogue*, ed. S. A. Stauffer (Geneva: LWF Studies, 1994), pp. 39-56.

- Fasting was an initiatory element in the ancient nature rites which developed into the third-century mystery religions.

- Initiation meals were part of the mystery rites.

- Certain mystery rites practiced anointing.

- Facing to the west and to the east may reflect influence from the cult of the sun.

- Drinking milk and honey was an ancient Roman custom for newborn infants designed to strengthen them against sickness and the influence of evil spirits.

- White garments were given to Roman boys as they entered manhood at the end of their fourteenth year. The mystery cult of Mithraism utilized a white garment in initiation.

- Foot washing of guests was a cultural sign of welcome and hospitality.[62]

Thus, much of the increasing complexity of baptismal rites, some argue, is likely the result of borrowings from culture as part of a process of inculturation to make Christianity look more at home in a Gentile milieu, with biblical texts subsequently employed to provide justification for the practice.[63] While such borrowings and adaptations cannot be proven with certainty, they help explain how a simple act in the New Testament became far more complex by the time of the *Apostolic Tradition* and beyond.

Baptism Elsewhere in the Early Church

Catechism in the early church. We have seen hints of a catechetical process in the *Didache* and noted a very extensive process in the *Apostolic Tradition*. What happened in succeeding centuries? Origen gives evidence of catechetical instruction in third-century Egypt and Palestine. The Bible itself stood at the center of this instruction. Origen's biblical homilies, given on a three-year rotating basis, indicate that catechumens had a significant grounding in both Old and New Testaments within a three-year period of instruction.[64] Catechism was by now seen as an essential aspect of the converting process, with the Council of Nicea warning in 325 that there was "need of time" and baptism should not occur quickly after conversion from heathenism to the Christian faith.[65]

Later in the fourth and fifth centuries, however, baptismal preparation became more compressed, such that the catechetical and penultimate processes became

---

[62]Ibid., pp. 43, 45, 47, 49, 51, 52, 53.
[63]Ibid., pp. 39, 50, 55.
[64]On this see Finn, *Early Christian Baptism . . . Italy, North Africa, and Egypt*, pp. 4, 193-94.
[65]Council of Nicea, Canon 2 (*NPNF*[2] 14:10).

fused into one intensive preparation process immediately prior to baptism. Despite the catechetical instruction being reduced to a forty-day period in *Egeria's Travels*, the document indicates that the catechesis still basically explained the message of Scripture, starting with Genesis.[66]

Egeria's description of instruction to the about-to-be baptized:

They have here the custom that those who are preparing for baptism during the season of the Lenten fast go to be exorcized by the clergy first thing in the morning, directly after the morning dismissal in the Anastasis. As soon as that has taken place, the bishop's chair is placed in the Great Church, the Martyrium, and all those to be baptized, the men and the women, sit round him in a circle. There is a place where the fathers and mothers stand, and any of the people who want to listen (the faithful, of course) can come in and sit down, though not catechumens, who do not come in while the bishop is teaching.

His subject is God's Law; during the forty days he goes through the whole Bible, beginning with Genesis, and first relating the literal meaning of each passage, then interpreting its spiritual meaning. He also teaches them at this time all about the resurrection and the faith. And this is called "catechesis." After five weeks' teaching they receive the Creed, whose content he explains article by article in the same way as he explained the Scriptures, first literally and then spiritually. Thus all the people in these parts are able to follow the Scriptures when they are read in church, since there has been teaching on all the Scriptures from six to nine in the morning all through Lent, three hours' catechesis a day. At ordinary services when the bishop sits and preaches, ladies and sisters, the faithful utter exclamations, but when they come and hear him explaining the catechesis, their exclamations are far louder, God is my witness; and when it is related and interpreted like this they ask questions on each point.

At nine o'clock they are dismissed from catechesis, and the bishop is taken with singing straight to the Anastasis, where there is terce. So there are three hours' of teaching a day for seven

---

[66]*Egeria's Travels* 46.

weeks. But in the eighth, known as the Great Week, there is no time for them to have their teaching if they are to carry out all the services I have described. So when seven weeks have gone by, and only the week of Easter remains, the one which people here call the Great Week, the bishop comes early into the Great Church, the Martyrium. His chair is placed at the back of the apse, behind the altar, and one by one the candidates go up to the bishop, men with their fathers and women with their mothers, and repeat the Creed to him. When they have done so, the bishop speaks to them all as follows: "During these seven weeks you have received instruction in the whole biblical Law. You have heard about the faith, and the resurrection of the body. You have also learned all you can as catechumens of the content of the Creed. But the teaching about baptism itself is a deeper mystery, and you have not the right to hear it while you remain catechumens. Do not think it will never be explained; you will hear it all during the eight days of Easter after you have been baptized. But so long as you are catechumens you cannot be told God's deep mysteries."[a]

[a]*Egeria's Travels* 46 (trans. J. Wilkinson, 3rd ed. [Warminster, England: Aris & Phillips 1999], pp. 162-63).

Augustine provides evidence of similar instruction given as a sermon to those seeking to enroll as catechumens (prior to the catechumenate itself).[67] The idea was to give applicants an overall sense of God's salvation history from Genesis to the end of time, not attempting to cover every detail, but at least to cover "the exact turning-points (of the history)."[68] Not only was the catechumenate a formal process; enrolment into the catechumenate was also a formal process, concluding with "signing" (making the sign of the cross) and (in Africa at least) giving salt (a symbol of cleansing) to the candidate.[69]

Eventually, as infant baptism became the norm, a prebaptismal catechumenate disappeared from the vision of the church. Even prior to this, the earlier rigorous

[67]Augustine *On Catechizing the Uninstructed* 3.5; 6.10 (*NPNF*[1] 3:285, 288-89).
[68]Ibid., 3.5 (*NPNF*[1] 3:285).
[69]Ibid., 26.50 (*NPNF*[1] 3:312); Augustine *Confessions* 1.11.

catechetical process had been undermined, both by the increasing enrollment of candidates irrespective of whether they evidenced faith and repentance, and also by the more superficial nature of the catechetical process itself. The universalizing of Christianity in Mediterranean society meant too many candidates for thorough screening and too much pressure to lower the standards. As a result, the "quality assurance program" (catechism) that ensured high entry standards for admission to the church became less and less effective. Infant baptism therefore simply put the last nail in the coffin of a rigorous catechism, and the process itself increasingly disappeared. Only in the twentieth century has the adult catechumenate been revitalized throughout the Catholic Church as part of the decisions of the Second Vatican Council.

Penultimate preparation for baptism in the early church. The *Apostolic Tradition* attests a double screening process, both to become a catechumen, and subsequently to become a baptizand. The fourth-century female pilgrim Egeria, in describing the compressed forty-day Lenten process in late fourth-century Jerusalem prior to baptism at Easter, confirms the persistence of significant screening of those in the final stages of the whole process:

> One by one the ones who are seeking baptism are brought up, men coming with their fathers and women with their mothers. As they come in one by one, the bishop asks their neighbours questions about them: "Is this person leading a good life? Does he respect his parents? Is he a drunkard or a boaster?" He asks about all the serious human vices. And if his inquiries show him that someone has not committed any of these misdeeds, he himself puts down his name, but if someone is guilty he is told to go away, and the bishop tells him that he is to amend his ways before he may come to the font.[70]

Those approved for baptism received a focused time of preparation in which the creed was taught and explained (and also the Scriptures if there was no earlier lengthy period of instruction). The creed was commonly given orally to the candidates two weeks prior to Easter (*traditio symboli*). Candidates then memorized the creed and professed it to the congregation (*redditio symboli*) on the Sunday prior to Easter (in the case of Rome and North Africa) or at the baptism itself (in the case of Syria).

As the prebaptismal period moved toward its climax, it featured a great amount of exorcism (though this appeared to be absent from Syria throughout most of our period of study).[71] Moving into Christ's kingdom required moving out of Satan's realm. This could not take place without intense and sustained struggle, hence the

---

[70]*Egeria's Travels* 45 (trans. Wilkinson, pp. 161-62).
[71]Bradshaw, *Search for the Origins*, p. 172.

prominence given to exorcism. Ritual was acted out drama: the defeating of Satan in battle, the breaking of his hold on the individual's life, the expulsion of Satan from that life. The exorcist thus had a vital role in the baptismal process. This was probably a major factor in the church at Rome alone having fifty-two exorcists in the middle of the third century.[72] Exorcism, administered frequently to the catechumens, culminated in the "scrutiny." In Augustine's situation, this solemn ceremony took place on Saturday evening, eight days before Easter. It involved the exorcist invoking the name of Christ and the Trinity, uttering vituperative biblical condemnations of Satan, imposing hands, hissing in the face of the baptizands, peremptorily commanding the Evil One to depart and physically examining the baptizand to see whether Satan had fully gone.[73] The drama of the exorcism must often have made it a terrifying experience.

The prebaptismal climax occurred on the final Saturday night. Augustine called it "the mother of all vigils." It lasted from the lighting of the paschal candle, signaling the arrival of evening, to cockcrow, heralding the dawn. It was filled with biblical lessons, responsive prayers and biblical homilies, and, for Augustine's church at least, the second recitation of the creed.[74]

The baptismal ceremony in the early church. Rites became increasingly elaborate in a ceremony that was "calculated to make a deep and lasting impression on the candidate's emotions."[75] Ambrose described at least thirteen steps in the process in fourth-century Milan:

1. The "opening." This rite, recalling Jesus' opening the eyes of the blind man using clay and spittle, took place just outside the baptistery and involved touching the candidate's ears and nostrils to invigorate "faith and piety."

2. First anointing. The whole body was rubbed with olive oil. Ambrose saw this as an exorcism that strengthened the candidate for the ensuing struggle with Satan.

3. Renunciation. Facing west, the candidate renounced the devil and his works.

4. Allegiance. Facing east, the candidate spoke words of allegiance to Christ.

5. Entry into the baptistery.

6. Exorcism and consecration of the baptismal water through prayer and tracing the sign of the cross on the waters.

---

[72]Eusebius *History of the Church* 6.43.11 (*NPNF*[2] 1:288).

[73]Finn, *Early Christian Baptism . . . Italy, North Africa, and Egypt,* p. 155.

[74]Augustine *Sermon* 219; Finn, *Early Christian Baptism . . . Italy, North Africa, and Egypt,* pp. 156-57.

[75]E. Yarnold, "Baptism and the Pagan Mysteries in the Fourth Century," *Heythrop Journal* 13 (1972): 247-67, quote p. 259.

7. Threefold immersion. Each immersion occurred after the candidate answered credal questions successively about the Father, Son and Holy Spirit.

8. Anointing of the head as the candidate emerged from the font. For Ambrose this was the rite that signified par excellence the gift of the Holy Spirit.

9. Foot washing (this was a distinctive practice of the church at Milan).

10. Robing in a white garment.

11. Signing with oil as a mark of reception of the Holy Spirit.

12. The kiss (a liturgical welcome into the Christian family).

13. A cup of mixed milk and honey.[76]

Significant divergence arose between East and West in relation to anointing. The West practiced both prebaptismal and postbaptismal anointing. The first strengthened one for the final break with Satan and the latter was associated with the gift of the Holy Spirit. The East practiced only prebaptismal anointing. The Eastern pattern viewed baptism itself as the particular moment of rebirth and the gift of the Holy Spirit, while the Western pattern focused more on the work of the Holy Spirit after baptism.[77] The Western approach increasingly led to the anointing aspect becoming detachable from the rite of baptism so that by the fifth century the rite of anointing (in contrast to baptism itself) was administered by the bishop alone.[78] Here, then, we see the seeds of the later development of confirmation as a separate sacrament. The fifth-century Eastern church also came to have a postbaptismal chrismation. However, divergence between the two regions persisted, with the Eastern understanding still clearly associating the reception of the Holy Spirit with the moment of baptism, and also with the postbaptismal anointing, whereas in the West that reception focused much more on the postbaptismal anointing.

Postbaptismal rites in the early church. Increasing awe and mystery marked fourth-century worship and were reflected also in baptismal practice. Baptism became a "hair-raising," "spine-chilling," "awesome mystery about which it is forbidden to speak."[79] Dramatic postbaptismal rites became progressively more elaborate. A composite description of late fourth-century practice shows that the newly baptized uttered the Lord's Prayer as they emerged from the waters, prayed prayers of intercession, dressed in white garments, received lighted candles (and some-

---

[76]For this complex rite see Finn, *Early Christian Baptism . . . Italy, North Africa, and Egypt,* pp. 60-61.

[77]Finn, *Early Christian Baptism . . . West and East Syria,* pp. 20-21.

[78]Pope Innocent I (402-417) reserved postbaptismal anointing to the bishop alone, because only he had the "plenitude" of the priesthood (Finn, *Early Christian Baptism . . . Italy, North Africa, and Egypt,* pp. 77-78).

[79]John Chrysostom *Catechetical Homilies* 6.15, discussed in Yarnold, "Baptism and Pagan Mysteries," p. 247.

times garlands) and proceeded to the Eucharist chanting the Twenty-third Psalm.[80] In the East, a week of celebrations followed. At this point the "mystery" of baptism was now explained to the newly baptized. According to Cyril of Jerusalem, the rite had become so sacred that its full meaning could not be given to candidates prior to baptism.[81] Yarnold, however, couples this with a missiological explanation—the use of secrecy as a "bait," "to arouse curiosity and to attract outsiders to become members of this fascinating and mysterious society."[82]

The validity of schismatic or heretical baptism. The church has always agreed that there is only one baptism. Where baptismal water has been applied a second time, it has always been on the basis that the first "baptism" was invalid, lacking the real quality of baptism. Issues arose when baptism occurred outside mainstream catholic church life. This typically happened when a schismatic or heretic (the two states not being sharply distinguished in the first centuries) administered baptism.

The issue of the validity of such baptism arose in the middle of the third century when Novatianist schismatics sought readmittance to the church. Bishop Stephen of Rome (254-257) held that their Novatianist baptism was valid, depending not on correctness of the minister, but on correctness of form (in the threefold name). Readmittance to the catholic church should therefore be marked not by baptism but by a simple laying on of hands. Bishop Cyprian of Carthage and his fellow North African bishops took an all-or-nothing stance, vigorously opposing this policy:

> To acknowledge the baptism of heretics and schismatics is in effect to approve them. It is impossible for their baptism to be partly void and partly valid. Whoever can baptize, can also give the Holy Spirit. But if the baptizer cannot give the Holy Spirit, because he is outside the church and therefore is not endowed with the Holy Spirit, he cannot baptize those who come; since both baptism is one and the Holy Spirit is one, and the Church founded by Christ the Lord upon Peter is one also, having its source and principle in unity. Hence it results, that since with them all things are futile and false, nothing of that which they have done ought to be approved by us. For what can be ratified and established by God which is done by them whom the Lord calls His enemies and adversaries?[83]

To Cyprian, baptism involved the bestowal of the Holy Spirit. Heretics and schismatics, being outside the church, were "dead men" and could not bestow the Holy

[80]T. M. Finn, *Early Christian Baptism and the Catechumenate: West and East Syria,* Message of the Fathers of the Church 5 (Collegeville, Minn.: Liturgical Press, 1992), p. 16.
[81]*Egeria's Travels* 46.
[82]Yarnold, "Baptism and Pagan Mysteries," p. 258.
[83]Cyprian *Letter* 69.3 (*ANF* 5:376, English modernized).

Spirit.[84] There was no such thing as part baptism. As heretics could not give the whole, they could not give anything in baptism.

The alternative viewpoint held that baptism was the act of God, not of a man. Therefore, human failure, for example, its administration by defective clergy, did not invalidate the baptism. A remarkable example of this viewpoint appears in a story of Rufinus at the beginning of the fifth century. The story relates that when Athanasius was a boy, he baptized some other children in play. He was observed by Bishop Alexander, who, having ascertained that the necessary baptismal questions had been answered and the water applied, declared that no further baptism was to occur, but that it only needed completion.[85] Whether the events of the story actually happened or not, the narrative highlights the point that the church was beginning to see baptism in *ex opere operato* fashion—as long as the right words were spoken and the rites administered, baptism occurred. Such a view meshed well with the argument that the form of words used in baptism pointed to baptismal conversion being God's act (and therefore not invalidated by defects in the baptizand or baptizer), as John Chrysostom explained in the late fourth century:

> For this reason, when the priest is baptizing, he does not say, "I baptize so-and-so," but, "So-and-so is baptized in the name of the Father and of the Son and of the Holy Spirit." In this way he shows that it is not he who baptizes but those whose names have been invoked, the Father, the Son, and the Holy Spirit.[86]

The opposing views of Stephen and Cyprian still lacked final resolution when Augustine faced the century-old Donatist schism at the beginning of the fifth century. Augustine's distinction between the validity and the fruitfulness of a sacrament became fundamental to Catholic thinking. Validity depends on the act of Christ embodied in the sign rather than on the moral character or ecclesiastical situation of the minister; fruitfulness depends on the dispositions of the recipient. Baptism was the act of God, the priest being no more than the instrument, so that baptism was valid irrespective of who baptized, so long as it was given "in the words of the gospel" (in the name of the Father, Son and Holy Spirit).[87] So even Marcionite, Arian and Gnostic heretical baptism were valid if given in the name of the Trinity.[88] Accordingly, once Donatists were reconciled to the Church, their already valid bap-

---

[84]Cyprian *Letter* 70.1 (*ANF* 5:377).

[85]Rufinus *Church History* 1.14.

[86]John Chrysostom *Baptismal Instructions: Series of Papadopoulos-Kerameus* 3.14 (in E. C. Whitaker, *Documents of the Baptismal Liturgy* [London: SPCK, 1970], p. 36). The same point was made some decades later by Narsai *Homily* 21, who explained the passive voice thus: "It is not he that baptizes but the power that is set in the Names" (in Whitaker, *Documents of the Baptismal*, p. 55).

[87]Augustine *On Baptism* 7.53.102 (*NPNF*[1] 4:513).

[88]Ibid., 3.15.20 (*NPNF*[1] 4:442).

tism would then become efficacious.[89] Likewise people who approached baptism in deceit did not need a further baptism when they genuinely repented.[90] Even in the case of the persisting sinner, baptism had validity: while it might not save in the end, it was still baptism, as was the baptism of Simon Magus, of whom it was declared that he had no part in the inheritance of Christ (Acts 8:9-24).[91]

Figure 9.3. Baptistery at Stobi (Macedonia) dating from the fifth century (Courtesy of Daniel Waugh)

Infant baptism. Scholars generally accept that in the first century or two of Christianity baptism primarily involved adult converts. Whether there were exceptions to the basic pattern from the beginning is a matter of debate. Strong communal identity, involving a sense that the whole family was entering into the new community, may have led to infants also being baptized along with the rest of the family. Such an argument is buttressed by the fact that Jewish circumcision (which in some ways is parallel to baptism) was administered to infants. Moreover, the New Testament tells us that "households" were baptized (Acts 16:33; 1 Cor 1:16).

---

[89]Ibid., 3.13.18; 6.9.14 (*NPNF*[1] 4:440-41, 483-84).
[90]Ibid., 1.12.18 (*NPNF*[1] 4:419).
[91]Ibid., 1.10-13.14 (*NPNF*[1] 4:418).

and these may well have included children.[92] However, the argument for infant baptism in the earliest years of Christianity is an argument from implication only and cannot be claimed as more than a possibility. An indication that infant baptism did not occur, or at least that it did not occur commonly, comes from a mid second-century statement of Justin Martyr. Justin contrasts the lack of choice at birth with the choice one exercises in being baptized.[93] As infants lack choice, this points to adult baptism being the norm if not the universal rule.

Whatever its beginnings, infant baptism soon became a more frequent practice, though still not the norm, by the late second century.[94] Irenaeus of Lyons refers to "infants, children, adolescents, youths and old men" who are "born again to God."[95] Hippolytus bears witness to infant baptism at Rome also: "First baptize the little ones; if they can speak for themselves, they shall do so; if not, their parents or other relatives shall speak for them."[96] Tertullian is evidence of the practice in North Africa too. While he discourages the practice, he utilizes practical rather than theological grounds: those baptized too young may later fall into sin. Better to baptize when the greatest threat of serious sin, especially fornication, is past.[97]

The evidence of the emergence of infant baptism provokes the question, assuming that the practice was not present in the first years of the church, how and why did the church embrace the practice? On the basis of tombstone evidence that closely connects the date of baptism of infants with the date of their death, Everett Ferguson has mounted a strong case for infant baptism beginning as "emergency baptism." As baptism became more and more crucial to salvation, parents and the church would be anxious to administer baptism to those clearly at risk of death whatever their age might be.[98] Because the threat of death was never far away, emergency baptism of infants could later become the general custom.

Practice appeared to predate theology. Theological underpinning of infant baptism came particularly via Origen and Cyprian and was linked to the concept of orig-

---

[92]See, for example, the argument of J. Jeremias, *The Origins of Infant Baptism,* trans. D. M. Barton (London: SCM Press, 1963), pp. 12-32.

[93]Justin Martyr *First Apology* 61 (*ANF* 1:183).

[94]Note David Wright's argument that infant baptism became common only in the fifth century: "The glaring *lacunae* of any agreed theology of infant baptism defies comprehension if the practice had been common, let alone standard, for centuries" (D. F. Wright, "Augustine and the Transformation of Baptism," in *The Origins of Christendom in the West,* ed. A. Kreider [Edinburgh: T & T Clark, 2001], pp. 287-310, see p. 305).

[95]*Against Heresies* 2.22.4 (*ANF* 1:391).

[96]*Apostolic Tradition* 21 (trans. B. S. Easton).

[97]Tertullian *On Baptism* 18 (*ANF* 3:678).

[98]E. Ferguson, "Inscriptions and the Origin of Infant Baptism," *Journal of Theological Studies* 30 (1979): 37-46.

inal sin. Earlier views commonly portrayed the very young as in a state of innocence. Second-century Aristides, for example, stated that Christians gave thanks to God on the death of an infant because it had departed life without sin.[99] Nearly a century later, Origen posed the question, "Why baptize babies?" His answer focused on original sin: "There is in all persons the natural stain of sins which must be washed away by water and the Spirit."[100] Cyprian articulated this view even more clearly, observing that "an infant . . . being born after the flesh according to Adam . . . has contracted the contagion of the ancient death at its earliest birth."[101] Such logic would call for baptism immediately at birth. Into the fourth century, however, many children of Christian families were not baptized until adulthood, among them Ambrose, Basil of Caesarea, Gregory of Nyssa, Gregory of Nazianzus, John Chrysostom and Jerome.[102] Gregory of Nazianzus in fact encouraged delay at least until the age of three:

> I give my advice to wait until the end of the third year, or a little more or less, when they may be able to listen and to answer something about the Sacrament; that even though they do not perfectly understand it, yet at any rate they may know the outlines; and then to sanctify them in soul and body with the great sacrament of our consecration. For this is how the matter stands; at that time they begin to be responsible for their lives, when reason is matured, and they learn the mystery of life (for sins of ignorance owing to their tender years they have no account to give), and it is far more profitable on all accounts to be fortified by the font, because of the sudden assaults of danger that befall us, stronger than our helpers.[103]

The logic of original sin and of baptism being the locus of salvation drove the early church in the direction of infant baptism. Thus the fourth-century *Apostolic Constitutions* urged the faithful to baptize their infants.[104] Eventually, the increasingly common practice of infant baptism was underpinned by authoritative theological argument by Augustine, which in turn fostered infant baptism becoming increasingly standard practice. Augustine, in locking horns with Pelagius over the issue of grace and free will, appealed to the practice of infant baptism. Why would it be administered unless there was sin to be washed away? The fact that it was administered was a sure sign that there was (original) sin to be dealt with from the

---

[99]Aristides *Apology* 15.11. Also Hermas *Similitudes* 9.29 (*ANF* 2:53); Athenagoras *On the Resurrection* 14 (*ANF* 2:156).

[100]Origen *Commentary on Romans* 5.9. See also *Homily on Luke* 2.22; *Homily on the Book of Leviticus* 12.2-8. For discussion of this see Jeremias *Origins of Infant Baptism*, pp. 69-75.

[101]Cyprian *Letters* 58.5 (*ANF* 5:354).

[102]D. F. Wright, "At What Ages Were People Baptized in the Early Centuries?" *Studia Patristica* 30 (1997): 389-94, see p. 393.

[103]Gregory of Nazianzus *Oration* 40.28 (*NPNF*[2] 7:370). Note, however, that earlier in the same oration he apparently recommends the baptism of babies (40.17).

[104]*Apostolic Constitutions* 6.3.15 (*ANF* 7:457).

time of birth itself. Therefore baptism was fundamental to salvation. As a result, a deceased unbaptized baby was locked out of heaven. Such a baby consequently faced condemnation, though it would be "the mildest condemnation of all."[105] This perspective fostered the long-standing Catholic view that unbaptized babies went to "limbo." Views such as those expressed by Augustine gave powerful impetus to the trend toward baptism in the first days of an infant's life.

Penance

Baptism was seen as an efficacious rite that accomplished cleansing from sin. However, its cleansing dealt only with sins already committed.[106] What of subsequent sins? And if cleansing of postbaptismal sins was problematic, was it problematic for all sins or were there less serious (venial) sins and deadly (mortal) sins? The church seemed to allow for "lesser" sins to be dealt with through personal confession, prayer, almsgiving and other acts of love.[107] But what of the "bigger" sins? Baptism was a once-in-a-lifetime experience. A second baptism was not possible. The dilemma of serious postbaptismal sin may have been felt within the time of the New Testament itself (Heb 6:4-6; 1 Jn 5:16-17). The issue certainly vexed the church for several centuries thereafter. The eventual solution involved a solemn public process, which has come down through the centuries as penance. This was, in the words of Tertullian, "a second reserve of aid against hell."[108]

Hermas in the second century was vexed by the issue of postbaptismal sin. Hermas's solution to the problem of moral lapse was to allow for one solemn time of postbaptismal repentance. The danger, however, was that Christians might trade on this, knowing that they could commit sins but always have a way back to God. Hermas felt this dilemma keenly. He therefore limited this second chance to one postbaptismal repentance that should be offered only to the already baptized. Those yet to be baptized should not be advised about the possibility of this repentance lest they abuse it. After utilizing this once-only repentance, no further second chance existed, no further possibility of repentance and forgiveness.[109] The once-only nature of penance became standard, at least in the early Western church.[110] Thus for Tertullian, penance, the second hope, was also the last hope,

---

[105]Augustine *On the Merits and Remission of Sins and on the Baptism of Infants* 1.21 (*NPNF*[1] 5:23).

[106]Cyprian *Treatise 8: On Works and Alms* 2 (*ANF* 5:476). See also K. Rahner, *Theological Investigations 15: Penance in the Early Church*, trans. L. Swain (New York: Crossroad, 1982), pp. 171-73, 185.

[107]J. N. D. Kelly, *Early Christian Doctrines*, 5th ed. (London: A. & C. Black, 1977), p. 216; Cyprian *Treatise 8: On Works and Alms* 2—5 (*ANF* 5:476-77).

[108]Tertullian *On Repentance* 12 (*ANF* 3:665).

[109]Hermas *Mandates* 4.3 (*ANF* 2:22).

[110]Ambrose *On Repentance* 2.10.95 (*NPNF*[2] 10:357).

"never more" available thereafter.[111] In tracing this thought back to Hermas, we should note, however, that though Hermas carefully circumscribed the use of penance, his intention was not to found a system of church discipline to keep certain people out evermore, but rather to develop a solution that drew backsliders back into salvation in the church.[112]

Tertullian significantly developed a theology of penance (using the term *exomologesis,* so chosen because of the element of confession in the process). Penance was a second, once-in-a-lifetime, rescuing plank when the ship foundered on the rocks of sin in the stormy seas.[113] It thus functioned as a kind of second baptism.[114] As with Hermas, it was a once-only, second chance. Fundamentally, penance in Tertullian involved repentance through prolonged and dramatic public humiliation and confession. In his view, repentance should not be an interior matter only ("exhibited in the conscience") but also expressed "in some exterior act" (i.e., the ritual of penance).[115] Appropriate acts were acts of mourning for sin. Tertullian laid down the sort of behavior appropriate to a penitent who was seeking God's mercy: sackcloth and ashes, plain food and drink, groaning, weeping, making outcries, prostrating oneself before the presbyters, kneeling before the congregation and beseeching them to pray for the penitent.[116] Reintegration into the church society thus came through ritualized acts as well as through a change of heart.

The issue of church forgiveness of major sins. Much confusion surrounded the application of penance at first. Were some sins too small to require this process? Were others too serious to be covered through penance? In the first centuries minor sins did not necessarily involve church-mediated forgiveness, but often they did. Thus Cyprian acknowledges the appropriateness of penance even for "smaller sins."[117] Whether or not smaller sins required penance may have been uncertain, but it was certain that major sins did. The problem was to distinguish the two types. While the early church seems to have made distinctions between various gravities of sin, it lacked clear-cut definitions to distinguish the various levels precisely. There were lists of the more serious sins, but they seemed to vary a great deal. Behind the distinctions, however, lay the sense that some sins destroyed the grace of baptism (such sins later being labeled "mortal" sins) while lighter ones did

---

[111]Tertullian *On Repentance* 7.7 (ANF 3:663). See also Ambrose *On Repentance* 2.10.95 NPNF² 10:357).

[112]L. W. Barnard, "The Shepherd of Hermas in Recent Study," *Heythrop Journal* 9, no. 1 (1968): 29-36, see p. 34.

[113]Tertullian *On Repentance* 4 (ANF 3:659).

[114]Ibid., 7.

[115]Ibid., 9.

[116]Ibid.

[117]Cyprian *Letter* 9.2 (ANF 5:290).

not (later labeled nonmortal or "venial" sins).[118]

In addressing the issue of penance for serious sin, Tertullian limited its scope by classifying some sins as remissible by the church and some as irremissible.[119] Tertullian would therefore not allow church reconciliation at all for the three big sins: murder, idolatry and sexual sins (particularly fornication and adultery). In part at least, Tertullian made the big three sins unpardonable by the church on the basis of the prohibitions in Acts 15:29, interpreting the prohibition on eating blood as a prohibition on shedding blood.[120] Tertullian berated "the bishop of bishops" (possibly the bishop of Rome) for daring to offer to remit the sins of adultery and fornication. In Tertullian's view, such persons must stay excommunicate for life and be left to the judgment or mercy of God alone. God forbid that the church be polluted with such people.[121] Tertullian took an approach of extreme rigor, at one point adding in fraud, apostasy and blasphemy also as irremediable sins.[122] Tertullian's stance on irremediable sins expressed a novel rigorism, since penitent apostates (who had been guilty of idolatry) had been welcomed afresh into communion at Lyons in 177 without difficulty, and earlier Hermas seemed to allow for the reconciliation of an adulterer.[123]

Initially, church discussion of what became penance involved little more than individual repentance. Around the end of the second century, however, focus on individual repentance mutated into ritualized public penance. The focus shifted to reintegration into the community, and the church developed a ritual process somewhat similar to solemn rites required for initial entrance into the community (i.e., baptism). As a result, concern over repentance increasingly focused on church requirements for restoration.[124]

In the early third century, the church was sailing in little-charted waters on the matter of penance. Whether there was forgiveness for "big-three" sinners continued to vex the church, with rigorists like Novatian maintaining the negative opinion of Tertullian, but the majority taking a more pastoral approach.[125] The early third-century *Didascalia Apostolorum* shows the church's muddle on the issue. On

[118]K. Rahner, *Theological Investigations 15*, p. 252.

[119]Tertullian *On Modesty* 2 (ANF 4:76).

[120]Ibid., 12 (ANF 4:85-86). See also N. Brox, *A History of the Early Church*, trans. J. Bowden (London: SCM Press, 1994), p. 108.

[121]Tertullian *On Modesty* 1 (ANF 4:74-75).

[122]Ibid., 19 (ANF 4:97).

[123]Hermas *Similitudes* 6.5 (ANF 2:38).

[124]On this point see G. G. Strousma, "From Repentance to Penance in Early Christianity: Tertullian's *De Paenitentia* in Context," in *Transformations of the Inner Self in Ancient Religions*, ed. J. Assmann and G. G. Strousma (Leiden: Brill, 1999), pp. 167-78, see pp. 167-68.

[125]See, for example, Cyprian's stress on potential forgiveness for all penitents in *Letter* 51.21-23, 27-28 (ANF 5:332-33, 334-35).

the one hand the *Didascalia* appears to be lax. Thus bishops are urged to forgive adulterers just as Christ did the woman taken in adultery.[126] God's forgiveness of Manasseh, who had committed both murder and idolatry (2 Chron 33), was also used as an exhortation to bishops to forgive the penitent.[127] This data indicates forgiveness for all sins. However, the *Didascalia* sets down the penalty for sins as "two or three weeks or five or seven,"[128] extremely light for that time and therefore likely having only minor transgressions in mind. Moreover, the *Didascalia* also harshly states, "Whoever does evil after baptism, the same is already condemned to the Gehenna of fire."[129] Further, the *Didascalia* explicitly says of a postbaptismal adulterer, "he cannot be made clean."[130] And the *Didascalia* also seems to draw a distinction between mortal and lesser sins:

> To everyone therefore who believes and is baptized, his former sins have been forgiven; but after baptism also, provided that he has not sinned a deadly (or mortal) sin nor been an accomplice (thereto), but has heard only, or seen, or spoken, and is thus guilty of sin.[131]

The *Didascalia* thus articulates apparently contradictory viewpoints. It points to two perspectives then existing in the church: one indicating forgiveness of all sins without distinction, the other making a distinction between lesser (forgivable) sins and mortal (nonforgivable) sins. And the *Didascalia* wobbles between these two understandings.

The issue of forgiveness by confessors, or by clerics only. In the aftermath of outbreaks of persecution, many regarded the special status of charismatic confessors as giving them the authority to forgive sins. Both Tertullian and Cyprian felt constrained to confine the right to grant final forgiveness to the clergy. In ruling out such a role to confessors, however, the church was forced to adopt a position of greater leniency (the leniency of many confessors was the factor that caused many Christians to look to them for forgiveness in the first place). Eventually then, the church came to view penance as available for all sins, including the "big three."

The nature of the penitential process. Toward the end of the third century Gregory Thaumaturgus identified four classes of penitents:

- "Weepers" stood at the outer gate begging prayers of the faithful.

- "Waiters on the word" were in the porch, but must leave prior to the Eucharist.

---

[126]*Did. Ap.* 7.2.23.
[127]Ibid., 7.2.22-23.
[128]Ibid., 6.2.16.
[129]Ibid., 5.2.7 (trans. R. H. Connolly).
[130]Ibid., 26.6.22.
[131]Ibid., 20.5.9 (trans. R. H. Connolly).

- "Submitters" were in the church, but must leave with the catechumens.

- "Restored" ones could remain, and then receive the Eucharist.[132]

The four classes seem not to identify four degrees of sinfulness but rather four stages that penitents passed through in a gradual process on their way back to full communion. The Council of Ancyra (314) reflects this also, laying down that those who encouraged others to sacrifice in the time of persecution should be restored through a ten-year process: a "hearer" for three years, a "prostrator" for a further six years, and then a further year being present at the Eucharist without participation, prior to full readmission.[133] In the early church, restoration was completed through the laying on of the bishop's hands: "for the imposition of the hand shall be to him in the place of baptism: for whether by the imposition of hand, or by baptism, they receive the communication of the Holy Spirit."[134]

Eventually, the church laid down set periods of excommunication for different types of offences. Fourth-century Basil, for example, decreed ten years excommunication for abortion, one to four years for bigamy, eleven years for unintentional homicide, and so on.[135] Significantly, clergy involved in fornication were to be stripped of their clerical office but not excluded from communion, on the basis that they were not to be punished twice for the same offence.[136] Here lay the seeds of the medieval practice of "benefit of clergy," a relative exemption of clergy from criminal prosecution in the secular courts. Penance developed as a public process of reconciliation to God and the church. Only in the late sixth century did private penance first appear.

Undergoing penance was no light matter in late antiquity. As a rite to remit sins, it was parallel with baptism—and just as momentous. Like baptism, it could be undertaken only once in a lifetime.[137] Until repentance had been displayed

---

[132]Gregory Thaumaturgus *Canonical Letter* 11 (*ANF* 6:20).

[133]*Canons of Ancyra* 9 (*NPNF*[2] 14:66-67).

[134]*Did. Ap.* 10.2.41 (trans. R. H. Connolly).

[135]Basil *Letters* 188.2, 4, 11 (*NPNF*[2] 8:225, 228); see also *Apostolic Constitutions* 2.3.16 (*ANF* 7:402) (here repeating the text of *Did. Ap.* 6.2.16), which, while not referring to specific offences, alludes to penalties of "two, three, five, or seven weeks" of excommunication depending on the nature of the offence (presumably for relatively minor offences).

[136]Basil *Letters* 188.3 (*NPNF*[2] 8:225).

[137]Tertullian *On Repentance* 5; 7 (*ANF* 3:660, 662-63); Ambrose *On Repentance* 2.11.104 (*NPNF*[2] 10:358). Earlier, however, Ambrose may be open to more than one process of penance. He is urging people to be baptized. His argument is that if they then fall there is the possibility of penance. But if there is no baptism there can be no penance. In making this argument Ambrose likens baptism to having a cloak and penance to the cloak being "frequently mended": *On Repentance* 2.11.98 (*NPNF*[2] 10:357). This shows the extent of the confusion about the parameters of penance. On the whole, however, penance was limited to a once-in-a-lifetime process in the Latin church up to the sixth century (E. Ferguson, "Early Church Penance," *Restoration Quarterly* 36, no. 2 [1994]: 81-100, see p. 89).

through the ritual of penance, penitents were not to be received into communion.[138] Down to the sixth century, penitents had to wear distinctive garb and stand or kneel in special parts of the church. They were subject to extra fasts. Once reconciled, they were still subject to severe discipline for the rest of their lives in order to minimize the temptation to sin. This included prohibition from engaging in certain occupations (trading, legal practice, military service and the civil service). It also included a prohibition on marriage and a requirement for marital sexual abstinence if already married. The rigors of penance caused most to postpone it until their deathbeds when the church would recognize their intention and grant absolution, though if they recovered they would have to undergo the full process.[139] As with baptism, one needed great skill in timing. Play the winning card at the last minute, but when is the last minute? Unplayed, all is lost, as Ambrose warned:

> But for a sinner who has died without repentance, because nothing remains but to mourn grievously and to weep, you find him [David] groaning and saying: "O my son Absalom! My son Absalom!"[140]

The ongoing church affirmed the need for repentance for sins committed after baptism. Increasingly, however, it understood such repentance for major sins to be expressed through an extended once-only ritual process. The church's concern to avoid sin being treated lightly may actually have led to greater sin, as the terms of the once-only remedy may have seemed too restrictive to be availed of immediately by most Christians. In the meantime one's account with God was in debt; and some may have felt a temptation to incur further debt prior to dealing with all debts through a deathbed penance. We are, therefore, left with an open question as to whether the process of penance dealt with sin or fostered it.

For Further Reading

Chupungco, A. J. "Baptism in the Early Church and in Its Cultural Settings." In *Worship and Culture in Dialogue,* edited by S. A. Stauffer, pp. 39-56. Geneva: LWF Studies, 1994.

Dujarier, M. *A History of the Catechumenate: The First Six Centuries.* Translated by E. J. Haasl. New York: Sadlier, 1979.

Ferguson, E., ed. *Conversion, Catechumenate and Baptism in the Early Church.* Studies in Early Christianity 11. New York: Garland, 1993.

Finn, T. M. *Early Christian Baptism and the Catechumenate: West and East Syria.* Message of the Fathers of the Church 5. Collegeville, Minn.: Liturgical Press, 1992.

---

[138]*Apostolic Constitutions* 2.5.38 (ANF 7:414).
[139]A. H. M. Jones, *The Later Roman Empire,* vol. 2 (Oxford: Blackwell, 1964), pp. 981-82.
[140]Ambrose *Concerning Repentance* 2.11.100 (NPNF[2] 10:358).

————. *Early Christian Baptism and the Catechumenate: Italy, North Africa and Egypt.* Message of the Fathers of the Church 6. Collegeville, Minn.: Liturgical Press, 1992.

————. "It Happened One Saturday Night: Ritual and Conversion in Augustine's North Africa." *Journal of the American Academy of Religion* 58, no. 4 (1990): 589-616.

Hinson, E. G. "Baptism in the Early Church History." *Review & Expositor* 65 (1968): 23-31.

Jeremias, J. *Infant Baptism in the First Four Centuries.* Translated by D. Cairns. London: SCM Press, 1960.

Lewis, J. P. "Baptismal Practices of the Second and Third Century Church." *Restoration Quarterly* 26, no. 1 (1983): 1-17.

Rahner, K. *Theological Investigations 15: Penance in the Early Church.* Translated by L. Swain. New York: Crossroad, 1982.

Strousma, G. G. "From Repentance to Penance in Early Christianity: Tertullian's *De Paenitentia* in Context." In *Transformations of the Inner Self in Ancient Religions,* edited by J. Assmann and G. G. Strousma, pp. 167-78. Leiden: Brill, 1999.

Weinrich, W. C. "Cyprian, Donatism, Augustine, and Augustana VIII: Remarks of the Church and the Validity of Sacraments." *Concordia Theological Quarterly* 55, no. 4 (1991): 267-96.

Werblowsky, J. J. Z. "On the Baptismal Rite According to St. Hippolytus." *Studia Patristica* 2 (1957): 93-105.

Wright, D. F. "The Origins of Infant Baptism." *Scottish Journal of Theology* 40 (1987): 1-23.

Yarnold, E. "Baptism and the Pagan Mysteries in the Fourth Century." *Heythrop Journal* 13 (1972): 247-67.

10

EXPLORING THE PATHS
The Development of Early Christian Doctrine

In many traditions Christians repeat the creed each week as part of the liturgy. As the creeds are documents from early times it would be easy for worshipers to assume that the doctrines they express were fully articulated in the earliest decades of Christianity. It is not the case, however, that Christianity began with a comprehensive set of fully developed doctrines. The church did not begin in orthodoxy; rather, orthodoxy progressively emerged in the first five centuries.[1] There was a process of evolution. The task of this chapter is to explain something of those developments prior to the eruption of widespread doctrinal controversy in the fourth century.

The Unfinished Task of Clarifying Beliefs

While central aspects of Christian teaching were rooted in the beginnings of Christianity (e.g., Christ's death and resurrection, 1 Cor 15:3-7), much doctrinal exploration had to proceed through uncharted territory. Even the central aspects of Christianity invited inquiry: what was the precise meaning of particular terms and teachings? The problem was all the greater because great truths were frequently expressed in metaphorical picture language (e.g., "I am the bread of life"), rather than in precise propositional statements. Metaphors are rich evocatively but lack rational clarity. How are they to be understood? The New Testament documents contained the raw materials of later Christian doctrine, but left much undefined, or sketched in faint outline only or lying in tension with other biblical material.[2] In addition, the New Testament seldom laid down doctrine in fully systematic fashion. Paul wrote his epistles, for example, as occasional documents to address

---

[1]See R. Williams, "Does It Make Sense to Speak of 'Pre-Nicene Orthodoxy'?" in *The Making of Orthodoxy,* ed. R. Williams (Cambridge: Cambridge University Press, 1989), pp. 1-23, see p. 2.

[2]For example, note the different emphases of Paul and James on faith and works, the relationship between God's activity and human response, the right understanding of Jesus as Lord within a monotheistic theology.

particular contexts and problems. They were not written as a general or systematic theology. All these factors allow the biblical records to be read in quite different ways. Thus early Christianity was not a monolithic movement but rather "a kaleidoscope of varied traditions, beliefs, and hopes centered on the single figure of Jesus Christ."[3]

Unless the church brought greater coherence to the materials contained in its Scriptures, it could never stick together as a united movement. Christianity risked becoming fragmented into a multiplicity of disputing and competing sects. The fact that this has happened since the reemphasis on Scripture through the Protestant Reformation indicates the vulnerability of the early church also to such fragmentation.

For a time the early church did in fact, at least in some locations, display a tendency to break up into unconnected, even opposing, bits. George La Piana, for example, noted the problem of fragmentation in relation to Rome at the end of the second century:

> The main problem with which the Church of Rome was then confronted . . . was whether Christianity was to be a conglomeration of churches, schools, and sects, widely differing in doctrinal tenets and in liturgical practices but all coming under the general denomination of "the Christian Church," or whether it was to form a compact body of believers governed by the strict law of doctrinal unity and of practical uniformity.[4]

That this was a real issue can be seen in the fact that in Rome at the end of the second century, at least ten Christian bishops or heads of independent groups and schools all claimed to represent exclusively the true Christian tradition.[5] Defining authority, belief and sources of doctrine was an important task to stop such fracturing from persisting and multiplying.

After the apostolic era two major tasks confronted the church: clarifying appropriate attitudes to a largely hostile world and preserving unity in churches that had a bias toward fragmentation. Early writings largely reflect these concerns. Except where particular teachings arose that were judged false, little exploration of central tenets of Christian theology occurred in this subapostolic period. It was not long, however, before major issues concerning Christ arose. At the heart of Christianity lay the affirmation of both monotheism and the worship of Jesus as

---

[3]W. H. C. Frend, "'And I Have Other Sheep'—John 10:16," in *The Making of Orthodoxy*, ed. R. Williams (Cambridge: Cambridge University Press, 1989), pp. 24-39, quote p. 36.

[4]G. La Piana, "The Roman Church at the End of the Second Century," *Harvard Theological Review* 18, no. 3 (1925): 201-77, see p. 207.

[5]Ibid.

divine. How could both be true? Was Jesus really human? Was he really divine? What was his relationship to God the Father? Was there one God? Or two? Or three? Church thought, deeply embedded in Judaism, knew that there was one God. However, the New Testament data, while seldom explicit, pointed to Jesus as being divine, even God. For example, the Book of Revelation twice contains the message to worship God only (Rev 19:10; 22:8-9); yet in that same book Jesus repeatedly receives worship equivalent to that ascribed to God.[6] In holding together both monotheism and an elevated view of Jesus, the early church sooner or later had huge issues to clarify.

The issues did not simply concern the nature of God and of Christ and their interrelationship. The issues also concerned salvation. Toward the end of the second century, Irenaeus articulated salvation as a process of divinization (*theosis*) of the believer, a becoming like God (not, it should be said, becoming God, but rather participating in God).[7] Within such an understanding of salvation, if Jesus was not fully God, could he save? And if he was not fully human, could he save? Irenaeus asserted that Jesus became "what we are that he might bring us to be even what he is."[8] He also spoke of Jesus "imparting God to men by means of the Spirit, and . . . attaching man to God by means of his own incarnation."[9] The attaching of humanity to God happened through "recapitulation,"[10] through Christ, as a second Adam, reliving all the stages of humanity as a perfect but real human being.[11] In so doing, Christ gathered up all humanity into himself and redeemed all stages of human life.[12] Such an understanding of salvation depended on Jesus being both fully divine and fully human. Irenaeus's notion of salvation as divinization greatly influenced the life of the early church. Most of the theologies later judged to be false threatened this doctrine. We should therefore not dismiss the later christological debates and clarifications as hair-splitting. The process was undertaken intensely and exhaustively because salvation itself appeared to be at stake.

While this book cannot hope to explore all the doctrinal developments, this chapter and the following one will focus on the development of thought on the

---

[6]Compare particularly worship of Jesus (the "Lamb") in Rev 5 with worship of God in Rev 4.

[7]Irenaeus *Against Heresies* 4.38.4 (*ANF* 1:522). Such teaching has exercised major influence in later Eastern thinking. It has its roots in biblical material such as 2 Pet 1:3-4. On Irenaeus's notion of participation, see E. Osborn, *Irenaeus of Lyons* (Cambridge: Cambridge University Press, 2001), pp. 16-17.

[8]Irenaeus *Against Heresies* 5, preface (*ANF* 1:526).

[9]Ibid., 5.1.1 (*ANF* 1:527).

[10]Irenaeus frequently utilizes the Greek term *anakephalaiōsis* for this "recapitulation." The term (or its verbal form) appears only in Rom 13:9 and Eph 1:10 in the New Testament. Its usage in Eph 1:10 is the springboard for later teaching on recapitulation.

[11]Irenaeus *Against Heresies* 3.21.10 (*ANF* 1:454).

[12]Ibid., 2.22.4 (*ANF* 1:391).

nature of Jesus and his relationship with God the Father (and with the Holy Spirit). This development took place as the church worked through the christological and trinitarian debates.

The Challenge of Docetism

One of the earliest christological controversies was over Docetism, a viewpoint that was to pervade a number of later heresies, including Marcionism and Gnosticism. Docetic teaching, while accepting Christ's divinity, effectively denied his humanity—Christ only *seemed* (Greek *dokein*) to be human. Greek cultural understandings made this belief attractive: Greek philosophical thought viewed ultimate reality (God) as totally separate from this world—unchangeable and impassible (without feeling or emotion). Furthermore, matter was inherently impure and corrupt. How then could God come to earth, let alone die? Paul early recognized this difficulty— to the Greeks the cross was foolishness (1 Cor 1:23). A century later the pagan Celsus, in mounting a searching attack on Christian doctrine, majored on this point: "It cannot be the case that God came down to earth, since in so doing he would have undergone an alteration of his nature."[13] A generation later Tertullian also recognized the countercultural nature of Christianity and gloried in that fact:

> The Son of God was crucified; I am not ashamed because men must be ashamed of it. And the Son of God died; it is by all means to be believed because it is absurd. And he was buried, and rose again; the fact is certain because it is impossible.[14]

Docetic thought made Jesus a pretend man, God masquerading as human. Its presence agitated at least one of the later New Testament writers. The otherwise surprising test in 1 John that true believers are those who confess that Jesus Christ has come in the flesh was a reaction to docetic teaching (1 Jn 4:1-6).[15] The contrary viewpoint—Docetism—is described as the spirit of antichrist (2 Jn 7). Docetic challenge was particularly strong in the first part of the second century; hence the counter-insistence of Ignatius and Polycarp that Christ really had come in the flesh.[16]

Marcionite and Gnostic Teaching

The docetic challenge was a strand in Marcionite thought. Marcion, a native of Pontus who was expelled from the church of Rome in A.D. 144 because of his be-

---

[13]Celsus, *On the True Doctrine*, trans. R. J. Hoffmann (New York: Oxford University Press, 1987), p. 78.
[14]Tertullian *On the Flesh of Christ* 5 (ANF 3:525).
[15]See also the careful insistence on the physicality of Jesus in 1 Jn 1:1-2; 5:6.
[16]Ignatius *To the Trallians* 9—10; *To the Smyrneans* 1—3; *To the Ephesians* 7; *To the Magnesians* 11; Polycarp *To the Philippians* 7 (all ANF 1).

liefs, wrestled with the problem of the relation between the Old and New Testaments. In his view the two testaments were diametrically opposed, and Christianity did not build on Judaism. In Marcionite perspective, the world was not made by the primary God but by a subordinate, inferior, heavenly being, the *demiurge* or craftsman, who ruled over the world as a god of wrath and judgment. This god stood in stark contrast to Jesus' gospel of grace and love. Jesus came to reveal the true but previously unknown God, the Father of Jesus. In distinguishing between the God of the Old Testament and the God of the New Testament, Marcionite teaching created a sharp disjunction between Israel and the church and between the two testaments. Thus, in terms of spiritual value, it basically jettisoned the Old Testament; Marcion's canon of Scripture was effectively a truncated version of Paul's epistles and Luke's Gospel. While Marcion's views may not have been totally docetic,[17] they reflected something of that dimension in excising Jesus' birth narrative in Luke 1—2 so that Jesus would not be implicated in the processes of creation and sex. Though the mainstream church rejected Marcion's beliefs, his well-organized and very missionary-minded movement remained a challenge to mainstream Christianity for several centuries.

Gnostic teaching presented an even greater challenge to Christianity. Whereas Marcionism largely emerged from within Christianity, Gnosticism had more complex origins. Gnosticism itself was not a standard set of teachings but more a general approach, such as New Age teaching is in the twenty-first century. Gnosticism was strongly syncretistic, drawing from several strands of religious thinking,[18] including

- apocalyptic Judaism. This influence was reflected in Gnostic angelology, preoccupation with the planets and the zodiac, and the use of the name "Jahweh."[19]

- Christianity. Christian contribution can be seen in the comment of the Gnostic Heracleon, that "in the days that we were Hebrews, we were orphans. We had [only] our mother, but when we became Christians we acquired father and mother."[20]

---

[17]S. G. Hall, *Doctrine and Practice in the Early Church* (London: SPCK, 1991), p. 39.

[18]On this see K. Rudolph, *Gnosis: The Nature & History of Gnosticism*, trans. R. McL. Wilson (San Francisco: Harper & Row, 1987), p. 54.

[19]W. H. C. Frend, *Saints and Sinners in the Early Church* (London: Darton, Longman & Todd, 1985), p. 45.

[20]Heracleon, Fragment 22, cited by Origen *Commentary on John* 13.19 (trans. Frend, *Saints and Sinners,* p. 45). Tertullian's statement also shows that the Gnostic Valentinus had earlier aspired to become a Christian bishop: *Against the Valentinians* 4 (ANF 3:505). The Christian influence also appears in the statement of the Gnostic *Gospel of Philip* 52, "A heathen man does not die, for he has never lived that he should die. The believer is only alive since Christ came" (in Frend, *Saints and Sinners,* p. 44).

Figure 10.1. Sample of Gnostic material found at Nag Hammadi (Institute for Antiquity and Christianity)

- Platonism. Its influence came especially in its stress on the extreme transcendence of God, which then led to explaining the world as the creation of divine intermediaries.

Gnosticism commonly had some direct overlap with Christianity, leading even to the emergence of Gnostic gospels such as those of "Thomas" and "Philip." Essentially, however, the Gnostics had a different message. In Gnosticism the world resulted from some primeval disorder, originating from an inferior deity (*demi-*

urge). Humans were trapped by matter and needed to escape to the realm of spirit. Salvation-escape came via knowledge (*gnōsis*). This could come through the help of divine mediators, ascetic rigor and the learning of esoteric knowledge, especially through possessing the correct magic passwords and the most potent amulets required to pass through resisting heavenly powers blocking passage to the realm of light. Had Gnosticism been able to influence Christianity as a whole, it would have dissolved historic Christianity into a timeless myth. With that dissolution, salvation would have been by knowledge, possible only for the "pneumatic" spiritual elite.

We may want to ignore Gnosticism on the basis that it was rejected by the church and had largely disappeared by the sixth century. However, despite conscious rejection, Gnosticism left its "shadow" on the church.[21] In reaction to it, the church created doctrines that refuted Gnosticism, and articulation of doctrines in this way influenced the way the church viewed itself.[22] Moreover, Gnosticism's negative view of the world may have shaped the church's increasing tendency to be negative to many aspects of life in the body, despite Christianity's affirmation of the cosmos as made by God.[23] The discovery of a Gnostic library in 1945 at Nag Hammadi on the River Nile a few miles from a Pachomian monastery is also very significant. It suggests that separation between Gnosticism and Christianity may not have always been total and that Gnosticism may at times have had direct influence on Christianity.

The Response of the Church

That Gnostic-type thinking did not subvert Christianity was largely because of the reaction that movements such as Marcionism and Gnosticism provoked. Because these movements had some relationship with Christianity, mainstream Christian leaders had to provide tests for the faithful so that they could scent heresy and avoid it. A major test was apostolic succession. The church contrasted the novelty of Gnosticism with its own apostolic links that preserved the original apostolic teaching in unadulterated form. All teaching should agree with that of the apostolic churches, "those wombs and original sources of the faith."[24] Should Gnostics claim that their teaching corresponded with that of the apostles, let them verify this by demonstrating apostolic succession:

> Let them produce the original records of their churches; let them unfold the roll of

---

[21]Rudolph, *Gnosis*, p. 368.
[22]Ibid., p. 369.
[23]Ibid., p. 371.
[24]Tertullian *Prescription Against Heretics* 21 (*ANF* 3:252, English modernized).

The Festal Letter of Athanasius, A.D. 367, is the first to set down the twenty-seven books that now comprise the New Testament as canonical:

Again it is not tedious to speak of the [books] of the New Testament. These are, the four Gospels, according to Matthew, Mark, Luke, and John. Afterwards, the Acts of the Apostles and Epistles (called Catholic), seven, viz. of James, one; of Peter, two; of John, three; after these, one of Jude. In addition, there are fourteen Epistles of Paul, written in this order. The first, to the Romans; then two to the Corinthians; after these, to the Galatians; next, to the Ephesians; then to the Philippians; then to the Colossians; after these, two to the Thessalonians, and that to the Hebrews; and again, two to Timothy; one to Titus; and lastly, that to Philemon. And besides, the Revelation of John.[a]

---

[a]Athanasius *Letter* 39.5 (*NPNF²* 4:552).

---

their bishops, running down in due succession from the beginning in such manner that that bishop shall be able to show for his ordainer and predecessor some one of the apostles or of apostolic men,—a man, moreover, who continued steadfast with the apostles. For this is the manner in which the apostolic churches transmit their registers.[25]

Correct doctrine was thus defined in terms of correct sources. In contrast to the proliferating Gnostic sects, the defenders of orthodoxy presented the criterion of the monolithic church, universally extended in space, with unbroken continuity in time and unanimous in its possession of an immutable revelation. Vincent of Lerins summed up this development in 432: "In the Catholic Church itself we take great care that we hold that which has been believed everywhere, always, by all [*ubique, semper, ab omnibus*]."[26] Against Gnosticism, mainstream Christianity stressed teaching as handed down in the mainstream church.

In addition to the teaching of the apostolic churches, another correct teaching

---

[25]Ibid., 32 (*ANF* 3:258, English modernized). For earlier similar sentiment, see Irenaeus *Against Heresies* 3.3 (*ANF* 1:415-16).

[26]Vincent of Lerins *Commonitorium* 2.6 (in J. Stevenson, ed., *Creeds, Councils and Controversies: Documents Illustrating the History of the Church, A.D. 337-461*, rev. ed. [London: SPCK, 1989], p. 322).

source for the mainstream church was Scripture. The early church did not see Scripture in contrast to tradition; each supported the other. In its beginnings Scripture was not one bound book labeled "Scripture." It needed definition. The Gnostics and Marcionites had their lists of sacred books and their own writings. What then was "Scripture"? The church quickly affirmed the Old Testament as Scripture, thus preserving the doctrine of creation and the sense of some degree of continuity with Judaism. Irenaeus, around 180, was the first to refer unequivocally to a New Testament corpus also as Scripture.[27] The basic test for canonicity was whether the writing was understood to originate or have strong connection with an apostle. By the end of the second century the canon had virtually been settled, though debate over a few books continued for several centuries.

Evangelicals especially may wonder today why the church stressed its own authority in its bishops and through apostolic succession in addition to the teaching of Scripture. To that question there are several answers. In the first place most of the faithful were illiterate and needed the church to disclose what the Scriptures said. Moreover, a copy of the Scriptures (handwritten) was extremely expensive to produce and therefore not easily accessible to most individuals. Furthermore, the sacred writings were capable of many interpretations, especially in the hands of clever manipulators. Vincent of Lerins, noting that it seemed possible to elicit from the Scriptures "as many opinions as there are men," asserted that interpretation "should be laid down in accordance with the standard of the ecclesiastical and Catholic understanding of them."[28] The church thus became the filter through which the faithful should read Scripture.

A final touchstone for Christian truth lay in the development of a "rule of faith." Again tailored to aid the uneducated, the rule was a short statement of the central apostolic teachings, a rule against which the faithful could assess other teachings. The rule provided a lens through which to read Scripture and rebut error.[29] The rule contained in rudimentary form ideas similar to those of the later creeds, which were really developments of the rule. Commonly the rule would assert the oneness of God who is also creator; the birth, death and resurrection of Jesus; the Holy Spirit; and future judgment.[30] The fact that the exact wording of the rule varied considerably suggests that it was a summary of a known set of ideas rather than a fixed form of words. Two early writers who set down such a rule towards the end of the second century were Irenaeus and Tertullian. Against

---

[27]Irenaeus *Against Heresies*, passim.

[28]Vincent of Lerins *Commonitorium* 2.5 (in Stevenson, *Creeds, Councils*, p. 322).

[29]So argued Tertullian in *Prescription Against Heretics* 19 (ANF 3:251-52).

[30]See, for example, Irenaeus *Against Heresies* 1.10.1 (ANF 1:330); Tertullian *Prescription Against Heresies* 13 (ANF 3:249); Origen *On First Principles*, preface (ANF 4:240).

The "Rule of Faith" in Tertullian:

Now, with regard to this rule of faith—that we may from this point acknowledge what it is which we defend—it is, you must know, that which prescribes the belief that there is one only God, and that He is none other than the Creator of the world, who produced all things out of nothing through His own Word, first of all sent forth; that this Word is called His Son, *and,* under the name of God, was seen "in diverse manners" by the patriarchs, heard at all times in the prophets, at last brought down by the Spirit and Power of the Father into the Virgin Mary, was made flesh in her womb, and, being born of her, went forth as Jesus Christ; thenceforth He preached the new law and the new promise of the kingdom of heaven, worked miracles; having been crucified, He rose again the third day; (then) having ascended into the heavens, He sat at the right hand of the Father; sent instead of Himself the Power of the Holy Ghost to lead such as believe; will come with glory to take the saints to the enjoyment of everlasting life and of the heavenly promises, and to condemn the wicked to everlasting fire, after the resurrection of both these classes shall have happened, together with the restoration of their flesh. This rule, as it will be proved, was taught by Christ, and raises amongst ourselves no other questions than those which heresies introduce, and which make men heretics.[a]

[a]Tertullian *Prescription Against Heretics* 13 (ANF 3:249).

the timeless mythology of the Gnostics, Irenaeus stressed Christianity as a series of historical facts. The bedrock of Christianity was faith in a historical person and in a history of God's acts. Tertullian likewise singled out the incarnation of Jesus in the flesh, his crucifixion and his resurrection as being historical facts at the core of Christianity.[31] Appeal to what the church universally believed and identification of its core in a rule of faith effectively made the church a filter channeling the way Scripture was to be read.

[31]Tertullian *Prescription Against Heretics* 13 (ANF 3:249).

The Theological Contribution of Justin Martyr

A philosopher converted from a pagan background in the middle of the second century, Justin continued in philosophical mode as a Christian. This may explain his more lateral and adventurous expression of Christian truth. For Justin all truth is one, and is to be honored regardless of its origin. Justin could thus see value in wisdom drawn from non-Christian sources: "Whatever things were rightly said among all men are the property of us Christians."[32] It is not that Justin gave equal value to other religions as to Christianity; other religions were valuable to the extent that they expressed truth in line with Christianity.[33] Truths found in other religions were borrowed from the writings of Moses, which, according to Justin, were older and alone were fully true.[34] Alternatively, such writings drew from insights through the inspiration of the *logos* in which all people share.[35]

Justin went so far as to claim that great thinkers like Socrates and Abraham, by virtue of living "according to reason or the *logos [meta logou]*," were Christians even though living before Christ.[36] Clearly this brought a radically fresh and affirmative view of the world. That which was good did not need to be jettisoned, but might in fact be a preparation for the greater revelation of Christ. Justin's approach was pregnant with potential for meshing with culture and contemporary thinking, and full of evangelistic potential. It was also pregnant with peril, with the danger of substituting culture and contemporary thinking for apostolic Christianity.

One can see this double-edged potential with regard to Justin's view of the connection between God and the created world. In Hebrew thought, God is both high (transcendent) and near (immanent). His otherness does not keep him from close involvement in mundane affairs. In contrast, Platonic thought, which significantly influenced the thinking of Justin, made a fundamental disjunction between the ultimate (God) and creation—never the twain shall meet. Thus God was unchanging, whereas the world was full of change; God was impassible (not able to suffer), whereas suffering was inherent to this world. This understanding deeply shaped Justin's thinking:

> You must not imagine that the unbegotten God himself came down or went up from any place. For the ineffable Father and Lord of all neither has come to any place, nor walks, nor sleeps, nor rises up, but remains in his own place, wherever that is, quick to behold and quick to hear, having neither eyes nor ears, but being of indescribable might; and he knows all things, and none of us escapes his observation. And he is

[32]Justin Martyr *Second Apology* 13 (ANF 1:193).
[33]Ibid. Also *First Apology* 60.11 (ANF 1:183). On this see A. J. Droge, "Justin Martyr and the Restoration of Philosophy," *Church History* 56 (1987): 303-19, passim.
[34]Justin Martyr *First Apology* 23; 59 (ANF 1:170, 182).
[35]Justin Martyr *Second Apology* 10 (ANF 1:191).
[36]Justin Martyr *First Apology* 46 (ANF 1:178).

not moved or confined to a spot in the whole world, for he existed before the world was made. How then could he talk to anyone, or be seen by anyone, or appear on the smallest portion of the earth, when the people at Sinai were not able to look even on the glory of him who was sent from him?[37]

Such a perspective obviously has implications for both creation and the incarnation. If God is unapproachable, how can he have contact with the world? Justin answered that he did so by an intermediary, whom he described as

a Beginning, a certain rational power from Himself, who is called by the Holy Spirit, now the Glory of the Lord, now the Son, again wisdom, again an angel, then God, and then Lord and Logos; and on another occasion He calls Himself Captain, when He appeared in human form to Joshua.[38]

Here Justin again drew heavily on Greek thought in positing an intermediary between the impassible God and the material world. That sort of thought commonly viewed such an intermediary as *Logos,* divine reason or cosmic order, creating and indwelling the world. Justin was not a total innovator in borrowing this thought-form for Christianity. Earlier New Testament writers, especially the author of the Fourth Gospel, had drawn on this concept in communicating something of the significance of Christ (Jn 1:1-18; Lk 1:2; Col 1:25ff.; Heb 1:1-3; Rev 19:13). What Justin did was to give the concept of Logos even greater prominence, making it his key term in explaining not only Christ, but also the cosmos as a whole. The Logos in its entirety is in Christ alone, but its seeds in part are in all people.[39] Sparks from the divine fire (*Logos*) are thus present everywhere.

In all of this, Justin had produced a theology that was broad in its scope and resonated with its cultural context. For Justin this Logos of Greek thought was Jesus par excellence, the one who was crucified for the sins of the world. Justin's thought leaves ambiguity regarding the relationship between Jesus and God. Yet the ambiguity in his thinking is not surprising because Justin was writing an apology (a defense of Christian faith) rather than a systematic theological treatise.

Justin's expression of the relationship between Jesus and God was ambiguous regarding the separateness/identity between God and Jesus. His use of the Logos concept as central to his Christology can be understood as stressing the separateness of Jesus' being from that of God. Justin himself did say that the two were "numerically distinct"[40] and that Jesus was "another God."[41] Did he then expound di-

---

[37]Justin Martyr *Dialogue with Trypho* 127 (*ANF* 1:263); also *Dialogue with Trypho* 60 (*ANF* 1:227).
[38]Ibid., 61 (*ANF* 1:227).
[39]Justin Martyr *Second Apology* 7; 10; 13 (all *ANF* 1).
[40]Justin Martyr *Dialogue with Trypho* 62; 128; 129 (all *ANF* 1).
[41]Ibid., 56 (*ANF* 1:223).

Figure 10.2. Representation of Justin Martyr (Courtesy of University of Michigan)

theism: two gods? Justin most likely would have rejected this suggestion, for he also insisted that the reality of the Logos in no way diminishes the being of God who begot the Logos. There is a unity between the two as there is between the sun and its light, such that "the light of the sun on earth is indivisible and inseparable from the sun in the heavens."[42]

Justin's Logos terminology also leaves ambiguous the matter of Jesus' equality with or subordination to God. He employed the Logos concept because of the absolute transcendence of God. This suggests that "the Word then becomes a subordinate God that serves as a bridge between the world and that supreme God who exists only in absolute transcendence."[43] Contemporary understanding of the Logos concept would evoke the natural assumption that it makes Jesus less than God. However, Justin stressed in several places that Jesus is God.[44] Yet language of subordination remains, as Christians hold Christ "in the second place" and the Spirit "in the third."[45] Was this simply subordination in function or was it also subordination in being? Only after the fourth-century theological debates did the church achieve the clarity within orthodoxy that the Scriptural language of subordination meant subordination of function only and not of being.

Justin's theology marked a huge advance in theological richness. Moreover, it resonated with contemporary philosophical thought, thereby making Christianity

---

[42]Ibid., 128 (ANF 1:264).
[43]J. L. Gonzales, *A History of Christian Thought*, vol. 1, *From the Beginnings to the Council of Chalcedon* (Nashville: Abingdon, 1987), p. 107.
[44]Justin Martyr *Dialogue with Trypho* 48; 55—68; 126; 128 (all *ANF* 1).
[45]Justin Martyr *First Apology* 13 (ANF 1:167).

more accessible and attractive to educated people. This theology is thus rightfully viewed as "the first attempt of an intellectually satisfying explanation of the relation of Christ to the Father."[46] However, Justin's framing his theology on the assumption that God was impassible runs counter to biblical Christianity. Furthermore, this created a dilemma for fourth- and fifth-century theologians who shared that assumption: either Jesus was not really God (he was not impassible) or he was not really incarnate (passible). Justin's theological complexity and ambiguity left open major issues concerning the nature of God and the place of Christ in relation to God—issues that recurred again and again in the history of the church.

Early Forms of Explicit Trinitarian Thinking

The Bible itself lacks explicit trinitarian teaching, though it certainly contains material that became the seedbed of later trinitarian formulation. Trinitarian language emerged in the church as a reaction to error and to safeguard truth. It brought explicit clarification of what had previously been implicit.

Explicit trinitarian formulation first appears in A.D. 177 in Athenagoras, who in stressing that God is one, referred to God the Father, God the Son and God the Holy Spirit.[47] This one God was referred to, at that time, as a "Triad," particularly in Theophilus of Antioch. Writing about the same time as Athenagoras, Theophilus highlighted the threeness (*triados*) of "God and his Word and his Wisdom."[48] It was not long before a new word was minted to express both the threeness and the oneness of the three-one God. Tertullian, whose views will be discussed a little later in this chapter, coined the new term "tri-unitas" around the end of the second century.

In the meantime, a decade or two earlier, Irenaeus was beginning to formulate a much more developed trinitarian understanding than the church had previously expressed. Irenaeus was unequivocal in affirming that Jesus is God.[49] However, he largely articulated this in a way that stressed the oneness of God who outworks through his Word/Logos and his Spirit/Wisdom. Thus God himself made the world, but he did it by his "hands," that is, by the Son and Holy Spirit.[50] The difference is one of manifestation, "the Father [being] the invisible of the Son," and the Son, "the visible of the Father."[51] Jesus then is the "measure" of the "unmeasurable Father."[52]

---

[46]J. Lupi, "God and the Trinity in the Fathers: The First Two Centuries," *Melita Theologica* 51, no. 2 (2000): 127-62, quote p. 132.

[47]Athenagoras *A Plea for the Christians* 10 (*ANF* 2:133).

[48]Theophilus *To Autolycus* 2.15 (*ANF* 2:101).

[49]Irenaeus *Against Heresies* 3.19.2; 4.6.7 (*ANF* 1:449, 469).

[50]Ibid., 4.preface.4 (*ANF* 1:463).

[51]Ibid., 4.6.6 (*ANF* 1:469).

[52]Ibid., 4.4.2 (*ANF* 1:466).

Irenaeus expressed an "economic" trinitarianism. The term "economic" comes from the Greek word *oikonomia,* which originally referred to the ordering of tasks in a large household. The divine household also reflected such division of labor: "the Father planning everything well and giving his commands, the Son carrying these into execution and performing the work of creating, and the Spirit nourishing and increasing [what is made]."[53] The "economy," then, is God's plan for his creation, particularly his plan known in the coming of Jesus Christ. God is revealed in threeness in the economy of his works, though one in his essential being. The Son and the Spirit, though revealed in the "economy" as other than the Father, are at the same time inseparably one with him in his eternal being.[54] Such a viewpoint focused on the unity of God rather than focusing on the three "persons" in the Godhead, the focus that came increasingly to the fore in orthodox Eastern formulations after Nicea. Economic trinitarianism simply indicated God's operating in a threefold manner in contrast to "immanent" or "essential" trinitarianism, which stressed the threefold quality of God's essential being.[55]

Tertullian was the first to explicitly describe God as a "trinitas."[56] Tertullian formulated his views in response to one "Praxeas," who felt that the unity of God could be preserved only if the Father, the Son and the Holy Spirit were the very selfsame person (thus denying any distinctions in the Godhead).[57] According to Tertullian, though God is unity, nevertheless in his economy he expresses himself in three separate "persons," though yet of one substance. The words, "I and the Father are one," Tertullian pointed out, do not indicate a unity of persons, but rather a unity of essence, since the term used (in Latin) is *unum* (neuter) rather than *unus* (masculine).[58]

Tertullian laid down a formula for the future: God is three persons in one substance.[59] One may feel this corresponds with the trinitarian belief that has now prevailed for many centuries. Such, however, is not necessarily the case. Particularly problematic is the term "person" (Latin *persona*). To us a person is a separate being. However, a *persona* was originally the mask worn by an actor. This *persona* created a distinction between the actor and the character he played, but the term did not focus on the self-consciousness that we now associate with *person.* Thus

---

[53]Ibid., 4.38.3 (*ANF* 1:521-22).

[54]J. N. D. Kelly, *Early Christian Doctrines,* 5th ed. (London: A & C Black, 1977), p. 108.

[55]S. G. Hall, *Doctrine and Practice,* p. 71.

[56]Tertullian *Against Praxeas* 2; 4 (*ANF* 3:598, 600).

[57]Ibid.

[58]Ibid., 22.

[59]On this see E. Osborn, *Tertullian: First Theologian of the West* (New York : Cambridge University Press, 1997), p. 138.

Tertullian's formula may not have focused on three "persons" (in the modern sense) in the Godhead, but simply that there were three distinctions in the Godhead. Tertullian greatly advanced a trinitarian understanding of God, but by no means did his thought provide the final answer.

Focus on the Oneness/"Monarchy" of God, Downplaying His Threeness

If God is both three and one, where should the emphasis lie: in threeness or oneness? Monarchians felt that the Logos doctrine and the subsequent emergence of economic trinitarianism imperiled the unity of God, his "monarchy" (from Greek *monos,* "alone, only," and *arche,* "origin, ruler, first cause"). Tertullian coined the Latin word *monarchia* to describe this type of thinking, claiming that the monarchians "took fright at the economy" and sought refuge in "the monarchy."[60]

Monarchianism took two forms: dynamic monarchianism and modalistic monarchianism. The dynamic form largely revisited earlier adoptionism (the view that God "adopted" the man Jesus as his Son at his baptism or at some such time). The term "dynamic" comes from the Greek word *dynamis,* "power." Dynamic monarchians preserved the "monarchy" (oneness) of God by understanding Jesus as a special man upon whom the Spirit or power of God descended. In recent centuries Unitarians have developed similar teaching. While dynamic monarchianism troubled the church for a time, it was never a serious contender for mainstream adherence.

The greater difficulty was modalistic monarchianism. This view basically affirms that there is one God who nevertheless manifests himself in three modes. Distinction within the Godhead is basically distinction of names rather than distinction of substance. Thus what is said of one member of the Godhead can equally be said of another. It is therefore appropriate to talk of the Father dying on the cross—hence the term *patripassianism* (drawn from the Latin words for father and suffering) for this type of thinking. A major exponent of this sort of thinking was Sabellius; hence modalistic monarchianism is sometimes called Sabellianism. Sabellius viewed God as a monad (whom he described as *Huiopator,* "Son-Father") manifesting himself in three ways. He was fond of the analogy of the sun, which radiates both warmth and light.

In what way is this viewpoint defective? Many Christians today unwittingly hold a Sabellian theology, seeking, for example, to explain the Trinity by drawing from the analogy of water, an image similar to that of Sabellius's sun image. In the water analogy, a particular mass of water is described as being sequentially ice, wa-

---

[60]Tertullian *Against Praxeas* 3 (in Kelly, *Early Christian Doctrines,* pp. 109-10).

ter and steam. This is a clear and concrete image, but it actually expresses Sabellian thinking. Orthodox Christianity then and now has insisted that there are real distinctions within the Godhead, which nevertheless remains a unity.

Supporters of Sabellius charged opponents of their viewpoint with *di-theism*—having two Gods.[61] Opponents of Sabellius counterclaimed that Sabellius obliterated scriptural distinctions between the different members of the Trinity. While the church ultimately decided against Sabellius, the issue still nagged at church thinking. Concern over these matters partly underlay the Arian controversy a century later (see chapter 11).

The Theology of Origen

While the overall thinking of this intellectual giant needs a book on its own, here we will briefly discuss only Origen's thought in relation to the Trinity. In studying Origen's thinking, it is very helpful to be aware that one of his teachers was Ammonius Saccas, a lapsed Christian who was later also teacher of Plotinus, chief early exponent of Neo-Platonic thought. Such wider tutelage meant that Origen's system of thought was less confined to Scripture than that of most Christian thinkers, more shaped by contemporary thought, more philosophical in nature. In particular, his perspectives display strong parallels with Neo-Platonic thinking of his time.

In reaction to monarchianism, Origen presented a much more pluralistic picture, teaching that God is three *ousiae* or *hypostases* (which we might translate as "separate beings" or "independent existences"[62]). Scripture required this stance. The very names "Father" and "Son" imply plurality and mutuality: "the Son must of necessity be the son of a Father, and the Father, the father of a Son."[63] The distinction between Father and Son is therefore not one of concept only, but rather of real subsistence: "they are two, considered as persons or subsistences *[hypostases]*, [but] are one in unity of thought, in harmony and in identity of will."[64]

Origen seemed uncomfortable with any reference to Jesus as "the most high God," stressing rather his derived nature (and probably also his subordination).[65] In this Origen seemed to assume the truth of the late Platonic axiom that in the hierarchy of being, what is produced must be inferior to that which produces it.[66] Origen distinguished on the one hand between the very God (*Autotheos*, God of himself), the uncreated cause of all things, and on the other, the one who is God

---

[61]Hippolytus *Refutation of All Heresies* 9.6, 7 (*ANF* 5:128).

[62]Origen *Commentary on John* 1.23 (*ANF* 10:310).

[63]Ibid., 10.21 (*ANF* 10:402).

[64]Origen *Against Celsus* 8.12 (*ANF* 4:643-44).

[65]Ibid., 8.14 (*ANF* 4:644).

[66]H. Chadwick, *History and Thought of the Early Church* (London: Variorum Reprints, 1982), 4:189.

through participation in God's divinity: "the Word being with God makes him God."[67] Jesus is God in the second sense. Thus while God the Father ("the uncreated cause of all things") is "the God," *ho theos,* Jesus the Logos is simply "God," *theos* (without the definite article).[68] Jesus is God, not so much through his essential nature ("not possessing that of himself"), but through his relationship with God ("by his being with the Father").[69] Such language would suggest that Jesus is God in a derivative sense—a "diminished God."[70] However, because Jesus is begotten of God, he is still God in his essential nature.

Origen's sense of subordination within the Godhead may be understood as within the "economy" only, that is, subordination in the ordering of the divine relationships and functions rather than in their essential natures. It is debatable whether this is the case or whether there is essential subordination also because of the rich, diverse and ambiguous expressions of Origen's thought. Yet subordination there certainly is:

> The God and Father, who holds the universe together, is superior to every being that exists, for he imparts to each one from his own existence that which each one is; the Son, being less than the Father, is superior to rational creatures alone (for he is second to the Father); the Holy Spirit is still less, and dwells with the saints alone. So that in this way the power of the Father is greater than that of the Son and the Holy Spirit, and in turn the power of the Holy Spirit exceeds that of every other holy being.[71]
>
> We . . . declare that the Son is not mightier than the Father but inferior to him.[72]

In Origen's thinking God is absolute unity *(monas)* and simplicity *(henas).*[73] With God being utterly transcendent there must be a mediator between God and the world. That mediator, the Logos of God, did not appear as a one-event generation but is rather being eternally generated from the Father.[74] This generation means that the Logos shares the essential characteristics of God because like begets like. Such generation must be from eternity because if he were not eternally generated there would be a time when the Father became the Father. This would imply change in the nature of God (not-Father becoming Father), something not conceivable in this Platonic-type thinking. Divine changelessness meant that what

---

[67]Origen *Commentary on John* 2.1 (ANF 10:323).

[68]Ibid., 2.2 (ANF 10:323). Here Origen is basing his arguments on the presence and absence of the definite article in the opening verses of John's Gospel.

[69]Ibid.

[70]E. J. Fortman, *The Triune God* (London: Hutchinson, 1972), p. 68.

[71]Origen *On First Principles* (Greek fragment) 1.3.5 (in Stevenson, *New Eusebius*, p. 202).

[72]Origen *Against Celsus* 8.15 (ANF 4:645).

[73]Origin *On First Principles* 1.1.6 (ANF 4:243).

[74]Origin *Homily 4.9 on Jeremiah.*

is said of God must be timelessly true: "if part of what is said of God is that he is one term of a relation [Father], the other term [Son] must also be eternal."[75]

Origen's doctrine of the eternal generation of the Son was a crucial development in christological understanding. It meant that the threeness of God's being was eternal and not just evoked by the needs of the economy.[76] Some earlier thinkers, while acknowledging the preexistence of the Son, nevertheless saw him as having a beginning. Tertullian, for example, specifically indicated that there was a time when no Son existed with God, and that therefore God was not always Father.[77] Origen's doctrine of the eternal generation of the Son proved vital in responding to Arius's assertion in the following century that generation implies that the Son had a beginning.

In grappling with Origen's complex theology, we need to recognize that he was not writing a systematic theology but rather writing for particular contexts and issues. As a consequence, his statements on particular issues are not altogether consistent. This is the case with his trinitarianism. It is dangerous to base one's views of Origen's thinking on isolated statements. Rather, one should take a wide-ranging look at the whole to appreciate the richness and tension (and perhaps even contradiction) in his thought. While recognizing this, one can also see that his writings were pregnant with possibility for competing protagonists, each trawling Origen's material for ideas that supported one's own cause. That, in fact, is what some squabbling theologians did in the succeeding century.

This brief survey of the early doctrinal developments prior to Nicea has highlighted enormous developments in Christian reflection. Much of this development happened in response to other perspectives that the mainstream church came to view as error. In the process, theological articulation became progressively more complex and sophisticated. Increasingly this involved utilizing the thought forms of Greek philosophy. This facilitated Christianity's becoming the faith of a society and not just the faith of a sect within society. However, the development also created the risk of moving away from aspects of Judeo-Christian thinking as expressed in Scripture, particularly the direct activity of the transcendent God in his created world. The solving of old problems often created new ones in their place—problems that led to intense and divisive theological debate in the fourth and fifth centuries.

[75]R. Williams, *Arius: Heresy & Tradition*, 2nd ed. (Grand Rapids, Mich.: Eerdmans, 2002), p. 138.
[76]W. G. Rusch, *The Trinitarian Controversy* (Philadelphia: Fortress, 1980), p. 15.
[77]Tertullian *Against Hermogenes* 3 (ANF 3:479); also *Against Praxeas* 6—7 (ANF 3:601). Contrast Irenaeus, for whom the Son was "eternally co-existing with the Father" *Against Heresies* 2.30.9; also 4.20.3 (ANF 1:406, 488).

For Further Reading

Barnes, T. *Tertullian: A Historical and Literary Study.* Oxford: Clarendon Press, 1971.

Crouzel, H. *Origen.* Translated by A. S. Worrall. Edinburgh: T. & T. Clark, 1989.

Droge, A. J. "Justin Martyr and the Restoration of Philosophy." *Church History* 56 (1987): 303-19.

Gonzales, J. L. *A History of Christian Thought.* Vol. 1, *From the Beginnings to the Council of Chalcedon.* 2nd ed. Nashville: Abingdon, 1987.

Grant, R. M. *Irenaeus of Lyons.* New York: Routledge, 1997.

Hall, S. G. *Doctrine and Practice in the Early Church.* London: SPCK, 1991.

Kelly, J. N. D. *Early Christian Doctrines.* 5th ed. London: A. & C. Black, 1977.

Minns, D. *Irenaeus.* London: Geoffrey Chapman, 1994.

Ramsey, B. *Beginning to Read the Church Fathers.* London: SCM Press, 1993.

Trigg, J. *Origen.* Atlanta: John Knox Press, 1983.

11

MAPPING THE MIND OF THE CHURCH
Orthodoxy Defined

Many worshipers today use a fourth-century creed as part of their weekly liturgy without any awareness of the intensity of struggle surrounding the beginnings of these documents, both prior to their articulation and prior to their general acceptance in the early church. Despite several centuries of reflection, when Constantine came to the imperial throne in A.D. 312, Christianity still had not approached any consensus in defining Jesus' essential being and his relationship to God. Origen highlighted ongoing major doctrinal differences dogging the church half a century earlier:

> [M]any . . . who profess to believe in Christ differ from each other, not only in small and trifling matters, but also on subjects of the highest importance, as, e.g., regarding God, or the Lord Jesus Christ, or the Holy Spirit.[1]

When the church still faced the threat of persecution, these issues probably had less prominence. Facing death, as Samuel Johnson once asserted, concentrates a person's mind wonderfully. The life-and-death context of persecution made other issues more pressing. One such pressing issue was the pursuit of unity in the church. Perspectives changed markedly, however, when long-term peace came with Constantine. The church now had more freedom to indulge in the luxury of discord. It is therefore not altogether surprising that deep trinitarian division surfaced in the church within a decade of Constantine's gaining power in Rome.

The Role of the State in the Theological Debates
That debates of several centuries should be significantly resolved, at least in the West, within one hundred and forty years of the advent of imperial favor toward Christians is also not surprising. Prior to Constantine the church had little power

---

[1]Origen *On First Principles,* preface 2 (*ANF* 4:239).

to enforce its decisions. It could make declarations, though these tended to be provincial or regional only in scope. It could also depose clerics (most particularly bishops) who strayed too far from major mainstream Christian beliefs. Such measures were, however, not enough to bring the whole church into one viewpoint on crucial issues. The church needed greater coercive strength to achieve that. This came through the Roman empire increasingly becoming a Christian empire, with church and state intertwined. Imperial power could now be used to establish a united church.

It was not the case, however, that the will of the emperor alone could create uniformity. Rather, the combination of substantial church consensus and imperial will together left little room for dissent to survive. The views and actions of the emperors were vital in the clarification of orthodoxy only when that meshed with strongly supported church stances.

Throughout the centuries, emperors had seen themselves as having a spiritual role, whether as *pontifex maximus* under paganism, or as a kind of "bishop" as Constantine did.[2] It was natural for Christian emperors, therefore, to get involved in church affairs. Their influence could be significant in several ways. First, they could bring issues to a head by instigating the holding of a church council, as Constantine strikingly did in bringing together the Council of Nicea in 325. Second, their moral influence might lead the church to decide one way rather than another, as happened at the Councils of Constantinople in 381 and Chalcedon in 451. Third, they could take direct measures to enforce decisions of church councils, which they commonly did in the period now under discussion. One imperial measure frequently employed in the fourth and fifth centuries was exiling those leaders whose views were regarded as erroneous. Another measure promulgated by Theodosius I in 392 was the provision of fines and confiscations for heresy:

> We decree that whosoever has remained in clerical errors, and either ordains clergy, or undertakes clerical office, should be fined ten pounds of gold each, and the land moreover, on which the forbidden acts are being attempted should, if the connivance of the owner is evident, be added to the resources of our treasury.[3]

These emperor-instigated measures contributed significantly to increasing consensus of the church with regard to its central doctrines, especially in the West (though major christological debate persisted in the East for some generations). A byproduct of this consensus (linked as it was to some extent with coercion) was the decline of innovative and adventurous theology. The stage was set for the later

---

[2] Eusebius *Life of Constantine* 4.24 (*NPNF*[2] 1:546).
[3] *Codex Theodosius* 16.5.21 (in J. Stevenson, ed., *Creeds, Councils and Controversies: Documents Illustrating the History of the Church, A.D. 337-461*, rev. ed. [London: SPCK, 1989], p. 152).

emergence of medieval, scholastic theology, designed more to explain and defend what was already known.[4]

The Outbreak of the Arian Controversy

The century or more prior to the council of Chalcedon in 451 was marked by extremely fervent and divisive debate. What was remarkable was that it affected not only the theologians of the church but also its grassroots members. This was probably because salvation itself seemed at stake in the outcome of the debates. If Christ was truly God, then he could save. On the other hand, if he was truly God (and it was generally understood that God was impassible and could not suffer), then how as God could he really suffer on the cross for the sins of the world? And if he was God, was he also really human such that he gathered humanity into himself in saving fashion?

Arius, the instigator of the first wave of debate, created a mass support movement. As an aspect of this support, he supposedly taught Alexandrian dock workers to chant his doctrines.[5] A generation later, Gregory of Nyssa gave a witty description of the then theologically charged situation in the East (thus showing that the issues remained grassroots concerns):

> If in this city you ask anyone for change, he will discuss with you whether the Son is begotten or unbegotten. If you ask about the quality of the bread, you will receive the answer that "the Father is greater, the Son is less." If you suggest that a bath is desirable, you will be told that, "there was nothing before the Son was created."[6]

The Arian debate may be viewed as a polarized response to the views of Arius. However, this may overrate his significance. "Arian-type" issues had already created doctrinal tension prior to Arius. Furthermore, the debate persisted long after his death. Again, few of his writings were preserved (suggesting that followers may not have valued them altogether highly enough to safeguard them). And many Arians denied that they were followers of Arius. Arius's significance was that he brought to prominence a doctrinal crisis that had been gradually gathering, providing a spark that triggered an explosion.[7]

Fundamental to the debate was the issue of the divinity of Jesus. In the wider Greco-Roman world, the word "God" (Greek *theos,* Latin *deus*) could have various

---

[4]J. N. D. Kelly, *Early Christian Doctrines,* 5th ed. (London: A & C Black, 1977), p. 3.

[5]Philostorgius *History of the Church* 2.2 (in F. M. Young, *From Nicaea to Chalcedon: A Guide to the Literature and Its Background* [London: SCM Press, 1983], p. 59).

[6]Gregory of Nyssa, *On the Deity of the Son and the Holy Spirit* (trans. W. H. C. Frend, *The Early Church* [London: Hodder & Stoughton, 1965], pp. 186-87).

[7]R. P. C. Hanson, *The Search for the Christian Doctrine of God: The Arian Controversy 318-381* (Edinburgh: T & T Clark, 1988), p. xvii.

shades of meaning. There could be lower grades of "God" (demi-gods), and even human beings could embody something of the divine—hence the misunderstanding in Acts 14:11. Such a context thus raises the questions, "How divine was Jesus, and what did *divine* mean?"[8]

What we now call the Arian controversy seems first to have erupted in Alexandria in 318. The fifth-century historian Socrates described the opening shots in the long war:

> Alexander [bishop of Alexandria] . . . in the fearless exercise of his functions for the instruction and government of the church, attempted one day in the presence of the presbytery and the rest of his clergy, to explain, with perhaps too philosophical minuteness, that great theological mystery—*the* UNITY *of the Holy Trinity.* A certain one of the presbyters under his jurisdiction, whose name was Arius, possessed of no inconsiderable logical acumen, imagining that the bishop was subtly teaching the same view as Sabellius the Libyan, from love of controversy took the opposite opinion to that of the Libyan, and as he thought, vigorously responded to what was said by the bishop. "If," said he, "the Father begat the Son, he that was begotten had a beginning of existence: and from this it is evident that there was a time when the Son was not. It therefore necessarily follows, that he had his subsistence from nothing."[9]

This description indicates a major concern of the Arian party: that their opponents were Sabellian, denying any substantial distinctions within the Godhead. We can note also a major concern of the anti-Arian party: that Arius was effectively denying the divinity of Jesus, especially in his affirmation that the Begotten must have a beginning.

What Arius believed apart from this is open to question, as information from him comes primarily from his enemies. However, his chief opponent, Athanasius, set down the contents of a document entitled the *Thalia* or *Banquet,* which scholars believe to be substantially from Arius. Among its affirmations are the following:

- "We praise God as without beginning because of him who has a beginning."

- "The Son has nothing proper to God in his substantial nature. For he is not equal, no, nor one in essence with him."

- "There is a Triad, not in equal glories."

- "The Father is foreign in essence from the Son."

- "The Son who was not, but existed at the will of the Father is only-begotten God."

---

[8]R. P. C. Hanson, "The Doctrine of the Trinity Achieved in 381," *Scottish Journal of Theology* 36 (1983): 41-57, see p. 50.

[9]Socrates *Church History* 1.5 (*NPNF*[2] 2:3, emphasis in original).

- "Being Son, he really existed at the will of the Father."[10]

- "God was not always a Father, but afterwards he became a Father."

- "The Son had an origin of creation."

- "The Word is not the very God. Though he is called God, yet he is not very God," but only "by participation of grace. He is God in name only."[11]

From this material we can note the assertion that the Son is not like God, even though he is also called "only-begotten God." He is not of the same substance with God and is essentially different from him. He is less than God is, and with a lesser glory. He is not the Son by nature but only by the Father's will. Though the Son may be divine, his divinity is derivative and his status inferior.

Arius had found a markedly rational solution to the conundrum of the Trinity. It explained the "begottenness" of the Son in its natural sense: that "begotten" implies a beginning and an inferiority to that which "begot" him. It also dealt with the soteriological dilemma, which was particularly acute for minds shaped by Greek philosophy. Christian soteriology presented God as feeling and suffering in Christ. But how could God, the highest form of reality, experience change through feeling and suffering, when, by accepted understanding, God's essential nature meant that he could not change? In the fourth century as much as in the first, the notion of an incarnate and suffering God was "foolishness" to the Greeks (1 Cor 1:23). Arius's solution addressed the problem head on. It took seriously the humanity of Jesus, albeit at the expense of his divinity. It created a Christianity that resonated better with Greek philosophy. The result was "two unequal gods, a High God incapable of human experiences, and a lesser God who, so to speak, did his dirty work for him."[12] It provided a neat rational solution, and it could claim some biblical support: that Jesus asked why he should be called "good," that the Son did not know the day nor hour of his return, that he asserted that the Father was greater than he (Mk 10:18; 13:32; Jn 14:28).

In thus addressing both trinitarian and soteriological issues, Arian teaching appeared to solve some problems—but only at the expense of creating others. Arian perspectives denied both other significant New Testament data and also traditions of the church. Athanasius, bishop of Alexandria from 328, pinpointed the threat of Arian teaching, not only to the majesty of Jesus, but also to the concept of salvation itself. Despite acknowledging in some sense the divinity of Jesus, Arian teaching ef-

---

[10]The foregoing extracts are from Athanasius *On the Councils of Ariminum and Seleucia* 15 (*NPNF*[2] 4:457, English modernized).

[11]The three preceding extracts are from Athanasius *Four Discourses Against the Arians* 1.2.5-6 (*NPNF*[2] 4:309).

[12]Hanson, *Search for the Christian Doctrine of God*, p. 122.

fectively reduced the Son to the level of a created being—a creature—as he was not from eternity, but existed by the will of God. A creature, however, cannot save creatures; only the Creator can. Only if the Son is fully God can he save.[13]

The Arian dispute operated in a subtle and rarefied atmosphere, largely incomprehensible to most Christians today. It was not, however, a matter of "small and very insignificant questions,"[14] despite Constantine's use of that language to describe the controversy in a letter to Arius and his initial adversary, Bishop Alexander of Alexandria. Fundamental questions concerning the nature of God and salvation were at stake. However, the doctrines at issue were complex and subtle, involving fine distinctions. The problem was to distance orthodox doctrine from one error without falling into the opposite error—which commonly seemed to be happening. The fineness of the distinctions led to protagonists reacting to opponents' statements on the basis that they embodied a previously defined heresy, even though that was commonly not the case. It was a confusing debate. From the vantage point of a century later, the historian Socrates likened the situation to two armies hacking and stabbing at each other at nighttime: "It seemed not unlike a contest in the dark; for neither party appeared to understand distinctly the grounds on which they slandered one another."[15]

The Solution of Nicea

The Arian controversy appeared solved by the Council of Nicea in 325. The touchstone of orthodoxy focused on the key term *homoousios,* that is, "of the same being or consubstantial." Jesus was *homoousios* with the Father. This term had critical importance in narrowing options concerning the way to understand Jesus to be divine. Jesus was no demi-God, but "very God from very God." *Homoousios* was the spear in the side of Arianism. The fact that the term *homoousios* was not itself a biblical term indicates a recognition that the problem lay with the meaning of biblical language itself, and thus it could not be resolved by utilizing biblical language alone. It needed a term such as *homoousios* in order to reject Arian perspectives emphatically.

This *homoousios* solution, for a time at least, however, proved to be a papering over the cracks. There are a number of reasons for the failure of Nicea to effect consensus at that time:

- The gathering at Nicea was subject too strongly to the dominance and shadow

---

[13]Athanasius *Letter* 60.8; *Letter* 61.3 (*NPNF*[2] 4:577-78, 579).
[14]Eusebius *Life of Constantine* 2.71 (*NPNF*[2] 1:517).
[15]Socrates *Church History* 1.23 (*NPNF*[2] 2:27). For an earlier similar image see Basil *On the Holy Spirit* 30.76 (*NPNF*[2] 8:48).

Figure 11.1. The ruins of St. Sophia cathedral, seat of the Council of Nicea, in modern Iznik, Turkey (William Allen)

of the emperor, so that the church did not really feel the freedom to articulate all viewpoints and to take the time to come to a genuine consensus.

- The term *homoousios* was not drawn from Scripture. Did it then really express the mind of apostolic Christianity? For its part the anti-Nicene faction could point to explicit Scripture to justify a subordinationist view of Jesus. Jesus himself said, "The Father is greater than I" (Jn 14:28). Moreover, the church fathers commonly held a subordinationist perspective prior to Nicea.[16] Apart from Athanasius, virtually every theologian, East and West, accepted some form of subordinationism up to the year 355, thus making that belief the "accepted orthodoxy."[17]

- The term *homoousios* had negative associations through being too closely associated with Paul of Samosata, who was deposed as bishop of Antioch in 268 for having heretical views. What Paul really believed cannot be fully determined, as

---

[16]By way of example only, see Tertullian, who emphasizes difference within the mode of being of Father and Son over against the modalistic Monarchians, through subordination of the Son: *Against Praxeas* 9 (*ANF* 3:603-4). See also the subordinationism of Ignatius in *To the Magnesians* 7; 13; *To the Philadelphians* 7; *To the Smyrnaeans* 7; 8 (all in *ANF* 1:62, 64, 84, 89).
[17]Hanson, *Search for the Christian Doctrine of God*, p. xix.

we access his views through the filter of his enemies' accounts. However, he appears to have been a dynamic monarchian, so anxious for the unity of God that he denied the real union of the Word with humanity in Jesus, asserting that Jesus was "pure man." While the Word was in Jesus, Paul wished to deny that the Word had a subsistence of its own, as this might imperil the unity of God. He therefore asserted that the Word is *homoousios*—consubstantial, of single identity—with the Father. The association of the term *homoousios* with this earlier heresy made it suspect after Nicea. Was it a monarchian term?

- Despite its apparent precision, *homoousios* still provided scope for diverse interpretation. Certainly it could imply ontological unity: that Father and Son were of the same substance. Alternatively it could mean that generically Father and Son had the same "God-stuff," that both had the attributes of deity.[18]

- The root issue at Nicea was less the unity of God and more the full divinity of the Son. This fostered the viewpoint that delegates could assent to Nicea, but interpret *homoousios* as "kindred substance" rather than as "same substance," thus affirming the Son's divinity rather than the substantial unity of God.[19]

- *Homoousios* left no room for Arianism. However, in slamming the door against Arianism, Nicea seemed to many Eastern bishops to leave the door open to Sabellianism. *Homoousios* sounded Sabellian. So too did the Nicene anathema against those holding that the Son was "of a different essence or being *[hypostasis or ousia]* from the Father." The notion that the Father and Son were of one *hypostasis* challenged the earlier teaching of Origen that, in order to avoid Sabellianism, it was necessary to say that the divine Triad is "three *hypostaseis*."[20] Many of the Eastern leaders, fearing Sabellianism more than they feared Arianism, viewed proponents of Nicea as Sabellian in their thinking. The staunchly pro-Nicene Athanasius, for example, was fond of the illustration, previously used by the Sabellians, that Son is to Father as radiance is to light, distinguishable as two, but essentially one and the same substance.[21] As a result of widespread Eastern unease with the Nicene formula, Nicea in many ways provided a catalyst for further debate rather than providing its resolution.

---

[18]Ibid., p. 170 (quoting Loofs).

[19]One who was unhappy with the term *homoousios* but accepted it on the basis that it simply indicated kindred substance to God (resembling him rather than creatures) was Eusebius of Caesarea: see Socrates *Church History* 1.8 (*NPNF*² 2:11-12).

[20]See H. Chadwick, "Orthodoxy and Heresy from the Death of Constantine to the Eve of the First Council of Ephesus," in *The Cambridge Ancient History,* vol. 13, *The Late Empire, A.D. 337-425,* ed. A. Cameron and P. Garnsey (Cambridge: Cambridge University Press, 1998), pp. 561-600, see p. 565.

[21]Athanasius *Four Discourses Against the Arians* 2.18.41; 3.25.11; 3.25.14; *Defense of the Nicene Definition* 5.20 (*NPNF*² 4:370, 400, 402, 164).

A Swing Toward Arianism

Given these concerns, it is not surprising that the church, especially in the East, fairly quickly swung away from the Nicene formulation. Imperial shift aided this, especially when the pro-Arian Constantius was sole emperor in the decade after 351. Constantius sought resolution of the doctrinal and ecclesiastical division by having the church take a minimalist theological approach to trinitarian issues, rather than defining orthodoxy too closely—a "lowest common denominator" perspective. This approach, permitting both "liberal" Arian and "conservative" Nicene teaching, was effectively a triumph for Arian-type thinking. The Second Creed of Sirmium, promulgated from an influential Western council in 357, displayed this victory. This creed stressed the subordination of the Son to the Father and forbade discussion of the term *ousia* and its related terms, *homoousion* and *homoiousion*. The pro-Nicene Hilary labeled the declaration, "the blasphemy of Sirmium."[22] While this creed may have seemed a disaster to the supporters of Nicea, it eventually contributed to their ultimate victory. The creed was patently Arian, enabling everyone to see where they stood: for it or against it. It caused a clarification of position in which anti-Arian parties became aware of their previously unrecognized common concerns.[23]

The "blasphemy of Sirmium" led on to the Fourth Creed of Sirmium, emanating from major twin councils of Ariminum (West) and Seleucia (East), both of which simply affirmed that the Son was like the Father:

> But whereas the term "essence" (*ousia*), has been adopted by the Fathers in simplicity, and gives offence as being misconceived by the people, and is not contained in the Scriptures, it has seemed good to remove it, that it be never in any case used of God again, because the divine Scriptures nowhere use it of Father and Son. But we say that the Son is like the Father in all things, as also the Holy Scriptures say and teach.[24]

The triumph of Arianism may have now seemed complete. In the words of Jerome some decades later, "the whole world groaned, astonished to find itself Arian."[25] By this time, however, the situation was much more complex than a simple Arianism-versus-Nicea polarity. In the mid 350s four distinct groupings became evident:

• The Homoousians (Greek *homoousios*, "of the same substance") held to the Nicene position that the Son was of "one substance with the Father." Athanasius

---

[22]Hilary of Poitiers *On the Councils* 1.10 (*NPNF*[2] 9:6).

[23]Hanson, *Search for the Christian Doctrine of God,* p. 347.

[24]Quoted in Athanasius *On the Councils* 1.8 (*NPNF*[2] 4:454).

[25]Jerome, *Dialogue Against the Luciferians* 19 (*NPNF*[2] 6:329).

was the most outstanding representative of this party.

- The homoiousians (Greek *homoiousios,* "of like substance") were the heirs of those with misgivings about Nicea, basically because it seemed to smack of Sabellianism. In opposing both Arianism and Sabellianism, homoiousians affirmed that the Son was of "like substance with the Father." They wanted to emphasize the Godness of the Son in a way that more clearly preserved the distinction between Father and Son. Basil of Ancyra and then the Cappadocian Fathers particularly argued in this fashion.

- The homoeans (Greek *homoios,* "like") took an Arian stance in simply affirming that the Son was "like the Father," an intentionally vague term that could allow a diversity of interpretation including that propounded by Arius. They agreed with the strict Arians that Christ was a creature, but still held that he was like the Father.

- The anomoeans (Greek *anomoios,* "unlike") are commonly referred to by scholars as Neo-Arians. The anomoeans were thoroughgoing Arians in asserting that the Son was "unlike the Father." If Father and Son are fundamentally related through being "unbegotten" and "begotten," then their essences are different at their most significant point. They are therefore unlike each other. Any likeness can only be in their outward works or activities, not in their nature.[26]

The Triumph of Nicene Theology

The creeds of Sirmium, which appeared to be the triumph of Arianism, were in fact ultimately the trigger for its death. It made the conservative homoiousians, who were "orthodox" apart from mistrusting the term *homoousios,* realize that by far the greater threat to "orthodox" belief was not the Nicene party but the Arians. Arian views, now starkly expressed in the Sirmium creeds, were abhorrent not only to the homoousians but also to the homoiousians. These creeds thus provided strong motivation for the two parties to recognize their common interests in responding to the threat of Arianism and realize that their theological differences were more of terminology than of essence. A rapprochement between the two groups, therefore, soon came. Combined, their numbers and strength far outweighed that of the Arian sympathizers. Their coming together meant the eventual death knell of Arianism.

The pro-Nicene Athanasius sought to win over key homoiousian leaders in the 360s by approving latitude of language where essentially there was commonality of thought:

---

[26]On this, see S. G. Hall, *Doctrine and Practice in the Early Church* (London: SPCK, 1991), p. 145.

Those, however, who accept everything else that was defined at Nicea, and doubt only about the Coessential, must not be treated as enemies; nor do we here attack them as Ario-maniacs, nor as opponents of the Fathers, but we discuss the matter with them as brothers with brothers, who mean what we mean, and dispute only about the word. For, confessing that the Son is from the essence of the Father, and not from other subsistence, and that he is not a creature nor work, but his genuine and natural offspring, and that he is eternally with the Father as being His Word and Wisdom, they are not far from accepting even the phrase, "Coessential."[27]

A crucial council held at Alexandria in 362 signaled the growing rapprochement of Homoousians and Homoiousians. Its purpose was to deal with factions within the church at Ephesus. However, among its conclusions the council made a distinction between *ousia* and *hypostasis*. Prior to that point the terms were commonly held to be synonymous. That understanding continued the deadlock between those insisting that the Godhead was one *hypostasis* (upholding his unity) and those who insisted that there were three *hypostases* (upholding distinctions within the Godhead). Athanasius himself had previously been so wary of the term *hypostasis* that he had tended not to use it at all, particularly as Origen had talked earlier of three *hypostases* in order to safeguard the notion that distinction between Father, Son and Spirit was more than one of words only. The new distinction articulated at Alexandria allowed the two parties to agree with each other: It was appropriate to talk of three *hypostases* but within one *ousia*. At the same time it was accepted that one could still talk of God as being one *hypostasis*. The language of three *hypostases* was acceptable if one did not imply Tritheism, and the language of one *hypostasis* was acceptable if one did not imply Sabellianism.[28]

The decisions of the council at Alexandria led to the ending of the major difference between the homoousian and the homoiousian parties. Rapprochement between the two main parties facilitated the resolution of the debate over Arianism. The tide was now clearly turning in favor of "orthodoxy." Victory came in 381 at the Council of Constantinople, which reaffirmed the Nicene position with minor word changes to the earlier credal statement. Thereafter, Nicea became a basically unchallenged litmus test for orthodoxy. By the end of the fourth century Arianism had largely disappeared from public view in the Roman Empire.[29]

The Cappadocian Contribution to the Debate over Arianism

While the A.D. 362 Council of Alexandria facilitated the subsequent victory of the

---

[27]Athanasius *On the Councils* 3.41 (NPNF[2] 4:472).

[28]Athanasius *Tome to the People of Antioch* 6 (NPNF[2] 4:484-85).

[29]While Arianism quickly shrank to invisibility within the Roman Empire, it persisted outside the empire among Germanic converts of the Arian missionary Ulfilas.

Nicene position, unfinished business still remained in distinguishing between the previously synonymous Greek terms *ousia* and *hypostasis*. While one term (*ousia*) might now be seen as acknowledging oneness and the other (*hypostasis*) threeness, how could these apparent synonyms be used to differentiate in this way? The problem appears most clearly because in the Latin trinitarian formula, God is three *personae* in one *substantia;* yet *substantia,* which was utilized for the oneness, is the literal equivalent of the Greek term *hypostasis,* which was now being utilized for the threeness. Clearly any distinction between *ousia* and *hypostasis* would require subtle argument.

For his part, Athanasius apparently had little concern for the distinction between the two terms for some time, using *hypostasis* interchangeably with *ousia* as late as 369, stating, "*hypostasis* is *ousia* and means nothing else but very being."[30] Differentiation was crucial, however, for the Cappadocian Fathers (Basil of Caesarea, Gregory of Nazianzus and Gregory of Nyssa) in order to avoid monarchianism. Basil explained why it was vital to make the distinction:

> It is indispensable to have clear understanding that, as he who fails to confess the community of the essence or substance (*ousia*) falls into polytheism, so he who refuses to grant the distinction of the *hypostases* is carried away into Judaism.[31]

While not further defining that difference in that letter, Basil in other letters identified the difference as that between the general and the particular. He defined *hypostasis* as the individual subsistence of a thing, while *ousia* was the essence that is common to the species:

> The distinction between *ousia* and *hypostasis* is the same as that between the general and the particular; as, for instance, between the animal and the particular man. Wherefore, in the case of the Godhead, we confess one essence or substance so as not to give a variant definition of existence, but we confess a particular hypostasis, in order that our conception of Father, Son and Holy Spirit may be without confusion and clear.[32]

On such an argument, *ousia* relates to that which is general (*to koinon,* "the common," i.e., God-stuff, God, the Godhead), while *hypostasis* relates to that which is distinctive (*to idion,* "the belonging to an individual," i.e., Father, Son and Spirit). It should be noted, however, that Basil does not necessarily think of three "self-consciousnesses." What he does talk about in relation to the three *hypostases* is "differentiating properties whereby one is distinguished from another."[33] What

---

[30]Athanasius *To the Bishops of Africa (ad Afros)* 4 (*NPNF*[2] 4:490).
[31]Basil *Letter* 210.5 (*NPNF*[2] 8:251).
[32]Basil *Letter* 236.6 (*NPNF*[2] 8:278); see also *Letters* 38 (*NPNF*[2] 8:137-41) and 214.4 (*NPNF*[2] 8:254).
[33]Basil [sometimes attributed to Gregory of Nyssa] *Letter* 38.2 (*NPNF*[2] 8:137).

were, however, the differentiating properties?

The Cappadocians located the differentiation in their relations of origin. The Father was unbegotten, the Son (eternally) begotten of the Father, and so on. The distinction then lies in the internal causal relations of the Persons: ingenerateness, begottenness and procession (understood in the context of the Trinity and not according to their normal human usage).[34] As Gregory of Nazianzus exclaimed of the Spirit, "What titles which belong to God are not applied to him except only Unbegotten and Begotten?"[35] Distinctions in the Godhead were thus essentially ones of causation: "One Person is distinguished from another [because] one is the Cause and another is of the Cause; and again in that which is of the Cause we recognize another distinction. For one is directly from the first Cause and another by that which is directly from the first Cause."[36] So we have a Cause (Father), a directly Caused (Son) and a mediately Caused (the Holy Spirit—caused by the Father through the Son).

While this perspective indicates differentiation, it hardly clarifies the nature of that differentiation. Here the church faced "mystery" that transcended comprehension. As Athanasius had earlier said, "It is impossible to know what God is, yet it is possible to say what he is not."[37] God is thus knowable in the sense of what he is not (negative theology) rather than in his essential being. In their trinitarian understandings, the Cappadocians essentially argued that the distinction between the Persons can be learned only from God's self-disclosure in Scripture.[38] The Son is "begotten" of the Father (Jn 1:18 KJV) and the Spirit "proceeds" from the Father (Jn 15:26). How much, though, does this clarify matters? What is the difference between being begotten and proceeding? Gregory of Nazianzus had little answer beyond the language of Scripture with regard to "begetting" and "proceeding," other than to say that the matter is part of the unfathomable mystery of God:

> What then is Procession? Do you tell me what is the Unbegottenness of the Father, and I will explain to you the physiology of the Generation of the Son and the Procession of the Spirit, and we shall both of us be frenzy-stricken for prying into the mystery of God.[39]

---

[34]H. O. J. Brown, *Heresies: The Image of Christ in the Mirror of Heresy and Orthodoxy from the Apostles to the Present* (New York: Doubleday, 1984), pp. 150-51.

[35]Gregory of Nazianzus *The Fifth Theological Oration (On the Holy Spirit)* 29 (NPNF[2] 7:327).

[36]Gregory of Nyssa *On "Not Three Gods"* 29 (NPNF[2] 5:336).

[37]Athanasius *First Letter to Monks: Letter* 52.2 (NPNF[2] 4:563).

[38]H. O. J. Brown, *Heresies*, p. 150.

[39]Gregory of Nazianzus *The Fifth Theological Oration (On the Holy Spirit)* 8 (NPNF[2] 7:320).

Debate over the Holy Spirit

While earlier debate had focused almost exclusively on the relations between Father and Son, the preceding quotation indicates that the debate had now raised trinitarian questions concerning the Holy Spirit. This ancillary debate on an appropriate understanding of the Holy Spirit had erupted in the middle of the fourth century. Up till that point, the church had given little thought to the nature of the Spirit in relation to God. However, for a score of years, beginning in the late 350s, fierce debate raged in relation to the Holy Spirit. Those taking a nontrinitarian stance on this point were labeled *Pneumatomachians* or "Spirit-fighters." Their views varied, some claiming that the Spirit was simply a creature, others that the Spirit was intermediate between God and creation. Their key spokesman, Eustathius of Sebaste, stated, "I can neither admit that the Holy Spirit is God, nor can I dare to affirm him to be a creature."[40] The Spirit-fighters quoted a number of texts that might imply the Spirit's inferiority, and noted Scriptural silence in relation to his divinity. It was the Cappadocian Fathers (Basil, Gregory of Nyssa, Gregory of Nazianzus) who played the most crucial role in refuting this viewpoint. In the process they extended the theological debates already raging in the East from a focus on Christology to a broader focus on trinitarianism.

The Cappadocians faced major argument that Scripture was largely silent as to the divinity of the Spirit. Response to this line of reasoning came from Gregory of Nazianzus. He articulated a theory of development in relation to the revelation of the persons of the Trinity, indicating that revelation came gradually only as humanity was able to receive it:

> The Old Testament proclaimed the Father openly, and the Son more obscurely. The New manifested the Son, and suggested the deity of the Spirit. Now the Spirit himself dwells among us, and supplies us with a clearer demonstration of himself.[41]

At the same time there was a crucial text to support the orthodox trinitarian perspective: the trinitarian baptismal formula in Matthew 28:19 said to baptize "in the name of the Father and of the Son and of the Holy Spirit."[42] The fact that this embedded trinitarian language in foundational Christian liturgy was crucial. Argument from liturgical practice—that the church had used this language from the beginning and that this language was trinitarian—provided a powerful weapon in doctrinal debate.

One challenge to the trinitarian position on the Spirit was the jibe that if the

---

[40]In Socrates *Church History* 2.45 (*NPNF*[2] 2:74).
[41]Gregory of Nazianzus *The Fifth Theological Oration (On the Holy Spirit)* 26 (*NPNF*[2] 7:326).
[42]The first argument used against those rejecting the ranking of the Spirit with the Father and Son in Basil *On the Spirit* 10.24; also 17.43; and *Letters* 159.2; 226.3 (*NPNF*[2] 8:16, 27, 212, 269).

Spirit was of the Godhead, then the Father had two Sons. Here the differentiation between the mode of origin of the Spirit from that of the Son became crucial. The language of being "begotten" attaches only to the Son; in the case of the Spirit Scripture uses different language—the language of "proceeding" (Jn 15:26).[43] The Son is "begotten" from the Father, but the Spirit "proceeds" from the Father.

In his defense of the divinity of the Spirit, Gregory of Nyssa used pictorial language to clarify the distinction between being "begotten" and "proceeding." Such language indicated that though the Son and Spirit are both caused by the Father, their origin arose in different fashion:

> It is as if a man were to see a separate flame burning on three torches (and we will suppose that the third flame is caused by that of the first being transmitted to the middle, and then kindling the end torch) and were to maintain that the heat in the first exceeded that of the others.[44]

This understanding of distinctiveness of origin became standard for the Eastern church. Thus the Father directly produces the Son, whereas the Spirit comes from the Father through an intermediary—the Son. The Council of Constantinople in 381 also largely brought to a close the debate on the standing of the Holy Spirit, affirming the consubstantiality of both Son and Spirit with the Father.

Not only were Arianism and Pneumatomachianism largely at an end; so also was a subordinationist view of Christ. While Athanasius was the pioneering champion of full equality of Son (and implicitly Spirit) with Father, it was the Cappadocian Fathers who caused the triumph of this perspective, extinguishing the long tradition of subordinationist thought in the process. Christian doctrine now held as central the perspective that Father, Son and Spirit are equally God. Earlier Scriptural and patristic language indicating subordination were now understood as pointing to subordination only in relation to the manifestation of God in the world in Christ (in his *economy*) and not within the Godhead itself.[45]

The Trinitarian Teaching of Augustine

The final great early church contribution to the doctrine of the Trinity came from Augustine. His trinitarian views were less forged in the heat of doctrinal battle than were those of many of his theological predecessors. In keeping with a trend that had long persisted in the West, he emphasized the unity of the Godhead much more than the distinction of persons. Instead of commencing his trinitarian understanding with the Father from whom the Son is begotten and from whom the

---

[43]Gregory of Nazianzus *The Fifth Theological Oration (On the Holy Spirit)* 8 (*NPNF*[2] 7:320).
[44]Gregory of Nyssa *On the Holy Spirit* (*NPNF*[2] 5:317).
[45]For example, Gregory of Nazianzus *Third Theological Oration* 18 (*NPNF*[2] 7:307-8).

Spirit proceeds (which leads to a focus on threeness), he began by examining the divine nature itself (which leads to a focus on oneness). The God-Trinity is the basic Divinity, unfolding itself into Father, Son and Spirit.[46] Starting with the God-Trinity means that Father, Son and Spirit are not three separate individuals as are, say, three human beings.[47] Rather, each is substantially the same as the others. They share one single will. As a consequence, their operation is inseparable, so that any operation of one is the operation of the entire Trinity.

Does this unity obliterate the notion of three "persons"? Augustine would have preferred not to use "person" language, as it might imply three Gods. However, he used such language to avoid the error of modalism. He employed the language of "persons" not because it was good language, but because it was the best option within inadequate language, "a conventional way of expressing what is otherwise inexpressible."[48] Otherwise one would have no language on the matter at all.[49] Augustine thus moves into the sphere of "negative theology": statements aimed to avoid error rather than to advance positive understanding:

> It sought then what three it should call them, and answered, substances or persons; by which names it did not intend diversity to be meant, but singleness to be denied: that not only unity might be understood therein from the being called one essence, but also Trinity from the being called three substances or persons.[50]

How then is there threeness at all? For Augustine, the distinctions within the Trinity are better described in terms of relations rather than of persons. The Godhead includes threeness in relationships:

> He [the Father] is the Father not in respect to himself, but to the Son; nor is the Son in respect to himself, but to the Father; nor is the Spirit so as regards himself, in as far as he is called the Spirit of the Father and of the Son.[51]

More positively, God is love, and love requires an object. In Augustine's analysis love can be analyzed into the one that loves, the one that is loved, and the love itself that unites.[52] This analogy in particular helps explain the procession of the Holy Spirit. The Spirit is the bond of love that exists between the Father and the Son:

---

[46]E. Portalié, *A Guide to the Thought of St. Augustine*, trans. R. J. Bastian (London: Burns & Oates, 1960), p. 131.
[47]Augustine *On the Gospel of Saint John*: Tractate 39.3-5 (NPNF[1] 7:222-23).
[48]J. L. Gonzales, *A History of Christian Thought*, vol. 1, *From the Beginnings to the Council of Chalcedon*, 2nd ed. (Nashville: Abingdon, 1987), p. 331.
[49]Augustine *On the Trinity* 5.9-10.10-11; 7.4.7 (NPNF[1] 3:92, 109).
[50]Ibid., 7.4.9 (NPNF[1] 3:111).
[51]Augustine *On the Gospel of Saint John*: Tractate 39.4 (NPNF[1] 7:223); also *On the Trinity* 5.5.6 (NPNF[1] 3:89).
[52]Augustine *On the Trinity* 8.10.14; 15.6.10 (NPNF[1] 3:124, 204).

Figure 11.2. Centuries of ecclesiastical debate over the Trinity summed up in a mosaic on the floor of St. Paul's crypt, London (Laurie Guy)

> Therefore the Holy Spirit, whatever it is, is something common both to the Father and the Son. But that communion itself is consubstantial and co-eternal; and if it may fitly be called friendship, let it be so called; but it is more aptly called love. And this is also a substance, since God is a substance, and "God is love," as it is written.[53]

Mystery in relation to God's threeness remains in Augustine's thought. Augustine was not altogether surprised by his difficulty. God in the end is a mystery, above the human mind to fathom. However, God is creator, and the world as God's creation shows "traces," *vestigiae*, of God's own being.[54] We can therefore utilize aspects of creation as analogies to help us in our understanding of the mysteries of God's nature, limited though analogies necessarily are. The most significant of these analogies or "traces" is the human mind itself, because humanity is made in the image of God.[55] The human mind can be viewed from three angles: the human mind itself, the human mind that knows itself, and the human mind that loves itself.[56] Clearly here is both threeness and oneness. To consider the human mind

---

[53]Ibid., 6.5.7 (*NPNF*[1] 3:100).
[54]Ibid., 15.2.3 (*NPNF*[1] 3:200).
[55]Ibid.
[56]Ibid., 9 (*NPNF*[1] 3:125-33).

from another perspective, memory, will and understanding are closely cojoined in the human mind—again traces of threeness in unity—traces of Trinity.[57] Augustine explores a number of features of human psychology to demonstrate that essential unity may yet have threeness. Thus the mystery of the Trinity is not foolishness.

Augustine's stress on the unity of the Godhead sailed close to Sabellianism, though he denied entering those waters. His view of the Spirit as the love between the Father and the Son later provoked conflict with the Eastern church in the famous *filioque* dispute. In that controversy the East challenged Western language that "the Spirit proceeds from the Father *and the Son [filioque]*" on the grounds that there can only be one ultimate source and that is the Father. For its part the East preferred to say that the Spirit "proceeds from the Father through the Son." That debate did not come to a head until the eighth century. In the fifth century, at least in the West, debate over the Trinity largely subsided. What did boil furiously in the fifth century, however, was debate over the nature of Christ, and it is to this issue that we now turn.

The Nature of Christ

In its formative centuries the early church could hardly avoid debate over the nature of Christ. If Christ was somehow God, how could he then be also human? The early solution of Docetism was that Christ was not really human—he only seemed to be. The alternative explanation of dynamic monarchianism went in the opposite direction: Christ was not really God but was rather a man especially empowered by God from the time of his baptism. Both solutions were rejected. Tertullian expressed mainstream thinking at the end of the second century: Christ was both God and man.[58] Though one person, he was composed of "two substances," which remained distinct.[59] How did the Word become flesh? Tertullian himself asked whether this was by the Word being transfigured into flesh, or whether it was by the Word clothing himself in flesh.[60] The first option was rejected because the eternal God is unchangeable and transfiguration implies the destruction of that which had previously existed. If transfiguration had occurred, then the two substances would mix and produce a third substance, which would be neither God nor man. As a consequence of this line of thinking Tertullian asserted rather that Christ clothed himself with flesh. Thus the Word remains nothing else than God, and the flesh nothing else than man, a twofold state with the property of each nature being wholly preserved.[61]

---

[57]Ibid., 10.12.19 (*NPNF*[1] 3:143).
[58]Tertullian *Against Praxeas* 2 (*ANF* 3:598).
[59]Tertullian *On the Flesh of Christ* 13 (*ANF* 3:533).
[60]Tertullian *Against Praxeas* 27 (*ANF* 3:623).
[61]Ibid.

On the whole the church was content with that explanation, until issues on the nature of Christ erupted afresh in the fourth century. The Nicene solution regarding the Godness of the Son seemed to contradict the fundamental assumption that God cannot suffer. If Christ suffered, and Christ was God, then God would suffer. What way was there through this dilemma? Speculation from Apollinarius, bishop of Laodicea, on the nature of Christ's divine-human nature sought a way through the maze. Instead it opened another front of debate in the 360s.

The Apollinarian Controversy

An unanswered question springing from views such as those of Tertullian involves the nature of Jesus' inner self. Did the Logos in Jesus replace any human soul? There were two options. A tendency emerged in the Alexandrian church to say that the Word united with human flesh without there being a human soul (a "Word-flesh" Christology). A contrasting perspective, which the Antiochene church tended to favor, said that the Word united himself with a complete humanity, soul as well as body (a "Word-man" Christology).[62] If the Logos did not replace the human soul in Jesus, were there then two souls in Jesus? If the Logos did replace the human soul in Jesus, was he fully human? Did he really suffer temptation if the Logos replaced the human soul?

Debate erupted afresh on the relationship of the divine and the human in Jesus in the fourth and fifth centuries. Prior to discussing the views of four key theologians on this issue I have provided a diagram on the following page to depict their views on this complex matter. Any pictorial representation obviously has its defects; the diagram is simply an imperfect but hopefully helpful learning aid for reference as you read the views of each theologian. The diagram only focuses on distinctive features of each theologian: it does not provide a total explanation of their theology in relation to Christ. This means that the diagrams are not fully equivalent. In particular, diagrams relating to the views of Apollinarius and Nestorius do not indicate their views on the eternal nature of Christ as Son of God (these views in fact being similar to those of Athanasius and Cyril on this matter).

Apollinarius brought the issue of the interrelationship of Christ's humanity and divinity to a head in the 350s, leading to major controversy in the 360s and 370s. In his view, the stumbling block to the notion that Christ had a human soul was that human souls are by nature *treptos* (fallible, unstable, succumbing to the flesh). Had Christ had a human soul, he could not have been Savior of fallen humanity. What was needed was a soul that was *a-treptos* (not fallible). Apollinarius argued that in contrast to normal humanity, where the "soul" unites with flesh, in the case

---

[62]For discussion of this distinction, see Kelly, *Early Christian Doctrines*, p. 281.

VARYING FOCUSES WITH REGARD TO THE NATURE OF CHRIST

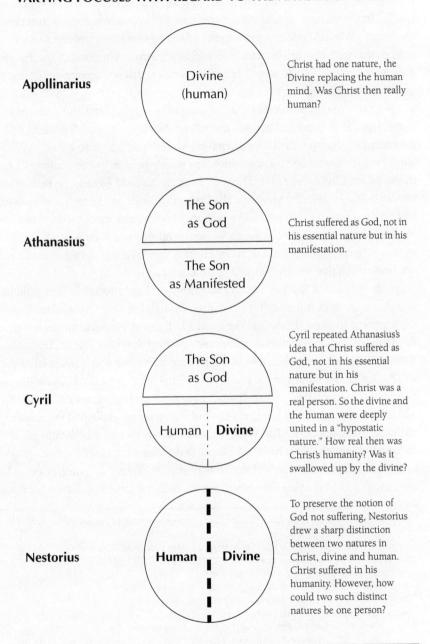

Apollinarius   Divine (human)   Christ had one nature, the Divine replacing the human mind. Was Christ then really human?

Athanasius   The Son as God / The Son as Manifested   Christ suffered as God, not in his essential nature but in his manifestation.

Cyril   The Son as God / Human ¦ Divine   Cyril repeated Athanasius's idea that Christ suffered as God, not in his essential nature but in his manifestation. Christ was a real person. So the divine and the human were deeply united in a "hypostatic nature." How real then was Christ's humanity? Was it swallowed up by the divine?

Nestorius   Human ¦ Divine   To preserve the notion of God not suffering, Nestorius drew a sharp distinction between two natures in Christ, divine and human. Christ suffered in his humanity. However, how could two such distinct natures be one person?

Figure 11.3. Varying focuses with regard to the nature of Christ

of Christ, the Logos united with flesh.[63] This means that the divine mind (Logos) replaced the finite human mind in Jesus, who can thus be called "the flesh-bearing God."[64] In Christ there is "one nature composed of impassible divinity and passible flesh."[65] While Apollinarius's thought had the rigor of logic, it meant that Christ did not really possess full humanity according to normal understandings. He had a divinized humanity. He would not, therefore, experience ignorance, agony or growth in knowledge.

Moreover, Apollinarius's thought cut across the old recapitulation view of Irenaeus, that the incarnate Christ was the second Adam, living a perfect life in order to redeem humanity, which he gathered into himself in his incarnation.[66] Within a recapitulation-type soteriology, which was widely held in fourth-century Christianity, could Christ really save if he was not really human? As early as the Council of Alexandria in 362, the view that the Logos displaced any human soul in Jesus was rejected on these grounds.[67] As Gregory of Nazianzus argued, "If anyone has put his trust in him [Jesus] as a man without a human mind, he is really bereft of mind and quite unworthy of salvation. For that which he has not assumed he has not healed; but that which is united to his Godhead is also saved."[68]

Major opposition to Apollinarius came from the Cappadocian fathers. Athanasius also had major influence on the matter through his extensive explorations of the relationship of the divine and the human in the Son. Emphatically, in his view, the Son was God. But prevailing understanding held that God was unchangeable. If the Son was unchangeable, how could he become human and how could he suffer? Athanasius's solution to the problem of Christ's nature focused not on the cohering of the divine and human "parts," but rather on his condescension for humanity in a way that joins humanity to God.[69] Athanasius explained the matter in terms of "appropriation." The Word "condescended" to take a body and make it his own.[70] Through this, what is not proper to the Word in himself becomes proper to the Word for our salvation.[71] Human attributes, including suffering, can thus be attributed to the incarnate Word because the body he took was indeed his body.

---

[63]M. F. Wiles, "The Nature of the Early Debate about Christ's Human Soul," *Journal of Ecclesiastical History* 16 (1965): 139-51, see p. 148.
[64]*Fragment* 109, in Kelly, *Early Christian Doctrines*, p. 291. See Gregory of Nazianzus *Letter* 102 (*NPNF*² 7:444) noting such Apollinarian usage.
[65]*Letter to Dionysius* 6, in Kelly, *Early Christian Doctrines*, p. 291.
[66]Irenaeus *Against Heresies* 2.22.4; 3.18.1; 3.21.10; 3.22.3 (all in *ANF* 1).
[67]Athanasius *Tome to the People of Antioch* 7 (*NPNF*² 4:485).
[68]Gregory of Nazianzus *Letter* 101 (*NPNF*² 7:440).
[69]K. Anatolios, *Athanasius: The Coherence of His Thought* (London: Routledge, 1998), p. 147.
[70]Athanasius *On the Incarnation of the Word* 18; 21.4; *Four Discourses Against the Arians* 2.21.64 (*NPNF*² 4:45-46, 47, 383).
[71]Anatolios, *Athanasius*, p. 146.

At the same time, that body was external to his essence; so the Word in his essential nature did not suffer: "It was fitting that the Lord in putting on human flesh, put it on whole with the affections proper to it . . . though they did not touch him according to his Godhead."[72] The outcome was paradox: the Son both suffered and did not suffer. Athanasius made this paradox explicit in his *Letter to Epictitus*: "It is strange that he it was who suffered and yet suffered not. Suffered, because his own body suffered; suffered not, because the Word, being by nature God, is unable to suffer."[73] Athanasius's solution meant that the Word really connected with humanity and gathered it to himself, while at the same time remaining God and so bringing our humanity "into the Father's presence," so that our "salvation and deification might be sure."[74]

This solution still left open, however, how the divine and the human cohered in the Son. The Council of Constantinople in 381 anathematized Apollinarianism. Nevertheless, latent issues still remained, which had the potential for yet further division in the future. That time came half a century later.

The Nestorian Debate

Behind so much of the debates of the fourth and fifth centuries lay problems caused by the foundational perspective that God is impassible. This assumption also became a major factor in the debate sparked by Nestorius, bishop of Constantinople from 428. How could one acknowledge a real incarnation while avoiding the notion that God suffered? Nestorius's solution stressed the dual nature of Christ's person so that it was his humanity, not his divinity, which suffered. He detonated the controversy through questioning the appropriateness of using the title *Theotokos*, "God-bearing," to honor Mary the mother of Jesus. Nestorius strongly opposed the term as confusing Christ's two natures and excessively focusing on his divinity at the expense of his humanity. If *Theotokos* were still to be used, it should be balanced by the term *anthropotokos*, "man-bearing." It would be better still, however, to avoid both terms in favor of *Christotokos*, Christ-bearing. Making this point involved risk at a popular level as well as theologically, as the objection to the term might seem to denigrate Mary, who was increasingly revered.

Nestorius's rival, Cyril of Alexandria, seized the opportunity to attack him for his views. Cyril argued that Nestorius's perspective implied the heretical position that there were two Sons, linked only by a moral union.[75] Clearly high levels of

---

[72]Athanasius *Four Discourses Against the Arians* 3.26.32 (NPNF[2] 4:411, English modernized).

[73]Athanasius *Letter 59 (to Epictitus)* 6 (NPNF[2] 4:572, English modernized).

[74]Athanasius *Four Discourses Against the Arians* 2.21.70 (NPNF[2] 4:386).

[75]*Letters* 3; 10; see Kelly, *Early Christian Doctrines*, p. 311.

ecclesiastical rivalry lay behind Cyril's challenge: "At no phase in the evolution of the church's theology have the fundamental issues been so mixed up with the clash of politics and personalities."[76]

However, deep issues of theology were also a fundamental driving force in the debate. While Nestorius held to the unity of the two natures of Christ, he insisted that the two natures of the incarnate Christ remained unaltered and distinct in the union. This meant that the impassible Word was not involved in any change or suffering and that Christ lived a genuinely human life. Nestorius's view of Christ regarded him as one person who combined in himself two distinct elements. The stress on two separate natures meant that one should not utilize the notion of *communicatio idiomatum* (literally, the sharing of attributes). *Communicatio idiomatum* expresses the view that because of the unity of Christ's person, the properties of one nature are communicated to the other so that it is appropriate to attribute to his divinity what properly pertains to his human attributes and experiences, and vice versa. In Nestorius's view, one should predicate the attributes and experiences of Christ to the appropriate nature—to his divinity or humanity—or to the God-man. Nestorius's difficulties with *communicatio idiomatum* understandings raised suspicions about Nestorius's teachings, because *communicatio idiomatum* perspectives were already widespread in the church. From that perspective, Nestorius failed to integrate adequately the divine and human dimensions of Christ.

In contrast, while Cyril acknowledged the two natures of Christ, he denied their separation. After the union of the Word with flesh, there was really one nature in Christ—a "hypostatic union" of the two natures. The two natures came together in one "hypostatic nature," the "enfleshed nature of the Word."[77] Cyril used the analogy of fire and charcoal. When fire penetrates charcoal, distinct identities remain but the two are now in no way separated. Such an image seemed to suggest that the Word swallowed up Christ's humanity to which it was united. This invited the objection that Christ did not have genuine human experience if his humanity was so fused to his divinity; this understanding would sacrifice the symmetry of the relation between the divine and the human in Christ.[78]

Behind the issue of how the two natures of Christ (divine and human) cohered lay the issue of the impassibility of God. Cyril, wanting to stress the real incarnation of the Word in humanity, spoke paradoxically of the "impassible suffering of

---

[76]Kelly, *Early Christian Doctrines,* p. 310.

[77]Cyril *Against Nestorius* 2, proem. (in Kelly, *Early Christian Doctrines,* p. 319).

[78]J. Pelikan, *The Christian Tradition: A History of the Development of Doctrine* (Chicago: University of Chicago Press, 1971), 1:248.

the Son."[79] Elsewhere he utilized thought already spelled out in Athanasius: "He suffers in his own flesh and not in the nature of the Godhead."[80] To opponents this made Cyril dangerously "theopaschite" (one who believes that God suffered). Such, according to Nestorius, must be resisted: "Even if the Emperor treats us with violence, we shall not be persuaded to admit a suffering God."[81] Yet was Cyril's position in relation to the suffering of Christ altogether different from that of Nestorius, who once used similar language? According to Nestorius, Christ was "impassible according to his divinity but passible according to the nature of his body."[82]

The issue then was a fine one. Cyril recognized qualified impassibility: God the Word emptied himself, temporarily limiting his divine power.[83] The eternal Word suffered as God-in-the-flesh and not as God outside of the framework of the incarnation.[84] To Nestorius, Cyril's language of impassible suffering was either contradictory or double talk.[85] In contrast, Nestorius held to unqualified divine impassibility.[86]

In his concern to protect the impassibility of God (his real "Godness"), Nestorius created a firewall between the divine and suffering by so emphasizing that Christ had two natures that one could then say that it was only the humanity of Christ that suffered. But how could there really be one person if the two natures were so separated? Nestorius answered that there was a "conjunction" (Greek *synapheia*) of the two natures in intimate union. This indicates that both Cyril and Nestorius were concerned to avoid a simple attribution of suffering to God and both were prepared to acknowledge both distinction and unity in Christ's nature. The difference between the two involved partly a question of emphasis. Did the stress lie on the unity or on the distinction? Additional issues included Nestorius's denials of two widely accepted beliefs and practices: the *communicatio idiomatum* (sharing of attributes of Christ's nature) and the description of Mary as *Theotokos*. These denials fed fuel to the fiery ongoing debate.

Without sketching all the complex events of the Cyril-Nestorius dispute, suffice it to say that a Council at Ephesus in 431 (subsequently regarded as the third great ecumenical council) deposed Nestorius, and a rival council deposed Cyril. The first of the two councils proved to be the more effective and led to Nestorius's exile

---

[79]Cyril *Second Letter to Succensus* 4.18 (in J. J. O'Keefe, "Impassible Suffering? Divine Passion and Fifth-Century Christology," *Theological Studies* 58 [1997]: 39-60, see p. 45).

[80]Cyril *That Christ Is One* (in O'Keefe, "Impassible Suffering?" p. 50).

[81]*Letter to Those of Ephesus* 1.1.7.77, in P. Gavrilyuk, "*Theopatheia*: Nestorius's Main Charge against Cyril of Alexandria," *Scottish Journal of Theology* 56, no. 2 (2003): 190-207, quote p. 192.

[82]Nestorius *Letter to Cyril* 2.4 (in Pelikan, *The Christian Tradition*, p. 231).

[83]Gavilryuk, "*Theopatheia*," p. 203.

[84]Ibid., p. 201.

[85]Ibid., p. 193.

[86]Ibid., p. 190.

till his death in about 451. However, the confused and turbulent dispute after 431 left two large unreconciled groups in the wider church. A middle way through the impasse needed to be found. Consequently a compromise was reached between the Antiochenes and the Alexandrians in the "Formula of Union" in 433. As it was substantially a doctrinal statement that the Antiochene bishops had drafted in 431, it appeared a victory for the Nestorians, particularly as its language of "a union of two natures" emphasized two natures after union. Nevertheless, *Theotokos* had been pronounced orthodox and Nestorius remained condemned. Even the "Formula of Union," however, did not end the debate.

One, Eutyches, seems in rather muddled fashion about 448 to have begun affirming that Christ had one nature only after his incarnation and that his incarnate humanity was unlike our humanity. Flavian, bishop of Constantinople, excommunicated Eutyches. The matter went to a council at Ephesus in 449 (the "robber council"[87]) chaired by Dioscorus, bishop of Alexandria. Council proceedings not only rehabilitated Eutyches and declared him orthodox, but also led to violence against Flavian, who was so badly beaten that he subsequently died. Now Alexandria seemed to have triumphed.

A change of emperor, however, brought yet another reversal. The advent of the new emperor led to the whole matter of the relation between the divine and the human in Jesus being reexamined at the Council of Chalcedon in 451. There the voice of Pope Leo of Rome prevailed. He had earlier written a famous dogmatic letter or *Tome* for the "robber council," but that council had not even considered it. Now that there was a new emperor sympathetic to Leo's views, such views proved decisive at Chalcedon. The *Tome* was received with acclamation. It was specifically endorsed by the council and strongly influenced Chalcedonian pronouncements that sought to resolve the doctrinal controversy. The council affirmed the following:

- The Son is truly God and truly man.

- Jesus had a rational soul as well as a body.

- The divine natures coexist without confusion (rejecting Eutychianism) and without separation (rejecting Nestorianism).

- The natures are separate principles of operation but they always act in harmony with each other.

- Mary is *Theotokos*, which also means that *communicatio idiomatum* language—

---

[87]The council is known by this name because Pope Leo of Rome was so appalled by its proceedings and outcome that he called it a "den of robbers."

saying, for example, that the Son of Man came down from heaven and that the Son of God was crucified—is valid.[88]

For the West, the bitterest times of doctrinal dispute had now come to an end. On the major disputed issues the church had now reached a substantial consensus: orthodoxy regarding the nature of Christ was defined. For the East, the situation after Chalcedon was much more complex than it was for the West. Those stressing the one nature of the incarnate Christ felt defeated, particularly as Dioscorus was deposed from his patriarchate at Alexandria. Eventually this led to the Monophysite schism of those emphasizing one *physis*, "nature" of the incarnate Christ.[89] This viewpoint persists today in the Armenian Apostolic Church and in the Coptic, Ethiopian and Syrian Orthodox churches.

After Chalcedon, Nestorius was still treated as a heretic and Cyril as orthodox. This happened despite Cyril's tendency toward "heavenly flesh" views of Christ that may have inadequately emphasized Christ's real humanity. Moreover, Nestorius specifically endorsed the convictions of Leo's *Tome* after Chalcedon, which raises the question of whether Nestorius should really be treated as heretical at all. Perhaps this illustrates how fine and confusing the distinctions had become and how much the debate intertwined with political factors. Still, the credal statement of Chalcedon did largely bring finality, at least for the West. Thereafter its formulas became the lens for the reading of John's great christological affirmation: "the Word became flesh and lived among us" (Jn 1:14).

For Further Reading

Anatolios, K. *Athanasius: The Coherence of His Thought*. London: Routledge, 1998.

Brown, H. O. J. *Heresies: The Image of Christ in the Mirror of Heresy and Orthodoxy from the Apostles to the Present*. New York: Doubleday, 1984.

Gavrilyuk, P. "*Theopatheia*: Nestorius's Main Charge against Cyril of Alexandria." *Scottish Journal of Theology* 56, no. 2 (2003): 190-207.

Gonzales, J. L. *A History of Christian Thought*. Vol. 1, *From the Beginnings to the Council of Chalcedon*. Nashville: Abingdon, 1987.

Gregg, R. C., and D. E. Groh. *Early Arianism: A View of Salvation*. London: SCM Press, 1981.

Groh, D. E. "The Arian Controversy: How It Divided Early Christianity." *Bible Re-*

---

[88]On this see Leo *Letter* 28.5 (part of Leo's *Tome*).

[89]The schism emerged only very gradually, so that it was eighty years after Chalcedon before there were any moves to establish an anti-Chalcedonian hierarchy in the eastern empire: W. H. C. Frend, "Heresies and Schism as Social & National Movements," in *Schism, Heresy and Religious Protest,* ed. D. Baker, Studies in Church History 11 (Cambridge: Cambridge University Press, 1972), pp. 37-56, see pp. 49-52.

view 10, no. 1 (1994): 20-32.

Hall, S. G. *Doctrine and Practice in the Early Church.* London: SPCK, 1991.

Hanson, R. P. C. "The Doctrine of the Trinity Achieved in 381." *Scottish Journal of Theology* 36 (1983): 41-57.

———. *The Search for the Christian Doctrine of God: The Arian Controversy 318-381.* Edinburgh: T & T Clark, 1988.

Kelly, J. N. D. *Early Christian Doctrines.* 5th ed. London: A. & C. Black, 1977.

LaCugna, C. M. *God for Us: The Trinity and Christian Life.* New York: HarperCollins, 1991.

O'Keefe, J. J. "Impassible Suffering? Divine Passion and Fifth-Century Christology." *Theological Studies* 58 (1997): 39-60.

Rusch, W. G., ed. *The Trinitarian Controversy: Sources of Early Christian Thought.* Philadelphia: Fortress, 1980.

Stevenson, J., ed. *Creeds, Councils and Controversies: Documents Illustrating the History of the Church, A.D. 337-461.* Rev. ed. London: SPCK, 1989.

Williams, R. *Arius: Heresy and Tradition.* London: Darton, Longman & Todd, 1987.

Young, F. M. *From Nicaea to Chalcedon: A Guide to the Literature and Its Background.* London: SCM Press, 1983.

CONCLUSION

This book has traced dramatic change in the life of the early church. At the end of the period the dynamic movement had become a highly structured and hierarchical institution. Moreover, connection to that institution had become fundamental to identification as a Christian.

The church, in clarifying and exploring the implications of its central convictions, developed a sophisticated, complex and often abstruse set of doctrines. No matter that these doctrines were much less comprehensible to its rank-and-file membership than those articulated at the beginning of its history. It was enough that the church as a whole had worked out its beliefs. These could be guarded and explained by the learned doctors of the church and utilized as a filter to shut down heretical ideas.

In the large cities at least, the gathering of the faithful had become a grand affair. Impressive, richly decorated buildings, splendidly robed higher clergy and elaborate ritual all served to remind believers of the central and glorious place of their religion in society. Its services were an awe-inspiring spectacle, led by a special category of people, the clergy.

A further special group of people had also emerged in the church: the monks. While growth in holiness might often be stunted in the cooler climate of a society-embracing church, a higher way of living seemed more easily nurtured in a hot-house monastic tradition. Monastic withdrawal from the world in asceticism and worship might also be balanced by social caring for the needs of society. In an increasingly crumbling society, the monks came also to be major preservers and bearers of education. In addition, their communal strength prepared them for a role as the shock troops of medieval missionary endeavor.

Church life in its first five hundred years was a river of change as the church developed and clarified its boundaries. The beliefs that it defined provide a doctrinal reference point to the present. Its writings embody a wealth of insight and spirituality for the church of all ages. They point back to the original gospel as well as on from the original gospel. The early church serves as a continuing reminder that the church must always be reforming if it is to remain true to its beginnings.

adoptionism. The belief that Jesus was a perfect man who was adopted as Son of God. The adoption was commonly understood by those who held this belief to have occurred when the Spirit descended at Jesus' baptism.

Anchorite. See monasticism.

apology. A type of writing that sought to explain and defend Christian beliefs and practices to a largely hostile pagan society.

apostolic fathers. A group of Christian writers of the late first century and the second century.

Arian. A supporter of Arius who viewed the Word (Christ) as not eternal and not fully God.

asceticism. The practice of severe self-discipline for the sake of spiritual advancement (Greek *askein* = "to exercise").

basilica. Originally a large public building, usually with an apse and colonnades. Later the term came to be applied to a church building of this nature.

caesaropapism. State rule over the church, even with regard to doctrine.

canon. A rule of the church (Greek *kanōn* = "rule").

catechumens. Those enrolled as preparing for Christian baptism (Greek *katechein* = "to teach"). The catechumenate relates to the structuring of that preparation time in instruction, etc.

catholic. While today *Catholic* is commonly linked to the Roman Catholic Church, at the time of the early church it simply referred to the church as a whole as opposed to separated parts that were either heretical or schismatic (Greek *katholikos* means "according to the whole").

coenobite. See monasticism.

communicatio idiomatum. The notion that because of the unity of Christ's person, his divine and human attributes and experiences may be expressed interchangeably. Thus what properly pertains to Christ's divinity may be attributed to his humanity and vice versa.

compline. The last hour of prayer for the day in the divine office.

confessors. Those who, though not martyred, had suffered for their faith in time of persecution.

decretal. A papal letter viewed by the pope as having the force of law within the church. It was usually written to an individual or group in response to some particular question or issue.

demiurge. In Platonic thought, the "craftsman" (Greek *demiourgos*) who was creator of the world.

divine office. The daily liturgical round of prayers, etc. especially within monastic communities.

divinization. The process of increasingly "partaking of the divine nature" (2 Peter 1:4) through union with Christ.

Docetism. The belief that Jesus Christ was not really human but only seemed to be so (from the Greek *dokein*, "to seem").

Donatism. The stance of the schismatic Donatist church which began in the fourth century in North Africa. It differed little from catholic Christianity apart from holding a position of greater rigor on issues that arose from the persecution of Christians. Its name derives from one of its early leaders, Donatus.

dynamic monarchianism. An adoptionist form of monarchianism (stress on the oneness of God). This perspective asserts that Jesus was a unique man divinely energized by the power (Greek *dynamis*) of God.

economic trinitarianism. This is an early form of trinitarian thought expressing the threeness of God in his operations in the world (Greek *oikonomia* = an "arrangement" or the "management of a household"). The term "economic trinitarianism" makes no statement about the internal relations within the Godhead (= "immanent trinitarianism").

epiphany. The term comes from the Greek *epiphaneia* = "appearance". Today the feast is celebrated on January 6 to commemorate the visit of the Magi to Bethlehem and the Christ child. In the fourth century it variously celebrated the birth of Jesus, the visit of the Magi, Jesus' baptism, and the miracle at Cana.

Eremite. See monasticism.

exomologesis. See penance.

ex opere operato. A Latin term applying to the sacraments. It reflects a theological understanding that a sacrament is valid even where the officiant or recipient of the sacrament is unworthy.

Gnosticism. A variety of early religious movements (especially from the second century), that taught salvation by *gnōsis*, secret knowledge. Some of these movements borrowed from or had links with Christianity.

hagiography. Biographical writing focusing on the lives of holy person/s (saint/s). They are usually presented in idealized fashion.

hypostatic union. The doctrine of the consubstantial union of the divine and human natures of Christ in the one person (Greek *hypostasis*).

labarum. Constantine's military standard after his visionary experience at Milvian Bridge. It was adorned with a cross decorated
with a wreath within which were the first two letters of Christ's
name: *chi* (the letters *Ch* written as *X*) and *rho* (the letter *R* written as *P*).

Lent. The forty-day pre-Easter period of penitence and fasting.

Logos. The Greek word literally means word or thought or reason.
For the Stoics, the term applied to the rational principle ruling the world. All
people shared in that logos. Christians utilized the term so that Christ was the
Logos *par excellence.* The term was very important in creating a cultural bridge
connecting Christianity with non-Christian understandings.

Marcionism. The teaching of the second-century heretical teacher, Marcion, who
taught radical discontinuity between Old and New Testaments and between the
God of the Old Testament and the Father of Jesus.

metropolitan. The bishop of the principal city *(metropolis)* of a province.

modalistic monarchianism. A doctrine so stressing the oneness of God that it denied essential distinctions within the Godhead. What others might call the
"persons" of the Trinity were regarded by modalistic monarchians as different
modes of expression by the one God. The belief could also be termed "patripassianism" (based on the notion that one could legitimately state that the Father
suffered on the cross) or "Sabellianism" (so-called because of a leading exponent of the belief named Sabellius).

monarchianism. See modalistic monarchianism and dynamic monarchianism.

monasticism. The practice of a structured withdrawal from the world in order to
enhance one's spiritual development. Coenobitic (from the Greek for life together) monasticism was communal monasticism. Eremitic (from the Greek
erēmos = "desert") and anchoritic (from the Greek *anachōrein* = "to withdraw")
monasticism was solitary monasticism, though in practice some structured
contact with others usually occurred (= semi-eremitic monasticism).

mono-episcopacy. The pattern of bishops that occurred when the senior presbyter or bishop in the team of presbyters leading the church in a local area became
the sole bishop while the others in the team remained designated as presbyters.

montanism. A Christian movement originating in Phrygia in the second century
having a strong emphasis on revelation from the Holy Spirit and on the imminent advent of the New Jerusalem.

oblation. The offering of bread and wine to God in the eucharist.

patriarchs. From about the fourth century these were the bishops of Rome, Constantinople, Antioch, Alexandria and, later, Jerusalem. The patriarchs held the
highest ecclesiastical offices in the church and exercised wide supervision.

patripassianism. See modalistic monarchianism.

patristic. That which relates to the writers/theologians of the early church period.

penance. The church-controlled ritual process of outward acts of self-abasement as part of repentance for major sins. The outward process included confession of guilt (Greek *exomologēsis*) and the discipline of the church including excommunication, absolution and restoration.

pontifex maximus. Originally this was the highest office in ancient Roman religion. The title came to attach to the emperor from Augustus onwards. Later the title was appropriated by the bishop of Rome.

recapitulation. The concept, developed particularly by Irenaeus, that Christ as the second Adam, recapitulated or gathered up all the experiences of humanity into himself and in so doing inaugurated a new, redeemed humanity.

Sabellianism. See modalistic monarchianism.

see. The area or diocese under the authority of a bishop.

subintroductae. Those ascetic men and women whose domestic arrangements entailed their living together in a hopefully celibate situation with an ascetic member of the opposite sex in "spiritual marriage".

Theotokos. The title of Mary as "bearer of God".

Table of Key People and Anonymous Writings

(c. = circa; b. = born; d. = died; fl. = flourished)

Person/Work	Dates	Primary Location	Significance
Ambrose	c. 339-397	Milan	Powerful bishop. Influence on church-state relations. Promoted monasticism. Influence on hymnody.
Antony	c. 251-356	Egypt	Exemplar of early solitary monasticism.
Apollinarius	310-c. 390	Laodicea	Bishop and theologian. Taught that the Logos replaced the normal human soul in Jesus. Views condemned by the church.
Apostolic Constitutions	Late fourth century	Syria	Manual of church order.
Apostolic Tradition	c. 215	Rome	Manual of church order.
Arius	d. c. 335	Alexandria and elsewhere	Heretical teaching that the Son is not co-eternal and co-equal with the Father. Triggered the Arian controversy.
Athanasius	c. 295-373	Alexandria	Bishop of Alexandria and theologian. Champion of "orthodoxy" against Arianism. Promoted monasticism.
Augustine	354-430	Hippo in North Africa	Key theologian and bishop. Opposed Donatism. Promoted monasticism.
Basil	c. 330-379	Caesarea in Cappadocia	Major theologian-bishop. Promoted Nicene doctrine and influenced trinitarian understanding. Promoted monasticism.
Callistus	d. c. 222	Rome	Bishop of Rome from 217. Opponent of Hippolytus. Moderate/lax on church discipline.
Cassian, John	c. 360-c. 435	Marseilles	A shaper of monastic thinking.
1 Clement	c. 96	Rome	Stress on divine order of ministry, promoted its permanence and priestliness.
Clement of Alexandria	c. 150-c. 220	Alexandria	Major scholar and teacher.
Constantine	c. 272-337	Rome & Constantinople	First emperor to embrace Christianity. Fostered close and intertwined church-state relationships.
Cyprian	c. 200-258	Carthage	Bishop and writer. Stressed salvation is only through the "catholic" (universal) church, which is united through the interlinking of its bishops.
Cyril of Alexandria	d. 444	Alexandria	Bishop of Alexandria from 412. Opponent of Nestorius. Stressed the "hypostatic union" of the divine and human in Christ.

Table of Key People and Anonymous Writings (continued)
(c. = circa; b. = born; d. = died; fl. = flourished)

Person/Work	Dates	Primary Location	Significance
Cyril of Jerusalem	c. 310-386	Jerusalem	Bishop of Jerusalem. His *Catecheses* are a significant window into belief and practice.
Damasus	c. 304-384	Rome	Influential bishop of Rome.
Didache	c. 100	Syria	Manual of church order providing window into the early church's life.
Didascalia Apostolorum	Early third century	Syria	Important manual of church order.
Donatus	d. 313	North Africa	Key second leader of the "Donatists."
Egeria	fl. 380s	Gallaecia (Spain) or Aquitania (France)	Diary of her pilgrimage to eastern holy places provides a window into those situations.
Eusebius of Caesarea	c. 265-c. 339	Caesarea in Palestine	Bishop of Caesarea from 314 and major church historian. Preserved much earlier material in his ten-volume church history (our most important source of church history for years prior to 300). Other writings include a *Life of Constantine* and *On the Martyrs of Palestine*.
Eusebius of Nicomedia	d. 341/342	Nicomedia and Constantinople	Successively bishop of Berytus, Nicomedia and Constantinople. A leader opposing the solution of Nicea. Later an influential advisor of Constantine and Constantius II.
Gregory Thaumaturgus	c. 213-c. 270	Neo-Caesarea in Pontus	Missionary bishop. Miracle-worker (= the meaning of *Thaumaturgus*).
Hilary	c. 315-367	Poitiers (France)	Western defender of Nicea.
Hippolytus	c. 160-235	Rome	Schismatic bishop. Theological writer. Stress on strict moral discipline.
Hosius	d. c. 358	Cordova (Spain)	Key religious adviser of Constantine. Defender of Nicea against Constantius II.
Ignatius	d. c. 110-115	Antioch	Letters stressing the monarchical bishop.
Irenaeus	c. 130-c. 200	Lyons	Major theologian.
Jerome	c. 347-c. 420	Rome, Bethlehem	Biblical scholar producing the Vulgate (Latin) translation. Controversialist. Promoter of asceticism.
John Chrysostom	c. 350-407	Antioch & Constantinople	Powerful preacher (hence the later nickname *Chrysostom* ("Golden-mouth"). Promoter of monasticism. Bishop of Constantinople.

Table of Key People and Anonymous Writings (continued)
(c. = circa; b. = born; d. = died; fl. = flourished)

Person/Work	Dates	Primary Location	Significance
Julian	c. 331-363	Constantinople	Emperor and nephew of Constantine. Sought to turn the Roman empire back to paganism.
Justin Martyr	c. 100-165	Rome	Apologist. Creative thinker whose Logos teaching provides a bridge for pagans.
Leo	c. 400-461	Rome	Bishop of Rome. Powerful promoter of its primacy.
Marcion	fl. 140s	Rome and elsewhere	Originator of a major Christian heresy (marcionism).
Martin	c. 335-c. 400	Tours	Bishop and monastic pioneer in Gaul (France). Miracle-worker.
Minucius Felix	fl. early third century	North Africa	Writer of a major apology defending Christianity.
Montanus	fl. 156-7 or 172	Phrygia	Key founder, along with Prisca and Maximilla, of the prophetic Montanist movement.
Nestorius	c. 381-c. 452	Constantinople	Protagonist of Cyril of Alexandria. Stressed the separateness of the two natures of Christ.
Novatian	d. c. 258	Rome	Schismatic bishop. A rigorist regarding treatment of apostates in time of persecution. Major treatise on the Trinity.
Origen	c. 185-c. 254	Alexandria and Caesarea in Palestine	Key theologian and speculative thinker. Strong ascetic emphasis. Fostered allegorical reading of Scripture.
Pachomius	c. 287-346	Upper Egypt	Key pioneer of communal monasticism.
Paul of Samosata	fl. 260s	Antioch	Bishop deposed for modalistic heresy.
Paula	347-404	Rome and Bethlehem	Wealthy noblewoman. Close friend of Jerome. Founder of convents.
Perpetua	d. 203	Carthage	Heroic woman martyr. Writer of much of a diary detailing her final times.
Pliny the Younger	c. 61-c. 112	Bithynia & Pontus	Roman governor. Writer of famous letter to Emperor Trajan asking for guidance on how to treat Christians.
Polycarp	c. 70-c. 155	Smyrna	Bishop. Disciple of John and teacher of Irenaeus. Famous martyr.
Sabellius	Early third century	Rome	Taught modalistic monarchianism, a view rejected as heretical.
Shepherd (of Hermas)	c. 100 and later	Rome	A document written in apocalyptic style providing a window on the early church at Rome.

Table of Key People and Anonymous Writings (continued)
(c. = circa; b. = born; d. = died; fl. = flourished)

Person/Work	Dates	Primary Location	Significance
Simeon Stylites	c. 390-459	North Syria	Influential preacher and pioneer of the stylite/pillar expression of monasticism.
Tatian	c. 120-after 174	Syria	Composed a harmony of the Gospels (the *Diatessaron*). Embraced an ascetic form of Gnosticism.
Tertullian	c. 160-c. 220	Carthage	First major theologian writing in Latin. Rigorist. Proponent of Montanism.
Theodosius	c. 346-395	Constantinople and Milan	Powerful emperor. Promoted the Nicene faith. Dealt a death-blow to paganism by outlawing pagan sacrifice.
Theophilus	d. 412	Alexandria	Powerful bishop. Used violence against paganism. Intrigued to bring about John Chrysostom's downfall.
Thomas, Gospel of	Second century	Syria	A Gnostic-leaning Gospel that also conveys some material independent of the canonical Gospels and possibly quite early.
Victor	d. 198	Rome	Influential bishop stressing the leading role of Rome.

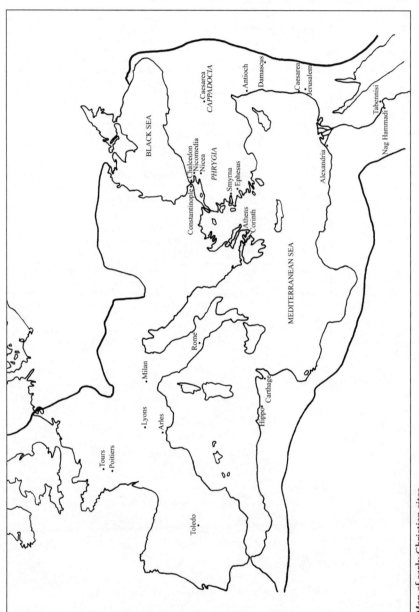

Map of early Christian sites

Modern Author Index

Barnes, T. D., 51

Bowe, B. E., 36, 38, 48

Brakke, D., 90, 102, 145

Brown, P., 27, 137, 142, 143, 156, 160, 161, 162-63, 164, 177

Chadwick, H., 7, 27, 102, 122, 125, 154, 181, 207, 264, 275

Clark, E. A., 140, 180, 184, 185, 191

Cloke, G., 167, 182, 185-86, 191

Ferguson, E., 27, 53, 65, 81, 92, 132, 199, 204, 208, 209, 215, 216, 239, 245, 246

Fox, R. L., 24, 25, 27, 52, 59, 96-97, 205

Frend, W. H. C., 10, 12, 27, 28, 50, 52, 56, 58, 70, 71, 77, 78, 81, 100, 101, 124, 128, 142, 156, 249, 252, 270, 293

Goehring, J. E., 143, 145, 152, 158, 164

Guy, L. D., 32, 223

Hall, S. G., 27, 252, 262, 267, 277, 294

Hanson, R. P. C., 89, 110, 294

Jeremias, J., 168, 169, 172, 191, 217, 239, 240, 247

Kelly, J. N. D., 16, 27, 106, 133, 241, 262, 263, 267, 268, 286, 288, 289, 290, 294

Kreider, A., 77, 201, 215, 239

La Piana, G., 249

MacMullen, R., 17, 77-78, 82, 132, 163, 166

Martin, R. P., 193-94, 216

Murphy-O'Connor, J., 10, 23

Osiek, C., 44, 49, 166, 167

Rouselle, A., 148, 151

Rousseau, P., 25, 28, 71, 119, 139, 146, 147, 149, 153, 156, 157, 164

Shaw, B. D., 167

Stark, R., 10, 167, 168, 182

Stevenson, J., 10, 28, 50, 63, 64, 110, 142, 143, 255, 256, 265, 269, 294

Swidler, L., 169, 170, 174, 181

Troeltsch, E., 16-17

Volz, C. A., 94, 98, 111

Wegman, H., 229

Subject Index

adoptionism, 44, 263, 296

Agape meal. *See* love feast

Alexander, bishop of Alexandria, 55, 126, 237, 271, 273

Alexandria
  church in, 89, 103, 106, 108, 145, 270, 271, 286, 292, 293, 298
  council of (in 262), 278-79, 288
  persecution of Christians in, 51, 54, 55

almsgiving. *See* social concern

Ambrose, 78-80, 94, 123, 125, 128-31, 185, 188, 200, 209, 219-20, 221, 225-26, 234-35, 240, 241, 242, 245, 246

Ammianus Marcellinus, 97

Ancyra, council of (in c. 315), 100, 142, 143, 189, 245

Antioch, church in, 12, 15, 85, 102, 103, 127, 274, 286, 292, 298

Antony, 55, 134, 143-46, 147, 148, 149, 152, 189

Apollinarius, 286-89

apostles, 34, 38, 85, 86

Apostolic Constitutions, 98, 187-88, 190, 195, 211, 214, 240, 245, 246

Apostolic Fathers, 29-49, 296

Apostolic Tradition, 26, 58, 61, 84, 94, 100, 187, 195, 197, 199, 204, 210, 211, 220, 226, 227-30, 233, 239

Arianism, 8, 90, 126, 127, 128, 129, 145, 237, 264, 270-80, 282, 296

Arius. *See* Arianism

Arles, council of (in 314), 124

Arsenius, 148, 149, 157, 185

Athanasius, 84, 90, 107-8, 128, 134, 145-46, 157, 237,

255, 271, 272-73, 274, 275, 276-77, 278, 279, 280, 282, 286-87, 288-89

Athenagoras, 67, 137-38, 240, 261

Augustine, 12, 94, 110, 119-120, 123, 125, 142, 158-59, 177, 181, 182, 183, 199, 206-7, 208, 215, 219, 220, 221, 232, 234, 237-38, 240-41, 282-85

baptism, 32-33, 42, 93, 95, 99, 217-41, 242
  in blood, 58
  ex opera operato, 201, 218, 237, 297
  infant, 94, 220, 224, 232, 238-41
  "nakedness" in baptism, 221-24

Barnabas, Epistle of, 30, 32

Basil of Caesarea, 95, 120, 140, 155-58, 186, 220, 240, 245, 273, 279-80, 281

Basilicas, 25, 26, 118-19, 296

Benedict, rule of, 157, 159, 213

bishops, 34, 43, 46, 84, 85, 86, 91, 92-93, 95, 101, 103, 109, 121, 143, 179, 298
  their authority and power, 21, 22, 41-42, 48, 96, 97-99, 122-23
  metropolitans, 22, 84, 102, 103

Blaesilla, 148, 184

Blandina, 68

Callistus, 12

Cappadocian fathers, 277, 278, 279, 281, 282, 288.
  See also Basil of Caesarea, Gregory of Nazianzus and Gregory of Nyssa

Carthage, 19, 51, 52, 71, 102, 106, 108, 236

Cassian, John, 136, 146, 148, 151, 157, 158, 159-61

catechumenate, 33, 89, 220, 223, 226, 227, 228, 229, 230-33, 234, 245, 296

celibacy. *See* sexual concerns

Celsus, 10, 75, 92, 251

Chalcedon, council of, 8, 20, 103, 108, 127, 158, 190, 269, 270, 292-93

Christianization, 12-13, 19, 77, 163, 214

Christmas, 214-15

Christology, 44, 248-67, 268-80, 285-93

Chrysostom, John. *See* John Chrysostom

church
  catholicity of, 42
  church-state relationships, 20, 51-81
  importance of, 48, 99
  institutionalization, 20-21, 83-111

Clement, First, 30, 35-39, 43, 48, 63-64, 84, 86, 93, 96, 104, 105
  dating, 30-31

Clement of Alexandria, 55, 89, 92, 93, 140, 141, 176, 177, 187, 199, 206, 208-9, 210, 219

Clement, Second, 30, 35-36

Communicatio idiomatum, 290, 291, 292, 296

Confessors, 60, 61-62, 71, 178, 244, 296

confirmation, 235

Constantine, 10, 19, 51, 72-73, 97, 112-28, 126, 131, 221, 268-69, 273-74
  conversion, 113-17
  favors the church, 12, 19, 25, 122

Constantinople, 22, 103, 105, 116, 121, 159, 292, 298
    council of, 20, 127, 269, 278, 282, 289
Constantius II, 128, 276
Cornelius (bishop of Rome), 10, 71, 75, 97
"curse of the *minim*," 14
Cyprian, 21, 52, 61, 62, 71, 72, 93, 95, 96, 97, 99, 102, 106, 138, 200, 209, 210-11, 224, 236-37, 239-40, 241, 242, 243, 244
    view of the church, 21, 84, 117-18, 119
Cyril, bishop of Alexandria, 286-87, 289-93
Cyril of Jerusalem, 199-200, 201, 221, 224, 227, 236
Damasus, 122
deaconesses, 189-91, 222
deacons, 20, 34, 41, 42, 75, 77, 84, 85, 86, 87, 93, 95, 100-101, 103, 121, 142, 222, 226, 228
Diatessaron. See Tatian
Didache, 14-16, 21, 26, 31-35, 37, 48, 84, 181, 196, 197, 200, 203, 208, 210, 211, 212, 224, 226, 230
    dating, 30-31
Didascalia Apostolorum, 77, 95, 96, 181, 187, 188, 190, 214, 222, 243-44
Dioscorus, 292, 293
Docetism, 40, 198, 251, 252, 285, 297
Domitian, 51, 63-64, 75
Donatism, 94, 106, 108, 110, 124-26, 237, 297
Dura-Europos, 23-24, 224-25
dynamic monarchianism. *See* monarchianism
Easter, 102, 106, 194, 202, 213-14, 226, 228, 232, 233, 234
Egeria, 227, 231-32, 233

Elvira, council of (in 306), 142, 189, 212
Encratites, 136
Ephesus, 194, 278
    council of (in 431), 291
    council of (in 449), 108, 292
Epiphany, 214-15, 297
Essenes, 135, 218
Eucharist, 33, 40, 42, 67, 93, 95, 96, 101, 188, 195-202, 228, 236
Eusebius of Caesarea
    as historian, 10, 11, 34, 45, 53, 54-55, 60, 67, 68, 72, 75, 78, 81, 88, 89, 91, 95, 113, 119, 127, 213
    as bishop, 275
Eusebius of Nicomedia, 127
Eustathius of Antioch, 127
Eustathius of Sebaste, 281
Eutyches, 292
exorcism, 17, 77, 101, 141, 181, 222, 226, 227-28, 231, 233-34
fasting, 16, 31, 33, 81, 87, 133, 141, 147-48, 150, 151, 184, 187, 188, 210, 211, 214, 226, 228, 230, 231, 246, 298
Firmilian, 222
Flavian, 292
Galen, 137, 149-51
Gnosticism, 137, 139, 180, 237, 251-57, 297
Gregory of Nazianzus, 22, 121, 155, 156, 214, 240, 279, 280, 281-82, 288
Gregory of Nyssa, 94, 199, 240, 270, 279, 280, 281-82
Gregory Thaumaturgus, 100, 244-45
Hadrian, 65
Hegesippus, 11, 36, 92, 105
Helena, 116
Hermas. *See* Shepherd

Hilary of Poitiers, 12, 25, 119, 201, 276
Hippolytus. *See also Apostolic Tradition*
homoousios, 126, 273-75, 276-77, 278
Hosius, 126, 128
hymns. *See* singing
Ignatius, 16, 21, 39-43, 48, 53-54, 84, 87, 91, 93, 100, 104, 105, 138, 176, 183-84, 188, 197-98, 206
    dating of letters, 30-31
Innocent I, 235
Irenaeus, 48, 65, 68, 84, 88, 91, 92, 105, 106, 136, 139, 180, 200, 212, 239, 250, 251, 255, 256, 257, 261, 262, 266, 274, 288, 299
itinerant ministry, 21, 34, 84, 87
Jerome, 80, 93, 121-22, 134, 139, 140, 148, 150, 151, 177, 181, 184, 185, 189, 240, 276
Jerusalem, 86, 103, 233, 298
Jews. *See* Judaism
John Cassian. See Cassian, John
John Chrysostom, 12, 15, 16, 96, 99, 121, 134, 138, 140, 146, 157, 177, 180, 199, 201, 202, 206, 208, 219, 221, 222, 223, 228, 235, 237, 240
    anti-Jewish preaching, 15, 16
Josephus, 169, 210
Judaism
    proselyte baptism, 218
    relationship of Christianity to Judaism, 13-15, 22, 40-41, 194
Julian, 18-19, 118
Julius I, 107-8
Justin Martyr, 13, 17, 23, 51,

73, 77, 89, 100, 101, 138, 178, 208, 209, 220, 221, 239, 258-61
  on worship, 13, 195, 196, 197, 202-3, 204, 207, 212, 219, 226
Justina, 129
kiss, holy kiss, 67, 195
Lactantius, 11, 24
laity, 37, 84, 93, 94-95, 96, 103, 142, 202, 209, 210
Lent, 214, 231, 298
Leo I, 22, 108, 109, 110, 292, 293
Logos, 258, 259, 260, 261, 263, 265, 286, 288, 298
love feast, 33, 42, 197, 206, 209
Lyons. *See* persecution at Lyons
Lucretius, 155
Macarius of Alexandria, 148, 185
Maccabees, 56
Macrina, 167
Marcionism, 237, 251-52, 254, 256, 298
Martin of Tours, 81, 125, 160
martyrdom, 50-82
  of Polycarp, 50, 65-67.
    See also persecution
Maximus the usurping emperor, 125
Melania the Elder, 167, 185
Melania the Younger, 167, 185
Meletians, 146
metropolitans. *See* bishops, metropolitans
Milan, edict of, 73, 117,
Minucius Felix, 12, 197
modalistic monarchianism. *See* monarchianism
monarchianism, dynamic, 263, 275, 285, 297
  modalistic (Sabellianism, patripassianism), 263,

264, 271, 274, 275, 277, 278, 279, 298
monasticism, 21, 133-64, 295, 298
monophysite schism, 293
Montanism, 84, 87-89, 141, 180, 181, 298
Nag Hammadi, 253, 254
Neocaesarea, council of c.314-315, 142
Neo-Platonism, 140, 142
Nero, 51, 62-63, 79
Nestorius, Nestorian controversy, 108, 286-87, 289-93
Nicea, council of, 84, 101, 102, 103, 126-27, 140, 213, 230, 269, 273-78, 286
North Africa. *See* Carthage
Novatian(ism), 71, 88, 99, 236, 243
Olympias, 134
ordination, 93-94, 122, 142, 157, 180, 181, 187, 190
Origen, 54-55, 58, 76, 77, 78, 84, 89, 199, 230, 239-40, 256, 264-66, 268, 275, 278;
  ascetic views of, 142
Oxyrhynchus, 158
Pachomius, 149, 151-54, 157, 161, 213
Palladius, 148, 157, 185
patriarchates, 22, 103, 298-99
patripassianism. *See* modalism
Paul, saint, 9-10, 11, 13-14, 23, 62, 85, 104, 105, 135, 172-76, 193, 206, 209, 218;
  death of, 63
Paul of Samosata, 97, 126, 274-75
Paula, 134, 184, 185, 213
Pelagius, 240
penance, 46, 71, 131, 217, 220-21, 241-46, 299
Pentecost, 214, 226
Perpetua, 51, 60, 61, 68-70

persecution, 50-82
  at Alexandria, 51, 55
  under Decius, 70-71, 78, 106
  the "great persecution," 52, 72-73, 78
  at Lyons, 50-51, 67-68, 243
  in North Africa, 51, 52, 68-70
  under Valerian, 71-72
Peter, saint, 104, 105
  death of, 63
Philo, 135, 168
philosophy, influence on Christianity, 19, 20
Pliny the Younger, 10, 51, 64-65, 75, 190, 197, 206
Plotinus, 140-41, 264
Pope. *See* Rome, bishop of
Polycarp, 14, 30, 39, 41, 42-43, 50, 51, 58, 78, 102, 106, 138, 187, 251
  martyrdom, 65-67
Porphyry, 140-41
presbyters, 41, 43, 84, 85, 86, 87, 89, 91, 93, 95, 99-101, 103, 179, 222, 226, 228, 242
priests, 34, 37, 95, 109
  and marriage, 142-43. *See also* presbyters
Priscillian, 125
prophets, 34-35, 47-48, 85, 178
recapitulation, 250, 288, 299
Rome, church in, 10, 23, 31, 36, 39, 43, 59, 62-64, 75, 100, 138-39, 229, 249
  bishop of (Pope), 22, 84, 97, 102, 103, 104-10, 249, 299
Rufinus, 237
rule of faith, 256-57
Sabellianism. *See* monarchianism
sexual concerns, 31-32, 135,

137, 139-40, 141, 142,
151, 153, 160, 177, 184,
188, 222, 227, 243, 244,
246
Shepherd of Hermas, 43-48,
86, 91, 105, 139, 241-42,
243
   dating, 30-31, 43
Simeon Stylites. *See* Stylites,
Simeon
singing, 141, 204-7, 211, 231
Siricius, 101, 125
Sirmium, council and creeds
of, 276, 277
social concern of Christians,
18-19, 20, 31, 46-47, 75,
100, 117-18, 120, 207-10,
241
Socrates (historian), 11, 116,
117, 271, 273, 275, 281
Sozomen, 11
Stephen (bishop of Rome),
106, 236, 237
Stylites, Simeon, 161-63
Subintroductae, 139-40, 299
subordinationism, 260, 264,
265, 274, 276, 282

Sulpicius Severus, 81
Sunday, 40, 117, 197, 202,
209, 212-13
Tacitus, 62-63, 73
Tatian, 89, 136
teachers, 34, 84, 85, 89-90
Tertullian, 14, 19, 20, 54, 57-
58, 60-61, 67-68, 74, 77,
84, 88, 93, 94, 95, 135,
138, 139, 180-81, 189, 197,
198-99, 204, 206, 208, 209,
210-11, 226, 239, 241-42,
243, 244, 254-55, 257, 261,
262-63, 266, 285
   against worldly
      philosophy, 19, 20, 76
   montanist views of, 141-
      42
Testament of Our Lord, 77,
210
Thecla, 219
Theodoret, 11, 127, 130, 131,
161, 163
Theodosius, 59, 117, 121,
130, 131, 269
Theophilus of Alexandria,
157

Theophilus of Antioch, 261
Theotokos, 289, 291, 292, 299
Thomas, Gospel of, 137
tithing, 95, 208
Trajan, 10, 51, 64-65, 74-75,
168
trinitarianism, 127, 261-63,
268-85, 297
Ulfilas, 124, 278
Valentinian III, 109-10
Valentinus, 137, 252
Victor (bishop of Rome), 106
Vincent of Lerins, 255, 256
virgins, 90, 138, 139, 143,
177, 183-85, 188-89
wealth. *See* social concern
widows, 10, 75, 94, 95, 121,
182, 184, 186-89, 190, 209,
227
women, 165-92
worship, 25-27, 193-216,
295
   in homes, 22-25, 26, 27,
      46, 75, 178, 194, 210,
      211